Rigos Bar Review Series™

Uniform Multistate Professional Responsibility Exam (MPRE) Review
Third Edition
(Course 5319)

Wolters Kluwer
Law & Business

AUSTIN BOSTON CHICAGO NEW YORK THE NETHERLANDS

James J. Rigos
230 Skinner Building
1326 Fifth Avenue
Seattle, WA 98101
Telephone: (206) 624-0716
Fax: (206) 624-0731
rigos@rigos.net

To contact Aspen Publishers' Customer Care, e-mail customer.care@aspenpublishers.com, call 1-800-234-1660, fax 1-800-901-9075, or mail correspondence to:

Aspen Publishers
Attn: Order Department
PO Box 990
Frederick, MD 21705

Printed in the United States of America.

1 2 3 4 5 6 7 8 9 0

ISBN 978-0-7355-9788-4

This book is intended as a general review of a legal subject. It is not intended as a source for advice for the solution of legal matters or problems. For advice on legal matters, the reader should consult an attorney.

Magic Memory Outlines® and Make Your Own Exam® are registered trademarks owned by Rigos Professional Education Programs, Ltd.

About Wolters Kluwer Law & Business

Wolters Kluwer Law & Business is a leading provider of research information and workflow solutions in key specialty areas. The strengths of the individual brands of Aspen Publishers, CCH, Kluwer Law International and Loislaw are aligned within Wolters Kluwer Law & Business to provide comprehensive, in-depth solutions and expert-authored content for the legal, professional and education markets.

CCH was founded in 1913 and has served more than four generations of business professionals and their clients. The CCH products in the Wolters Kluwer Law & Business group are highly regarded electronic and print resources for legal, securities, antitrust and trade regulation, government contracting, banking, pension, payroll, employment and labor, and healthcare reimbursement and compliance professionals.

Aspen Publishers is a leading information provider for attorneys, business professionals and law students. Written by preeminent authorities, Aspen products offer analytical and practical information in a range of specialty practice areas from securities law and intellectual property to mergers and acquisitions and pension/benefits. Aspen's trusted legal education resources provide professors and students with high-quality, up-to-date and effective resources for successful instruction and study in all areas of the law.

Kluwer Law International supplies the global business community with comprehensive English-language international legal information. Legal practitioners, corporate counsel and business executives around the world rely on the Kluwer Law International journals, loose-leafs, books and electronic products for authoritative information in many areas of international legal practice.

Loislaw is a premier provider of digitized legal content to small law firm practitioners of various specializations. Loislaw provides attorneys with the ability to quickly and efficiently find the necessary legal information they need, when and where they need it, by facilitating access to primary law as well as state-specific law, records, forms and treatises.

Wolters Kluwer Law & Business, a unit of Wolters Kluwer, is headquartered in New York and Riverwoods, Illinois. Wolters Kluwer is a leading multinational publisher and information services company.

Introduction

Welcome and thank you for purchasing the Rigos Uniform Bar Review Series Multistate Performance Responsibility Exam (MPRE) self-study review course. This is all you need to pass the United States "Uniform" MPRE administered by the National Conference of Bar Examiners (NCBE). Please begin by carefully reviewing the introductory information in this preface. It contains valuable information about the MPRE exam and insights into the question characteristics. Reviewing the Preface also serves as your orientation and planning session.

Editorial Direction

Jim Rigos is an Attorney-CPA, a graduate of Boston University Law School, Editor-in-Chief of the creating team of this Uniform Bar Review Series, owner of Rigos Professional Education Programs, Ltd., and an author for Aspen Publishers. He has written and lectured for professional law and accounting associations and BAR and CPA exam review programs for over 30 years. For many years he has also served as a national Director of the American Association of Attorney-CPAs. The publisher also has created a series of CLE and CPE courses focusing on professional ethics. Professors Sam Donaldson, Tom Lininger, Joe Keeney, Alex Ruskell, and Tania Shah contributed to the third edition of this MPRE volume.

Acknowledgments

This work product was substantially enriched because of the robust encouragement and editorial involvement of many thoughtful individuals. Jon Cavanagh, Laura Colberg, Matt Conrad, Tracy Duany, Lisa Goldoftas, Leah Golshani, Steve Johnson, Gina Lowe, Laura McCabe, Carolyn Plant, Aaron Rocke, Joanna Roth, Tom Smith, Kevin Stemp, Jason Stonefeld, Sidney Tribe, and Tracy Wood made significant drafting contributions. Law school Professors Janet Ainsworth, Jim Bond, Mark Chinen, David DeWolf, Sam Donaldson, Christian Halliburton, Gregory Hicks, Tom Lininger, John Parry, Chris Rigos, and Karl Tegland made important suggestions on substantive improvements and reviewed the Rigos Uniform Bar Review Series textbooks. A special thanks to our past students for their many suggestions of substantive improvement and creative new learning aids. Their recommendations and successes are a part of every page of this Rigos Bar Review Series. Thanks also to the guidance of the Aspen Publishers' team in Boston that brought this all to fruition.

RIGOS BAR REVIEW SERIES
OTHER RELATED COURSES

If you **liked** this Uniform Multistate Professional Responsibility Exam (MPRE) course and related software, you **will love** our other Multistate "full service" Uniform Rigos Bar Review Series publication sold by Aspen Publishers. Included are

1. UNIFORM MBE OBJECTIVE MULTIPLE-CHOICE EXAM—2 volumes

- Presents succinct explanations of the **most frequently tested black letter law** principles **without overwhelming you with unnecessary concepts.**
- **Hundreds of acronyms, tips, and solution approaches** help you easily memorize legal concepts.
- **"Magic Memory Outline"®** software to assist you in synthesizing and summarizing the law in your own words.
- **Learning questions with complete answer rationales within each chapter help reinforce learning as you go,** targeting your weaker areas, so that when you reach the more difficult practice questions, you are more confident.
- More than **1,700 multiple-choice exam questions** provide extensive MBE-style practice, as well as full answer rationales.
- **Two mock 3-hour/100-queston practice MBE-patterned exams** allow you to simulate and test yourself in an actual MBE experience.
- **"MBE Secret Weapon"™** provides maximum efficiency and more correct answers.
- The **"Make Your Own Exam™" feature on the free included CD-ROM** allows you to randomly select varying topic questions.

2. UNIFORM MEE SUBJECTIVE ESSAY EXAM

- **Succinct exposition of the most frequently tested essay black-letter law** principles. This test is very concise and focused, containing only the information you need to answer the MEE essays.
- **Hundreds of acronyms and Rigos Bar Review Series tips** to assist you in memorizing legal elements and perfecting your essay approach.
- **Five essay questions with summarized pointer grading guides and full answers per subject** for all NCBE MEE subjects, the six MBE subjects, and professional responsibility.

3. UNIFORM MPT PERFORMANCE TEST

- Succinct explanations of the most frequently tested MPT tasks contain **only the information you need** to pass the MPT portion of the exam.
- **"Tips and Traps" section** helps familiarize you with typical distracters used by the examiners to confuse the Performance Test exam-takers.
- **Advice on the best approach, time scheduling, and format** for answering each of the four types of MPT questions helps strengthen your abilities to organize and focus your answers efficiently.
- **Seven simulated exam questions** categorized by topic **with full sample answers** provided help you gauge your progress and reinforce MPT practice.

Ask your bookstore about Rigos Bar Review Series products from Aspen Publishers, or visit us online at *http://lawschool.aspenpublishers.com.*

RIGOS UNIFORM BAR REVIEW SERIES

PROFESSIONAL RESPONSIBILITY EXAM REVIEW (MPRE)

Third Edition

Table of Contents

Uniform Multistate Professional Responsibility Exam (MPRE) Review
Third Edition
(Course 5319)

RIGOS UNIFORM BAR REVIEW SERIES

PROFESSIONAL RESPONSIBILITY EXAM REVIEW (MPRE)

INTRODUCTION AND ORIENTATION

Table of Contents

RIGOS UNIFORM BAR REVIEW SERIES

PROFESSIONAL RESPONSIBILITY EXAM REVIEW (MPRE)

INTRODUCTION AND ORIENTATION

I. OVERVIEW

Welcome to the review for your first "uniform" bar exam. This introduction is an overview of the Rigos Professional Responsibility Exam (MPRE) Review Course. It describes the MPRE process, question characteristics, and related suggested approaches. Also detailed is our recommended organized preparation program you should follow to ensure you score high on the MPRE at the first sitting. The information in this preface is important. It should be thoroughly studied and understood before you start your Rigos MPRE review program.

A. Summary of Introductory Chapter's Coverage

There are two aspects to preparing and scoring well on the NCBE Uniform MPRE: learning the ABA's Model Rules and practicing applying the rules to multiple-choice style of objective questions. While covered in much depth later in this Introduction chapter, a brief summary of your responsibilities follows.

1. Learning the Rules: This Rigos text covers all the Model Rules in an outline – narrative format. It is sufficiently comprehensive to be helpful in a law school class yet focused enough on the MPRE exam to allow you to score well here. Your first job is to use our Magic Memory Outline templates software to summarize the rules. You will only do this once.

2. Learning to Apply the Rules to the Exam: Application is important because, unlike law school, the MPRE uses only multiple-choice questions to test your knowledge. Students should refer to the NCBE's web site (www.ncbex.org) for current official sample questions. Our Question Maps cross-reference the textual coverage to our related questions.

3. Rigos Learning Questions: Our questions are more varied than the MPRE in terms of format, length, and degree of difficulty. You will struggle with some of our rigorous and complex questions but they will teach you all the nuisances and distracters that are at play in the most difficult 20% of the questions. Many students miss these so it is important.

4. Use Software: Work the chapter's questions during or at conclusion of preparing your Magic Memory Outline. In the middle of the course start using our The "Make Your Own Exam" software. These drills will train you to bounce from subject to subject. Overall, the Rigos approach is to over prepare you and you will find the actual exam seems easy.

B. Focused, Positive Mental Attitude

What the mind can conceive, dedicated hard work can achieve. You must believe you can and will pass the bar exam and become a successful attorney.

1. Join the Winning Team: Our review programs have more than 100,000 professional alumni who used our structured system to pass their professional entrance exams. Therefore, your objective of scoring high on the MPRE at the first sitting is very attainable.

2. Success-Focused Program: Exam confidence is the result of a well-organized and well-executed preparation program. Students following the complete Rigos "seamless process" preparation program are geared for exam success.

C. MPRE Exam Details

1. Administration: The MPRE is a testing product of the National Conference of Bar Examiners ("NCBE") and offered three times per year (March, August, and November) in numerous national locations. The MPRE is 120 minutes in length and includes 60 multiple-choice questions, of which 50 are scored. There also may be a few additional questions that concern the student's assessment of the test itself and testing environment.

2. Offerings: The exam is required in all but a handful of states. More than 60,000 students sit for the MPRE each year. Both the actual MPRE test booklets and this review text are printed in 12-point type.

3. Registration: To apply to sit for the MPRE, an applicant should contact:

National Conference of Bar Examiners
MPRE Application Department
301 ACT Drive, P.O. Box 4001
Iowa City, Iowa 52243-4001
Telephone: (319) 341-2500
Online Registration: http//www.ncbex.org or www.act.org/mpre

4. Governing Authorities: The MPRE exam focuses on ethical dilemmas encountered in the practice of law and the context of a lawyer serving as a judge. The primary source of normative rules are those promulgated by the American Bar Association (ABA).

a. Lawyer Code and Rules: Both the 1983 ABA Model Code of Professional Responsibility (MCPR or Code) and 2010 edition of the Model Rules of Professional Conduct (MRPC or Rules) are tested, but the Rules are favored. While a few provisions are in the Code but not in the Rules or vice versa, usually a situation is treated similarly so the question answer outcome is the same. State variations from the ABA model and add-on provisions – even if common – are not usually tested. Indeed, in some questions they serve as attractive distractors.

b. Judicial Conduct: The current ABA Model Code of Judicial Conduct (MCJC) provides the authoritative outcome for the 5 to 7 questions testing judicial ethics.

c. Other: Questions presenting issues of legal malpractice should be answered by applying general tort and contract principles. Litigation sanctions by a court such as contempt, Civil Rule 11 fines, fee forfeiture, or disqualification may be tested. A lawyer's potential criminal liability is occasionally tested where the lawyer aided and abetted a client in committing criminal or fraudulent acts.

II. QUESTION DETAILS

An MPRE test question usually focuses on the application of only one discrete Rule – not the broader based multi-rules testing typically found in the factual setting of ethics essay questions. The subjects tested and relative weights are covered in Part D below on pages 6 through 8. The exam tests the subjects in a random order.

A. Question Source

1. Organization: The NCBE has an MPRE six-member drafting committee that monitors all the MPRE subjects tested. The Committee has a broad representation of law school professors, professional bar examiners, and practicing attorneys.

2. New Questions: New questions are created on an ongoing basis to refresh the test bank of potential questions and promote breadth of topic coverage. Law school professors, practitioners, and bar disciplinary authorities are fertile sources for new questions. Proposed new questions are subject to multiple reviews by committee members to ensure they fairly test the subjects and are well drafted, accurate, and unambiguous.

3. Broad Input: Each participating state bar admission authority may also submit comments to the Committee prior to accepting a new question. A thorough review of all questions is made before every final exam is published.

B. Grading System

1. Scoring: All scored questions must be psychometrically sound. Every right answer you choose is worth one point, regardless of the question's degree of difficulty or time it takes to complete. There is no penalty for wrong choices. The average score students achieve is about 38 to 42 correct out of the scored 50 possible.

a. Scaled for Difficulty: The final number of right answers reported for a particular exam depends on that exam's overall difficulty. The NCBE has a scaled ("equating" is its descriptive term) difficulty system of 50 to 150, with 100 the mean.

b. Ensure Consistency: The examiners' analysis of answers and the scaling system are intended to correct the effect of any bad questions on a particular exam. The performance standard is based on the examinees who took the exam in March of 1999. This ensures grading consistency and comparisons from exam to exam.

2. State Passing Rate: Each jurisdiction decides how to treat the MPRE scaled score. The passing scaled score range goes from approximately 70% in Mississippi to 85% in New York. Nationally, about 75% of the students receive a "passing" scaled score, although this percentage varies from state to state. In states that permit students from non-ABA-approved law schools to sit, the pass rate may be significantly lower. For a breakdown of statistics go to http://www.ncbex.org/bar-admissions/stats.

a. State Rules Control: Many states also require students to answer essay ethics questions using the local jurisdiction's rules as a part of the general bar exam. Most states accept MPRE scores from other jurisdictions.

b. Particular State: For details of the passing statistics and particular grading method used in your jurisdiction, you should check with your individual state bar admission authority. Go to www.abanet.org/barserv/stlobar.html for an online listing of state-by-state bar exam information.

C. Question Approach

1. Question Facts: The facts are presented in either single or multiple paragraph format. Over the past few years the fact patterns have tended to become longer, creating more time pressure on the candidate.

2. Call of the Question: The MPRE questions concentrate on analysis and the detailed ABA Code or Rule section rules, not the usual broad concepts found in law school or state bar exam subjective essay questions. The specific factual events of a question provide the foundation to test the applicable ethical rule.

a. Facts Lead to Requirements: The factual events lead to a requirement sentence containing a "call of the question." This is your direction to decide which is the best among the four given alternatives. Detailed analysis of all four alternatives is necessary; instinctive answers are often wrong because fine-line distinctions are frequent on the MPRE.

b. Requirement Position: The student is required to determine whether the act or inaction of a lawyer or judge is proper or subjects the lawyer or judge to potential discipline. Note that "not improper" is the functional equivalent to "proper." Usually two answers go in each direction, and each conclusion – yes or no – is followed by a statement of a legal rationale. About two-thirds of the correct alternatives conclude that the lawyer is subject to discipline. The reasoning is thus more important than the likely outcome.

c. Key Words: The MPRE uses key words or phrases in the requirement to test the degree to which a lawyer must comply with the particular Code or Rule provision.

(1) "Shall" or "Subject to Discipline": Under this required behavior directive, potential discipline will result from non-compliance. The controlling rule itself usually begins with the wording "a lawyer shall" or "a lawyer shall not." About 45% of the questions use this mandatory compliance standard.

(2) "Should," "May," or "Proper": This requirement recommends conduct that is suggestive or acceptable, but a failure to comply will not automatically subject the lawyer to discipline ("Is it proper for A to . . . ."). The recommended aspirational conduct may not always be required. The question may adopt a negative approach such as "is the lawyer's conduct improper?" Approximately 25 to 35% of the questions fall into this negative approach category. The "proper" versus "improper" approach distinction is very important and can easily trip up a candidate's analytic approach to identifying the best alternative.

(3) Other: About 10% of the questions have keywords that are not directly related to professional discipline. These include "Is the lawyer subject to liability for malpractice?", "subject to litigation sanction?", "subject to criminal liability?", "subject to disqualification?", "must the judge recuse herself?", and "must the lawyer/judge report?" Civil Rule 11 sanctions or general principles of contract and tort law may also be tested.

3. Multiple Violations: Frequently the lawyer's act or inaction has potentially been a violation of multiple disciplinary rules. Usually the highest level disciplinary rationale controls. Some of the violated provisions may not even be identified in any alternative.

D. Subjects Tested

The ABA Model Rules of Professional Conduct (MRPC or Rules) and Code of Judicial Conduct (MCJC) are the testing focus. The Preamble and Comments to the Rules contain further detail and explanations that may also be tested. The Rigos text distributes the required substantive knowledge over six equally weighted chapters. The NCBE content specification outlines provide rough testing percentage distributions as follows:

1. Regulation of the Legal Profession (6-12%)

- Powers of Courts and Other Bodies to Regulate Lawyers
- Admission to the Profession
- Regulation After Admission – Lawyer Discipline
- Mandatory and Permissive Reporting of Professional Misconduct
- Unauthorized Practice of Law – by Lawyers and Non-lawyers
- Multi-jurisdictional Practice
- Fee Division with a Non-Lawyer

- The Law Firm and Other Forms of Practice
- Responsibilities of Partners, Managers, Supervisory and Subordinate Lawyers
- Restrictions on Right to Practice

2. **The Client-Lawyer Relationship (10-16%)**

- Formation of Client-Lawyer Relationship
- Scope, Objective, and Means of the Representation
- Decision-making Authority – Actual and Apparent
- Counsel and Assistance Within the Bounds of the Law
- Termination of the Client-Lawyer Relationship
- Client-Lawyer Contracts
- Fees

3. **Client Confidentiality (6-12%)**

- Attorney-Client Privilege
- Work Product Doctrine
- Professional Obligation of Confidentiality – General Rule
- Disclosures Expressly or Impliedly Authorized by Client
- Other Exceptions to the Confidentiality Rule

4. **Conflicts of Interest (12-18%)**

- Current Client Conflicts – Multiple Clients and Joint Representation
- Current Client Conflicts – Lawyer's Personal Interest or Duties
- Former Client Conflicts
- Prospective Client Conflicts
- Imputed Conflicts
- Acquiring an Interest in Litigation
- Business Transactions with Clients
- Third Party Compensation and Influence
- Lawyers Currently or Formerly in Government Service
- Former Judge, Arbitrator, Mediator, or Other Third Party Neutral

5. **Competence, Legal Malpractice, and Other Civil Liability (6-12%)**

- Maintaining Competence
- Competence Necessary to Undertake Representation
- Exercising Diligence and Care
- Civil Liability to Client, Including Malpractice
- Civil Liability to Nonclients
- Limiting Liability for Malpractice
- Malpractice Insurance and Risk Prevention

6. **Litigation and Other Forms of Advocacy (10-16%)**

- Meritorious Claims and Contentions
- Expediting Litigation
- Candor to the Tribunal
- Fairness to Opposing Party and Counsel
- Impartiality and Decorum of the Tribunal
- Trial Publicity
- Lawyer as Witness

7. **Transactions and Communications with Persons Other than Clients (2-8%)**

- Truthfulness in Statements to Others
- Communications with Represented Persons
- Communications with Unrepresented Persons
- Respect for Rights of Third Persons

8. **Different Roles of the Lawyer (4-10%)**

- Lawyer as Advisor
- Lawyer as Evaluator
- Lawyer as Negotiator
- Lawyer as Arbitrator, Mediator, or Other Third Party Neutral
- Prosecutors and Other Government Lawyers
- Lawyer Appearing in Nonadjudicative Proceeding
- Lawyer Representing an Entity or Other Organization

9. **Safekeeping Funds and Other Property (2-8%)**

- Establishing and Maintaining Client Trust Accounts
- Safekeeping Funds and Other Property of Clients
- Safekeeping Funds and Other Property of Third Persons
- Disputed Claims

10. **Communications about Legal Services (4-10%)**

- Advertising and Other Public Communications about Legal Services
- Solicitation – Direct Contact with Prospective Clients
- Group Legal Services
- Referrals
- Communications Regarding Fields of Practice and Specialization

11. **Lawyers' Duties to the Public and the Legal System (2-4%)**

- Voluntary *Pro Bono* Service
- Accepting Appointments
- Serving in Legal Services Organizations
- Law reform Activities Affecting Client Interests
- Criticism of Judges and Adjudicating Officials
- Political Contributions to Obtain Engagements or Appointments
- Improper Influence on Government Officials
- Assisting Judicial Misconduct

III. MPRE QUESTION CHARACTERISTICS

A. Comments and Pitfalls

Tests show that understanding and avoiding the MPRE question traps, distracters, and pitfalls may add up to 10% more right choices on uncertain questions. The exam tests not only your knowledge of the applicable legal and judicial ethics, but also your MPRE question analytical skills. The skill necessary to score high is best developed by working practice questions. Most candidates get the easy questions correct; it is the performance on the more difficult and nuanced 15 to 20% that often determines the student's ultimate rank and score.

1. Format: All the MPRE questions are multiple-choice with four alternatives. All levels of difficulty are represented, and there is no pattern to the sequence.

2. Preferred Answer Objective: Typically one pair of answers concludes the lawyer is subject to discipline, while the other pair concludes the lawyer is not subject to discipline. The rationale thus becomes the determining factor.

a. Objective: The best answer is the most nearly correct, or conversely, the least incorrect answer. There is usually some truth in more than one alternative; the best alternative must be the most completely correct, and it must relate to the facts. Still the best alternative may not be a perfect statement of the rule, and there may be more than one disciplinary rule violated that could lead to discipline. Appreciate the difference between the command adverbs "may" (suggestive) and "shall"/"must" (mandatory).

b. Problems: Two of the four alternatives are often the same or very close in outcome, and both may sound reasonable. An alternative may reach the right conclusion for the wrong reason or for a reason less compelling than the other rationale. Watch out for incomplete definitions of the determinative rules, particularly those rules that have more than one requirement, where only one requirement is stated in the answer.

3. Negatives: Negatives may appear in the facts, the call, or the alternatives. This means that the correct choice is the worst, least helpful, or most false alternative. The student must reason very carefully through the alternatives and reverse the normal frame of reference. Picking the alternative involving an "improper conduct" call may be a form of negative. The "true-false" approach discussed in item 4 below is often quite helpful in dealing with negatives. If looking for the negative, the false or incorrect alternative is the best choice.

4. Try a True-False Approach: For some questions it may help to use a true-false analysis for each of the four alternatives. This is where you evaluate each answer option by asking the question, "Is this statement true or false?" The true-false approach is especially useful for questions having a negative call. Ideally you will end up with a 3-1 split; the odd one out is usually the correct answer.

5. Absolutes: Be on the alert for sweeping exclusionary words such as "all," "always," "none," "never," "under no circumstances," or "solely." An alternative containing such words is so broad that it is unlikely to be correct. Ask yourself, "Is there any exception?" The more narrowly stated alternative usually is preferable to an "open door" option and "sometimes" or "usually" are more attractive determining words than absolutes.

6. Nonsense Theory: Occasionally, the MPRE will include answer options containing a nonsense principle, concept, or theory such as an equitable maxim like "clean hands are required in equity." A good rule of thumb is that such an alternative is wrong unless you have seen the disciplinary rule theory in the Rigos texts.

7. Distracters: Red herrings are often present in the question. The examiners are very clever in creating attractive factual distracters. They are designed to support logic that leads to one of the wrong alternatives.

8. Analyze Modifiers in the Four Answer Alternatives: Many answer alternatives begin with the conclusion (e.g., "Lawyer is subject to discipline," or "Lawyer is not subject to discipline"). This is then followed by a conditional or limiting modifying word ("because," "since," "if," "only if," or "unless") and a statement of a supporting ethical reasoning or rationale. Picture the three-element skeleton below.

a. "Because," "Since," or "As": These conditional modifiers indicate the following rationale is usually the reasoning necessary to satisfy the legal conclusion.

(1) Example: "Alice will be subject to discipline because she represented both adverse parties, thus creating a conflict of interest." "Alice will be subject to discipline" is the conclusion, "because" is the conditional modifier, and "she represented . . . interest" is the legal rationale.

(2) Reasoning Requirements: The "because" reasoning must be consistent with the facts and events given in the question. The reasoning must also resolve the central legal issue in the question.

b. "If" and "Only If": This limiting modifier indicates the following rationale need only be possible under the facts in the question; it is not required to be totally consistent, as in "because" or "since" questions.

(1) Example: "Betty is not subject to discipline if (or "only if") she communicated the conflict to the client." "Betty is not subject to discipline" is the conclusion, "if (or only if)" is the conditional modifier, and "she communicated the conflict to the client" is the legal rationale.

(2) Reasoning Requirement: The "if" modifier can – and usually does – go beyond the given question's facts and events to create a more compelling factual argument to support the legal conclusion. "Only if" is similar, except it creates an exclusive condition that must be satisfied for the alternative to be the best answer. An "if" or "only if" modifier also requires you to reason through the other three alternatives to be sure there is not a better "if" or "only if" argument.

c. "Unless": This conditional modifier typically is followed by a rationale that addresses more of the required legal reasoning than the other modifiers. Notice that "unless" usually is a mirror image of "if," and the usual form of "no, unless. . . ." is the only way the alternative outcome could occur.

(1) Example: "Carol is subject to discipline unless she makes disclosure of the falsity to the court." "Carol is subject to discipline" is the conclusion, "unless" is the conditional modifier, and "she makes disclosure to the court" is the legal rationale.

(2) Reasoning Requirement: This "unless" reasoning limitation must be necessary for the application of the controlling rule. If there is any other reason or way the result can occur, an "unless" alternative is usually incorrect. Again, you should reason through all the other alternatives to be sure there is not a better argument.

9. MPRE Seductive Distracters: Beyond the usual multiple-choice question tricks, there are a few MPRE-unique distracters focusing on the ethical rules.

a. Focus on Lawyer's Mental State: The lawyer's knowledge, belief, or motivation often are important. Many Rules require the lawyer to believe reasonably some conclusion will or will not result from the advocacy situation. Whether a lawyer would be allowed to withdraw from a matter often turns on the motivation and mental state of the lawyer. One of the Rules requires a lawyer with actual knowledge of another attorney's misconduct to report it to the appropriate authority.

b. No Harm, Still Foul: One of the alternatives often states facts suggesting "harmless error." An example is where a defendant's attorney introduced false evidence, but the jury still found the defendant liable. The result does not excuse the ethical violation.

c. No Fee, Still Foul: One of the alternatives often states the attorney took no fee for the representation. The ethical violation is not excused even if the lawyer receives no financial benefits from the engagement.

d. Client Agreement Preferred: Many of the ethical restraints require the attorney to communicate to the client the risks and danger of a particular ethical dilemma. The objective of informed consent is more likely met if the client affirmatively agrees, preferably in writing. Therefore, the client "agreed" or "agreed in writing" are better options than wording indicating merely that the client "was informed" or received "a confirming communication."

e. Client Agreement May Be Insufficient: Some of the ethical restraints have requirements in addition to client consent or agreement. An example is fee payment by a third party, which must not interfere with the attorney-client relationship. If interference is clear, mere client consent is insufficient to foreclose a disciplinary charge against the lawyer.

10. Remember Our Default Rules: A systematic approach to correct answer selection helps. An enlightened guessing system is helpful on up to 20% of the questions. By eliminating wrong answers, you can usually reduce the choice to two alternatives and apply the following default rules. They provide a logical basis for an educated guess.

a. Precision: The more exact the alternative, the better. Vagueness is never encouraged in the law. The three incorrect alternatives in such a question will contain distracters to create confusion.

b. Easier to Prove: An answer choice that the facts suggest is easier to prove is preferred to one that has more complicated legal requirements.

c. Opposite Answer: If only two of the four alternatives are opposite (e.g., "P is subject to discipline because X. . . ." as contrasted with . . . . "P is not subject to discipline because X. . . ."), one of the two opposites is likely to be the best answer to the question.

d. Longest Alternative: Everything else being equal, the longer alternative is slightly more likely to be the correct answer than a shorter one. A correct answer must usually contain all the required qualifying provisions and reasoning of the governing ethical rule necessary for the best choice. A fragmented alternative with fewer words is usually less attractive. This concept favors the more detailed alternative; this is usually the one with the most technical words and specific terminology.

e. Eliminating Wrong Answers: It may be helpful to understand there are three common reasons why an MPRE answer choice is wrong:

(1) Legal Rule Misstatement: The statement of the rule may be wrong or, more frequently on the MPRE, may be an incomplete statement of the rule.

(2) Factual Misstatement: The facts required to support the alternative may not be stated in the question fact pattern at all. An example is the required client consent that must be confirmed in writing to abate a conflict of interest. The alternative's facts may go clearly and impermissibly beyond what is given in the question. In a few instances, the facts of the alternative directly contradict the facts in the question. Read the question carefully.

(3) Legal or Factual Irrelevancy: The law or facts in the answer may be accurate as stated, but not focus on the central ethical determinant in the question. An example is a lawyer's business transaction with a client that was fair, but there was not a reasonable opportunity for the client to obtain independent representation. Again, the central determinant concern usually involves the strict application of an ABA Model Rule.

B. Approach to MPRE Questions

Parts of this section refer to practicing questions on paper. If you want to use the CD-ROM feature, make sure you also review the instructions in Section V *infra* at 16.

1. Stay Within Time Allocation: There are 60 questions in the 2-hour session. This is an average of 2 minutes per question.

a. Pace Yourself: Carefully manage your time as you proceed through the questions. The trend is towards longer fact patterns but you should answer every question.

b. Procedure: It is important to work as quickly as possible without sacrificing thoroughness and accuracy. Read intensely and analyze the fact pattern carefully because you likely will have time to read the question only once. If a particular question gives you difficulty, either skip it, or make your best educated guess and mark it in the margin.

2. Analyze Facts and Law: You need to analyze both the facts and the law. Try to understand the facts of the question separately from the four alternative choices. The events in the question develop chronologically. As you read the facts, circle all people's names in the question book; every new person adds another potential legal relationship and possible ethical dilemmas. Analyze the factual events in the question carefully; selecting a wrong answer usually occurs because the candidate failed to appreciate the consequences of a significant fact. For extremely complicated questions, it may be helpful to quickly create a chronological skeleton diagram of the events.

3. Go Through Questions Twice: Initially, go through all the questions in order. Time is so precious it is usually best to answer every question in order the first time through. Still, some students use a two-step approach.

a. First Time Through: The first time through, every question should be put into one of three categories. You can do this with notes to yourself in the margins, on a separate sheet of paper, or in your head.

(1) Sure of Subject: If you are reasonably competent in the subject, answer all the subject's questions and move on. This applies even if you are not sure of the exact issue being tested. Circle your alternative choice – A, B, C, or D – on the question sheets.

(2) No Clue? Skip It: If you have great difficulty with a question's subject or if the particular question would take too long, skip it. Do not get frustrated by the skipped questions or spend more than 10 seconds before deciding to skip.

(3) Unsure? Take Your Best Shot: If you have some idea, but are unsure which alternative is the best answer, make your best educated guess. After you eliminate the wrong alternatives, you will usually be down to two choices. Perhaps use the default rules discussed above. If you spend more than 20 seconds on the question, you must commit; there is just not enough time to waste on second-guessing. Answer the question, but put a mark in the margin so you can come back later and check the answer if you have remaining time.

b. Second Time Through: After you have gone through all 60 questions once, look at the time left and count the skipped questions. Calculate the time per question you have left. Keep on your new time schedule and answer every question.

(1) Do Skipped Questions First: The second time through, work the skipped questions first. Do not exceed the average remaining time. Do not get hung up; some of the series' questions intentionally have long and complicated fact patterns. If still unsure after a reasonable intellectual effort, use your educated guess default rules discussed above.

(2) Review Marked Questions Last: After the skipped questions are completed, turn to questions you marked in the question book to determine if you see anything new. The questions you have worked in the meantime may have jogged your memory. If you are still uncertain, go with your first judgment; it is likely your best shot at the correct answer.

4. Answer Sheets Are Critical: Attention to detail here is vital. A mistake in marking the right number on the official bubble answer sheet can be fatal. Always circle your answer choice on the examination book just before you mark the answer sheet so you have a cross-check. After every 10 questions, you should consciously cross-check the numbering on both documents to be sure you did not make a transposition error. This is especially necessary if you skipped answering some questions the first time through.

IV. RECOMMENDED PREPARATION PROGRAM

A. Substantial Effort Necessary

A significant time commitment is necessary to achieve MPRE success. The details of the rules tested take time to absorb and synthesize into your own Magic Memory Outlines®. This knowledge must then be directed toward the MPRE multiple-choice method of testing.

1. Disassemble Book: Carefully take the book apart at the perforated lines a few pages at a time and place everything in a three-ring binder. This will allow you to study more efficiently by spreading out the various parts of your book for easy reference.

2. Further Reference Site: To ensure you have the most current information on the MPRE, we have created a web site page containing updates and related information. Go to http://www.rigos.net/new/MPRE_Resource_Site.asp.

3. You Must Work Questions: Familiarization with the examiners' fine-line distinctions and various tricks is best mastered by working hundreds of MPRE-patterned questions. This Rigos text contains a compendium of several hundred questions of varying degrees of easy, average, and hard difficulty. Overall, our questions are more complex and contain more tricks than the MPRE, so you may find the actual exam questions seem somewhat superficial. The focus is on the most frequently asked topics on the MPRE.

4. Time Commitment: The necessary preparation time depends on how long ago you had professional responsibility in law school. Efficiency and concentration in the MPRE learning process helps reduce the required time.

a. Time Variables: Our high-scoring students report an average of 5 hours per chapter or about 30 hours average in total, including working our final exam. Your law school professional responsibility course helps build a foundation.

b. Do It Right: It is a mistake to underestimate the necessary effort required to score high on the MPRE. This is a very competitive exercise, and you never know when you cross the passing line. The prudent approach is to aim for a healthy margin of safety.

5. Schedule and Calendars: A well-organized effort is necessary. Use our weekly planning sheet and calendars. Work backward from the MPRE exam date. Pages 19 and 20 of this preface contain an overall four-week planning sheet and sample week-by-week calendar.

6. 120-Minute Time Blocks: Get used to studying in 120-minute solid blocks of time without a break. This is the actual MPRE time. You may have to work up to this.

B. Six Element Success Program

The Rigos Series MPRE Review is most effective when used in a structured learning environment. A multi-step approach works best because the student is exposed to the substantive ethical rules and question nuances from many different viewpoints. The Rules take time to sink in and we recommend on page 19 a four-week preparation program. The result is a complete preparation program and a seamless process that leaves nothing to chance. The total integrated effort is more effective than the sum of the individual parts.

1. Preview Whole Text Quickly: Start by quickly reading all the text pages of this professional responsibility course in one sitting. This will acquaint you with the MPRE subjects upon which the exam questions are based. Then go through every chapter individually in much detail. Be sure to allocate sufficient time for the important four learning steps described below. Your Rigos Review covers only what is tested on the MPRE, not the broader coverage found in many law school ethics courses or other bar review courses.

2. Detailed Chapter Learning Session: The second step is learning. You may attend a live class or listen to ours at www.rigos.net. You must also read and study each chapter's text slowly and carefully. You must learn the ethics rules thoroughly, and the fine-line distinctions are important. Read intensely and underline, circle, and/or highlight the important words in the text. Pay particular attention to the "MPRE Tips" that point out areas of testing concentration or technique suggestions. Highlighted in the text and tips are important facts or legal rules upon which the fine-line distinction answers frequently turn.

3. Preparing Your Own Magic Memory Outline®: This is essential to success. Many students do this just after completing a section of the text or at least after every MRPC.

a. Summarize Your Knowledge: You need to prepare a summary of every chapter in your own words. This is best accomplished using the Magic Memory Outlines® that are both printed in the book and provided on the CD-ROM software templates. The electronic outline corresponds to the bold headings in the printed text. An example is on page 1-21.

b. Capture the Essence: Your job is to summarize the text by capturing the essence of the rule and entering your summarized wording into your own outlines. Aim for concise, yet comprehensive statements of the rule. Focus on the required technical elements of the ethical restraint. Integrate any helpful "learning question" information into your outline.

c. Memorize Your Outlines: After you have completed your own Magic Memory Outline® for the whole chapter, read it over carefully once or twice. You need to commit the black letter law on your Magic Memory Outline® to rote memory. Every week between your 6 outline preparations and the actual MPRE exam, read over your completed Magic Memory Outlines® at least once.

4. Work Chapter's Questions:

a. Work Practice Questions: Next, work the practice questions at the end of the chapter. These questions are not necessarily in the same order as the topics in the chapter, but the chapter's Question Maps will serve as a cross-reference. The questions preceded by a bold "F" at the right refer to final exam questions. Our questions are more difficult than the actual MPRE; most candidates get the easy ones right, so your performance on the more difficult questions will make the difference. The more questions you work, the better, and this Rigos course has more questions than any other MPRE review program.

b. CD-ROM Option: The same questions printed in the book are on the CD-ROM, so you can use the software to work the questions. On the CD-ROM Question Map software, a question pertaining to that topic will pop up if you click on the topic. See page 16.

c. Do a Few at a Time: Work the chapter questions in small bites. Make sure you stop after every or no more than a few questions to check the answer rationales while the facts are still fresh in your active memory. Some students refer to the answer rationale after every question. Mask down on the answer sheet so you don't peek ahead. In this third edition we have positioned every question and answer so it does not go over to a succeeding page.

d. Learn from Your Mistakes: The objective is to learn from your mistakes by reviewing the answer rationales while you still remember the details of the question. It is good to struggle with the difficult ones; they will help you become familiar with the MPRE nuances, tricks, and fine-line distinctions. These make the difference. Put a red star alongside (or if you're using the CD-ROM, note elsewhere on paper) every question you missed. Missed questions should be worked again just prior to taking the actual MPRE.

5. Take the Practice Exam: At the end of the book is a simulated MPRE exam. There are 60 questions in random order. On the real exam only 50 of the 60 are counted, but there is no way of knowing which are only included for validation purposes. While many of the questions in our text are intentionally difficult and complex, the final exam has the same format and approximately the same overall difficulty as the actual MPRE.

a. Solid Block of Time: It is best to create actual exam conditions for the practice exam. Time yourself and work as quickly as you can without sacrificing accuracy.

b. Correct Your Answers: The answers do not come directly after the individual questions. Correct all your answers only after you complete the full practice exam.

(1) Learn from Your Mistakes: When you refer to the answer rationales, be sure you understand why you picked the wrong choice. The fine-line distinctions are critical. Again, it is usually worthwhile to review the answer rationales to all of the four alternatives because they reinforce the details of the relevant issue. More than one answer rationale may be identical if the alternatives are incorrect for the same reason.

(2) Mark Mistakes: Again, put a red star in the margin alongside every question you missed and work them again right before sitting for the actual MPRE. If you are using the software, print out or note the questions you missed on a sheet of paper.

6. Update and Memorize Magic Memory Outlines®: As you work the chapter and the practice exam questions, you may want to supplement and update your Magic Memory Outlines®. Key determinative facts have a tendency to repeat themselves on the MPRE, even though the facts of the questions may be superficially different. Your self-prepared Magic Memory Outlines® should be committed to memory by reading them over many times.

7. Other Tips:

a. Keep Working Questions: Continue to work practice MPRE questions by mixing topics from different chapters. With more than 350 questions in our book, every topic is covered. You can make your own exams with the CD-ROM software. You may work 5, 10, or 20 random questions at a time. When you have a few spare minutes, pick a number of questions and work your own short exam. Review every chapter and practice exam question you missed in your preparation process shortly before sitting for the actual exam (these questions should have a red star alongside them). Learn from your mistakes.

b. Study Time Blocks: Concentration during your study time is critical and will increase the efficiency of your effort. We recommend you build your studying time block to a full 120 minutes. This will not be easy at first, but the Rigos CD-ROM "Make Your Own Exam™" software will help. This will help you build up your stamina and concentration intensity so you will not have to take breaks during the actual exam.

V. HOW TO USE THE CD-ROM SOFTWARE QUESTION AND ANSWER

There are many ways to work the questions contained on the software. You can mix and match the techniques below. With several hundred questions, you won't soon run out of new challenges. Be sure to work many on paper which is the format of the exam.

A. Work Straight Through Chapter Questions

You should work practice questions from one chapter at a time, usually in order.

1. How It Works: The chapter questions will appear one at a time, beginning with Question Number 1. You can work questions in sequential order until you want to stop.

2. How to Use It: Go to the main page and click the chapter you want to work (for example, Chapter 1, Client Relations – Competence, Scope of Representation, and Fees). The questions will appear in the same order as in the text, and you can work them from beginning to end. Read the fact pattern and call of the question thoroughly, then click on your selection of "A," "B," "C," or "D." When you make your answer selection, a window will open and indicate whether your choice was correct or incorrect, and present the answer rationale. You should click on the four answer alternatives until you get the right answer. The arrow at the bottom of the screen allows you to "jump" to other than the next sequential question.

B. Final Exam

1. How It Works: The final exam is a mock MPRE with the same number of questions, difficulty range, and time constraints as the actual MPRE. The CD-ROM version is timed at 120 minutes for the 60-question exam. It is designed to be both your final review of what you have learned as well as a practice run for the MPRE. It should give you confidence when you take the real MPRE.

2. How to Use It: When you are ready, go to the main page and click "Chapter 7, Final Exam." Unlike your practice sessions, the correct answers will not be revealed on the screen until you have completed the whole exam.

C. Make Your Own Exam™

This feature allows you to create organized practice sessions in sets of 5, 10, 20, or a specified number of questions of your own choosing with the click of a mouse.

1. How It Works: The questions appear in random order from all of the six MPRE topics. You should review all of the answer rationales to gain a depth of subject understanding. You can use this software feature as many times in a row as you wish, and you will constantly get new combinations of different questions. You should work many questions without stopping, to build stamina.

2. How to Use It: To use this feature, simply click the "Make Your Own Exam™" button on the main page. Choose the number of questions that you want to work: click "5," "10," "20," or type any whole number into the white box and click "X." The questions will come on the screen one at a time or you can print them out so you can work your drill on paper. Read the fact pattern and call of the question thoroughly, then click on your selection of "A," "B," "C," or "D." When you select an answer, a window will show whether your choice was correct or incorrect, and why. You may find it helpful to read all four answer rationales to gain a more thorough understanding of the subject.

VI. EXAM SITE TIPS

A. Be Punctual

1. Consider a Convenient Hotel: If you live far away or could have transportation delays, consider booking a hotel room near the test center site. Many authorities advise staying alone so there are no distractions. It is best to walk from your hotel room to the exam site; this avoids the uncertainties and stresses of traffic, bus, train, or subway travel.

2. Arrive Early: Don't be rushed on the morning of the exam. On the exam day, arrive early at the test center before the scheduled starting time. Avoid hurrying or arriving late because it is disconcerting and may adversely affect your composure. Check in at the registrar's desk. Look over the facilities and restroom locations.

3. Improve Morning Performance: If you are usually a late riser, practice getting up early every morning for the week before the exam. Start your day by using the Rigos "Make Your Own Exam" software to create a short exam from varied subjects.

B. What to Bring with You

1. Admission Information: Students should bring to the exam site the written instructions and the Admission Ticket provided by the NCBE. Also bring two pieces of backup identification bearing your signature and photo. Unauthorized devices such as cameras, cell phones, normal computers, recording devices, scanners etc., are not allowed in the exam room.

2. Comfort and Practicality: Dress comfortably in clothes that make you feel the best. In some states you can bring a cushion to soften the chairs if you like. Hats and headphones are not allowed in the testing room. Some students find earplugs aid their exam concentration. If your state allows earplugs in the actual exam, use them while working questions during the preparation period.

3. Snacks: Food and beverages usually are not allowed in the exam room, but a water bottle often is. Do not consume a large meal or copious liquids just before the exam.

4. Administrative Concerns: Restroom breaks are possible, but are ill advised. They use up valuable time and break mental concentration. Time is very precious in this intellectual exercise. Your studying should have expanded your ability to sit and concentrate for a two-hour block.

C. Focus Only on the MPRE

1. Preserve Your Mental Energy: Get a full night's sleep before you take the MPRE. Fight to keep mentally sharp and intense for the full testing session. If you find your mental intensity weakening in the last hour, pause, close your eyes, and take four deep breaths.

2. Concentrate on the Task: Imagine you and the exam booklet are in a glass box. During the 120 minutes in the MPRE session, the only thing that you should think about is making your best effort on this exam. Personal problems should be left outside the exam room. Don't daydream or allow your thoughts to wander.

D. Be Confident

1. Relax: Consciously relax. Deep, slow breathing will facilitate this mental state. Don't listen to the pre-exam chatter of nervous candidates. You do not want their test anxiety to affect you. It is too late to add anything to your knowledge, and this distraction will only confuse and drain you. It is better not to talk to anyone. If other candidates are bothering you, take a little walk away from them to relax.

2. Confidence and Poise: Get psyched up to make the MPRE your finest intellectual effort. Approach the exam with mental confidence and poise. Think of the MPRE as a game that you are going to win. Don't get discouraged by any difficult questions. Think of them as opportunities to use your keenly-developed MPRE analytical skills. Work as quickly as you can without sacrificing accuracy. Many of your competitors have not followed a thorough review program and are really there "for practice." Rigos students are there to pass.

3. Contemplate the Moment: Just before the examiner says, "Start your exam," contemplate the moment. Close your eyes and picture the bar admission ceremony in which you will be sworn in. For lawyers, this is our professional rite of passage, and you will only do it once. Prepare yourself mentally to go for every grading point and make a commitment not to leave the session early. The most important race of your professional life has just begun.

E. Go the Distance

Fight to the end of the exam. Don't leave any questions unanswered. The difference between a passing and failing score can get down to one or two extra correct questions. Rework questions. Only the inexperienced or foolish leave any bar exam session early.

VII. CONCLUSION

Scoring high on the MPRE exam is very doable the first time you take it. The Rigos "seamless program" works well for those students willing to work at it. There is simply no shortcut to planning and following a thorough, complete preparation program.

Plan to spend the necessary time and distribute all six substantive chapters and the final exam over at least four weeks until the exam. Use the planning calendar and weekly planning sheet on pages 19 and 20. This allows you to break down your effort into manageable modules. Leave time at the end for the practice exam and a final review of your Magic Memory Outlines®. Plan your success program and stay on schedule week-by-week.

After you get your results, please take the time to fill out the Course Evaluation Form at the end of this book. It will help us improve our course for students who will follow you, and we may publish your ideas and thoughts. Good luck on the MPRE and we hope you will think of the Rigos Uniform Bar Review Series when you prepare for the full bar exam.

James J. Rigos
Editor-in-Chief
Rigos Uniform Bar Review Series

RIGOS UNIFORM BAR REVIEW SERIES

PROFESSIONAL RESPONSIBILITY EXAM REVIEW (MPRE)

OVERALL FOUR-WEEK MPRE PREPARATION PLANNING CALENDAR

PACE OF 2 LEARNING SESSIONS A WEEK OVER 3 WEEKS AND ONE FINAL WEEK OF REVIEW

MPRE Candidate__________________________Exam Date___________________

Students should use the below paced chapter-by-chapter program to schedule your MPRE review. After you work through the various functions, list the date completed.

Week4

Chapter	Learning Session	Complete M.M.O	Work all Q&As
1	____________ Date Completed	____________ Date Completed	____________ Date Completed
2	____________ Date Completed	____________ Date Completed	____________ Date Completed

Week 3

Chapter	Learning Session	Complete M.M.O	Work all Q&As
3	____________ Date Completed	____________ Date Completed	____________ Date Completed
4	____________ Date Completed	____________ Date Completed	____________ Date Completed

Week 2

Chapter	Learning Session	Complete M.M.O	Work all Q&As
5	____________ Date Completed	____________ Date Completed	____________ Date Completed
6	____________ Date Completed	____________ Date Completed	____________ Date Completed

Week 1

Exam Week: Monday – Thursday, ___________. Take the Rigos final exam on page 301. Continue using the software feature to Make Your Own Exams® of 60 questions each.

Friday, _____________. Read over all your Magic Memory Outlines® and review all questions and answer rationales you missed during your detailed review. Relax in the evening and get a good night's sleep.

Exam Date, ________________________, 20____. Sit for and score high on the MPRE!

RIGOS UNIFORM BAR REVIEW SERIES
PROFESSIONAL RESPONSIBILITY EXAM REVIEW (MPRE)

WEEKLY AND DAILY PLANNING SHEET

WEEK: From Monday ________________ to Sunday __________________.

THE BAR EXAM IS ________ WEEKS AWAY

MPRE WEEKLY OBJECTIVES

	MPRE Subject Studied	Prepare Magic Memory Outlines	Memorize MMO and Acronyms	Do All Chapter Questions	Use "Make Your Own Exam" Software
Mon					
Tues					
Wed					
Thurs					
Friday					
Sat/ Sun					

DAILY SCHEDULE BY HOUR

Time	Monday	Tuesday	Wednesday	Thursday	Friday	Saturday	Sunday
6-7:00am							
7-8:00							
8-9:00							
9-10:00							
10-11:00							
11-12:00							
12-1:00pm							
1-2:00							
2-3:00							
3-4:00							
4-5:00							
5-6:00							
6-7:00							
7-8:00							
8-9:00							
9-10:00							
10-11:00							

RIGOS UNIFORM BAR REVIEW SERIES

PROFESSIONAL RESPONSIBILITY EXAM REVIEW (MPRE)

Chapter 1

Client Relations – Competence, Scope of Representation, and Fees

Magic Memory Outline®

A. Competence – Legal knowledge, skills, thoroughness required for case
1. Proficiency Required – or can research but not charge C for excess time. May associate with other expert Ls with client consent
2. Required Standard – held to the general L due care reasonable competency unless L is holding out as an expert, thereby creating a higher performance duty
3. Emergency Situation – only best efforts required under emergency
4. Maintaining Competence – Must keep your specialized knowledge current
5. Legal Malpractice Relationship – Breach of contract, fiduciary duty, or malpractice claims, but ethical rules do not establish legal standard

B. Scope of Representation and Authority Allocation
1. Representation Objectives – C determines representation objectives
2. Lawyer's Decisions – Means and procedural tactics for L with C approval
3. Client's Decisions – **AJET** – C has exclusive decision authority whether to accept settlement offers, jury waiver, enter plea, or testify in person at trial
4. No Endorsement – of C's political, social or moral positions by L
5. Counsel a Crime or Fraud – if for future, may be aiding and abetting the C
6. Client Urging MRPC Violation – consult with C and must withdraw
7. Client Authority – required to act on C's behalf with third parties
8. Limit of Representation – discrete aspect OK, if reasonable and C consent

C. Diligence – carefulness, timeliness, and promptness required by L
1. Dilatory Practices – No unreasonable delay and/or procrastination
2. Legal Rules – SOL concern – must calendar and control docket dates
3. Representation Completion – L should inform C, preferably in writing

D. Communication – Must keep C timely informed in reasonable detail
1. Informative Explanations – C should participate in significant decisions
2. Written v. Oral – Representation letter sets C's expectations
3. Special Situations – two exceptions to duty to disclose to C
   a. Court Order or Rules – may prohibit or limit sensitive information
   b. Client Imprudent Reaction – If C will cause harm to themselves
4. Communicate Mistakes – to C of L's error and incidents
5. Communicate Termination – when relationship terminates so it is clear that there is no C expectation of future monitoring by L

RIGOS UNIFORM BAR REVIEW SERIES
PROFESSIONAL RESPONSIBILITY EXAM REVIEW (MPRE)

Chapter 1

Client Relations – Competence, Scope of Representation, and Fees

MPRE Tip: A Lawyer-Client relationship may be expressed or implied, often created by a lawyer's failure to affirmatively reject a client's reasonable belief of representation.

A. Competence – MRPC 1.1

Lawyers must be legally competent. Competent representation requires the legal knowledge, skills, thoroughness, and preparation reasonably necessary for the legal matter.

1. Proficiency Required: Competent representation is usually based on personal experience. Lack of experience in a given area is not conclusive evidence of incompetence because all persons who graduate from law school and pass the bar exam are presumed competent to research and practice any area of law. However, a lawyer cannot charge the client for excessive research time spent learning details of the substantive law that an experienced lawyer would know. A lawyer may associate with another attorney who has the required competency, but the client must consent to the arrangement.

2. Required Standard: The standard is usually that of a general practitioner, but may be elevated if the lawyer held himself out as an expert such as an LL.M. in taxation.

3. Emergency Situation: In an emergency, a lawyer may make a best effort until it is possible to consult with or refer the client to a more competent practitioner.

4. Maintaining Competence: A lawyer must keep abreast of changes in the area of practice. Usually this means participating in relevant continuing legal education (CLE).

MPRE Tip: Incompetence is often combined on the exam questions with delay (MRPC 1.3) and a failure to communicate with the client (MRPC 1.4).

5. Legal Malpractice Relationship: Legal malpractice theories include breach of contract (reasonable care implied), tort (misrepresentation or negligence), or fiduciary duty (confidentiality or honest dealings). The MRPCs do not create a cause of action against a lawyer and do not necessarily set the standards of practice for purposes of civil liability. Evidence of a disciplinary violation may not be introduced in a malpractice lawsuit. However, an expert may incorporate the concepts underlying the MRPCs into an opinion on the reasonable legal standard of care and fiduciary duty to which the lawyer should have adhered. The client generally must prove that but for the lawyer's malpractice, the client would have prevailed in the underlying matter ("case within a case").

B. Scope of Representation and Authority Allocation – MRPC 1.2

This Rule includes a variety of representation matters including who – the client or lawyer – makes which decisions and addresses related ethical restrictions on the client's directions over the lawyer. The scope of the lawyer's undertaking is also examined.

1. Representation Objectives: The client has the ultimate authority in determining the representation objectives. This includes all of the major outcome-determinant decisions.

2. Lawyer's Decisions: Unless specified to the contrary, the lawyer has implied authorization to decide the legal tactics used to achieve the objectives. This includes making most strategic and procedural decisions such as causes of action to plead, the extent of discovery, professional courtesy to be extended to opposing counsel, and trial witness presentation choices. The lawyer should consult with the client on such details.

3. Client's Decisions – AJET: The client has the ultimate authority to make major litigation decisions. These include the questions of whether to (1) accept or reject a settlement offer; or in a criminal case, (2) jury trial waiver, (3) entering a plea, or (4) testifying at trial.

4. No Endorsement: A lawyer's representation of a client does not constitute approval or an endorsement of the client's political, social, or moral views and activities.

5. Counsel a Crime or Fraud: A lawyer shall not counsel or assist a client in perpetrating conduct that the lawyer knows is criminal or fraudulent. Prohibitions include planning and concealing ongoing unlawful activities, which is aiding and abetting; the lawyer must withdraw. However, the lawyer may attempt to determine the validity, scope, meaning, or application of the law to a past offense and discuss the legal consequences. A lawyer may in good faith counsel a client on how to gain legal standing necessary to challenge the law.

6. Client Urging MRPC Violation: If the client expects assistance from the lawyer not permitted by the MRPCs, the lawyer must consult with the client concerning the ethical limitations on the lawyer's conduct. The lawyer must tell the client that he cannot violate the disciplinary rules. If the client insists, the lawyer must attempt to withdraw.

7. Client Authority: In some states, a lawyer shall not willfully purport to act as a lawyer for any person without the prior authority of that person.

8. Limit of Representation: Clients usually retain a lawyer contractually to handle all aspects of a matter, such as pursuing or defending all legal representation in a predefined cause of action. In many states, the scope of representation by a lawyer may be "limited" to a particular discrete aspect of a matter, such as only the trial court representation, but not an appeal. Scope restrictions must be reasonable under the circumstances. The client must give informed consent after consultation.

MPRE Tip: A lawyer unilaterally making the client's **AJET** decisions is frequently tested.

C. Diligence – MRPC 1.3

A lawyer shall act with reasonable diligence and promptness in representing a client.

1. Dilatory Practices: The lawyer must act promptly and forcefully in pursuing the client's interests. Dilatory practices include an unreasonable delay in filing a lawsuit, procrastination in pursuing the matter, or neglecting to return the client's calls or requests for information concerning the status of the case. If a lawyer is leaving the practice of law, substituted counsel must be appointed to handle the ongoing client representation. The client must be informed of the situation and the succeeding attorney. The client may decide to go elsewhere.

2. Legal Rules: Court deadlines control. A plaintiff's lawyer's worst nightmare is a statute of limitations violation – usually failure to file a claim timely is automatic malpractice. Effective calendaring and docket control systems are critical.

3. Representation Completion: Diligence includes carrying through the representation until the case is complete and/or the lawyer properly withdraws. The client must be informed of completion and any appeal possibility – preferably in writing – so she understands the lawyer's responsibility has ended and she needs to look elsewhere for advice and monitoring.

MPRE Tip: To violate MRPC 1.3, the lawyer's delay must be patently unreasonable.

D. Communication – MRPC 1.4

A lawyer shall keep the client reasonably informed about progress and developments in the status of the matter, any issues requiring informed consent, and any limitations on the lawyer. Any MRPC limitations should be explained if the client's expectations could involve a violation. All bona fide offers of settlement must be communicated to the client.

1. Informative Explanations: An explanation may be necessary so that clients can participate in making informed decisions and have a full understanding upon which informed consent is based. Any request for information by the client should be answered timely. Client telephone calls, emails, and letters should be returned promptly. If for some reason the time schedule or agreed timeline slips, the lawyer should inform the client before the due dates.

2. Written v. Oral: Oral communications are worth the paper they are written on. While the expectations of both parties start with the representation agreement, it is also a good idea to send a letter at various intervals summarizing the status of the matter and what is ahead.

3. Special Situations: There are two exceptions to the communication duty.

a. Court Order or Rules: A court order may prohibit or limit the lawyer from sharing sensitive information with the client. For instance, a judge may issue a protection order forbidding the lawyer from communicating to the client trade secrets of a competitor that the lawyer learned in the discovery process.

b. Client Imprudent Reaction: If the disclosure of adverse information would cause the client to harm herself, the lawyer may delay the communication.

4. Communicate Mistakes: Ethical rulings direct that any mistake a lawyer makes must be communicated to the client. This could create a conflict of interest requiring client consent to allow the lawyer to go forward in the representation.

5. Communicate Termination: The client must be informed when the attorney-client relationship has ended. This requirement intends to make it clear to the client that the lawyer's responsibility has terminated, and she is no longer monitoring the client's situation or changes in the law that may have adverse consequences.

MPRE Tip: A failure to communicate (MRPC 1.4) and failure to act in a diligent manner (MRPC 1.3) both suggest an incompetent lawyer (MRPC 1.1).

E. Fees – MRPC 1.5(a)

A lawyer may not charge excessive fees (or recover excessive expenses), regardless of how characterized or calculated. Therefore, all charges that are ultimately the responsibility of the client shall not be unreasonable.

1. Reasonable Factors: In determining the reasonableness of a fee, there is no single bright-line test. Rather consider the following **SANTA** (case-related) and **REBER** (attorney-related) factors.

a. Skill Required: A complex antitrust class action will require more skill than an uncontested divorce and thus may be billed at a higher rate.

b. Amount Involved: Value added is currently a favored justification for higher fees. An attorney pursuing a personal injury case seeking millions of dollars in damages could bill more per hour than for a small dollar collection action.

c. Novelty and Difficulty: The novelty and difficulty of prevailing in the case is a factor in determining appropriate fee levels.

d. Time Involved / Opportunities Foregone: The time and labor required are probably the most widely accepted factors in setting fees. A case that the client knows will absorb all a lawyer's time and preclude other employment may be billed at a higher rate.

e. Average Customary Fee: This is the amount normally charged in the locality for similar legal services.

f. Relationship: The nature and length of the attorney's professional relationship with the client is a factor in determining the fee level. Frequently a lawyer demands a fee and cost advance from a new client.

g. Expertise: An attorney who is the world's expert on corporate tax-free reorganizations would command a higher billing rate than a novice.

h. Basis of Fee: Whether the fee is fixed, hourly, or contingent is an important factor in determining the reasonableness question.

i. Experience / Reputation: The more experience in the area and better the reputation of the attorney, the higher the attorney's fee is to be expected.

j. Result: The result matters; winning attorneys usually are paid more than losing attorneys.

MPRE Tip: No one factor is conclusive in the **SANTA REBER** analysis. If the fee is questioned, the burden is on the lawyer to show that the fee is not unreasonable.

2. Double Billing: The ABA in Formal Opinion 93-379 stated that double billing the same time or work product to two clients is improper. This may involve billing two clients for the same research or the same transportation time.

3. Fee Agreement Required – MRPC 1.5(b): Fee agreements (alone or as a part of a more inclusive representation agreement) are often determinant or quite important to the reasonableness of the amount to be charged.

a. Includes: There must always be a fee agreement that allows the client to receive a reasonable and fair disclosure of all material elements of the engagement and billing practices. Some states require a writing if the fee exceeds a threshold amount, such as $1,000 in California, or involves a flat fee or nonrefundable fee arrangement. The MRPCs suggest a simple written memorandum avoids misunderstandings and clarifies expectations. Still, the Rule does not preclude an oral agreement as long as the lawyer is able to prove that the oral agreement gave the required reasonable and fair disclosure.

b. New Client: When the lawyer does not have an established business relationship with the client, an agreement is required. This communication will preferably be communicated before or within a reasonable time after commencing the representation.

c. Substantially Different: If the services to be performed or the fee details are substantially different from a previously-existing arrangement between the lawyer and client, the new factors involved in determining the charges must be communicated to the client.

d. Change in Circumstances: If developments occur that make an earlier fee estimate impossible, a revised estimate should be timely submitted to the client.

e. External Fee Split: The client must receive a written fee statement if a fee split involves a lawyer external to the firm. The fee division must be proportional to services performed or both lawyers must assume joint responsibility. Fee splits with non-lawyers are not allowed. See also MRPC 5.4(a) *infra* at 194.

f. Writing Request: Upon the request of the client in any matter, the lawyer shall communicate in writing the rate or basis of the fee.

g. Withdrawal Writing: Depending on the particular situation at hand, the lawyer may conclude that the safest course of action is to withdraw rather than complete the representation. The client's non-payment of fees, failure to provide required information, or expressed intent to defraud the court may create such a situation. If the matter is in litigation, a formal motion to withdraw may be necessary. See also MRPC 1.16 *infra* at 110 for additional detail concerning withdrawals.

4. Client Fee Objection: The question of fee reasonableness usually develops when a client objects to a billing. If there was a client fee prepayment, the disputed amount should remain in trust pending a resolution. A lawsuit by a lawyer to collect a fee from a client usually draws both a counterclaim for malpractice and a complaint to the disciplinary authority alleging the fee is unreasonable.

> **MPRE Tip:** Any disputed portion of client advances and prepayment funds should be left in trust pending a resolution.

F. <u>Contingency Fee Agreement</u> – MRPC 1.5(c)

A fee may be contingent in whole or in part on the outcome of the matter except in the two situations where a contingent fee is prohibited; see subsection 3 below. If a fixed fee is partially refundable, it is functionally to be classified as a contingent fee.

1. Writing Requirement: A contingent fee is determined by the outcome of the representation. Such an agreement must always be in writing and signed by the client. A contingent fee cannot be unreasonable in amount considering the effort and outcome. The writing should clearly state the method by which the lawyer's fee is to be determined. Details of the percentages that would accrue to the lawyer in the event of settlement, trial, or appeal should be explained. Examples, including case outcome dollar hypotheticals, may also be helpful.

2. Treatment of Costs: The agreement must set forth litigation and other expenses to be deducted from the recovery. In addition, whether such expenses are to be deducted before or after the contingent fee is calculated must be disclosed.

3. Prohibited Matters – MRPC 1.5(d): A lawyer cannot enter into a contingency fee arrangement for the following matters:

a. Domestic Relations: This includes an attempt to secure a dissolution or custody of a child, or the amount of property awarded, alimony, or child support. In contrast, a contingent fee is proper for collection of alimony or support in arrears.

b. Criminal Matter: Representation in a criminal case may not be undertaken on a contingency basis.

4. Client Termination: The client may terminate an "at-will" lawyer at any time. Substantial completion is usually achieved if the lawyer obtains a firm settlement offer in an amount that the client had approved. If substantial completion has been delivered, a recovery is allowed under a theory of *quantum meruit* for the reasonable value of the services rendered. The court may allocate contingent fee recoveries between terminated plaintiff's counsel and successor lawyers taking over the representation.

5. End of Case: Upon conclusion of a contingency matter, the lawyer must provide the client with a written statement of account. This should itemize the dollar recovery outcome, all chargeable costs, and the calculation of amounts going to both the lawyer and the client.

> **MPRE Tip:** Contingency fee representation is a very frequent MPRE testing area.

G. <u>Division of Fees</u> – MRPC 1.5(e)

The rules on an allowable division of fees between lawyers depends on whether they practice in the same law firm.

1. In Same Firm: There are no restrictions on intra-firm split of fees paid by a client for representation. Many firms have formula revenue and expense allocation systems. For example, a rainmaking partner may receive some portion of the billing for supervising the law firm's representation of certain of her clients. Similarly, the firm may pay a former partner a percentage of fees earned after her retirement or sale of her interest.

2. Not in Same Firm: This involves a single fee billing to a client when the lawyers do not practice in the same firm. This facilitates association of external expertise on a client's matter. There are two allowed methods of permissive fee splits.

a. Proportional: Fees proportional to services each lawyer performs, or

b. Non-Proportional / Joint Responsibility: An external fee division not proportional to services performed by each lawyer may be proper if each lawyer assumes joint responsibility for the whole representation.

c. Client Consent: Under either of the above external splitting arrangements the client must consent to the fee-splitting details, including the share each lawyer is to receive. The client disclosure must include the inherent material risks and advantages of externally splitting fees and divided responsibility. The client agreement to consent must be confirmed in writing. For instance, the client could agree that her friend, the overseeing lawyer, would receive a substantially higher fee per hour than the lawyer doing most of the work.

> **MPRE Tip:** Splitting a fee with an external lawyer who neither works on the case nor assumes responsibility creates a potential disciplinary action against both lawyers involved.

3. Referral Services: External referral fees may be paid only to a bar association or local bar-approved referral service. Any other forwarding, referrals, or commissions on fees may not be paid to any person, even if that person is another lawyer. See *infra* at 197.

4. Overall Reasonable Restraint: Finally, the total fee all the lawyers receive in the matter and the fee allocation scheme must be reasonable.

Chapter 1

Client Relations – Competence, Scope of Representation, and Fees

Question Map

Numbers immediately following the topic are the chapter question numbers. The **boldface** numbers preceded by "F" are the final exam question numbers. For example, for the topic "A. Competence" below, questions 9, 22, and 32 are in the chapter questions on pages 1-33, 1-37, and 1-40, respectively; questions **F12** and **F41** are in the final exam on pages 7-278 and 7-288, respectively.

A. Competence – 9, 22, 32 .... **F12, F41**
   1. Proficiency Required – 9 .... **F32**
   2. Required Standard – 17........ **F44**
   3. Emergency Situation – 20........
   4. Maintaining Competence – 21 ....
   5. Legal Malpractice Relationship – 19, 24, 30, 32, 33 .... **F31, F32**

B. Scope of Representation and Authority Allocation ....
   1. Representation Objectives – 10, 28 .... **F34**
   2. Lawyer's Decisions – 10, 16, 28........ **F34**
   3. Client's Decisions – 2, 7, 10, 28, 30........ **F59**
   4. No Endorsement – 29 ....
   5. Counsel a Crime or Fraud – 1, 22, 34, 35........
   6. Client Urging MRPC Violation – 34 .... **F59**
   7. Client Authority – 16 .... **F55**
   8. Limit of Representation – 13 ....

C. Diligence – 6, 23, 32........ **F41**
   1. Dilatory Practices – 6........
   2. Legal Rules – 23 ....
   3. Representation Completion........

D. Communication – 8, 9, 23, 30........
   1. Informative Explanations – 16........
   2. Written v. Oral ....
   3. Special Situations – 14........
      a. Court Order or Rules – 14........
      b. Client Imprudent Reaction – 14........
   4. Communicate Mistakes – 14........
   5. Communicate Termination ....

Chapter 1

Client Relations – Competence, Scope of Representation, and Fees

Questions

1. Charles wanted to buy a laptop computer for his daughter in high school. He went to George's Computer Shop, and George showed him a fancy laptop computer with all the bells and whistles, saying with a smirk, "I 'acquired' this last night, and I will sell it to you for $100." Charles knew this price was too low to be legitimate, but he bought the computer anyway.

On his way home, Charles went to Alice Attorney's office to have her draft a lease for his rental property. Alice had handled property matters for Charles in the past. Charles showed her the laptop and relayed George's comments. Alice remarked that Charles should not tell anyone about the great deal he got on the computer because the laptop was probably stolen.

Was Alice Attorney's conduct proper?

- **(A)** No, because Alice advised Charles how best to commit a fraudulent or illegal act.
- **(B)** No, unless Alice refused to provide representation without an adequate reason.
- **(C)** Yes, because Alice recognized that the laptop was a great deal and didn't want to obstruct Charles' gift to his daughter.
- **(D)** Yes, unless Alice accepted Charles as a client.

2. Lawyer Nancy Negotiator received a call from Mike, who was in jail for possession of an illegal substance. Mike wanted Nancy to bail him out and represent him in the matter. Mike told Nancy he didn't care what Nancy had to do, as long as he was cleared of the charges and maintained his good reputation.

In a pre-trial conference, the prosecutor offered a plea bargain to Nancy – enter a guilty plea to a lesser charge – in exchange for a reduced sentence. Nancy turned down the offer on the spot as she was sure that she could convince the jury not to convict. Unfortunately, Mike was convicted at the trial.

Was it proper for Nancy to reject the plea?

- **(A)** No, because Mike was later convicted.
- **(B)** No, because Nancy did not advise Mike of the plea offer.
- **(C)** Yes, if Mike would have rejected the plea anyway.
- **(D)** Yes, because an Nancy has a duty to advocate zealously for her client.

3. Debra Debtor retained Lawyer Betty Bankexpert to represent her in a federal bankruptcy proceeding. Due to Debra's insolvency, Betty required Debra to pay half of the estimated fee in advance. Betty estimated the total fee would be approximately $10,000, so she wanted Debra to pay $5,000 now. Debra did not have that much cash, so she decided to find another lawyer.

Is Betty subject to discipline?

(A) Yes, because Betty would not begin work until she was paid 50% of the estimated fee.
(B) Yes, because Betty required 50% of the fee to be paid in advance.
(C) No, if Debra was a new client.
(D) No, because Betty may require payment in advance.

4. In which of the following situations would it be proper for Loretta Lawyer to enter into a fee arrangement whereby Loretta would receive 20% of any recovery realized by the Client?

I. Client owns an undivided one-half interest in a boat marina with his ex-wife. He now wants Loretta Lawyer to seek a partition of the property.

II. Client's ex-husband stopped paying support five months ago. She wants Loretta Lawyer to attach and levy on Ex's wages.

III. Client wants Loretta Lawyer to file a paternity suit to prove ex-Boyfriend is the father of her child, so she can establish a right to collect child support payments from him.

(A) I only.
(B) I and II only.
(C) I and III only.
(D) II and III only.

5. Ellen was in an automobile accident. Two days later, she called attorney Rebecca Ready on the phone and told her the details of her personal injury. Ellen had no fault in the accident, and the at-fault driver had full liability insurance. Ellen decided that she wanted to file a formal lawsuit. Rebecca orally committed to handle the case for a 60% contingency fee of the recovery.

Is Rebecca subject to discipline?

(A) No, unless 60% is not the normal percentage in the local community.
(B) Yes, a contingent fee agreement must be in writing.
(C) No, because the case is very complicated, and this fee is a reasonable amount.
(D) Yes, a contingency fee agreement needs to be in writing, and 60% is likely not a reasonable percentage under the circumstances.

6. Alpha Attorney agreed to represent Beta and take the deposition of defendant Chi. Several months elapsed, and the deposition had not been taken. Beta called Alpha, complaining about the lack of progress on her case. During the phone call, Alpha again promised to take the depositions immediately. Two additional months went by and the depositions had not been scheduled.

Is Alpha subject to discipline?

(A) Yes, Alpha was not diligent and was not truthfully communicating with her client.
(B) Yes, unless Beta's case did not suffer.
(C) No, because Alpha is very busy and hasn't had time to get around to Beta's case.
(D) No, unless the trial date is coming up soon.

7. Delta was representing Epsilon in a long-delayed lawsuit and finally received a generous settlement offer from the defendant. The offer stated that the offer was open for only three days. Delta called Epsilon to discuss the settlement, but despite repeated attempts, could not reach her on the phone. After two days had elapsed, Delta herself called the opposing counsel and told her that Epsilon had accepted the settlement offer at $250 per hour.

Is Delta subject to discipline?

(A) No, if Delta could not reach Epsilon and felt she needed to accept within three days.
(B) No, because accepting the settlement offer was in Epsilon's best interest.
(C) Yes, the decision to accept or reject a settlement offer belongs solely to the client.
(D) Yes, but only if it was not a reasonable settlement amount.

8. Blair Bigman was a wealthy businessman who hired lawyer Esther Estateplanner to prepare a comprehensive estate plan to protect his family after his death. Esther created a Last Will and Testament containing a rather complicated testamentary trust. The trust provided for discretionary distribution to Blair's wife and children. Esther subsequently retired from the practice of law but failed to inform the Bigmans. Five years later, the Internal Revenue Service (IRS) changed the trust distribution tax law. Blair and his family were unaware that the IRS's trust tax law had changed. No one from the law firm notified Blair about the change in the law.

The law firm and/or Esther are

(A) Not subject to discipline because Blair and his family are no longer their clients.
(B) Not subject to discipline unless Blair and his family are damaged.
(C) Subject to discipline if they did not inform Blair that the attorney-client relationship had ended.
(D) Subject to discipline because Blair was not informed of the change in the IRS's trust tax law.

9. Paula Prosecutor worked for the County Prosecutor's office for five years after law school. All her work there involved prosecuting felonies. Due to a cutback in public funding, her position was eliminated, so she hung out her shingle to practice law. Her first client asked Paula to research and draft a memorandum covering a complicated corporate reorganization. Paula never took any corporate or tax courses in law school, but needed the work and the money, so she accepted the case after receiving a $3,500 cash retainer.

Which of the following is the most acceptable for Paula?

(A) Attend a seminar on corporate reorganizations, read all the references contained in the seminar workbook, and charge the client for the time.
(B) Attend a seminar on corporate reorganizations, read all the references contained in the seminar workbook, and not charge the client for the time.
(C) Associate with another lawyer with extensive corporate reorganization experience without informing the client.
(D) Decide the engagement is too difficult and withdraw from the case after tendering the client a fee statement for $2,500.

10. Mary Magician was a very experienced and skillful criminal trial attorney. Georgianne Guilty hired her because she had heard of her criminal trial success. Georgianne had a long history of robberies and came across as a common criminal when she spoke. Still, Georgianne felt that if she could personally testify at trial, the jury would believe her. Mary felt strongly that Georgianne did not understand the best legal strategies and that her desire to testify was a grave error because she would be very exposed in the rigorous cross-examination. Accordingly, against Georgianne's wishes, Mary waived a jury trial and refused to call her at the bench trial.

The trial court found that the state did not meet its required burden, so Georgianne was acquitted.

Mary is

(A) Subject to discipline because she overrode Georgianne's wishes as to general trial strategy.
(B) Subject to discipline because she did not allow Georgianne to testify.
(C) Not subject to discipline because Georgianne was not convicted.
(D) Not subject to discipline because an experienced lawyer can choose the appropriate trial strategy.

11. Esther is working on a case for Big Bucks Inc. and has to decide the proper amount to bill the client for two discrete tasks. The first is a comprehensive memorandum on a technical corporate stock security offering matter. Two months before she had researched an almost identical problem for another client, which took 10 hours. To create the Big Bucks memorandum, Esther spent 2 hours changing the names on the prior memorandum and quickly researching the law to be sure it had not changed.

Esther also had to drive to a distant court to argue a motion on behalf of Big Bucks that would normally take 3 hours of billable time. However, another client's motion was fortuitously scheduled in an adjoining courtroom the same day, and she was able to accomplish both motions in 4 hours.

Esther's billing rate is $250. She should properly bill Big Bucks the following total dollars for both preparing the memorandum and arguing the motion.

(A) $1,000
(B) $1,250
(C) $3,000
(D) $3,250

12. Olive Overspender was an attorney in private practice. She had some personal financial problems and decided to double-bill her client, Mega Corporation. Mega had never questioned any tendered billing so she felt it was low risk. . Later, Olive's associate quit the law firm and complained to the Bar Association.

If the applicable disciplinary authority determines that some portion of Olive's double billing practices is unethical, the best argument Olive could reasonably and legitimately muster to avoid discipline for the over billing practices would likely be

(A) Everyone does it.
(B) She had been instructed to double bill by the senior partner in her law firm.
(C) The value of her services to the client were many times the dollar amount she would bill under the double billing system.
(D) The client gave prior written consent to the double billing system.

Debra Developer was a property owner who wanted to develop her property Greenacres. Debra hired Zelda Zoningexpert, a lawyer, to prepare and present the development plan to the County's zoning board. The planned development project required variances from the regular building code. Zelda was successful in securing some, but not all of the variances from the zoning board.

Debra wants to appeal some of the denied variances. Zelda is leery of handling that representation because all of her experience was with the zoning board, and she had never handled an appeal. Debra is insistent that Zelda "finish what she started" because she believes it would be too expensive to educate a new attorney on the technical details of the project.

Is Zelda subject to discipline if she refuses to take on the appeal?

(A) Yes, because a lawyer is obligated to pursue the matter until its conclusion.
(B) Yes, but only if the lawyer affirmatively agreed to handle the appeal within the scope of the representation.
(C) No, unless the client expected the lawyer to handle the appeal.
(D) No, if the representation agreement excluded any appeal.

14. A lawyer should ordinarily promptly inform the client of any decision or circumstance reasonably necessary to permit informed decisions.

Which of the following is an improper reason for not disclosing such information to the client?

(A) A court rule in the jurisdiction prohibiting the release of information about certain categories of anonymous whistleblowers.
(B) A court order prohibiting the attorney from disclosing trade secrets learned in the discovery process.
(C) Information disclosing that the lawyer failed to file a claim timely.
(D) Information that might cause the client to take her own life.

15. Sally Solo is a lawyer from an old and well-connected family in Everytown. She clerked for a local judge after law school and developed a fine reputation in the legal community. Sally then opened a robust solo practice specializing in bankruptcy and debtor rights. She was approached by Betty Breakup, a lawyer who specializes in family law who was trying to build her law practice. Betty proposed that Sally refer any family law claims to her and that in return, she would remit 10% of any fee earned on referrals by Sally.

This agreement is improper

- **(A)** Unless Sally either works on the referred cases or assumes joint responsibility.
- **(B)** For Betty, but not Sally.
- **(C)** For Sally, but not Betty.
- **(D)** Unless the fee distribution is proportional to the work each lawyer performed.

16. Cathy Cautious was an attorney whose practice consisted of litigating consumer product defects. Her client, Gloria Gullible, purchased a lemon automobile based on outrageous express oral misrepresentations made by the car salesman. Cathy is reluctant to assert fraud because the jury could easily find Gloria's reliance was unreasonable and deny any recovery. To assert negligence would likely produce a victory but there would be a substantial offset under the applicable comparative negligence statute in the jurisdiction.

Is it proper for Cathy to assert only the negligence claim?

- **(A)** Yes, because a lawyer decides the means and procedures to achieve the legal objective.
- **(B)** Yes, if the lawyer decides the client's interests are best served by pleading negligence.
- **(C)** No, because a reasonable basis argument may be made that the fraud claim has substantial merit.
- **(D)** No, unless Gloria agrees with the strategy after consultation on all the details.

17. Connie Corporatelaw was the general business attorney for Bigbuck Ltd. Bigbuck was sued by a community group alleging the corporation had polluted the local water supply. Connie negotiated with the plaintiffs' attorney and was getting close to a settlement. A vocal minority of the class plaintiffs disagreed with the community group lawyer and demanded the plaintiff hire a new lawyer.

One month before the scheduled trial the plaintiffs changed lawyers. It became obvious to the defense that there would not be a pre-trial settlement. Connie was not a competent trial lawyer and associated with Terri Triallawyer from another law firm to assist her.

Was Connie's association with Triallawyer proper?

- **(A)** Yes, because Bigbuck Ltd. was aware that Connie associated with Triallawyer.
- **(B)** Yes, if Bigbuck Ltd. was informed in writing and consented to the association and fee sharing arrangement.
- **(C)** No, unless Connie attended the trial with Triallawyer.
- **(D)** No, if the late association meant there was not enough time left to prepare adequately for trial.

18. Cathy Contingency is a criminal defense attorney who has been approached by Alice Abusive for a potential client. Alice was involved in an altercation with her neighbor and the Prosecutor is considering whether to charge her with a crime. Alice has no money and therefore insists that Cathy take her case on a contingency basis.

Cathy may properly

- **(A)** Take the case on unless the Prosecutor charges Alice with a felony rather than a misdemeanor.
- **(B)** Not take Alice's case on.
- **(C)** Take the case on as long as the fee agreement is written.
- **(D)** Not take the case on unless Alice is independently represented in negotiating the terms of the representation.

19. Debra Defamation's legal practice was limited to bringing claims by public figures defamed by media reporting and/or harassed by reporters. Patty Politician saw one of Debra's advertisements and called seeking an appointment. During the meeting, Debra told Patty, "I am very busy and your case is rather complicated, but I can refer you to another defamation lawyer whom you should see before the statute of limitation runs on your claim."

Patty was hopeful that Debra would free up the time to take on her case and thus did not contact another lawyer. Some time later, Patty called Debra back to see if her schedule had improved. Debra said, "No, but the statute of limitations has now run on your claim anyway." It was later determined that Patty did have a meritorious claim for invasion of privacy against the media reporter.

Is Debra subject to civil malpractice liability?

(A) Yes, because a lawyer must tell a potential client the specific date the statute of limitation expires.
(B) Yes, only if she charged the potential client for the appointment.
(C) No, because Debra did not violate any duty owed the potential client.
(D) No, because Debra offered to refer the potential client to another defamation lawyer.

20. Terri Taxlawyer received an LL.M. in tax law and joined a large firm that handled business work for large corporations. All her work at the firm involved the taxability of large corporate divisions and reorganizations. One Friday evening she received a telephone call from her friend, Tom Trouble, who lived in the same apartment house. Apparently, Tom had been stopped for driving his automobile with a defective taillight, and the police found marijuana in the automobile trunk. Terri explained to Tom that she had no experience in criminal law. Tom pleaded with her to bail him out, and Terri agreed to try.

Terri read over the criminal law and procedure outlines she received in her bar review course two years previously. However, because she did not understand the "in plain sight" and search and seizure rules, Terri was not able to get Tom released. Monday morning, Tom's cellmate referred him to a competent criminal lawyer who secured Tom's release in two hours.

Was Terri's conduct proper?

(A) Yes, because this was an emergency situation where referral was not practical.
(B) Yes, because Tom was a personal friend of Terri, not an ongoing client of the law firm.
(C) No, because Terri did not have the required proficiency to undertake a criminal law representation.
(D) No, unless Terri did not charge Tom for the representation.

21. Carol Competent was a new associate in a law firm and asked her supervisor about the firm's continuing legal education (CLE) policy. She was informed that the firm did not pay for CLE or give time off for it. The stated reason was that the State Bar Association did not require any annual CLE in the jurisdiction. Carol was paying off her student loans and decided to save her money and work more hours.

Is it proper for Carol not to attend any continuing legal education programs?

(A) Yes, unless the State Bar Association offers free continuing legal education courses.
(B) Yes, if Carol undertakes sufficient ongoing education to keep abreast of changes relevant to her area of practice.
(C) No, unless Carol purchases malpractice insurance.
(D) No, because maintaining a lawyer's competency requires attending continuing legal education courses.

22. Diane Defense had a client named Sally Shifty. Sally owned a business that was being investigated by a legislative committee trying to determine if the business was connected to organized crime. Sally received a subpoena to appear and give testimony and asked Diane to accompany her. The committee members pressed Sally hard with some questions that were very sensitive and could potentially create criminal liability. Diane advised Sally not to answer on the basis that she was exercising her constitutional right to silence. The attorney for the committee warned Sally that if she continued to refuse to answer, criminal charges would be asserted against her. Sally, based on Diane's advice, continued to refuse to answer and was subsequently convicted for the offense.

Is Diane subject to discipline?

(A) Yes, because in effect, she advised Sally to commit a crime.
(B) Yes, because her advice to Sally was apparently not legally correct based on the subsequent conviction.
(C) No, if Diane reasonably believed that Sally had a legal right to refuse to answer the propounded question.
(D) No, unless she knew the committee had the right to charge a witness with a criminal offense if they refused to testify.

23. Alice Aggressive was an attorney with a practice limited to personal injury cases. Irene Injured was in her car when a commercial truck ran her off the road. Seeking representation, Irene contacted Alice, asking if she would pursue her claim. Alice said that she would take on the case if Irene would pay a retainer of $5,000 and agree to pay one-third of the recovery as a fee. They signed a written representation agreement and Alice said she would begin working on the case immediately.

Alice did contact the attorney for the trucking company and set up an appointment to discuss a settlement. Unfortunately, she did not keep the settlement appointment and refused to return calls from either the trucking company attorney or Irene. After repeated unreturned telephone calls and requests for communications regarding the status of the matter, Irene in desperation contacted Sarah Secondlawyer. Sarah reviewed the case and informed Irene that the statute of limitations expired in two months. At Irene's direction, Sarah filed the lawsuit before the statute had run. Alice then refunded the $5,000 retainer.

Is Alice Aggressive subject to discipline?

(A) Yes, because Alice neglected Irene's case and failed to communicate.
(B) Yes, unless Alice's time was completely occupied with work from other clients that was undertaken before Irene's case came up.
(C) No, because Alice returned Irene's $5,000 retainer.
(D) No, because Irene's case was properly filed before the statute of limitations expired, so no damage was done.

24. Nancy Negligent voluntarily undertook representation of a case for a client named Debra Difficult. At the end of the case, Debra was very unsatisfied with the outcome and found a new lawyer who told her Nancy committed malpractice and violated the rules of professional conduct. Debra filed a grievance against Nancy with the local bar association's disciplinary counsel, which resulted in official discipline being imposed. Debra's new attorney then filed a civil lawsuit against Nancy for malpractice on the same matter as the disciplinary action.

What effect should Nancy's professional discipline have in the civil malpractice action?

(A) It is controlling and conclusive on the negligence issue.
(B) It creates a presumption of negligence, which the lawyer may rebut.
(C) It is some evidence that the jury may consider.
(D) It should not be introduced at all in the civil malpractice case.

25. Harriet Heavybill represented Able Builders, Inc., a local general contractor, in a complicated dispute involving claims to and against a subcontractor. Harriet had been billing Able at $100 per hour, which was the firm's standard rate. The law firm met at their fall retreat and decided to raise their hourly fee to $150. Harriet neglected to inform Able of the hourly increase, and Able continued, as in the past, to pay the total monthly billings on the tenth of the following month.

Is Harriet subject to discipline?

- **(A)** Yes, unless the billing rate per hour is clearly stated on the monthly billings that Able received.
- **(B)** Yes, unless the billing rate change was communicated to Able.
- **(C)** No, unless Able had previously requested notice of any fee change.
- **(D)** No, unless Able contested the total fee as being unreasonable.

26. Sally Selfish was an attorney who limited her practice to personal injury actions. Sally represented Ida Injury in an action against an insurance company to recover for physical injuries she suffered in an automobile accident. After a period of intense negotiations, the insurance company finally paid the agreed settlement amount.

Which of the following actions will not subject Sally to potential discipline?

I. Present a written contingent fee estimate to Ida at the beginning of the representation.
II. Require Ida to sign the contingent fee agreement.
III. Present a written statement to Ida upon conclusion that discloses the details of the final remittance including cost allocations.
IV. Require Ida to sign the written statement disclosing the details of the final remittance to the client upon conclusion.

- **(A)** I and III.
- **(B)** I and IV.
- **(C)** II and III.
- **(D)** II and IV.

27. Connie Corporatelawyer has a law firm that handles only general corporate matters. The CFO of Conglomerate, Inc. has just told Connie that they intend to reorganize various parts of their corporate subsidiaries and want to be sure the IRS does not impose a tax on the reorganization. Connie was relatively inexperienced in the topic and felt it prudent to contact Theresa Taxlawyer in a different law firm to get a formal opinion on the taxability of Conglomerate's reorganization plan. Theresa studied the transaction, prepared a detailed written memorandum of law, and billed Connie for $5,000 – 20 hours at $250 per hour. Connie spent 10 hours on the review of Theresa's memorandum and copied it onto her own letterhead without disclosing the author. She then sent it to Conglomerate's CFO along with a bill for $7,500.

Was the division of fees proper?

(A) Yes, because a lawyer may split fees as she sees fit, as long as the total amount the client pays is not unreasonable.
(B) Yes, as long as the lawyer sending the client the final billing includes only the time she spends on the review.
(C) No, unless each lawyer takes joint responsibility for the whole representation.
(D) No, because Conglomerate, Inc., was not informed of the division of the fee outside Connie's law firm.

28. In a dispute involving the interpretation of a contract, lawyer Alice is representing the plaintiff Betty, and lawyer Connie is representing the defendant Dorothy. Negotiations between the attorneys were not successful in resolving the matter, and Alice began to draft the complaint as the statute of limitations was about to expire. Two days before the statute of limitations expiration date, Alice's daughter was seriously injured in an accident and hospitalized. The daughter called Alice to ask if she could drop what she was doing and travel to her home to watch over her four children. Alice wanted to do the right thing – help her grandchildren – and called Connie to ask her to sign a forbearance agreement allowing a two-week extension of the date the statute of limitation was to expire.

May Connie properly agree to the requested forbearance agreement?

(A) Yes, because Alice could merely file a simple complaint and amend upon her return.
(B) Yes, as long as Dorothy is consulted on the requested professional courtesy forbearance.
(C) No, because the statute of limitations is a state law that cannot be changed.
(D) No, unless this is the type of courtesy that should normally be extended to opposing counsel.

29. Emily Equitable is a lawyer and a partner in a medium-sized law firm in New York. One of the firm's clients Emily has worked for is Addiction Sticks, Inc., a large tobacco wholesaler. New York has under consideration a statute that would make tobacco smoking illegal in a public place. Addiction Sticks is opposed to the measure and is financing a large opposition effort. Emily has been a long-time active member of Americans Against Public Smoking (AAPS), which is one of the major supporting organizations of the proposed non-smoking statute. Emily has been asked by other members of AAPS to support the measure publicly.

It would be proper for Emily to

I. Take a public position on the issue, but attempt not to present her views in such a way that might unduly prejudice Addiction Sticks.
II. Speak publicly in support of the statute, but be clear she is speaking on her own behalf and not for Addiction Sticks.
III. Say nothing publicly that is inconsistent with Addiction Sticks' position on the statute.
IV. Say nothing publicly about the statute because her prior representation of Addiction Sticks constitutes an implied approval of the client's political, economic, social, and moral positions.

(A) I only.
(B) II only.
(C) I and II only.
(D) III and IV only.

30. The National Exquirer Magazine wrote a series of articles detailing the practices of certain companies in overbilling the government. In one of their juiciest articles, they identified a company owned by Pattie Private. Their accusation of her fraud resulted in many of Pattie's customers going elsewhere. In fact, the investigative reporter had confused Pattie's company with another having a similar name.

Pattie hired Loretta Libellawyer to bring suit against National Exquirer and told her, "I probably will not agree to accept less than $250,000 in settlement or $400,000 recovery at trial." The week before trial, Loretta received a settlement offer from National Exquirer of $200,000. Loretta could not contact Pattie, so she called the defendant and rejected the offer. The bench trial the next week resulted in a plaintiff's verdict of $500,000.

Did Loretta's actions subject her to civil malpractice liability?

(A) Yes, because the client always retains the sole authority to accept or reject all settlement offers.
(B) Yes, because Loretta violated her duty to keep her client informed about all significant developments in the case.
(C) No, because there are no damages.
(D) No, because Pattie did not authorize Loretta to accept a settlement below $250,000.

31. Sally Sufferer was one of the patients injured as a consequence of the defendant's faulty prescription medicine. The Drug Company's defendant admitted liability and hired an adjuster to negotiate settlements with the two dozen victims and their families. Sally's physical injuries were the same as those for which 20 other defendants had received a settlement amount between $225,000 and $250,000. When the defendant's claim adjuster tendered her an offer, Sally asked Pattie Predator, a lawyer, to consult with her in reviewing the offered settlement. Pattie agreed and reviewed the agreement, telling Sally it looked fine to her. After Sally signed and the papers were sent off to the defendant's claim adjuster, Sally asked Pattie what she was going to be charged as a legal fee. Pattie said, "Oh, I always charge one-third of any recovery of a personal injury claim."

Is Patty subject to discipline?

- **(A)** Yes, if one-third of the recovery is unreasonable as compared to the amount normally charged in the locality for similar legal services.
- **(B)** Yes, if the dollar fees have no rational relationship to the time and effort required.
- **(C)** No, because Sally could have gone to another lawyer.
- **(D)** No, if Sally agreed in writing and did not contest the fee.

32. Connie Client hired a lawyer named Roberta Reckless to file a negligence claim against Debra Driver. Connie had gone on a joy ride with Debra even though Connie knew Debra was drunk at the time. The drunk Debra was unable to drive properly and got into an accident, causing Connie serious injuries. The trial court held the defense of contributory negligence applied and that it negated Connie's claim against Debra in total. The highest court in the controlling jurisdiction had just replaced contributory negligence with comparative fault for a claim that predated Connie's claim.

Roberta was distracted by other problems at the time and forgot to file the appeal within the 30-day time frame that was required by the applicable court rule. Connie was told by many other lawyers that the appellate court would certainly have reversed the trial court.

Roberta Reckless is subject to:

	Professional Discipline	Malpractice Liability
(A)	No	Yes
(B)	Yes	No
(C)	No	Yes
(D)	Yes	Yes

33. Debra Dishonest was charged with robbery and was represented by Alice Asleep, who charged a $10,000 retainer. At trial, the prosecutor was halfway through presenting the case and suffered a heart attack. Over the judge's objections the prosecutor's office refused to assign another lawyer to continue the prosecution. Two days later, since no substitute prosecutor had shown up, the judge entered a judgment of acquittal and discharged the jury.

Three months later, the prosecutor's office brought identical charges against Debra. Debra was so pleased with the result in the first case she kept Alice on for her attorney in the second case. Alice filed no pre-trial motions in the second trial. After considering all the evidence, the jury entered a guilty verdict, and the judge imposed a prison sentence. Debra was shocked at the inconsistent result and hired a new lawyer to pursue an appeal. Before Alice had to begin serving her prison sentence, the appellate court reversed the conviction on the basis of double jeopardy and clear incompetence of Alice Asleep.

Is Alice subject to civil liability for malpractice?

(A) Yes, but because Debra was found guilty, only nominal damages may be recovered.

(B) Yes, if Debra can show the jury would not have convicted her had Alice exercised reasonable care.

(C) No, even if Debra can show that she did not commit the robbery in question, because that question is for the jury.

(D) No, because the court of appeals reversed before Alice had to begin serving her sentence.

34. Iola Infringer operates a company that copies CD-ROMs and videos of musical groups, and markets the copied product as an original work product. Iola became a little worried by a rumor she had heard from a salesperson. The salesperson was told that a musician who had not received royalties on his songs had hired a lawyer and that this lawyer was asking questions about Iola's legal compliance. After learning this, Iola made a consultation appointment to see Carol Copyright, an attorney whose practice is limited to defending copyright infringement actions.

In the meeting it became apparent to Carol that Iola's business activities consisted primarily of distributing illegally-duplicated, copyrighted works of legitimate musical groups. Carol explained the detection procedures used by legitimate music and software companies. She further explained and recommended the best procedures that would be helpful to Iola in avoiding infringement detection and defending against civil or criminal actions for pirating authors' protected work product.

Is Carol subject to discipline?

(A) Yes, because she counseled a client in how to perpetrate ongoing criminal or fraudulent conduct.

(B) Yes, unless Carol withdrew, because the activity violates the MRPCs.

(C) No, because a lawyer may discuss the consequences of a crime or fraud with a client.

(D) No, because a lawyer may counsel a client in how to avoid criminal prosecution.

35. Pattie Propertyowner is an advocate for homeless groups. She has recently become concerned about a new statute passed by the legislature that makes it a crime for private landowners to allow unpermitted homeless people to camp on their property. Pattie met with a lawyer named Connie Constitution who stated that the new statute could easily be overturned as an unconstitutional restraint on the use of private property. However, to bring the question to issue and provide legal standing to contest the statute would require that a lawsuit be brought. One way this result could be achieved would be if the state attorney general prosecuted Pattie based upon a violation.

Following Connie's advice, Pattie allowed a large number of homeless people to camp on her property without a permit. The attorney general learned of the homeless people on Pattie's property and charged her with a violation of the statute.

Is Connie subject to discipline for advising Pattie to commit the violation?

- **(A)** Yes, because Connie advised her client to do something Connie knew was illegal.
- **(B)** Yes, unless Pattie signed a consent agreement stating that she was aware Connie's advice could lead to charges of a violation of the statute.
- **(C)** No, only if the statute is ultimately determined to be unconstitutional.
- **(D)** No, because the advice covered how to gain the standing necessary to challenge the constitutionality of the statute.

36. Paula Plaintiff was a permanent resident of State A who was seriously injured in State B while at her vacation home. She hired her regular lawyer Alice Attorney to represent her in pursuing the claim. Alice was only admitted to practice law in State A. The proper jurisdiction to pursue the claim was State B, so Alice associated with Nancy New, an attorney in State B, to try the case. Nancy was paid 50% of the $1,000,000 attorney fees charged.

This fee allocation is proper if

- **(A)** Nancy did 50% of the work.
- **(B)** Both attorneys were responsible for the whole case.
- **(C)** Alice was admitted to practice law in State B.
- **(D)** Only if Paula approved of the fee split allocation and such consent was confirmed in writing.

Chapter 1

Client Relations – Competence, Scope of Representation, and Fees

Answers

MPRE Tip: Put a piece of paper over the answers and "mask down" while working through the questions so you don't accidently peek at the next answer.

1. **/A/** A lawyer shall not counsel a client to engage, or assist a client, in conduct that the lawyer knows is criminal or fraudulent. [MRPC 1.2(d)] Since Alice strongly suspected the laptop was stolen, she should not have advised Charles to conceal the fact that Charles was probably in possession of stolen goods. **(B)** is incorrect because Alice did not refuse to represent Charles, and in fact, it is because Charles was her client that her actions were a violation. **(C)** is incorrect because her action was a violation regardless of her motive. **(D)** is incorrect because Charles was already her client.

2. **/B/** A lawyer shall abide by the client's decision whether to accept an offer of settlement as well as the plea to be entered. [MRPC 1.2(a)] Since a plea bargain is an offer of settlement, it must be communicated to the client, and the client must make the decision. The plea to be entered is also a client decision. It was improper for Nancy to make the decision without consulting her client. **(A)** is incorrect because a good or bad outcome of the matter does not excuse Nancy's violation. **(C)** is incorrect because the fact that the client would probably reject the offer does not excuse Nancy from communicating the offer to her client. **(D)** is incorrect because zealously advocating for her client has nothing to do with her failure to communicate the offer and abide by the client's decision.

3. **/D/** There is no rule against demanding and collecting an advance towards the estimated total a fee. The only requirement is that the lawyer return any unearned portion of the advances at the end of the case. [MRPC 1.5] **(A)** is incorrect because the lawyer may collect an advance before she starts to work. **(B)** is incorrect because the lawyer may require an advance on the fee. **(C)** is incorrect because whether or not the client is a new or old client is not relevant to the central issue of fee advances.

4. **/B/** A lawyer shall not enter into an arrangement for, charge, or collect any fee in a domestic relations matter, the payment or amount of which is contingent upon the securing of a dissolution or annulment of marriage or upon the amount of maintenance or support, or property settlement in lieu thereof (except in post-dissolution proceedings). [MRPC 1.5(d)] Situation I is a post-dissolution partition of property, and thus a contingent fee is allowed. Situation II does not involve the amount of support, only the enforcement and collection of a prior-determined payment, so a contingent fee is allowed. Situation III is not allowed since this domestic relations matter seeks to establish child support, including the amount of child support.

5. **/D/** A contingent fee agreement shall be in writing. [MRPC 1.5(c)(1)] Also, the percentage needs to be reasonable under the circumstances. D is the most complete correct answer. **(A)** is not the best answer because, while the alternative is correct (and includes a double negative), it is not as complete as D. **(B)** is not the best answer because, while the alternative is correct, it is not as complete as D. **(C)** is incorrect because this fee is not reasonable under the circumstances.

6. **/A/** A lawyer shall act with reasonable diligence and promptness in representing a client. [MRPC 1.3] It is also professional misconduct for a lawyer to engage in conduct involving dishonesty, fraud, deceit, or misrepresentation. [MRPC 8.4(c)] Rebecca is not being diligent in delaying the depositions. She is also not being truthful to her client by making promises she does not keep. **(B)** is incorrect because even if Ellen's case did not suffer, it does not excuse the violation. **(C)** is incorrect because the lawyer is in violation no matter what her excuse is. **(D)** is incorrect because the lawyer is still in violation even if the trial date is not imminent.

7. **/C/** A lawyer shall abide by a client's decision whether to accept an offer of settlement. [MRPC 1.2(a)] **(A)** is not the best answer because the decision belongs to the client, and Attorney Rebecca had to communicate the offer to Ellen. **(B)** is incorrect because even if the offer was in Ellen's best interest, she as a client had to make the decision. **(D)** is incorrect because even if the settlement was a reasonable amount, Ellen as a client had to make the decision.

8. **/C/** The client must be informed when the attorney-client relationship has ended, so it is clear that the lawyer is not monitoring the client's situation. [MRPC 1.4] **(A)** is incorrect because if Blair reasonably believes that Esther is still representing them by monitoring the applicable trust law, Esther is subject to discipline. **(B)** is incorrect because a failure to communicate reasonably may be an ethical violation independent of whether a malpractice action for damages exists. **(D)** is not the best answer because the thrust of the question is the failure to communicate the representation termination. If the termination was properly communicated, there would clearly be no duty to inform the client of the change in the IRS's trust tax laws.

9. **/B/** The best answer because a lawyer may research an area of the law to acquire the necessary competency as long as the client is not charged for excess research time to learn details that a competent lawyer should know. [MRPC 1.1] **(A)** is incorrect because the client should not be charged for excess research. **(C)** is incorrect because such a lawyer association should be communicated to the client and consent obtained. **(D)** is incorrect because the client should not be billed for time in which no benefit was received. In addition, a reasonable lawyer with no experience in complicated corporate reorganizations would likely have refused the representation in the first instance.

10. **/B/** The best answer because a lawyer must abide by the client's decision whether to take the stand and testify in a criminal trial [MRPC 1.2(a) and 3.3a *infra*]. **(A)** is incorrect because the lawyer may usually make the decisions as to general trial strategies. **(C)** is incorrect since a disciplinary violation is not excused merely because no harm has resulted from the violation; here, Mary is subject to discipline even though Georgianne was not convicted. **(D)** is incorrect because while the rationale is correct – an experienced lawyer may usually choose the trial strategy – it does not follow that discipline may not be imposed under this fact pattern.

11. **/A/** The ABA in Formal Opinion 93-379 stated that dual billings for the same time is improper. The measure of time detriment to the lawyer is to prevail over the value benefit to the client. Thus, only the active time spent – 2 hours ($500) – should be billed for the memorandum, and only 2 hours (one-half the total 4 hours) for arguing the motion ($500) – should be billed to Big Bucks. **(B)** is incorrect because this alternative would allow 3 hours to be billed for arguing the motion. **(C)** is incorrect because this alternative would allow 10 hours to be billed for the memorandum. **(D)** is incorrect because this alternative would allow billing both 10 hours for the memorandum and 3 hours for arguing the motion.

12. **/D/** The best and highest-level alternative. Many (but not all) of the ABA disciplinary rules (such as conflicts of interest) provide for an exception if the client gives informed consent, especially if the consent is written. The lawyer's burden to show that the overall fee is not unreasonable is facilitated if the client agrees. [MRPC 1.5] **(A)** is incorrect because "everyone" is an absolute, all-inclusive category and even if accurate, it does not mean the practice is proper. **(B)** is incorrect because all this alternative justifies is a disciplinary proceeding against the firm's senior partner as well as Esther. **(C)** is not the best answer because while the amount of value of the services to the client is one factor to be considered in determining if the fee was reasonable, it is not conclusive.

13. **/D/** The best answer because the attorney-client relationship is consensual, and the best evidence of both parties' expectations is their representation agreement. **(A)** is incorrect; while the default rule may be that the representation includes appeals, this function can be decided to the contrary in the representation agreement. **(B)** is not the best answer because of the condition "only if." There are likely other ways or reasons why the lawyer could be required to take on the appeal besides lawyer agreement. **(C)** is not the best answer because the terms of the representation agreement may override a client's expectation on an issue. [MRPC 1.2, comment 6]

14. **/C/** The comments to MRPC 1.4 require a lawyer to make full communication to the client unless an exception applies. A lawyer's malpractice should be communicated to the client. **(A)** is incorrect because the ABA comments to MRPC 1.4 authorize non-disclosure pursuant to a court rule. **(B)** is incorrect because the ABA comments to the MRPC 1.4 allow a court (gag) order prohibiting disclosure of trade secrets a lawyer learns in the discovery process. **(D)** is not the best answer because the ABA comment to MRPC 1.4 allows a lawyer to delay communicating information to a client that might cause the client to react imprudently. [Note that the double negative in the requirement is the equivalent to requiring and identifying the proper reason.]

15. **/A/** The rule is that a fee-splitting arrangement between lawyers not in the same firm may be made only if both lawyers work the case or assume joint responsibility, and the client approval is confirmed in writing. Note that while this is the best answer, the critical client consent element still missing. **(B)** is incorrect because both the payer and the payee are acting improperly in this fee-splitting arrangement. **(C)** is incorrect because both the payer and the payee are acting improperly in this fee-splitting arrangement. **(D)** is not the best answer because it is not necessary that the fee be proportional to the work performed if the client approves (and same is confirmed in writing), and both lawyers either work on the case or assume responsibility for the case. [MRPC 1.5(e)]

16. /D/ This is not one of those AJET decisions that is reserved to the client nor is it a representation objective normally left to the lawyer. Thus, it is one of those decisions that is jointly made after the lawyer has consulted with the client on the details. Only alternative D focuses upon the required client consultation. [MRPC 1.2] **(A)** is incorrect because this type of decision is usually jointly made by the lawyer and the client. **(B)** is not the best answer because it omits the necessary communication from the lawyer to the client explaining the details of the decision. **(C)** is not the best answer because the quantum of support for either action (fraud or negligence) is not the central issue in the question.

17. /B/ The client must consent to the sharing of fees arrangement between lawyers not in the same firm and at least receive a written confirmation of their agreement. [MRPC 1.5(e)] **(A)** is not the best answer because splitting the fees between lawyers not in the same firm requires client consent at least confirmed in writing, which goes beyond mere client awareness. **(C)** is incorrect because attending the trial is irrelevant if the client has not consented to the association in writing. **(D)** is not the best answer because this fact pattern implies lack of competency that is what association with another lawyer is intended to overcome and normally a reasonable continuance may be sought from the court.

18. /B/ A lawyer may not take a criminal case on a contingency basis. **(A)** is incorrect because the level of criminal charges – misdemeanor or felony – is not relevant to the prohibition against a lawyer taking a criminal case on a contingency basis. [MRPC 1.5(d)(2)] **(C)** is incorrect because all contingency cases must have a written agreement: this requirement does not go to the prohibition on contingent fee compensation for a criminal case. **(D)** is incorrect because whether or not the client is independently represented is irrelevant to the prohibition on contingent fee compensation for criminal cases.

19. /C/ In order for there to be legal malpractice liability, there must be a breach of the representation contract or a failure to exercise a reasonable duty of care, and neither of those theories appear present in these facts. [MRPC 1.1 and general legal malpractice principles.] **(A)** is incorrect because the exact date the statute of limitation expires often involves facts beyond the details of an initial potential client meeting. **(B)** is incorrect because charging or not charging a potential client for an initial appointment is not conclusive on the question of malpractice or whether a duty had arisen. **(D)** is incorrect because offering to refer a potential client to another lawyer is not conclusive on the question of malpractice.

20. /A/ In an emergency, a lawyer may make a best effort until it is possible to locate a more competent practitioner.[MRPC 1.1, comment 3] **(B)** is incorrect because the presence or absence of a personal friendship between the lawyer and the client does not affect the required level of competency and proficiency. **(C)** is incorrect because while Tom did not have the required proficiency this was an emergency situation at the time. **(D)** is incorrect because whether a lawyer charges for representation is not necessarily determinant of legal malpractice and professional conduct.

21. /B/ To maintain competency in her area of practice, a lawyer must keep abreast of relevant changes in the law that they practice, regardless of where that knowledge is obtained. [MRPC 1.1] **(A)** is incorrect in that a lawyer must keep current in her area of practice even if the State Bar Association does not provide CLE classes. **(C)** is incorrect because malpractice insurance is not a substitute for a lawyer's ethical responsibility to keep current in her area of practice. **(D)** is incorrect because there may be other methods to stay current in a practice area besides attending formal CLE classes.

22. /C/ The best answer because if the lawyer had a reasonable belief that the client had a legal right to refuse to answer, discipline would not be imposed. Notice that a lawyer does not guarantee the client that there will not be adverse consequences if her advice is followed. The "reasonable belief" component of the alternative suggests that the required competency standard was met. [MRPC 1.1] **(A)** is incorrect because asserting a person's constitutional rights is not committing a crime. [MRPC 1.2(d)] **(B)** is incorrect because whether it was the best client advice is irrelevant; the lawyer does not guarantee that there will not be adverse results, and the consequences of answering the committee's questions may have been worse than a refusal to answer. **(D)** is incorrect because whether it was the best advice is irrelevant; the lawyer does not guarantee that there will not be adverse results, and the consequences of answering the committee's questions may have been worse than a refusal to answer.

23. /A/ A lawyer shall act with reasonable diligence [MRPC 1.3] and must communicate with clients as they request or otherwise as reasonable. [MRPC 1.4] **(B)** is not the best answer because a lawyer should control her workload so that each matter she assumes responsibility for can be handled adequately. **(C)** is incorrect because, while a failure to return the retainer might have been grounds for discipline, the return does not itself excuse the lack of diligence and failure to communicate reasonably. **(D)** is incorrect as it relates to an ethical violation. In a civil action it is less clear, but damages may have been suffered because the trucking company may now be less charitable or reasonable in the negotiations, any recovery might have earned some interest for the client, and the client would have avoided the frustration caused by a lawyer's refusal to communicate by returning telephone calls.

24. /D/ The preamble to the ABA Model Rules states that "violation of a Rule should not itself give rise to a cause of action against a lawyer nor should it create any presumption in such a case that a legal duty has been breached." **(A)** is incorrect because evidence of a disciplinary violation or alleged violation may not be introduced in a malpractice lawsuit. **(B)** is incorrect because evidence of a disciplinary violation or alleged violation may not be introduced in a malpractice lawsuit. **(C)** is incorrect because evidence of a disciplinary violation or alleged violation may not be introduced in a malpractice lawsuit.

25. /B/ A lawyer shall communicate to the client any change in the rate of the fee to be charged. [MRPC 1.5(b)] **(A)** is not the best answer because the rule contemplates client communication of a fee increase prior to or at the time of the change, not after the fact. **(C)** is incorrect because the duty to communicate a fee increase is not dependent on a client request (but a client request for the details of the billing must be promptly responded to). **(D)** is incorrect because this alternative implies that the lawyer did not communicate the fee increase contemporaneously, but rather only after the client contested the billing.

26. /C/ The best combination of alternatives from MRPC 1.5(c). I is incorrect because a written contingent fee estimate is insufficient; there must be an agreement signed by the client. II is correct because the client must sign the original contingent fee agreement. III is correct because the lawyer must present the client upon conclusion of the contingency a detailed, written statement containing cost allocations. IV is incorrect because it is not necessary that the client sign the written statement presented by the lawyer at the conclusion of the contingency.

27. /D/ A division of fees between lawyers not in the same law firm must be either proportional to the work performed, or involve joint responsibility for the whole matter and the client must consent to the division which is confirmed in writing; here, the client was not informed, so consent was not obtained. [MRPC 1.5(c)] **(A)** is not the best answer because there are restrictions on fee splits between lawyers not in the same firm. **(B)** is not the best answer because the major requirement absent in this case is the lack of client approval. **(C)** is incorrect because joint responsibility is only one of the requirements for splitting fees between law firms and is ineffective without client consent and written confirmation.

28. /B/ The best answer because extending this professional courtesy could be a major outcome determinant decision in the case, which at least requires client consultation. [MRPC 1.2(a)] **(A)** is not the best answer – even though likely a true statement – because the thrust of the question is the defendant allowing the plaintiff something she would otherwise not be entitled to. **(C)** is incorrect because the plaintiff is not trying to reach an agreement changing state law, but rather to suspend the defendant's right to affirmatively defend upon the issue of expiration of the statutory period. **(D)** is not the best answer – even though likely true – because it does not include consulting with the client about the professional courtesy to be extended.

29. /C/ The best answer because a lawyer's representation of a client does not constitute an approval or endorsement of a client's political, economic, social, or moral views [MRPC 1.2(b)], and a general statement of support of a proposed statute would likely qualify as a law reform activity [MRPC 6.4]. This degree of participation would not seem to limit materially the lawyer's general representation of Addiction Sticks in other matters. [MRPC 6.3(b) and 1.7(b)] This freedom of expression right is properly tempered in that the lawyer's remarks should be fashioned in such a way that they do not unduly prejudice the client. **(A)** is incorrect because it is an incomplete combination of alternatives involving proper conduct. **(B)** is incorrect because it is an incomplete combination of alternatives involving proper conduct. **(D)** is incorrect because the lawyer's prior representation of the client does not require she personally endorse all the client's political, economic, social, or moral positions.

30. /C/ The best answer because even if rejecting the offer of $200,000 was malpractice, the subsequent verdict of $500,000 eliminated any damages. **(A)** is not the best answer – even though a correct statement under MRPC 1.2(a) – because the question requirement refers to civil malpractice liability, not ethical violations. **(B)** is not the best answer – even though a correct statement under MRPC 1.4 – because the question requirement refers to civil malpractice liability, not ethical violations. **(D)** is incorrect because it misstates the facts in that Pattie did not consent to Loretta deciding settlement offers.

31. /B/ The best answer because a lawyer has the burden to show that even a contingency fee is not unreasonable, and the most basic criteria is the time and effort required. [MRPC 1.5] **(A)** is not the best answer – even though it is one of the criteria that an attorney might use to justify the fee – because the time and effort required are more often considered to be basic measures of reasonable value. **(C)** is incorrect because the facts given indicate the lawyer's services were completed, and it is the attempt to extract an unreasonable fee that is an ethical violation. **(D)** is incorrect because even if Sally agreed in writing and did not contest the fee, the facts given indicate the lawyer's services were completed, and it is the attempt to extract an unreasonable fee that is an ethical violation.

32. /D/ A lawyer's failure to exercise diligence [MRPC 1.3] is also an example of incompetence [MRPC 1.1]; both are grounds for professional discipline. In addition, it appears the failure to file the appeal timely created client monetary damages, so the lawyer also has potential civil malpractice liability. **(A)** is an incorrect combination of alternatives. **(B)** is an incorrect combination of alternatives. **(C)** is an incorrect combination of alternatives.

33. /B/ The trial court lawyer will be liable for malpractice in not raising the issue of double jeopardy at the beginning of the second trial. The "case within the case" standard requires the plaintiff to prove "but for" the lawyer's malpractice the damages would not have occurred. This implies that the jury would not have convicted the defendant. [Common law of negligence] **(A)** is incorrect because at least the legal retainer of $10,000 would be recoverable. **(C)** is not the best answer because the lawyer should have raised the double jeopardy issue at the beginning of the second trial. **(D)** is incorrect because there were nominal and actual damages suffered independent of the prison sentence which was avoided.

34. /A/ A lawyer shall not counsel or assist a client in perpetrating ongoing conduct that the lawyer knows is criminal or fraudulent; here it is clear this was an ongoing criminal enterprise of violating the copyright law. [MRPC 1.2] **(B)** is not the best answer because withdrawal is not ordinarily necessary merely because a lawyer is representing a client for a past crime or fraud; representation of such clients is not a per se violation of the MRPCs. **(C)** is not the best answer; while this is a true statement as it relates to past crimes or frauds, the facts here indicate that the lawyer counseled the client in perpetrating ongoing criminal or fraudulent activities. **(D)** is not the best answer; while a lawyer may generally consult as to past crime or fraud, the facts here indicate that the lawyer counseled the client in perpetrating ongoing criminal or fraudulent activities.

35. **/D/** While a lawyer shall not counsel or assist a client in perpetrating illegal conduct, good-faith consultation on how to gain the legal standing necessary to challenge the law is not improper. [MRPC 1.2(d)] **(A)** is incorrect because there is an exception to the general rule of not advising illegal action. **(B)** is incorrect because the client's consent is irrelevant to the restraint prohibiting a lawyer from counseling or assisting a client in perpetrating illegal conduct. **(C)** is not the best answer because the ultimate determination of the statute's constitutionality is not controlling if the lawyer violated an ethical restraint.

36. **/D/** The best answer because an external fee split always requires client consent which is at least confirmed in writing. **(A)** is not the best answer since fee allocation proportional to the work performed still requires client consent which is at least confirmed in writing. **(B)** is not the best answer because both lawyers assuming joint responsibility for the whole representation still requires client consent which is at least confirmed in writing. **(C)** is not the best answer because the issue of the unauthorized practice of law would apply only if the attorney doing the legal work – here Nancy New – was not admitted in the state of the litigation. [MRPC 1.5(e)]

RIGOS UNIFORM BAR REVIEW SERIES

PROFESSIONAL RESPONSIBILITY EXAM REVIEW (MPRE)

Chapter 2

Client Relations – Confidentiality and Conflicts of Interest

Magic Memory Outline®

RIGOS UNIFORM BAR REVIEW SERIES

PROFESSIONAL RESPONSIBILITY EXAM REVIEW (MPRE)

Chapter 2

Client Relations – Confidentiality and Conflicts of Interest

A. <u>Confidentiality of Information</u> – MRPC 1.6

1. In General: This subject includes both the evidence rules of the attorney-client privilege and work-product doctrine, as well as the ethical rule of confidentiality. If the matter is in litigation, the lawyer's duty of candor to the court may trump some of the client – focused confidentiality rules. See *infra* at 143.

a. Core Values: The core legal professional value here is to promote candid and complete communications from the client to the attorney so all the details and complexities of the problem become known. Only with this full information can lawyers provide the best possible comprehensive advice to their clients. If a client believes the lawyer will reveal her representation information to third parties outside the law firm, it necessarily puts a chilling effect upon the desirable candid communications. Confidential information usually may be shared within the firm for consultation or to prepare for trial.

b. Attorney-Client Privilege: The attorney-client privilege is an evidence rule of exclusion for non-public communications that an actual or potential client communicates to his lawyer. The client should not be worse off by the attorney disclosure. Preexisting documents do not become subject to the privilege merely by transmitting them to an attorney, but all work product created by a lawyer or her subordinates generally is privileged. The confidential privilege survives the death of the client. The general rule is there is no litigation privilege between jointly-represented clients – see MRPC 1.7 *infra* at 59.

2. Representation Information: In some jurisdictions the rule distinguishes between confidences and secrets. "Confidences" include the substance of client communications to the lawyer and a lawyer's work product protected by the evidentiary attorney-client privilege. "Secrets" refers to other information gained in the professional relationship concerning the client, the disclosure of which would be embarrassing or would likely be detrimental to the client. Profits made by the lawyer from the use of confidential client information may be disgorged.

3. Exceptions: There are important exceptions to the general rule of non-disclosure outside the law firm absent informed client consent. The lawyer should first seek to persuade the client to take the action necessary to obviate the need for disclosure and, if unsuccessful, warn that the lawyer will reveal the confidential information. If disclosure is still necessary, the scope of any disclosure should be minimized.

a. Future Death or Substantial Bodily Injury: A lawyer may reveal confidential information to the extent necessary to prevent the client from committing a future crime causing certain death or substantial bodily harm of a human. This includes a client's plan to take his own life. The overriding value of life controls. Even if the lawyer concludes that disclosure should be made, it is permissible only to the extent necessary to prevent the offense. This might not even require disclosure of the identity of the client.

MPRE Tip: A growing number of states elevate the future death or substantially bodily harm confidentiality exception "may" to "must" reveal.

b. Crime or Fraud Using Lawyer's Services: If the lawyer's services are being used to commit a fraud or crime, such may be disclosed to prevent future occurrences.

c. Lawyer Being Sued or Related: A lawyer may also reveal relevant client confidential information only to the extent necessary concerning a:

(1) Claim or Defense Against Client: Disclosure is allowed to establish a "claim or defense" on behalf of the lawyer in a controversy between the lawyer and the client. If the client brings a malpractice claim against a lawyer, she waives the confidentiality right, at least as it relates to the relevant details of the representation. A lawyer entitled to a fee may reveal client confidences to the extent reasonably necessary to effectuate collection.

(2) Lawyer's Involvement: A lawyer may disclose client crimes, fraud, or substantial financial injury in which the client used the lawyer's services. Such involvement could create complicity and lead to a criminal charge or civil claim against the lawyer because of client activities. A lawyer may also make disclosures in the process of securing legal advice about his own degree of compliance with the MRPCs.

(3) Bar Complaint: Disclosure may be made to respond to allegations in any proceeding concerning the lawyer's representation of the client (such as a bar association grievance filed by a client). Some jurisdictions, however, require client approval as a prerequisite to disclosure of confidential information in a disciplinary action against the lawyer.

d. Court Order: Disclosure may be made pursuant to a court order.

MPRE Tip: The above exceptions to the general rule of nondisclosure are frequently tested.

e. Sarbanes-Oxley Act (SOX): The ABA Model Rule now allows – but does not encourage - federal securities lawyers to externally disclose listed corporate client frauds.

(1) Breadth: Disclosure may be made to prevent the client from committing a crime, financial fraud, or breach of fiduciary duty that involved the lawyer's services, if reasonably certain to result in substantial injury to the financial interests or property of another.

(2) Report Internally: SOX § 307 states that a lawyer learning of evidence of (1) material, clear violations of federal security laws or (2) breach of fiduciary duty must disclose such evidence internally within the company. If the corporate chief legal officer (CLO) or CEO does not "appropriately respond" – basically stop the wrongdoing – the lawyer is required to then report the matter to the company's board of directors or audit committee. If that internal reporting fails to result in a corporate "appropriate response," external disclosure to the SEC is authorized to the extent necessary to prevent material and certain injury to the corporation or its investor-owners. See also MRPC 1.13 *infra* at 108.

(3) Representation Withdrawal: The lawyer may also make a "noisy withdrawal" if necessary. See MRPC 1.13 *infra* at 108-109 for organizational reporting and whistleblowing issues.

f. Third Party Notice: The lawyer may give reasonable notice to a third party of the fact that she has withdrawn from the representation. Also, any relevant opinion document or other "questionable information" prepared by the lawyer based on client provided fraudulent information may be withdrawn or disaffirmed.

g. IRS Form 8300: Another "no reveal" exception involves IRS Form 8300, which must usually be filed if the client pays the lawyer $10,000 or more in cash. The ABA suggests that unless the client approves, the lawyer can file the form but must leave the secret of the client's name and Social Security number off the form. The IRS can issue a summons, and if the U.S. District Court judge so orders, the lawyer could then make full disclosure.

h. Client Waiver: If the client communication is not private or the client releases a substantial portion of the information to third parties, confidentiality may be legally waived. This does not necessarily eliminate the lawyer's duty of confidentiality.

i. Breach of Fiduciary Responsibility: Many states also have an exception allowing a lawyer to reveal to the tribunal information that discloses any breach of fiduciary duty responsibility by a client who is a guardian, personal representative, receiver, or other court-appointed fiduciary.

MPRE Tip: Confidentiality issues are heavily tested. The extent and manner of disclosure under the above exceptions must be the minimum necessary under the circumstances.

B. Conflict of Interest: Current Clients – MRPC 1.7

MRPC 1.7, 1.8, and 1.9 have a variety of restraints to ensure there are no impairments to the fiduciary duty of a lawyer in rendering undivided loyalty and service to a client. A lawyer must decline new representation for a person whose interest concurrently conflicts with that of an existing client. If the conflict becomes apparent later after the representation is underway, the lawyer must withdraw from both clients. Under MRPC 1.10, this conflict disqualification is imputed to all lawyers in a firm.

1. Conflict Abatement Structure: Prohibited conflicts are often subject to representation exceptions that would allow the proposed conduct under certain circumstances. The client may be allowed to agree to the prohibited conduct in question as long as the lawyer reasonably believes that no harm will result. Different rules require slightly different degrees of disclosure and client approval. Consider the following four-step process approach:

A	**Conditional Modifier**		**Lawyer Must**		**Client Does**		**Objective Test**
L	shall/must – required	**U**	Notify	**A**	Nothing	**A**	lawyer
A	should – recommended	**N**	Communicate	**N**	Not object	**N**	reasonably
W	may/can – voluntary	**L**	Advise	**D**	Agrees/approves	**D**	believes
Y	should not -	**E**	Consult		Consents		that no harm
E	not recommended	**S**	Give written notice		Consents in writing		will result
R	shall/must not – prohibited	**S**	Confirms in writing		Informed consent		

MPRE Tip: The above distinctions are subtle. Look for the method of client conflict disclosure by the lawyer, related form of client approval, and whether a writing/signing is required or necessary to confirm an oral client approval. These may be tested on difficult MPRE questions.

a. Informed Consent: "Informed consent" has two components. First, there must be adequate information and explanation of the material risks and dangers that are potentially present under the dual representation. Examples are "what is good for one could be bad for the other" and "this dual representation may preclude the attorney-client privilege." Second, there must be an explanation of available alternatives such as "these limitations are avoided if you both have your own counsel."

b. Confirmed in Writing: "Confirmed in writing" can be achieved in one of two manners. First, the client consent requirement may be given in writing by the person or persons giving informed consent. Second, the client may give oral informed consent to the conflict and the lawyer promptly confirms the client agreement in a writing.

2. Client-to-Client: There are two degrees of present and potential concurrent client conflicts. The lawyer's benefit to one client is also a detriment to the other client.

a. Representation of Two Directly Adverse Clients – MRPC 1.7(a)(1): "Direct Adversity" is the highest level of present conflict of interest and applies to a matter that is in litigation. A lawyer shall not represent a client if the representation is directly in opposition to the interests of another of the lawyer's clients.

b. Lawyer's Responsibilities Materially Limited – MRPC 1.7(a)(2): This potential conflict applies if there is significant risk that a lawyer's action on behalf of one client will materially limit her future effectiveness in representing other client(s).

(1) Lower Level: "Materially limited" is a lower level of conflict than present "direct adversity," and formal litigation may not be involved. The conflict may arise because of the lawyer's responsibilities to another client, a third party, or her own interests.

(2) Examples: Examples include joint representation of the driver and passenger against a common defendant in an automobile accident; could the passenger cross-claim against the driver? Representing two direct business competitors in marketing or representing both a buyer and seller in the same transaction are favorite exam facts.

(3) Adverse Precedent: Ordinarily a lawyer may take inconsistent legal positions in different tribunals at different times on behalf of different clients. An exception applies if a lawyer advances a position of law or decision favoring one client that will create a precedent likely to seriously weaken the position taken on behalf of another client.

c. Exception – MRPC 1.7: Dual representation may be allowed if:

(1) No Harm to Attorney-Client Relationship: The lawyer must reasonably believe that the representation of one client would not adversely affect the competent and diligent representation relationship with the other client. This is an objective foreseeability standard of a prudent, disinterested lawyer.

MPRE Tip: The lawyer's belief that there will not be an adverse effect on the representation of either client must be objectively reasonable. Would a disinterested lawyer so conclude?

(2) Informed Consent Confirmed in Writing: Each client must give informed consent after receiving full disclosure of all material risks and dangers that the lawyer's conflict could create. This informed consent must then be confirmed in writing.

(a) Adverse Clients Identification: The lawyer's disclosure to the clients must usually include the identification of the other conflicting client(s) and lacks of the attorney-client privilege between clients in jointly represented matters.

(b) Confidential Information Authorization: Full disclosure to one client may require the other client's authorization if it contains his confidential information.

(3) Revoking Consent: Conflict consent may be withdrawn by either client, especially after the client becomes fully aware of the fact that the lawyer can no longer provide them 100% loyalty. The employment of the lawyer may also be terminated by either client. The lawyer ordinarily will be forced to withdraw from representing any and all the clients if the joint representation fails.

> **MPRE Tip:** Look for a situation in which an incident occurred that strongly suggests future representation of a client may be materially limited by the duty of loyalty to another client. The lawyer must withdraw from representing both clients without disclosing any confidences.

(4) Same Litigation Prohibition: The ABA Model Rule does not allow the above consent to abate a present directly adverse conflict if the matter is in litigation.

> **MPRE Tip:** In both direct adversity and materially limited situations, representation is only possible if (1) the clients give informed consent confirmed in writing and (2) there is not an adverse effect on the representation. Both requirements must be met.

(5) Fundamentally Antagonistic: The comments to the Model Rules state that if the clients are fundamentally antagonistic, they may not be capable of giving reasonable consent. A husband and wife dissolution may be a good example due to the high level of animosity that frequently develops between the parties in such a proceeding.

d. Related Attorneys: A possible conflict of interest relates to personal relationships between opposing counsel. A lawyer is prohibited from representing a party if an attorney who is related to the first lawyer represents a directly adverse party. Related attorneys include husband-wife, parent-child, or two siblings. The informed consent of both clients may abate this restriction, and a writing is not required. The prohibition is not imputed firm-wide so another lawyer in the firm could handle one of the representation positions.

> **MPRE Tip:** Zealous advocacy and confidentiality of client information are the twin concerns when related lawyers represent both parties in the same matter.

e. Organizational Clients: This conflict rule addresses organizational groups. Examples include a lawyer for one corporation in a corporate-affiliated group or one governmental agency that is a part of an upstream government control organization.

(1) General Rule: A lawyer representing one corporate or governmental unit does not necessarily represent any other constituent or affiliated organization. Thus, such a lawyer may accept representation of a case adverse to the affiliate.

(2) Exceptions: The no-conflict outcome does not apply if (1) the related affiliate is considered to be a client of the lawyer, (2) there is a prior understanding that the lawyer will avoid representation adverse to the affiliate, or (3) the representation would in fact place a material limitation on the loyalty afforded to either client.

f. Lawyer Board Member: A lawyer for an entity who is also an official member of the board of directors may be conflicted in advising board actions when the lawyer's prior work is at issue. This could create a go-forward conflict for the lawyer. The lawyer may be required to withdraw from the board to eliminate the conflict. Further, other board members should be advised that the attorney-client privilege does not apply if the lawyer is in a director's capacity. See also MRPC 1.13 *infra* at 108-109 for additional details.

> **MPRE Tip:** MRPC 1.8, discussed in detail below, contains a variety of restrictions and/or prohibitions where the conflict of interest is between the lawyer and the client. The client trust inherent in the fiduciary relationship creates a disparity in bargaining power. Any prohibition on a lawyer is generally imputed to all the lawyers associated in the law firm.

3. Current Client/Prohibited Transactions and Related: A lawyer's transactions with a client could create divided loyalties and thus are subject to special scrutiny.

a. No Business Relationship Unless TIC – MRPC 1.8(a): The lawyer shall not enter into a business relationship with a client (including an estate) she represents in the same transaction because there is a clear possibility of overreaching. Examples are loaning to or borrowing money from a client or entering into a partnership with a client. An exception allows the client transaction if all three **TIC** transaction elements are met:

(1) Terms of Transaction Are Fair: The financial transaction and all material terms must be fair at a reasonable market price and fully disclosed to the client in writing. The disclosure must be stated in language that the client can clearly understand.

(2) Independent Counsel: The client must be advised in writing to seek the advice of independent counsel in the transaction. Notice it is only a requirement that the client has reasonable opportunity to seek advice from another attorney, not that he actually receives it. The safest posture is if the client secures independent advice and financial valuation.

(3) Consent in Writing: The client must consent in a signed writing. The informed consent must go to both the transaction's essential terms and the lawyer's conflict of interest disclosure, not only the terms of the underlying transaction.

> **MPRE Tip:** The disparity in bargaining power is significant since the client inherently trusts the lawyer to protect her financial interest. This creates a presumption of overreaching and undue influence justifying setting aside a client-to-lawyer transaction, such as a bargain purchase or loan from a client.

b. Information Disadvantaging the Client – MRPC 1.8(b): The lawyer must not use information to a client's disadvantage unless the client gives informed consent. For instance, a lawyer may not purchase assets in competition with a client she is representing. In a later transaction or business dispute, the lawyer cannot use information derived from a prior representation to the client's disadvantage unless informed consent was given.

> **MPRE Tip:** To violate the disciplinary rule the lawyer's client must be financially disadvantaged and profits made by the lawyer may be disgorged.

c. Gifts from Clients – MRPC 1.8(c): A lawyer may accept a gift from a client only if the transaction meets general standards of fairness and does not involve undue influence.

(1) Solicitation and Instrument Preparation: A lawyer cannot solicit a gift or prepare an instrument bestowing upon herself or the lawyer's family members a substantial gift from a client. The client should have the objective and detached advice that a non-interested lawyer can provide; such a referral may be prudent. This prohibition includes a testamentary device, unless the lawyer is related to the donor. For instance, lawyers can prepare their family relatives' wills and name themselves and their children as takers.

(2) Allowed Gifts: Gifts given to a lawyer without a prepared instrument – say a cash bonus at the end of a case – are not per se improper as they are for a judge.

MPRE Tip: Preparing a will or trust instrument in which the lawyer is a beneficiary is frequently asked.

d. Agreement for Literary or Media Rights – MRPC 1.8(d): A lawyer may not negotiate an agreement to receive the client's publication rights to information based in substantial part on the lawsuit prior to the conclusion of the representation. A client waiver is ineffective. A lawyer has to wait until the case is over before the client can agree to give her the book and movie rights to the trial. This rule guards against a lawyer trying to publicize an upcoming book during a trial, which could jeopardize the client's position.

e. Financial Assistance – MRPC 1.8(e): A lawyer may not subsidize lawsuits. This includes advancing or guaranteeing financial assistance to a client for living expenses, advances for family support, or medical treatment. There are three exceptions:

(1) Litigation Expenses: A lawyer may lend a client funds to pay or guarantee a third party's payment of litigation costs – such as expert witness fees, court costs, medical examinations, and discovery costs – but the client must remain responsible for those costs. Still, repayment of these costs may be contingent on the outcome of the matter.

(2) Contingency Cost Allocation: There are three possible ways to charge costs in a contingency recovery. First, the costs come off the top before the percentage split between the attorney and client. That's probably all right because the client bears most of the costs. Second, the client bears 100% of the costs from his portion – that's permissible even though the client may not like it. Third, the lawyer bears all the costs from her share – in theory, that is a violation even though the client would usually prefer it.

(3) Indigent Client: Court costs and expenses may be paid on behalf of an indigent client regardless of whether these funds will be repaid. Some jurisdictions also have a class-action exception, which is justified because of the public service aspect, since it otherwise might be too difficult to get plaintiffs to join the class.

MPRE Tip: A lawyer may refer a client seeking funds to a financing institution or bank as long as the lawyer does not make or guarantee the loan.

f. Fee Payment by Third Parties – MRPC 1.8(f): Payment of attorney fees by a third party is not allowed. Examples include parents who pay for their child's DUI defense or the corporate payment of attorney fees incurred by a co-defendant officer. Another example is the defendant's insurance company that may be responsible for the ultimate damage claim and is also paying for the defendant's legal defense. Exceptions apply if:

(1) Informed Consent and No Interference: The primary client may consent after consultation – a writing is not required – if there is no interference by the third-party payor with the lawyer's independence, professional judgment, or loyalty to the client. A future conflict waiver demanded by an insurance company third party payor is problematic. It may be ineffective because the client may lack sufficient information about possible future payor third-party interference possibilities to give an informed consent until a conflict actually develops.

(2) Confidentiality: The client's confidential information must not be compromised. This is potentially sensitive because information the lawyer conveys to the third-party payor in a billing statement is protected by the confidentiality rules. The lawyer cannot disclose sensitive client information that could damage the client. An example is an insurance company issuing a "reservation of rights" as to claim coverage based on the lawyer's billing information. Insurers may not impose "litigation management guidelines" on a lawyer if it will harm the representation of the primary client insured. If any of these conditions occur, a lawyer may have to withdraw.

MPRE Tip: Legal fees paid by a third party require **CIC** – <u>c</u>lient informed consent, <u>i</u>ndependent professional judgment not impaired, and <u>c</u>onfidentiality must be maintained.

g. Aggregate Settlement if Multiple Clients – MRPC 1.8(g):

(1) Criminal Case: When a lawyer represents more than one client in a criminal matter, the lawyer must not participate in making an aggregate agreement as to guilty or *nolo contendere* pleas. The potential for conflict in representing multiple criminal defendants is grave – they may need to take inconsistent positions because what is good for one may be bad for another. Ordinarily a lawyer should decline to provide simultaneous representation of both clients. An exception applies if each client consents in a signed writing. The lawyer must make disclosure of the existence and nature of all the claims or pleas involved and the participation of each person in the settlement agreement.

(2) Civil Case: This lawyer representation restraint applies to multiple clients who would share as plaintiffs in an aggregate dollar settlement or co-defendants in a civil case with joint and several liability. There may be cross-claims or disputes relating to award recovery or cost allocations between the lawyer's multiple clients that should be determined. Again, there is an exception if each client consents in a signed writing after disclosure that includes all information about the claims being settled and the amount each client will receive or be required to pay.

MPRE Tip: This broadens the lawyer's potential conflict from representing both plaintiff and defendant to representation of two parties on the same side of the litigation.

h. Limiting Liability – MCPR 1.8(h): A lawyer who is representing a client shall not limit his own future or past liability for malpractice.

(1) Prospective Limitation: The lawyer's representation agreement cannot state that the "client agrees not to sue for malpractice if the lawyer fails to exercise reasonable care" unless the client is separately represented by counsel in the negotiation. A mere warning that "you should talk to a lawyer" is insufficient; actual independent representation is required.

(2) Malpractice Settlement: A client may assert a malpractice claim against her lawyer, for example, because the lawyer complied with the requirement that he communicate his lack of competent performance and the client is unhappy about it. The attorney and client may reach agreement as to an equitable settlement. The client must be advised in writing to seek independent counsel, but need not do so. However, there must be reasonable opportunity to seek outside counsel; settlement cannot be made "on the spot."

> **MPRE Tip:** Notice the client must actually have independent representation for prospective malpractice limitations. In contrast, after-the-fact limitations only require the client to receive written advice and a reasonable opportunity to seek counsel.

i. Proprietary Interest in Cause of Action – MRPC 1.8(i): A lawyer shall not acquire an actual ownership interest in the client's cause of action or legal claim. There is no exception, even if the client agrees. Still allowed are:

(1) Security: A lawyer may take a promissory note or acquire a lien granted by law to secure the lawyer's fee or expenses. This is a business or financial transaction with a client requiring the three **TIC** transaction elements.

(2) Contingency: A lawyer may contract with a client for a reasonable contingent fee in a civil case.

> **MPRE Tip:** Acquiring an ownership interest is often combined with business transactions [MRPC 1.8 (a)] and client property custodianship. [MRPC 1.15]

j. Sexual Relations with Clients – MRPC 1.8(j): Lawyers in most jurisdictions are prohibited from having sexual relations with current clients or representatives of their clients, such as the parent of a child in a personal injury action. This restriction is not imputed to other firm members who are not working on the representation. Also, an exception exists if there was a prior consensual relationship before the lawyer undertook the case and there is no adverse effect on the representation. This sexual relationship prohibition terminates at the end of the representation.

(1) Definition: The definition of "sexual relationship" is not in the Model Rule – and many people differ in their views of how much it takes to have a "sexual relationship." Some states attempt a definition such as California's "sexual intercourse or the touching of an intimate part of another...." Disciplinary cases focus on lawyers going to bed with their clients; in most states this meets the threshold definition.

(2) Consent Ineffective: A client's consent or waiver, even in writing, does not abate the violation. In such a situation, there could easily be overreaching by the lawyer where a client is emotionally vulnerable and therefore might feel forced to accept an imposed *quid pro quo* personal relationship.

(3) Risks: A sexual relationship could impact the attorney's fiduciary duty, in which the lawyer occupies the highest position of trust and confidence. From a lawyer's standpoint, your independence and objectivity may be put at risk – can you tell a lover client that her case objectively lacks merit or that she would make a bad witness? And if you lose her case, what will the consequence be on the relationship?

(4) Client Affections: If the client wants an affair, the attorney needs to say, "I am sorry." Explain to the client that you could get disciplined. Say no to gifts and invitations to dinners or drinks after work. If the client's aggressive affections do not stop, it would be prudent to transfer the client to another attorney in the firm.

MPRE Tip: The 1.8 restrictions (except 1.8(j)) usually are imputed to all lawyers in the firm.

C. Conflict of Interest: Duties to Former Clients – MRPC 1.9

Lawyer loyalty and confidence rules survive the representation, and these ongoing duties to a former client may conflict with a current client's interests. Under MRPC 1.10 (covered in the next chapter), the conflict disqualification is imputed to every lawyer in a law firm, unless the imputation can be overcome by screening.

1. Subject Matter Relationship: The current matter must be substantially related to the factual context of the prior client's matter. Detailed analysis of the nature and scope of the prior representation may be necessary. Was substantial confidential information in the prior matter at play? This provision relates to MRPC 1.7 in that if a lawyer withdraws from representing one client, the client then becomes a prior client.

2. Informed Consent Possible: A lawyer usually cannot, in the same or a substantially related legal dispute, represent another person who has an adverse interest to her prior client. Representation in different unrelated matters against a former client is usually allowed. This conflict may be waived if both the former and new client give informed consent after full disclosure, confirmed in writing.

3. Substantially Related Example: Suppose a lawyer represented both spouses in a property transaction, and three years later, the wife wants the same lawyer (or the lawyer's partner) to represent her in a divorce. If the same property is subject to the dissolution proceeding, the matter is probably sufficiently factually related to disqualify the lawyer. The lawyer needs both spouses' informed consent to the conflict or the attorney is subject to disqualification.

4. Confidential Information Restriction: Even if the former client consents to the representation and it is confirmed in writing, there is a separate restriction on using the former client's information to his disadvantage. The duty of confidentiality creates the "information specific" conflict that continues after the client-lawyer relationship has terminated.

5. Example: Suppose a corporate client asked a lawyer's opinion about hiring an employee whom the lawyer had defended in an embezzlement case five years ago. The lawyer probably cannot disclose to the corporation what she knows about her former client's fraud potential even though one could argue the matter is not exactly the same. The test is "substantial subject matter relationship." Still, the common nexus concerns the former embezzlement, so the similar subject matter test is arguably satisfied in this fact pattern.

MPRE Tip: For purposes of former client disqualification under Rule 1.9, the matter at issue must be substantially related to the prior client's matter. Note this subject-matter nexus is not necessary to create a disqualifying conflict under Rule 1.7 for present "direct adversity" and future "materially limited" conflicts where mere adverse client identity may be sufficient.

RIGOS UNIFORM BAR REVIEW SERIES

PROFESSIONAL RESPONSIBILITY EXAM REVIEW (MPRE)

Chapter 2

Client Relations – Confidentiality and Conflicts of Interest

Question Map

Numbers immediately following the topic are the chapter question numbers. The **boldface** numbers preceded by "F" are the final exam question numbers. For example, for the topic "A. 1. a. Core Values" below, question 24 is in the chapter questions on page 2-70; question **F49** is in the final exam on page 7-290.

Chapter 2

Client Relations – Confidentiality and Conflicts of Interest

Questions

1. Larry Litigator retained Nancy Negligent to represent him in a malpractice case against his former lawyer. Nancy is apprehensive about undertaking the representation because Larry has sued all his prior lawyers for amounts greatly in excess of the fees the lawyers earned in the representation. To ensure she does not end up in the same position, Nancy inserted a clause in the client representation agreement stating that "any claim arising out of this representation shall be limited in dollar amount to the fee paid." Case law in the jurisdiction has upheld such a damage limitation.

Is Nancy subject to discipline for including the damage ceiling in the representation agreement?

- **(A)** No, because Larry could have retained a different lawyer who did not have a damage ceiling provision in her agreement.
- **(B)** No, as long as Larry was independently represented in making the agreement.
- **(C)** Yes, unless Nancy explained to Larry the effect of the damage ceiling provision.
- **(D)** Yes, unless Nancy explained to Larry the effect of the damage ceiling provision, and Larry consents thereto.

2. Terry Thief made an appointment to discuss a matter with Deloris Defender. Terry arrived at the lawyer's office in a Porsche she had stolen the previous day. Terry parked the car in the law firm's parking lot. In the meeting with Deloris, Terry freely admitted that she had stolen the Porsche and was selling it to Sally Stripper, who specialized in stripping down stolen vehicles.

Deloris told Terry she owed a $200 fee for the meeting and that she had to pay a $1,000 retainer towards future representation. Terry said she would return later with the money. Terry left the state, but a police spotter reported the stolen Porsche as having been in the law firm's parking lot. An investigator questioned Deloris about the whereabouts of the Porsche and her involvement with the theft.

May Deloris properly disclose the information given to her by Terry?

- **(A)** No, because the details of the Porsche do not involve a future crime.
- **(B)** No, unless there were criminal charges commenced accusing Terry of theft.
- **(C)** Yes, if the disclosure is necessary to establish a defense on Deloris' behalf.
- **(D)** Yes, if Terry Thief did not pay the $200 fee to Deloris.

3. Magna Computer Services sells and leases computer systems to businesses. For years, it has used attorney Connie Conflict to draw leases and other corporate documents for them. Connie also has another client named Accurate Accounting, which has a number of offices in the area. Connie was talking to the office manager from Accurate, who mentioned that they were thinking about purchasing a new computer system. Connie suggested that they contact Magna Computer Services. Accurate and Magna entered into a computer lease agreement with attorney Connie to draw the lease at the sole expense of Magna. Connie believes that her dual representation will not adversely affect either client.

May attorney Connie Conflict properly prepare the computer lease agreement?

- **(A)** No, because it is improper for Connie's fees to be paid solely by one party.
- **(B)** No, because the separate interests of Magna and Accurate may become adverse if a dispute develops between them.
- **(C)** Yes, if such multiple representation is standard practice in the locale where Connie practices law, and the client consents.
- **(D)** Yes, only if both Magna and Accurate have given their consent and that is confirmed in writing.

4. Lorraine Landlord hired a lawyer named Elbert Environment to assist her in securing a rezone covering her proposed shopping center. Nancy Neighbor was very vocal against the project and attempted to reduce the size of the ultimate project. In the hearing, Lorraine became very hostile towards Nancy. Two years later, Nancy, who was shopping in the shopping center, slipped and fell because of Lorraine's negligence. Nancy approached Elbert Environment and asked if he would represent her in suing Lorraine. Elbert called Lorraine, who said, "No, I do not approve because you represented me in the rezone, and she was an adverse party." Elbert needs the fee and accepts Nancy's case against Lorraine's disapproval.

Is Elbert subject to discipline?

- **(A)** No, as long as no confidential information from the rezone proceeding is used by Elbert in Nancy's case.
- **(B)** No, because Elbert's representation of Lorraine in the rezone was successful.
- **(C)** Yes, because Elbert is representing a client with materially adverse interests to his former client Lorraine without consent.
- **(D)** Yes, because Elbert's prior client Lorraine refused to consent to his representation of Nancy.

5. Jimmie and Joan were married for thirteen years. After many unpleasant confrontations they concluded that they were incompatible and would therefore enter into a "friendly" divorce. They approach Marty Matlock, an attorney in the community widely known as a good family lawyer. In their first meeting, Marty informed them that he could not represent both parties since they had substantial marital property and their interest therein were fundamentally antagonistic.

They both asked Marty if he could represent only one of them and recommend another attorney for the other. He recommended his daughter Mary to represent Joan and both Jimmie and Joan accepted their two respective lawyer representation. The divorce went to trial and Joan received a large portion of the marital property. Jimmie was so outraged he filed an ethical complaint with the local bar association against both lawyers alleging Marty did not represent him zealously because he wanted his daughter to look good.

The Bar Association would likely discipline

(A) Marty only because Mary had no duty to and was properly adverse to Jimmie.
(B) Both Marty and Mary if each client did not give informed consent to the conflict.
(C) Both Marty and Mary if each client did not consent to the conflict in writing.
(D) Both Marty and Mary if each client did not consent to the conflict which was later confirmed in writing.

6. Denise Defendanyone is a defense attorney who specializes in DUI defense. Rochelle Reckless, a 21-year-old, full-time student, was charged with DUI and hired Denise to defend her. Rochelle became delinquent in paying her legal bill owed to Denise. Rochelle's favorite Uncle Harry sent Denise a check for $5,000 and asked her to apply it to Rochelle's account. Harry also told Denise not to tell his niece, Rochelle, since other family members were hoping Rochelle would be sentenced and spend time in jail to rehabilitate herself.

Is it proper for Denise to accept Harry's $5,000 check?

(A) Yes, only if Harry has signed a payment guarantee of Rochelle's legal expenses.
(B) Yes, only if Harry does not interfere with Denise's representation in the matter.
(C) No, unless Denise first communicates the situation to Rochelle, and she gives informed consent.
(D) No, because this would destroy the lawyer's independent professional judgment.

7. Doug Dumber is an aggressive drunk who enjoys going into taverns and starting fistfights. One Saturday night he went into the Roundabout Tavern. After drinking heavily for three hours, he picked a fight with Tim Timid. Tim tried to defend himself, but Doug was too strong, and Tim suffered a brutal assault. Doug was subsequently charged with criminal assault and is being prosecuted by Gail Getem. Doug hired a defense attorney named Gordon Getem. Two weeks later, Doug found out that Gordon and Gail were brother and sister. Gordon made sure that during the representation he did not talk to his sister Gail or any of his other family members. Doug was found not guilty by the jury.

In those jurisdictions that prohibit related attorney representation in the same lawsuit Gordon is

- **(A)** Not subject to discipline because the client was well aware of the family relationship.
- **(B)** Not subject to discipline because the client was found not guilty.
- **(C)** Subject to discipline because there was no consent by the client.
- **(D)** Subject to discipline because Gordon failed to refer the client to another attorney for consultation.

8. Laurie Lawyer was defending Gale Guilty, who was charged with murder and had confessed to the police. Before trial, Gale demanded that Laurie call two witnesses who would testify that Gale was elsewhere at the time of the murder. Laurie asked Gale to explain the contradiction between the confession and the alibi witness statements. Gale's answer was, "Just present the case." Laurie refused to present the two witnesses. Gale lost at trial and during her first year in prison was murdered. Her personal representative subsequently sued Laurie for malpractice.

May Laurie testify and present evidence of the attempt to suborn perjury by Gale?

- **(A)** Yes, if breaching her confidence is necessary to defend the case.
- **(B)** Yes, because the attorney-client privilege terminates at the death of the client.
- **(C)** No, because the past attempted subordination of perjury is a client confidence that is protected information.
- **(D)** No, unless the client has expressly waived the confidentiality rule.

9. Magna Motors built automobiles and installed the minimum safety airbags required by law. Magna's President was strongly encouraged by stock market security analysts to increase profits by cutting costs, and so he secretly ordered the production department not to install the airbags on select models sold in certain markets. During an open Board of Directors' meeting, the President disclosed that Magna had undertaken this action to reduce costs. The corporate attorney, Cathy, then asked, "What will happen when someone dies?" and the President said, "We will have to pay them off."

One of the new cars without airbags crashed, and a whole family was killed. The Prosecutor asserted various criminal charges against Magna and the President. Cathy undertook the defense. At trial, Cathy was called by the prosecution as a witness and asked when she first learned of the non-installation of the airbags. Cathy asserted the attorney-client privilege, but the judge held the privilege was not applicable and ordered her to answer. Cathy then testified fully and candidly about all her conversations with the President.

Is Cathy subject to discipline?

- **(A)** Yes, if she discloses confidential information of her client.
- **(B)** Yes, unless the jurisdiction allows a lawyer to disclose confidential information if necessary to prevent future criminal acts likely to result in death or substantial bodily harm.
- **(C)** No, because the information at issue was disclosed to third parties at an open Board meeting and thus not subject to the attorney-client privilege.
- **(D)** No, because Cathy was compelled by law to disclose the confidential information.

10. Florence Flamboyant was a well-known criminal defense attorney. She was approached by a rock star who had just been charged with child molestation. Florence agreed to undertake the defense. The Government was successful in convincing two of the victims to testify as witnesses, and the jury found the star guilty.

A television reporter approached Florence and her rock star client right after the trial and asked, "Why did you lose the case?" The rock star client stated, "I lost because this lawyer was incompetent, and I am going to hold her responsible for this travesty of justice." The reporter asked if Florence had any reply, and she said, "If this defendant would have paid those two witnesses not to testify, as he did the others, he would not have been convicted, so it's his own fault."

Is Florence Flamboyant subject to discipline for making this reply?

- **(A)** Yes, because she made the comment in a public forum.
- **(B)** Yes, because she intentionally revealed the client's confidential information.
- **(C)** No, because Florence also admitted her own wrongdoing.
- **(D)** No, because Florence has a right to reveal client confidential information to defend herself against allegations of wrongful malpractice liability.

11. Carol Client retained Laura Lawyer to represent her in a title defect case involving property Carol had purchased from Sally Seller. Laura was to receive one-third of any recovery. Unfortunately, Laura was quite busy with other cases and neglected to file the lawsuit until after the statute of limitations had run. She reported her misfeasance to Carol in a meeting, and the two then agreed on the spot that Laura would pay Carol $25,000 to settle the malpractice claim.

Is Laura subject to discipline for settling the malpractice claim in this matter?

- **(A)** Yes, unless $25,000 is a fair and reasonable estimate of the opportunity settlement Carol lost.
- **(B)** Yes.
- **(C)** No, because the liability of the Seller to Carol was never judicially established.
- **(D)** No, as long as the settlement agreement was written and specified that independent counsel should be consulted.

12. Elise Employee was a longtime employee of Big Bucks Corporation. She was injured in an automobile accident and became partially paralyzed. Big Bucks terminated her because she could no longer perform as before. Elise hired Alice Attorney to press her claim that Big Bucks failed to make reasonable accommodations in light of her disability. Big Bucks agreed to a very substantial cash settlement that they paid directly to Elise, who in turn paid Alice $25,000 in cash. At the time, Elise told Alice, "Do not report this cash or give the IRS any information about my case." Big Bucks apparently reported the cash settlement to the Internal Revenue Service (IRS). Two years later, an IRS agent seeking information on the details of the settlement and how the cash was handled contacted Alice Attorney.

Is it proper for Alice Attorney to provide the IRS with this client information?

- **(A)** Yes, only if a U.S. District Court Judge orders that disclosure must be made by the lawyer.
- **(B)** Yes, if Alice no longer represents Elise in any matter.
- **(C)** No, unless Alice believes that the disclosure would not be detrimental to Elise in that the income tax was paid.
- **(D)** No, because the IRS must collect taxes from everyone in order to raise revenue to support the legal and court system.

13. A and B were passengers in an automobile driven by C that got into an accident with a car driven by D. A, B, and C were all injured and asked Paula Plaintiffs-lawyer to represent them. It was unclear whether C or D was at fault. Nonetheless, the attorney for D called Paula and offered to settle all the claims that A, B, and C had for a total of $100,000. The settlement would be allocated $35,000 to A, $35,000 to B, and $30,000 to C.

To comply with professional conduct rules, Paula

- **(A)** May not inform A, B, and C of the total settlement amount or the amount received by the other two clients, unless they consent.
- **(B)** May inform A, B, and C individually of the total settlement amount, but must not inform any client of the amount received by the other two unless they consent.
- **(C)** Must inform A, B, and C individually of the total settlement, but need not inform each of the amount received by the others.
- **(D)** Must inform A, B, and C individually of the total settlement amount and the amounts received by the others.

14. Debra Defense was engaged by Patricia Politician to defend her in a criminal investigation of accepting bribes from lobbyists. Patricia had a large number of bona fide contributors who did not want their identities revealed. Accordingly, Patricia told Debra not to disclose any information about the case or any of her contributors to anyone. Later, Debra's law firm partner assisted in preparing the defense for trial. In the process, she asked Patricia what other contributions she had received. Patricia refused to answer the inquiry. The partner then asked the same question of Debra.

May Debra inform her law firm partner of the details of Patricia's other contributors?

- **(A)** Yes, because Debra's partner is a partner in the same law firm.
- **(B)** Yes, because Debra's partner is a lawyer.
- **(C)** No, unless Patricia gives specific approval.
- **(D)** No, unless the other contributors are part of the public record.

15. Attorney Betty Bankruptcy represents a corporation in a federal Chapter 11 bankruptcy reorganization plan. The corporation was owned jointly by a married couple, Adam and Eve. Eve approached Betty and asked if she would represent her in a marital dissolution action against Adam. This suit would be filed in state family court.

May Betty accept Eve's representation?

- **(A)** Yes, because the subject matter of each representation is totally unrelated to the other.
- **(B)** Yes, if both the corporation and Eve consent after consultation.
- **(C)** No, unless the federal bankruptcy court and state family court both approve of the representation.
- **(D)** No, because Betty's relationship with each client will probably be adversely affected by the other representation.

16. Nancy Newlawyer has just passed the bar exam and opened her solo practice facing large student loan payments. One of her first clients was Susan Startup, who asked Nancy to assist in taking her company public. The representation would take at least six months, and the fee was to be paid in non-marketable stock options in the corporation. Nancy wanted to help Susan, but was concerned. The engagement could take too much of her time and restrict her ability to work for other clients who could provide the cash to pay the student loans.

Susan offered to have a friend of hers, Barbara Banker, loan Nancy money until the public offering. Susan would guarantee the loan. Nancy drafted the stock option and loan agreements, but delayed the signatures for a week, notifying both Susan and Barbara that they might want to seek a lawyer's advice. Ten days later, Nancy, Susan, and Barbara all signed the documents, and Nancy received the loan.

Is Nancy subject to discipline?

- **(A)** No, because Susan suggested the loan agreement, not Nancy.
- **(B)** No, as long as the terms of the loan were fair and reasonable.
- **(C)** Yes, unless Nancy provided full security for the loan from Barbara.
- **(D)** Yes, because this is an indirect client business relationship, which is improper.

17. Amy Artcollector was a lawyer specializing in representing art collectors. One of her clients dealt in antique original American oil paintings. The client provided Amy with a rotating number of paintings for the walls of the law firm reception area and library. A prosecuting attorney was in Amy's office to negotiate a settlement and conclusion to another case. The prosecutor recognized one of the office wall paintings as one that had recently been stolen from the local museum. Amy was arrested and charged with possession of stolen property.

Is Amy subject to discipline if she discloses the particular client who brought the painting to her office?

(A) Yes, if the disclosure would put the client at risk.
(B) Yes, if the client specifically ordered Amy not to disclose that the office paintings on display were actually owned by the client.
(C) No, if the disclosure is necessary for Amy to defend herself against the possession of stolen property charge.
(D) No, because the attorney-client privilege does not apply if the lawyer was involved in criminal conduct.

18. Coral Cautious had just been through a very unpleasant investigation by the local bar association's disciplinary process. Coral had sued a client for non-payment of delinquent fees, and the client filed a bar complaint in response which was finally dismissed. She now has implemented a new end-of-case protective procedure in which she conducts an exit interview of the client. The interview is recorded with the client's knowledge, and every document in the file and the fee statement is reviewed. The client is asked if they have any questions about the lawyer's work or fees charged.

Is Carol subject to discipline for conducting and recording these exit interviews?

(A) Yes, because Carol is acting adversely to the client during the professional representation.
(B) Yes, because Carol is attempting to limit her liability for potential malpractice claims.
(C) No, because Carol is merely reviewing the file and answering any questions that the client may have about the representation.
(D) No, because the exit interview is conducted after Carol has completed the representation.

19. Alice Aggressive and Olivia Overbill started the law firm of Aggressive and Overbill. They found it was slow going at first and wanted to expand their cliental base. Their CPA recommended that one thing that might help would be if they make it easier for start-up business clients to pay their legal bills.

Which of the following would be proper for Aggressive and Overbill?

I. Assist clients in obtaining bank loans.
II. Allow clients to use credit cards to pay their bills.
III. Take an equity interest in the client company as the law firm's fee.
IV. If the case would be of significant interest to the public, require the client to give Aggressive and Overbill the literary and media publication rights.

(A) I and II only.
(B) II only.
(C) I, II and III only.
(D) I, II, III, and IV.

20. Carol Corporatelawyer is the general counsel of Great Expectations Inc. and serves on the board of directors. There is litigation against the company, and the plaintiff is seeking significant sanctions against both the corporation and Carol's law firm. The chairman of the board asked Carol to advise the corporate board on the matter.

Carol is most likely to become subject to discipline if she

(A) Does nothing.
(B) Considers the effect if she resigned from the board and the possibility of the corporation's obtaining legal advice from another lawyer.
(C) Advises the other directors that if she is present in the capacity of a board director, the attorney-client privilege may not cover the communications.
(D) Informs the board that the conflict of interest considerations might require her recusal.

21. Gayle Giftner was a lawyer specializing in estate planning. Most of her clients were quite wealthy and usually developed an attraction to Gayle because she was very friendly, helpful, and personable. Betty Bigbucks was especially appreciative of the work Gayle had accomplished in organizing her estate. Six months after completion of the engagement, Betty called Gayle, explaining she wanted to gift her a parcel of valuable real property.

Gayle will be least likely to be subject to discipline if she

(A) Accepts the gift herself directly.
(B) Suggests to Betty that she make a second large gift to Gayle's favorite charity.
(C) Drafts a legal warranty deed instrument conveying the property from Betty to Gayle.
(D) Drafts a testamentary trust instrument conveying the property to Gayle upon Betty's death in the future.

22. Aggressive & Overbill is a New York law firm specializing in divorce. One of their divorce clients, Frances Fantafast, retained the law firm to represent her in her fifth divorce. During her many office visits, Frances developed a crush on many of the male lawyers in Aggressive & Overbill. Harry Handsome is handling her case at the law firm.

Which of the below sexual actions will most clearly subject an Aggressive & Overbill lawyer to discipline?

(A) Harry continues an existing sexual consensual relationship with Frances that predated the client-lawyer relationship.
(B) Harry had a sexual relationship with Frances during the divorce representation, but Francis signed a written waiver.
(C) Stan Second, another lawyer in Aggressive & Overbill, had a sexual relationship with Frances during the divorce representation.
(D) Harry had a sexual relationship with Frances that began after the divorce representation was concluded.

23. Louise Landuse is a lawyer who specializes in commercial property development. She represents a number of property project developers. One morning, she received a telephone call from Denise Developer, who informed Louise that a large property owner had just agreed to sell development land to her. She also disclosed that Skymart had committed to become an anchor tenant in a shopping center she is going to develop on the property. Louise had previously been told by Denise's real estate broker that the seller of the adjacent parcel of property also wanted to sell.

Is Louise subject to discipline if she tells a business associate of the opportunity to buy the adjoining property?

(A) Yes, because this would be a use of information learned in the representation to the disadvantage of the client.
(B) Yes, unless Denise Developer gives informed consent to Louise to relay the news to a third party who intends to purchase the adjacent property.
(C) No, as long as Denise is not the purchaser of the adjacent property.
(D) No, as long as Denise does not directly or indirectly benefit from the purchase of the adjoining property.

24. Alice Administrative was a lawyer who specialized in state administrative law and agency oversight. She had a number of clients who were active in the consumer loan business. Alice also had real estate shopping center landlord clients. She learned during representation of Better Loans, Inc., that the State Banking Commission had interpreted a statutory provision in the relevant law as authorizing and encouraging the expansion of the consumer loan business in the state.

Is Alice subject to discipline if she discloses and uses this information to benefit her real estate shopping center landlord clients?

(A) Yes, because the lawyer learned the detailed information during representation of Better Loans, Inc.
(B) Yes, because Better Loans, Inc., may not want her to work with any other clients.
(C) Yes, as long as Better Loans, Inc., consents to Alice disclosing and using the information to the benefit of her other clients.
(D) No, as long as the use of the information does not disadvantage Better Loans, Inc.

25. Arron, Inc., is an energy resale corporation listed on the New York Stock Exchange. Iola Innocent represented the corporation as their corporate attorney. An employee hotline received an anonymous complaint stating that the company management had directed the accountants to inflate earnings artificially. The complaint alleged that the Chief Financial Officer (CFO) had fraudulently used special purpose accounting entities to misclassify liabilities as revenue.

Iola investigated and found the complaint was essentially accurate, and the amounts involved were very material. She then reported up the corporate chain to the disclosure committee of the Board of Directors and requested they stop the financial fraud. The Board, CEO, and CFO all refused and directed Iola to forget the whole matter and not inform the Security and Exchange Commission (SEC) of her concern.

Which of the following conduct would subject Iola to discipline from the bar association?

I. Do nothing.
II. Withdraw with notice to third parties.
III. Contact the SEC.
IV. Disavow to the SEC any document Iola helped prepare that contained fraudulent financial information.

(A) None of the above.
(B) Only one of the above.
(C) Only two of the above.
(D) Only three of the above.

26. Diane Divorce was an attorney with a family law practice. One of her clients, Dan Dangerous, was in the midst of a bitter divorce. During discovery in the dissolution proceeding, Diane became aware that Dan had physically abused his wife in the past. The wife succeeded in obtaining a restraining order prohibiting Dan from having any conduct with her or the children. The order was served on Diane as counsel of record for Dan. When Diane explained the situation to Dan, he became outraged and stated, "Now I am going to have to seriously hurt that woman, so she will understand the way it is."

Will Diane be subject to discipline if she informs the police of Dan's apparent intentions to seriously injure his wife?

- **(A)** Yes, because revealing this information could violate the lawyer's duty of confidentiality.
- **(B)** Yes, because the expression of intention to inflict substantial bodily harm constitutes a waiver of the lawyer's confidentiality duty.
- **(C)** No, because revealing Don's plans would be necessary to prevent the client from committing an act reasonably certain to result in death or substantial bodily harm of a human.
- **(D)** No, if Diane believes that she will be implicated in Dan's murder or battery of his wife and children.

27. Carol Consumer is a lawyer working for Care More, PLLC. One of the firm's clients is Deadly Dumper, Inc., a waste disposal company. Carol was in a meeting with the Chief Executive Officer when the Waste Disposal Manager entered the room. The Manager stated that she had just received a report that one of the disposal trucks was in an accident. The disposal truck overturned, and the toxic fluid drained into the city fresh water system. The engineers were not sure if the fully diluted strength of the toxins would affect the drinking water in the city. The CEO said, "Let's not do or say anything because the fines and adverse publicity if we get caught would be disastrous," and Carol disagreed. Carol then told the CEO she was going to inform the city officials and she formally withdrew.

Is Carol subject to discipline if she subsequently informs the city?

- **(A)** Yes, because the toxic waste information is a clear confidence of the client that may not be disclosed absent informed consent.
- **(B)** Yes, because this was past, not future, confidential information.
- **(C)** No, because the client did not approve the disclosure, and an attorney who withdraws from the representation has no further stake in the dispute.
- **(D)** No, only if Carol believes that disclosure of the toxic fluid drainage was reasonably necessary to prevent serious physical harm.

28. Geena Government is an Assistant Attorney General employed by the state government's Attorney General's Office. She is the legal advisor to the State Education Agency. The voters passed an initiative that mandated the state provide the Education Agency an additional $100 per student for cultural enrichment. Because of a declining economy, the state taxation revenue has decreased. The Governor decided that among the non-critical expense reductions possible, the new grant for cultural enrichment could be delayed. The Education Agency had already included the cultural enrichment revenue in their budget. The agency thus instructed Geena to file a lawsuit against the state government to require them to restore the revenue approved by the voters.

Is it proper for Geena to file the lawsuit?

(A) Yes, even though she works for the very government she is now directly adverse to.
(B) Yes, only if the state broader funding unit approves the lawsuit by affirmatively waiving the conflict of interest.
(C) No, because she works for the very government she is now directly adverse to.
(D) No, unless the state broader funding unit approves the lawsuit by affirmatively waiving the conflict of interest.

29. Betty Blackacre had been crossing over land of her neighbor for 21 years. She hired Loretta Landlawyer to file a quiet title action and seek an order that would record the easement in the official land index file. Betty did not then have any cash and agreed to give Loretta a fee in the amount of one-third of the value of the difference in value of Blackacre with and without the easement. Betty also agreed to pay Loretta a flat $10,000 if the quiet title action is not successful. Loretta asked for security for the fee, and Betty gave her a $15,000 bearer bond issued by First Bank.

Is Loretta subject to discipline?

(A) No, because a lawyer may acquire an ownership interest in the client's claim.
(B) No, if the lawyer can show that the total fee is not unreasonable.
(C) Yes, because demanding collateral in excess of the minimum agreed fee is improper.
(D) Yes, because a lawyer may not enter into a business or financial transaction with a client.

30. Teresa Taxpayer retained Alice Attorney to represent her in a dispute with the Internal Revenue Service (IRS). The fee was to be $200 per hour, billed monthly. The IRS alleged that Teresa had fraudulently omitted $100,000 from her tax return. Alice wrote a number of letters to the IRS and met with them on four occasions. Finally a compromise was reached at $50,000 of additional tax, and the IRS gave Teresa a bill for $75,000, including $25,000 of interest. The representation lasted six months.

Alice billed Teresa monthly, and she paid the first three months' billings. The last three months' invoices totaling $5,000 remained unpaid. Alice kept billing Teresa and included a late payment fee at 1% per month.

What collection action may Alice properly take?

I. None unless the representation agreement is in writing.
II. Write dunning letters to prompt Teresa to pay the bill.
III. Charge interest on delinquent balances.
IV. Assign the receivable to a collection agency.
V. File a civil collection action even if a breach of minor confidences results.

(A) Only two of the above.
(B) Only three of the above.
(C) Only four of the above.
(D) All five of the above.

31. Alwaysthere Insurance Co. insures CPAs in public practice against malpractice claims. The policy covers all legal defense costs, but has an exclusion for affirmative dishonesty and fraud. Alwaysthere has a panel listing of lawyers who agree to bill no more than $100 per hour, and the insurance policy states that the insurance company has the sole right to appoint counsel of its choosing. Alwaysthere is reviewing the standard form it uses to assign an attorney to defend a malpractice case and has asked your opinion about including the following provisions.

I. The parties agree that assigned counsel is representing both the insurance company and the insured.
II. The parties agree that the assigned counsel is representing the insured and not the insurance company.
III. Both the insurance company and the insured agree to waive any complaint of conflict of interest against the assigned counsel.
IV. If assigned counsel determines during the representation that there is a conflict between the interests of the insurance company and the insured, the insurance company will allow the client to replace defense counsel with an attorney the client selects and agrees to pay themself.

Which of the above provisions are proper?

(A) I only.
(B) II only.
(C) III only.
(D) Only two of the provisions.

32. Goodservice Law firm handles a variety of matters, but has a large practice concentration of representing workers who were injured on the job. Some of these clients have claims with various state agencies, and some are litigating directly against the employer in question.

A new associate has asked the senior partner which of the following payments are proper.

I. Making a living and medical care advance to indigent clients until they receive the state or employer award.
II. Guaranteeing a bank loan to the client for living expenses until he receives the state or employer award.
III. Advancing the client court and discovery costs and the costs of an original medical examination.
IV. Paying court costs for indigent clients even if these funds will not be repaid.

(A) All of the above.
(B) Only three of the above.
(C) Only two of the above.
(D) Only one of the above.

33. Deloris Defenseattorney represented the Green River Killer, whom the Prosecutor charged with multiple murders. His victims were ladies of the night whom he enticed to come for a ride with him. The Prosecutor suspected the defendant was responsible for almost 100 murders over a five-year period, but formally charged him with only a dozen offenses that could be easily proven. During the trial, the defendant told Deloris he had murdered 100 women and buried them all in a specific area around the Green River. The defendant was convicted and received the death penalty. After he was executed, a group of families of the other missing women victims came to Deloris, explaining they needed closure for their families and wanted to conduct a proper burial of the bodies.

May Deloris properly reveal to the authorities the location of the bodies?

(A) Yes, because Deloris' duty of confidentiality ended when the defendant was executed.
(B) Yes, because the duty to provide closure for the victims' families outweighs the duty of confidentiality absent a showing of prejudice.
(C) No, unless she is subpoenaed to give testimony in a court of law or before a grand jury.
(D) No, because this information is protected, and death of the client does not constitute informed consent to disclosure.

34. Patty Plaintiff was in an automobile accident and seriously injured. The at-fault other driver was insured by Stingyinsurance Co. The case did not settle, and Patty asked Wendy, a passenger in her car during the accident, to be a fact witness at trial. Wendy did not remember much of the accident details, so to improve her testimony, Patty gave her a large file of information accumulated by her attorney. Stingyinsurance Co. moved to compel production of the entire file.

If Patty's lawyer refuses to produce the file, is she subject to potential litigation sanction?

(A) Yes, because the defendant has a right to demand production of any documents that may lead to relevant information.
(B) Yes, because Patty has waived the attorney-client privilege as it relates to the confidential information in the file.
(C) No, because the requested information is protected by the attorney-client privilege.
(D) No, because it is not fair for Stingyinsurance Co. to have the advantage of the confidential file of information.

35. Alice Appeal is a lawyer specializing in appeals principally of building code interpretation issues. She has just represented Donna Developer in the court of appeals seeking to reverse a denial of a side yard variance from Progressive City Building Department. Her argument was that the difficulties of expensive commuting and falling suburban housing values increasingly demand more density and an easy way to accomplish this is to liberally grant variances for residential side yards between buildings. Oral arguments went well and the court of appeals decision is due in six months.

Shortly thereafter, Alice was approached by Nancy Nongrowth who had tried unsuccessfully with the same Building Department to block her neighbor from building into the neighbor's side yard. She has asked Alice if she will handle her appeal to the court of appeals.

Is it proper for Alice to take on Nancy's case?

(A) Yes, because Donna and Nancy are not directly adverse parties in the same matter.
(B) Yes, because the Donna matter is different than the Nancy matter.
(C) No, because the decision favoring one client could create a precedent with the court of appeals likely to weaken the position taken on behalf of the other client.
(D) No, unless the tribunal approves of the second representation because of Alice's expertise in residential side yard issues.

36. Attorney Alice represented Mary in a breach of contract action. Alice acquired information detrimental to Mary during the representation, but still prevailed in the action. Five years later, Alice formed a two lawyer partnership with Attorney Betty. Two years later, a new client, Nancy, asked Betty if she would represent her in a lawsuit against Mary.

Is Attorney Alice subject to discipline if Attorney Betty takes on the representation of Nancy?

(A) Yes, because Alice acquired information detrimental to Mary in the prior litigation.
(B) Yes, unless Alice forfeits her share of any fee that Alice and Betty may earn by representing Nancy.
(C) No, because Betty was not in partnership with Alice when Alice represented Mary and acquired knowledge of Mary that was detrimental.
(D) No, if Alice does not disclose to Betty any of the detrimental information she learned about Mary.

37. Laura and Larry Lovebird employed Wanda Willmaker to prepare joint wills. The dispositive scheme was a life estate to the survivor of the two with any remainder to the present alive and hereafter born children of their marriage. One year later, Larry Lovebird came into Wanda's office and announced that he was leaving Laura for Terri Trophy, and he needed to change his will. He asked Wanda to change the life estate portion of his will from Laura to Terri.

Wanda will engage in proper conduct if she:

(A) Changes the will as requested and does not reveal the change to Laura.
(B) Changes Larry's will as requested and reveals the change to Laura.
(C) Not change Larry's will as requested and does not reveal Larry's intent to change Laura's interests.
(D) Not change Larry's will as requested and reveal to Laura Larry's intent to change Laura's interests under the will.

38. Florence Flighty was a defendant in a lawsuit alleging she had infringed on copyright material in writing her new book, *Software for Dummies*. Because the case had complicated intellectual property issues, Florence hired lawyer Iola Information to represent her in the case. The agreed-upon fee was $300 per hour. The case went to trial, and the jury verdict went for the defendant Florence. Even though she won, Florence was unhappy and believed the loser should pay her unpaid legal fee balance of $40,000. Iola waited for payment, but finally filed a lien against a duplex Florence owned. Florence then decided to sell the duplex and offered to trade the lien release for 50% of the royalties from the new book *Software for Dummies*.

Is Iola subject to discipline if she accepts Florence's offer?

- **(A)** Yes, because a lawyer may not negotiate an agreement to give herself the clients' literary or media publication rights.
- **(B)** Yes, because filing a lien against a client's property to secure payment of legal fees is improper.
- **(C)** No, as long as Florence was independently represented by another attorney in the exchange.
- **(D)** No, as long as the value of the transaction was not so large as to render the total fee received unreasonable.

39. Alice Aggressive represented Elma Employee in an age discrimination wrongful discharge case against Floormat Corporation. Alice conducted massive discovery in the case and developed an in-depth understanding of how the human resource department of Floormat Corporation operated. The case finally did settle at a dollar figure that was reasonably satisfactory to Elma at the time.

Two years later, another ex-employee of Floormat, Sally Second, contacted Alice. Sally had heard of Alice from Elma. The facts and circumstances of the second claim against Floormat Corporation were virtually the same as the first case. This similarity and the confidential information learned in the Elma case allowed Alice a much more efficient and lower cost discovery process. This produced a higher dollar settlement award, and Alice received one-third of the enhanced settlement recovery. Elma heard of the large settlement and called Alice. Elma complained that she had paid for the original research used again in the second case and thus should share a part of Alice's large windfall fee.

Is Alice subject to sanction for using Elma's confidential information?

- **(A)** Yes, because Alice failed to communicate to Elma the use of her relevant information which might lead to informed consent.
- **(B)** Yes, because a lawyer may not use information of a client to the disadvantage of the same client.
- **(C)** No, because a lawyer may use and benefit from information acquired in a former case unless such use disadvantages the prior client.
- **(D)** No, because Elma's right to confidentiality terminated upon the settlement of her case and the attorney-client relationship.

40. Iola Injured suffered massive tumors in her liver and lungs, which she believed were caused by Cooken Chemical Company discharges into the stream that provided the water to her home well. She retained Sally Skillful, a toxic waste lawyer, to pursue the claim at $300 per hour. Sally filed suit on Iola's behalf. Cooken realized they had substantial exposure and hired Gloria Generous with instructions to settle the case. Gloria made a settlement offer of $2,000,000 cash that Iola and Sally felt was more that adequate. Gloria drew the settlement, and the parties signed the agreement. Sally sent Iola her final bill for $15,000, which represented 50 hours at the agreed rate of $300 per hour. Iola immediately paid the $15,000 bill and sent Sally a second check for $25,000 labeled, "Gift for a great lawyer with all my gratitude, Iola."

Is Sally subject to discipline if she cashes the $25,000 check?

- **(A)** Yes, if the $15,000 constituted adequate consideration for her work on Iola's claim against Cooken Chemical Company.
- **(B)** Yes, only if the gift does not meet general standards of fairness.
- **(C)** No, if Iola was advised to seek advice from an independent lawyer in the gift transaction.
- **(D)** No, if Iola was independently represented in negotiating the gift transaction.

41. Deloris Defendant undertook the criminal representation of Roberta Reckless, who was in an automobile accident and subsequently charged with Driving Under the Influence (DUI). Two days later, Deloris' law partner Grace informed Deloris that a longtime firm client Victoria was seriously injured in the same accident. Grace further stated that earlier in the day the law firm filed suit against the driver named Roberta Reckless. Deloris immediately withdrew from the criminal defense representation of Roberta. A week later, Deloris realized that Roberta had told her information that would be very helpful in defending against the prosecutor's criminal case.

Is it proper for Deloris to reveal the information to the prosecution?

- **(A)** Yes, because the information might help her former client Roberta.
- **(B)** Yes, because the attorney-client privilege ended when Deloris withdrew from representing Roberta.
- **(C)** No, unless Roberta expressly consents to the disclosure to the prosecutor.
- **(D)** No, because the information in question was acquired during the attorney-client relationship.

42. Sally Sleepy was injured in a collision with an automobile owned by Iola Innocence. Sally prepared a written accident report that she submitted to Magna Insurance Company. Magna hired a lawyer named Debra Defense to represent Iola in defending the case. Debra took the deposition of Sally, and the testimony seemed inaccurate to Debra as compared to Sally's original accident reports. After the deposition, Debra asked Sally about the inaccuracies in her testimony. Sally admitted to Debra she had lied in her report to Magna. Debra concluded that the falsity violated the policy requirement that the insured must cooperate in the defense and that the truthful disclosure breach might eliminate any insurance coverage duty of Magna.

It would be proper for Debra to:

(A) Inform Sally that she needed to stay with the story in her original report.
(B) Inform Sally that she needed to stay with the story in her deposition.
(C) Inform Magna Insurance of Sally's inaccurate statements.
(D) Seek the court's permission to withdraw from the representation without informing Magna Insurance of Sally's client confidences.

43. In which of the below four situations is the attorney-client privilege a viable defense?

I. A defendant reveals to a lawyer damaging information in the presence of the defendant's friend.
II. A defendant shows her banker all the records upon which she has claimed an attorney-client privilege.
III. A defendant's attorney retains a non-lawyer assistant to assist in preparing documents for trial.
IV. A defendant reveals confidential information to a lawyer during an initial interview, but decides not to hire the lawyer to handle the matter.

(A) One of the above.
(B) Two of the above.
(C) Three of the above.
(D) All of the above.

44. Connie Client called her attorney, Lita Lawyer, and stated that an inspector from a federal environmental agency had contacted her corporation regarding waste disposal. Connie explained how her corporation dealt with their disposal of the waste in question, and Lita agreed to conduct research. Lita soon realized that she didn't have the technical scientific knowledge needed to complete the necessary research. She therefore consulted with another partner in her law firm, Evelyn Environment, who had heavy experience in the environmental matters in question. Evelyn intended to make an oral diagnosis of the problem to Lita, but needed to understand one key fact. She thus called Connie with the question who was outraged that Lita revealed her confidential information about the waste disposal to anyone.

Is Lita subject to discipline?

(A) Yes, because she did not receive client consent before she made the unauthorized disclosures.
(B) Yes, if she revealed Connie's environmental dumping secrets to Evelyn Environmental.
(C) No, because she revealed the information to another attorney in her law firm, and Connie Client failed to limit expressly the authority to make such disclosures.
(D) No, as long as she did not disclose the identity of Connie Client and her corporation to Evelyn Environment.

45. An automobile accident occurred in Sweetville that involved a large semitrailer truck. The large truck changed from the center to the right lane without signaling, thereby forcing a car to collide with a concrete barricade. Both the car's driver, Diane Driver, and the passenger, Pattie Passenger, sustained substantial personal injury caused by the truck's change of lane. They asked Alice Attorney if she would represent them both in pursuing the negligence action against the company that owned the truck in question.

Which of the below would represent proper conduct by Alice?

I. Represent both the trucking company and Diane and Pattie in this matter with disclosure to all three clients.
II. Represent both Diane and Pattie after disclosure, confirmed in writing, that they could have potential crossclaims against each other and obtain both clients' informed consent.
III. If subsequent discovery indicates that Diane and Pattie have crossclaims, Alice should withdraw.

(A) None of the above.
(B) Only one of the above.
(C) Two of the above.
(D) All three of the above.

46. Mary Mafia was a foot soldier in the organized criminal family that controlled much of Big City. She was arrested along with a number of other family members fleeing from an arson attempt on a warehouse owned by another up and coming criminal family. When she was being booked into the jail, Mary asked to be represented by a public defender. She had one short meeting with the assigned public defender lawyer.

Later, a lawyer named Sally Sleepy met with Mary and told her that she had been paid by the criminal family to defend her. The offered defense was conditioned upon Mary accepting sole responsibility for the arson and not implicating anyone else from the family. Mary accepted, and Sally substituted into the case for the public defender. Sally immediately notified the prosecutor that her client changed her mind and would not accept the proffered probation sentence in return for testimony against other family members. The prosecutor believed Mary's change of position was solely motivated by threats delivered by Sally and filed a motion to disqualify Sally.

Is Sally properly subject to disqualification?

- **(A)** Yes, because the court has a responsibility to protect a criminal defendant from a third party interfering with a lawyer's independence.
- **(B)** Yes, because a third party cannot pay legal expenses of a criminal defendant.
- **(C)** No, because it is the criminal defendant's sole choice whom they chose to represent them in the matter.
- **(D)** No, as long as the client consents to the potential conflict of interest after consultation.

47. Abe and Barbara decided to end their business partnership and approached Connie Careful, a business attorney. They proposed that to save money, Connie should assist them both in the business dissolution. Connie agreed to so act and required them both to sign a common representation agreement, which stated that the attorney-client privilege may not apply to information Connie receives in the representation. Abe's banker called Connie and said Abe had approached the bank, asking for a loan to buy out Barbara.

Upon questioning by the banker, Connie discussed details of the partnership and assets of both Abe and Barbara. Barbara later learned of Connie's discussion with the banker and complained.

Did Connie act properly?

- **(A)** Yes, because she required both parties to sign a common representation agreement.
- **(B)** Yes, because the clients were put on notice that the attorney-client privilege would not apply.
- **(C)** No, because the scope of the implied consent was exceeded.
- **(D)** No, because a lawyer may not reveal client information without permission.

48. Sally Software was a lawyer with heavy experience in computer software copyright protection. She was approached by Marilyn Microhard, who was interviewing lawyers for representation in pursuing software copyright infringement claims against a Chinese corporation. The interview involved a two-hour PowerPoint presentation by Microhard detailing their corporate background and the history of other copyright claims they had successfully pursued. This discussion covered only public information or portions of documents contained in the court files of prior litigated cases. Sally had a bad feeling about the one-sided Microhard presentation and at the end of the interview stated she did not want to take on the case.

Microhard subsequently hired Smith & Jones to pursue the claim. Two months later, Sally's law firm partner Sarah received a telephone call from the same Chinese corporation, which informed Sarah they were being sued by Microhard in a claim alleging infringement. After review of the facts, Sarah entered into a representation agreement with the Chinese corporation to take on the defense. Smith & Jones learned that Sarah was a partner of Sally and that Sally had interviewed with Marilyn Microhard while considering taking the case. Based upon this meeting, Smith & Jones filed a motion with the trial court to disqualify both Sally and Sarah.

Is Sally and/or Sarah subject to disqualification?

	Sally	Sarah
(A)	Yes	Yes
(B)	Yes	No
(C)	No	Yes
(D)	No	No

49. Harriet Honest was an attorney who specialized in trust law. She was approached by Dorothy to draft a testamentary trust instrument that would receive all her assets upon her death. The trust instrument specified that Dorothy's daughter, Sally, was to be the trustee and receive the income for life. Dorothy's grandchildren were to receive the corpus upon the death of their mother. The trust instrument did not allow the trustee to invade the trust principal.

Harriet handled the probate of Dorothy's will and conveyed all the assets into the trust. Over the next two years, she gave legal advice to Sally on trust issues and other matters. Sally called and requested a meeting with Harriet to discuss some confidential issues regarding the management of the trust assets. In the meeting, Sally admitted she had taken substantial sums from the trust principal to support her gambling habit. Harriet explained that was illegal and that the funds should be returned to the trust. Sally refused.

If Harriet reports the embezzlement to the court department that handles estate and trust matters, is she subject to discipline?

(A) Yes, because this was confidential information of a client.
(B) Yes, because the information was voluntarily given to the attorney by the client.
(C) No, because a lawyer may reveal to a tribunal information that discloses a breach of fiduciary responsibility by a client who has used the lawyer's services in the commission.
(D) No, because the probate and trust were Harriet's client, not Sally.

50. Sally Startup is a venture capital lawyer specializing in taking privately-owned corporations public. Great Expectations Ltd. employed her in arranging their initial public offering. During her investigation, Sally learned of the great value of the corporation's software, which was protected by enforceable copyrights and was considered confidential by the corporation.

She thus believed the corporation's stock was worth much more than the initial offering price. Based on this insider knowledge, she purchased a large amount of the shares at market upon the initial offering. Sally did not seek client permission and none of the corporate personnel had knowledge of the purchase. Six months later, Sally sold the shares, thereby doubling her investment and realizing a substantial profit.

Is Sally subject to civil liability of disgorgement or professional discipline?

(A) Neither civil liability nor professional discipline because Great Expectations was not disadvantaged by her stock transaction.
(B) Civil liability of disgorgement only, but not professional discipline.
(C) Professional discipline only, but not civil liability.
(D) Both civil liability of disgorgement and professional discipline.

51. Alpha and Beta planned out how to successfully pull off a robbery of First Bank. They both rushed into the Bank and began firing their pistols in the air. One of the bullets ricocheted off the ceiling and killed a bank teller but it was not clear if the bullet came from Alpha's or Beta's pistol. The state charged them both with felony murder. They have both approached attorney Debra Defense and asked if she would defend them both.

Debra Defense must

(A) Explain to them both the potential risks and dangers of the conflict.
(B) Explain to them both the potential risks and dangers of the conflict and obtain their oral consent.
(C) Explain to them both the potential risks and dangers of the conflict and obtain their signatures in writing.
(D) Explain to them both the potential risks and dangers of the conflict and confirm their agreement in writing.

Chapter 2

Client Relations – Confidentiality and Conflicts of Interest

Answers

MPRE Tip: Put a piece of paper over the answers and "mask down" while working through the questions so you don't accidently peek at the next answer.

1. /B/ A lawyer shall not make an agreement prospectively limiting the lawyer's liability to a client for malpractice unless permitted by law, and the client is independently represented. [MRPC 1.8(h)] **(A)** is incorrect because the ability to retain a different lawyer does not suspend the requirement that Nancy comply with the MRPCs. **(C)** is incorrect because MRPC 1.8(h) requires independent representation, which goes beyond explaining the damage ceiling limitation provision. **(D)** is incorrect because MRPC 1.8(h) requires that there be independent representation, which goes beyond mere client consent.

2. /C/ The general rule of MRPC 1.6 is the evidentiary attorney-client privilege prohibits revealing information received from a client; Terry's Porsche theft would qualify. An exception applies allowing disclosure if necessary to establish a defense to a criminal charge or civil claim against the lawyer. **(A)** is incorrect; while the rationale is correct – ordinarily, only future crimes may be revealed – the exception of alternative C is a better answer. **(B)** is incorrect because whether criminal charges had been commenced against the client is irrelevant to the issue of revealing client's information; Deloris may respond to avoid complicity. **(D)** is incorrect; while the nonpayment of the bill is probably not protectable confidential information, it does not provide a justification for revealing the underlying substantive confidence or secret.

3. /D/ The best answer through the process of elimination. Both MRPC 1.7(a)(1) and (2) conflict of interest exceptions require that the attorney must reasonably believe the dual representation will not adversely affect either client's diligent representation, and both clients must give informed consent confirmed in writing. This conflict is not in litigation. **(A)** is incorrect because payment by one of the parties to the transaction is not payment by a third party, which may be prohibited under MRPC 1.8(f). **(B)** is incorrect because it is too simplistic, and this possibility may still be present even if the clients consent in writing after full disclosure. **(C)** is incorrect because the standard practice in the locale is irrelevant to the question of whether the attorney met the requirements of MRPC 1.7. In addition, it fails to include the key requirement that the clients both consent to the conflict after full disclosure, which is confirmed in writing.

4. /A/ The subject of the representation under MRPC 1.9 must be the same or substantially similar; here, the matter is arguably factually distinct. Therefore, representation is allowed, so long as no client information from the prior matter is used in this case. **(B)** is incorrect because the result in the prior matter is irrelevant. **(C)** is incorrect because it ignores the subject matter relationship test. **(D)** is incorrect; since the representation is not substantially similar, it is not necessary to get the consent of the prior client.

5. **/B/** A lawyer is prohibited from representing a party if an attorney who is related to the first lawyer represents a directly adverse party unless each client gives informed consent. **(A)** is incorrect because both lawyers would likely be subject to discipline since both clients must give informed consent. **(C)** is incorrect because a waiver of the related lawyers rule does not require written consent. **(D)** is incorrect because a waiver of the related lawyers rule only requires each client to give informed consent; under this particular conflict such consent does not necessarily have to be confirmed in writing [MRPC 1.7, comment 11].

6. **/C/** A lawyer may accept compensation for representing a client from one other than the client if the client gives informed consent [MRPC 1.8(f)]. Notice that only if the third party's payment is known to the client is informed consent possible. **(A)** is incorrect because a payment guarantee does not eliminate the ethical violation. **(B)** is not the best answer; while non-interference by the paying party is a requirement, the more important and prerequisite factor is informed client consent. **(D)** is not the best answer since this merely states the risk the Rule is intended to preclude.

7. **/C/** In many jurisdictions, a lawyer shall not represent a client in a matter where the lawyer representing the opposing party is related as a spouse, parent, child, or sibling, unless the clients both give informed consent [MRPC 1.7, comment 11]. "A matter" likely includes a criminal prosecution and defense matter. **(A)** is incorrect because client awareness of the relationship between counsels is not sufficient without informed consent after consultation. **(B)** is incorrect because the result achieved in the representation does not abate the conflict without informed consent after consultation. **(D)** is not the best answer because it is not necessary that the client be referred to another attorney, only that there be informed consent after consultation.

8. **/A/** The issue raised by the personal representative of the former client is the alleged malpractice of the attorney in refusing to call the witnesses who would perjure themselves; therefore, the lawyer's evidence of this may be introduced as a defense. **(B)** is incorrect because the attorney-client privilege normally survives the death of the client and may be claimed by the personal representative. **(C)** is incorrect because the attorney-client privilege is inapplicable when the client sues the lawyer. **(D)** is not the best answer because client confidences may be revealed in this circumstance even if the client has not waived the confidentiality rule [MRPC 1.6].

9. **/D/** The best answer because the court may order a lawyer to give testimony that divulges client confidential information, and this does not subject the lawyer to discipline. **(A)** is incorrect because it merely states the general rule without referring to any of the exceptions. **(B)** is not the best answer; while a lawyer may reveal confidences to prevent a criminal act likely to result in death or serious injury, in most jurisdictions that only applies if a lawyer decides to do so. Here, disclosure is pursuant to a court order. **(C)** is not as good an answer as D because the duty of confidentiality covers information derived from the representation, and the Board would likely be interpreted as part of the client, so waiver would not apply [MRPC 1.6].

10. /A/ The best answer because it was not reasonably necessary for the lawyer to reveal that client's confidential information in a public forum. This statement would probably be permissible if the lawyer were later sued by the client or becomes subject to legal sanctions of the court or a bar disciplinary action, but those possibilities are not yet ripe. [MRPC 1.6] **(B)** is not the best answer because it only includes the general non-disclosure rule and not the exceptions here on point. **(C)** is incorrect because while the lawyer may also be responsible for participating in bribing the witnesses, it does not excuse revealing the client's confidential information. **(D)** is incorrect because a malpractice liability claim has not yet been formally asserted.

11. /B/ The best answer because beyond written advice of the desirability of seeking independent counsel, there must be a reasonable opportunity to consult, which was not provided. [MRPC 1.8(h)] **(A)** is incorrect because even if $25,000 were a fair settlement, the client must be given a reasonable opportunity to seek independent counsel. **(C)** is incorrect because it is not necessary to establish the precise amount of damages to settle a professional malpractice case. **(D)** is not the best answer; while true as far as it goes, it excludes the critical requirement that the client have a reasonable opportunity to consult with independent counsel. A writing is insufficient if the reasonable opportunity is not possible.

12. /A/ IRS reporting falls under the constraints of that requiring non-disclosure of information that the client asserts is confidential. An exception applies (so disclosure may be made) if a U.S. District Court signs an order requiring an attorney to disclose. [MRPC 1.6] **(B)** is incorrect because a prior client's confidential information remains subject to the non-disclosure rules after the representation ceases. **(C)** is incorrect because it contradicts the given fact that the client ordered the attorney not to make disclosure to the IRS. **(D)** is incorrect because however laudable the rationale, it does not excuse the disclosure of the client's confidential information.

13. /D/ Multiple clients who would share as plaintiffs must give written consent if the lawyer becomes involved in an aggregate settlement. They must be informed of all the total settlement and the amount each client will receive. [MRPC 1.8] **(A)** is incorrect because the required disclosures are mandatory (shall or will), not discretionary (may). **(B)** is incorrect because in addition to disclosing the total aggregate settlement, the attorney must disclose the amount received by each. **(C)** is incorrect because the duty to inform all the clients of the total aggregate settlement, and individual amounts is mandatory, not optional.

14. /C/ The best answer because the client's specific direction not to disclose the contributors' identities will override the general rule that confidential client information may be shared internally within the law firm for consultation or in preparation for trial. The client could, of course, approve such disclosure, but that was specifically declined. [MRPC 1.6] **(A)** is incorrect because the client gave specific instructions not to disclose. **(B)** is incorrect because the fact that the recipient is a lawyer does not override the client's specific directions. **(D)** is incorrect (even though an attractive distracter) because whether the contributors are public is irrelevant since the client has specifically directed the lawyer not to make disclosure of this information.

15. /D/ Since Adam owns one-half of the corporation, and the business will be a major asset in the marital dissolution, there is a present fundamental antagonism between both clients. [MRPC 1.7] It does not seem that the issues and emotions will be reasonably reconciled. Thus, Betty's relationship in the two clients' matters will probably be adversely affected by the dual representation. **(A)** is incorrect because there is some common relationship, and the parties are fundamentally antagonistic. **(B)** is incorrect because consent may not be effective if a fundamental antagonism exists between the clients. **(C)** is incorrect because the consent or non-consent of the involved courts is irrelevant to the conflict of interest questions at issue here.

16. /B/ The best answer, even though this could be characterized as a client business relationship. Here it is not clear that the client expects the lawyer to represent her in the loan guarantee, but this alternative does meet the three **TIC** transaction requirements necessary to the exception. (<u>T</u>erms reasonable, <u>i</u>ndependent counsel, <u>c</u>onsent by the client in writing.) The facts indicate the client had a reasonable opportunity to seek independent counsel, and the client consent is in writing, so if the transaction terms are fair and reasonable, all requirements would be met. [MRPC 1.8(a)] **(A)** is incorrect because who suggested the transaction is not relevant in this situation. **(C)** is incorrect because full loan security goes perhaps to the fair and reasonable test, but docs not address the other two requirements. **(D)** is incorrect because regardless of whether the business transaction is direct or indirect, the three **TIC** requirements must be met.

17. /C/ The best answer because a lawyer may disclose client confidential information if necessary to establish a defense to a criminal charge based upon conduct in which the client was involved. [MRPC 1.6(b)(3)] **(A)** is incorrect because disclosure is authorized if necessary to defend against the results of the client's wrongdoing, regardless of the consequences to the client. **(B)** is incorrect because if the lawyer must defend herself resulting from the client's wrongdoing, disclosure is authorized even if the client directs to the contrary. **(D)** is not the best answer because the privilege applies to in-court testimony concerning client communications; the disclosure here is not in court, but even if it were, the lawyer is allowed to disclose client confidences to defend against a charge arising from client wrongdoing.

18. /C/ The facts do not indicate that the lawyer Coral knew had committed malpractice or was attempting in the exit interview to settle a malpractice claim. A good faith explanation of the history of the case and answering any remaining questions the client may have is not necessarily improper. MRPC 1.8 does not seem to have been violated. **(A)** is incorrect because the interview is not adverse to the client, but rather helps in explaining any unanswered questions. **(B)** is incorrect because the case is complete, and the restrictions do not apply since there is no attempt to limit malpractice liability. **(D)** is not the best answer because if the interview was deemed to be an attempt to settle a malpractice claim, it would be a violation regardless of whether the representation was completed or ongoing.

19. /C/ The best answer because it is the only correct combination of alternatives. "Assisting" clients in getting loans from a bank is different than "providing" financial assistance directly. [MRPC 1.8(e)] There is no ethical restriction on a law firm allowing a client to pay with credit cards. A law firm may receive an equity interest from a client for a fee as long as it is reasonable in amount [MRPC 1.5(a)], and the business transaction of receiving the ownership interest meets all three **TIC** requirements of MRPC 1.8(a). A law firm may not make an agreement giving the lawyer literary and media publication rights prior to conclusion of the case. **(A)** is incorrect because the alternative contains the wrong combination of the four fee matters. **(B)** is incorrect because the alternative contains the wrong combination of the four fee matters. **(D)** is incorrect because the alternative contains the wrong combination of the four fee matters.

20. /A/ The correct answer because a lawyer serving as a corporate director while simultaneously advising the board about a matter in which her law firm's interest may be adverse is under a conflict of interest requiring some affirmative action. It is improper for a lawyer in such a position to do nothing. [MRPC 1.7, Comment 35] **(B)** is not the best answer because this represents a proper procedure to abate or mitigate the conflict. **(C)** is not the best answer because this represents a proper procedure to abate or mitigate the conflict. **(D)** is not the best answer because this represents a proper procedure to abate or mitigate the conflict.

21. /A/ A lawyer may not solicit such a substantial gift from a client. However, a lawyer may accept a gift from client if the transaction meets general standards of fairness. This alternative does not indicate there was any solicitation or overreaching in procuring the gift and thus is the best answer. [MRPC 1.8(c)] **(B)** is incorrect because the lawyer suggesting a substantial gift be made to a third party for the lawyer's benefit is improper; here, there is solicitation, which distinguishes it from a voluntary gift. **(C)** is incorrect because a lawyer preparing a legal instrument on behalf of the client that gives the lawyer a substantial gift is engaging in improper conduct. **(D)** is incorrect because a lawyer preparing a legal instrument on behalf of the client that gives the lawyer a substantial gift is engaging in improper conduct.

22. /B/ The best answer because a lawyer who engages in a sexual relationship with a client concurrent with legal representation is subject to discipline, and any client waiver is ineffective. [MRPC 1.8(j)] **(A)** is incorrect because an exception to the "no sexual relationship" rule with a client is if there was a consensual relationship prior to undertaking the representation, and the lawyer's ability to represent the client will not be materially limited by the relationship. **(C)** is incorrect because the "no sexual relations" rule only applies to the lawyer performing the representation: other lawyers in the firm are not so restricted. **(D)** is incorrect because the disciplinary rule applies only to a sexual relationship that is concurrent to the legal representation.

23. /B/ The best answer because a lawyer shall not use information relating to the representation of a client unless the client gives informed consent. [MRPC 1.8(b)] **(A)** is incorrect because it states only the general rule without addressing the consent exception. **(C)** is incorrect because it is not necessary that the lawyer personally use the information if the information being used by the lawyer works to the disadvantage of the client or was considered confidential. **(D)** is incorrect because the prohibition applies if the information works to the detriment of the client; benefit to the lawyer is not the test.

24. /D/ The best answer. The prohibition on use of information relating to the representation of a client applies only if such use would disadvantage the client; here, there does not appear to be such a disadvantage or a direct benefit to the lawyer. [MRPC 1.8(b) commentary] **(A)** is incorrect because the mere fact the lawyer learned the information during the representation of the client does not necessarily mean a disadvantage to the client will result. **(B)** is incorrect because client informed consent to use of information relating to the representation is necessary only if it could work to the disadvantage of the client. **(C)** is not the best answer because it appears as if this information came from the State Banking Commission, not the client, so the client cannot claim a proprietary right in this information.

25. /A/ The best answer because the confidentiality Rule 1.6 has an exception allowing disclosure necessary to prevent a client from continuing a crime or fraud in the future that is reasonably certain to result in substantial injury to the financial interests of another. But the command adverb "may" is not "must," so disclosure action is not actually required. [MRPC 1.6] I would not subject Iola to discipline since the future fraud exception only allows disclosure; it does not mandate disclosure. II is specifically allowed under MRPC 1.6 if the lawyer has become complicit in the client's fraud. III is specifically allowed under Sarbanes-Oxley, and even though it may be contrary to some state laws or rules, the federal security law controls. IV is not improper because a lawyer may withdraw or disaffirm any of their documents that were prepared based upon client provided fraudulent information.

26. /C/ A lawyer may inform authorities of a client's confidential information if necessary to prevent the client from committing a future criminal act reasonably certain to result in death or substantial bodily harm; that appears to be the situation here. [MRPC 1.6(b)(2)] **(A)** is incorrect because the prohibition against revealing confidential information has an exception for acts involving future serious bodily harm. **(B)** is incorrect because this is an exception to the confidentiality rule, not a waiver. **(D)** is not the best answer since there was no present criminal charge or civil claim asserted at the time the disclosure was made.

27. /D/ The best answer because a lawyer's belief that a client's action will cause serious physical harm may justify disclosure to a preventive legal authority, at least to the extent necessary to prevent the offense. [MRPC 1.6(b)(1)] **(A)** is incorrect because it states only the general rule against disclosure of confidential information and does not include the exceptions. **(B)** is incorrect because, while the offense occurred in the past, the potential serious physical harm will occur in the future. **(C)** is incorrect because the exception to the general rule of non-disclosure may apply even if the lawyer has withdrawn from the representation.

28. **/A/** A lawyer for one government unit does not represent any other affiliated upstream broader government control organization, so Geena may sue the state government funding unit even though her agency unit is affiliated. [Comment 34 to MRPC 1.7] **(B)** is not the best answer because it is not necessary that the broader funding unit approve the lawsuit unless there was a prior understanding to the contrary, and no such agreement is stated in these facts. **(C)** is incorrect because there is an exception to the conflict of interest rules for affiliated organizational clients. **(D)** is incorrect because the conflict of interest rule only applies if there was a prior understanding to the contrary, and no such agreement is stated in these facts.

29. **/B/** The best answer through the process of elimination. [MRPC 1.5] **(A)** is incorrect because a lawyer may not acquire an ownership interest in the client's claim. [MRPC 1.8(i)] **(C)** is incorrect because there is no disciplinary rule that states collateral given to a lawyer may not exceed the minimum fee; the actual fee may exceed the minimum fee, and the better answer focused on the reasonableness of the total fee. **(D)** is incorrect; while there are required **TIC** transaction elements that must be met if a lawyer enters into a business or financial transaction with a client, such a transaction is not necessarily improper.

30. **/C/** Four of the five listed items are usually considered to be proper behavior in collection actions by a lawyer. I is incorrect because while there are some instances where the agreement must be written (contingency, etc.), representation at a flat hourly rate is not usually one of the cases. II is not usually improper because communications to a client intended to prompt legitimate past-due receivable payments are allowed. III is usually proper because interest is the cost for using the money. IV is likely not improper, but all the non-lawyer's collection conduct must be compatible with the professional obligations of the lawyer. [MRPC 5.3(a)] V is likely not improper because a lawyer entitled to a fee is permitted to provide some of the details of the services rendered in a collection action, even if some minor confidences are revealed. [Comment 9 to MRPC 1.6]

31. **/A/** The only correct alternative of those given is Item I stating that the assigned counsel is representing both parties (thereby creating a conflict of interest that may be abated if there is informed consent by both clients and no interference with the lawyer's independent professional judgment). [MRPC 1.8(f)] Item II is incorrect because it disregards the dual representation reality and both the informed consent and no interference requirements. Item III is incorrect because informed consent implies that the lawyer discloses to both clients the details of the significant risks that will materially limit the total loyalty to each client; that information is not normally available prospectively. Item IV is incorrect because it disregards both the requirement that the client may not be prejudiced by the conflict and the requirement that the insurance company may not interfere with the lawyer's professional judgment.

32. /C/ The correct answer is that items III and IV are proper payments, but I and II are improper. I is incorrect because making a living and medical care advance to a client is improper. II is incorrect because guaranteeing a bank loan to a client is the equivalent to making the loan, which is improper. III is proper because a lawyer may advance such expenses as long as the client remains ultimately liable for such costs. (Notice that an original medical examination is different from paying the client's ongoing medical expenses.) IV is proper because court costs may be paid for indigent clients (including class action participants in some states), even if the funds will not be repaid. [MRPC 1.8(e)] **(A)** is an incorrect combination of the proper payments. **(B)** is an incorrect combination of the proper payments. **(D)** is an incorrect combination of the proper payments.

33. /D/ The best answer because a lawyer may not reveal privileged client information given to them in confidence, unless there is informed consent to disclosure. Death is not the equivalent to or a substitute for consent. [MRPC 1.6] **(A)** is incorrect because the confidentiality duty survives the death of the client. **(B)** is attractive and commendable, but incorrect; relative benefits to the victim's relatives do not outweigh the lawyer's duty of confidentiality owed to the client. **(C)** is incorrect because the lawyer would have to claim the attorney-client privilege if subpoenaed.

34. /B/ If a client knowingly fails to claim the privilege and releases the information to third parties, the attorney-client privilege may be waived. [MPRE 1.6 and common law evidence] **(A)** is incorrect because an opposing party does not have the right to demand production of documents protected by the attorney-client privilege. **(C)** is incorrect because in this situation the client has waived the privilege. **(D)** is incorrect because while the result is perhaps unfair, the client has waived the attorney-client privilege, so the documents in question are discoverable.

35. /C/ When the same lawyer argues one side of a significant issue likely to create a precedent, she should not simultaneously represent another client seeking a reverse precedent. While this would likely be a waivable conflict, the facts do not indicate either client even knew of the other, much less gave informed consent confirmed in writing. [Comment 24 to MRPC 7.1] **(A)** is incorrect in that a conflict may exist if the lawyer's advocacy for one client materially limits her effectiveness in representing another client. **(B)** is incorrect because an impermissible conflict may exist even though the matter is different than the other appeal. **(D)** is incorrect because it is the potentially adverse clients that must approve, not the tribunal.

36. /A/ Attorney Alice has a duty of loyalty to her former client, Mary, that disqualifies her from representing an opposing party [MRPC 1.9]. Detrimental information was acquired, and the disqualification is imputed firm-wide unless there is proper screening. Screening is not mentioned in the facts and would seem difficult in a two partner law firm [MRPC 1.10]. **(B)** is incorrect because forfeiture of any fee does not cure the conflict and the imputed firm-wide disqualification. **(C)** is incorrect because the conflict of interest rules apply as of the date the subsequent representation is undertaken. **(D)** is incorrect; while disclosure of the past detrimental information is the danger, non-disclosure does not abate the conflict.

37. **/C/** The best answer because the lawyer's responsibility to one client has now become materially limited by her responsibility to another client [MRPC 1.7(b)]. A lawyer may not usually reveal a client's confidential information communicated to the lawyer with an intention that it not be revealed to others [MRPC 1.6(a)]. **(A)** is incorrect because the lawyer's responsibility to one client has now become materially limited by her responsibility to another client. **(B)** is incorrect because the lawyer's responsibility to one client has now become materially limited by her responsibility to another client. **(D)** is incorrect because the confidential information may not be revealed.

38. **/D/** The best answer because the lien and trade for the literary partnership are not improper, but they would likely be deemed part of the fees, and the lawyer has the burden to demonstrate that the total fee charged the client was not unreasonable [MRPC 1.5(a)]. **(A)** is incorrect because the prohibition on acquiring media rights terminates at the conclusion of the representation [MRPC 1.8(d)]. **(B)** is incorrect because a lawyer is entitled to file a lien against client property to secure payment of a legitimate fee. **(C)** is incorrect; while the trade of the lien for a literary partnership is a client business transaction, the client only has to be advised in writing to seek the advice of independent counsel, and actual representation by another lawyer is not necessary. [MRPC 1.8(a)]

39. **/C/** Unless the use of information from a prior case operates to the disadvantage of the prior client, subsequent use is not improper [MRPC 1.8(c)]. **(A)** is incorrect because it is not usually necessary that a lawyer inform a prior client before they use information acquired in prior representation unless the client is disadvantaged thereby [MRPC 1.6]. **(B)** is not the best answer because – while a correct statement – there is no indication the lawyer is using this information to the disadvantage of the former client. **(D)** is incorrect because the duty of confidentiality survives the termination of the attorney-client relationship [MRPC 1.9].

40. **/B/** The best answer because an unsolicited gift from a satisfied and grateful client may be accepted by a lawyer if the transaction meets general standards of fairness and does not involve solicitation and/or overreaching [MRPC 1.8(a)]. **(A)** is incorrect because even if the original agreed fee was adequate consideration, the client may make the lawyer a gift providing it was fair, and there was no overreaching. **(C)** is incorrect because it is not necessary that the lawyer advise the client to seek independent advice (although in some circumstances it might be prudent). **(D)** is incorrect because it is not necessary that the client be independently represented to validate a voluntary gift.

41. **/C/** The correct answer in that an attorney may only reveal client confidential information if the client expressly consents to the disclosure [MRPC 1.6(a)]. **(A)** is incorrect because even if disclosure would help the former client, confidential information disclosure requires client consent. **(B)** is incorrect because the attorney-client confidentiality rules survive the withdrawal of the attorney. **(D)** is incorrect because the time the confidential information was acquired during the attorney-client relationship is not relevant to whether disclosure may be made without securing client consent.

42. /D/ When the client admitted her initial report was false, the lawyer's responsibility to both clients became materially limited, and therefore it became impossible to represent effectively both the insured and insurance company. Thus, the lawyer should file a motion seeking permission to withdraw without informing the insurance company of the confidences of the insured. [MRPC 1.7(a)(2)] **(A)** is incorrect because upon the potential conflict coming into existence, it would be improper to inform or advise either client on a future course of action. **(B)** is incorrect because upon the potential conflict coming into existence, it would be improper to inform or advise either client on a future course of action. **(C)** is incorrect because upon the potential conflict coming into existence, it would be improper to inform or advise either client on a future course of action.

43. /B/ The only correct combination of alternatives. I is incorrect because the presence of the defendant's friend at the time and place the information was revealed to the lawyer precluded the creation of the attorney-client privilege. II is incorrect because the voluntary disclosure of a substantial portion of the information to a third party may constitute a waiver of the privilege. III is correct because an assistant to an attorney is covered by the attorney-client privilege as to both communications and work product created. IV is correct because the attorney–client privilege and confidentiality provisions attach to all information acquired in the role of attorney even if the prospective client, does not subsequently become an actual client. [MRPC 1.6 and 1.18] **(A)** is an incorrect combination of alternatives. **(C)** is an incorrect combination of alternatives. **(D)** is an incorrect combination of alternatives.

44. /C/ A lawyer's communication of a client confidential information to other lawyers in the same law firm for consultation purposes does not violate MRPC 1.6 unless the client had expressly limited the lawyer's authority to communicate their information to firm colleagues. **(A)** is incorrect because consent to consult internally within the law firm is implied unless the client specifies to the contrary. **(B)** is incorrect because permission to consent to consult internally within the law firm is implied unless the client specifies to the contrary. **(D)** is not the best answer because the question of disclosure of confidential information usually turns more on the sensitivity of the information than whether the owner's identity was revealed.

45. /C/ The only correct combination of alternatives. I is improper conduct because the stated parties' interests seem to be directly adverse, so joint representation is not usually allowed, since it would put the lawyer in the inconsistent position of representing both the plaintiff and defendants. [MRPC 1.7] II is proper conduct if there is no present conflict of interest, and the potential future crossclaim conflict is adequately disclosed. III is proper conduct because if a potential conflict evolves into an actual conflict, withdrawal may be necessary. **(A)** is an incorrect combination of alternatives. **(B)** is an incorrect combination of alternatives. **(D)** is an incorrect combination of alternatives.

46. /A/ The best answer because a court has a responsibility (especially in a criminal case where ineffective counsel is grounds for reversal on appeal) to ensure a third party who is paying fees for a criminal defendant does not interfere with the lawyer's independence or professional judgment [MRPC 1.8(f)]. The judge's decision applies even if the client has waived the lawyer's conflict of interest [MRPC 1.7]. **(B)** is not the best answer because a third party may pay legal expenses of a criminal defendant as long as there is no interference. **(C)** is incorrect because the court may interfere if a third party paying legal fees adversely affects the attorney-client relationship. **(D)** is incorrect because consent after consultation is effective only if there is no interference with the lawyer's independence.

47. /C/ The best answer because the clients were aware there might be no attorney-client privilege between the jointly-represented clients; here, the disclosure went beyond the two clients to a third party, so the scope of consent was exceeded [MRPC 1.6]. **(A)** is incorrect because it does not address the central concern of confidential information disclosure. **(B)** is incorrect because while both clients were aware that the privilege might not apply between them, the disclosure here was to a third party. **(D)** is incorrect because the scope of consent was exceeded here.

48. /D/ Neither Sally nor Sarah is subject to disqualification for their representation of the Chinese corporation because their interview with Microhard did not involve them receiving any non-public client confidential information. Information contained in an unsealed court file is considered in the public domain and thus also not usually confidential [MRPC 1.6]. While former clients are protected under MRPC 1.9, here the lawyer never entered into an attorney-client relationship, so this provision arguably does not apply. A privilege exists for confidential information of a prospective client, but as long as "significantly harmful" information is not shared, the lawyer (or law firm) will not be personally disqualified from later representing the other side in the same controversy [MRPC 1.18]. If Sally had been properly personally disqualified, this disqualification would be imputed to her partner Sarah (and any other lawyer in the firm) under MRPC 1.10(a) absent proper screening which is not discussed in the facts.

49. /C/ A lawyer may reveal information to a tribunal that discloses a breach of fiduciary responsibility by a client when the client has used the lawyer's services in furtherance of the offense [MRPC 1.6(b)(2)]. Here, the grandchildren remainder beneficiaries are unable to contest because the wrongdoer is their mother, the trustee who has breached her fiduciary duty. **(A)** is incorrect because the circumstances of this case fit the breach of fiduciary duty confidentially exception permitted in most jurisdictions. **(B)** is incorrect because the circumstances of this case fit the breach of fiduciary duty confidentially exception allowed in most jurisdictions. **(D)** is not the best answer because it appears that Harriet did consult with Sally on other matters, so the attorney-client relationship was likely formed (even though it might also have created a MRPC 1.7(b) conflict of interest).

50. **/B/** A lawyer using confidential information of a client without approval for her own profit is subject to potential civil liability and profit disgorgement, but not professional discipline, unless the client is disadvantaged; here, there does not appear to be a direct disadvantage to Great Expectations Ltd [MRPC 1.8(b)]. **(A)** is incorrect because potential civil liability and profit disgorgement results if a lawyer uses a client's information for her own profit without approval. **(C)** is incorrect because professional discipline is possible only if the client was disadvantaged. **(D)** is incorrect because professional discipline is possible only if the client was disadvantaged.

51. **/C/** A lawyer representing joint criminal defendants must disclose the risks and dangers inherent in such dual representation and secure both clients' consent to the conflict in writing [MPRC 1.8(g) (1)]. **(A)** is incorrect because a mere explanation of the risks and dangers involved in dual representation is insufficient without both clients' consent. **(B)** is not the best answer because the explanation of the risks and dangers involving dual representation must be accompanied by written, not oral client consent. **(D)** is not the best answer because merely confirming the client's consent to the dual representation is insufficient; there must be a written consent by the clients to abate such a conflict.

RIGOS UNIFORM BAR REVIEW SERIES

PROFESSIONAL RESPONSIBILITY EXAM REVIEW (MPRE)

Chapter 3

Client Relations – Disqualification, Client Funds, and Withdrawal

Magic Memory Outline®

RIGOS UNIFORM BAR REVIEW SERIES

PROFESSIONAL RESPONSIBILITY EXAM REVIEW (MPRE)

Chapter 3

Client Relations – Disqualification, Client Funds, and Withdrawal

A. Imputation of Conflicts and Disqualification – MRPC 1.10

The Rules regard a firm of lawyers as essentially one lawyer for purposes of disqualification and most MRPC 1.8 conflicts. An attorney might not be directly disqualified, but rather part of a law firm containing a lawyer who is personally disqualified. Para-legals, legal secretaries, and law students are not usually included in this attribution rule.

1. Conflicts of Interest: While lawyers are associated in a law firm, none of them shall knowingly represent a client when any one of them practicing alone would be prohibited from doing so because of a conflict of interest. If any one lawyer is disqualified, this disqualification is traditionally imputed to all other lawyers in the firm.

2. Joining a Firm: Changing law firms is more frequent today. When a lawyer who, as opposing counsel, represented an adverse party at their old firm becomes associated with a new firm, both the new firm and all members in it are disqualified under the general rule. Lawyers sharing office space may be characterized as one "law firm." Neither the firm nor the "personally disqualified lawyer" – PDL - may knowingly represent a person with adverse interests to the prior represented client in any same or related matter unless:

a. Screening: The PDL is timely screened from participating in or discussing the matter with members of the litigation team of the new firm. She also may not be apportioned any part of the fee. The burden is on the law firm to show sufficient screening.

b. Written Notice to Former Client: The former client of the PDL must receive notice of the conflict and the details of the screening mechanism used to prohibit dissemination of secret or confidential information.

c. Certificate: The PDL and a firm partner must submit to her former law firm and client a periodic certification of compliance. Judicial review and supervision of the screening procedures is possible to ensure compliance.

3. Leaving a Firm: A law firm may represent a person with interests directly adverse to a client represented by a lawyer who left the firm. Representation is only precluded if (1) the matter is the same or substantially related and (2) any lawyer remaining in the firm has relevant confidential information protected by MRPC 1.6.

B. Successive Government and Private Employment – MRPC 1.11

This applies to a government attorney who goes into private practice, such as a prosecutor, public defender, or representative attorney for a government agency.

1. Personal and Substantial Participation: Such a previous government lawyer may not represent a private client in a matter in which she previously **p**ersonally **a**nd **s**ubstantially – (PAS) - participated, unless the agency consents with confirmation in writing. The "matter" must involve the same or related parties. This disqualification is imputed to any other lawyer in the firm, but (1) a screening arrangement is possible with (2) written notice to the agency of the screening procedures employed, if (3) the screened lawyer does not share in the fee. The prohibition extends to use of any agency confidential information.

2. Employment Negotiation: A government lawyer may not negotiate for private employment with parties and attorneys appearing before the agency if the lawyer participated personally and substantially. If the lawyer did not participate in a matter for or against the party – i.e., she only worked for the same agency – it is not improper to pursue such employment.

3. Confidential Government Information: In subsequently representing a client in private practice, a lawyer may not use "confidential government information" that was prohibited by law from disclosure to the public. The prohibition extends to confidential government information about a person who is an adversary of the client. Information available under the Freedom of Information Act is not deemed confidential.

C. Former Judge, Arbitrator, Mediator, or Neutral – MRPC 1.12

This provision parallels MRPC 1.11.

1. Restrictions: A former or retired judge, adjudicative officer, or third-party neutral (including their law clerks) may not act as a lawyer in a matter in which she formerly served as a judge. Prior participation in the matter must have been – PAS - **p**ersonal **a**nd **s**ubstantial to disqualify the former judge – for example, she personally adjudicated a case where the client was a party. Mere remote involvement or incidental administrative responsibility is insufficient to create a conflict. A partisan member of an arbitration panel is not prohibited from subsequently representing that party.

2. Employment Negotiation: A judge or law clerk shall not negotiate for private employment with parties appearing in her court. This restriction does not block all work for a former litigant in front of the judge – only those matters in which the former judge or law clerk was involved. A law clerk nearing the end of a clerkship may negotiate for employment with a law firm appearing in the court; however, the clerk must first tell the judge of the employment search and specifically identify the law firms with which she is interviewing.

3. Consent or Screening Exception: Subsequent representation is permitted if all parties to that proceeding consent after disclosure. Even if no consent is given, a law firm may not be disqualified if its tainted lawyer is timely screened and written notice is promptly given to the parties and appropriate tribunal.

D. Organization as Client – MRPC 1.13

A corporate lawyer owes the primary duty of loyalty to the entity, not the directors, officers, employees, shareholders, or other human constituents. A lawyer for a business entity may usually also represent a majority owner.

1. Dual Representation: Dual representation of both the corporation and a human constituent may be a RPC 1.7 conflict, but informed consent by both clients may avoid the disqualification. A lawyer may not concurrently represent a constituent whose interest the lawyer determines is adverse to the organization, such as employee accused of committing a criminal act involving the corporation. The lawyer must tell the employee that they cannot represent them and that they should obtain independent representation.

2. Private Organization Internal Reporting: A lawyer should report violations of law to the involved wrongdoer(s). If not corrected, and the matter is clearly a violation of law that will result in substantial injury to the organization, the lawyer "may" (not "must") reveal "up the ladder" to the chief executive officer or full Board of Directors. The lawyer must minimize the risks of revealing the information externally. A lawyer discharged by a corporate manager for revealing such wrongdoing shall inform the Board of the discharge or withdrawal.

3. Public Organization External Reporting: If the corporation is publicly-traded, the lawyer "must" report to the SEC under the Sarbanes-Oxley Act. While noisy withdrawals are not encouraged, a lawyer may externally withdraw prior writings relied upon by third parties, even if this is not normally permitted by Rule 1.6.

4. Governmental Organizational Client: When a lawyer who is not a public officer or employee represents a discrete governmental agency that is part of a broader governmental entity, the lawyer's client is the particular governmental agency or unit represented, not the broader upstream governmental entity. An exception may apply if provided otherwise in writing by both governmental agencies in question.

E. <u>Client with Diminished Capacity</u> – MRPC 1.14

Usually we assume a client has the ability and decision-making capacity to maintain a normal client-lawyer relationship, including making adequately considered decisions and assisting in preparation of her case.

1. Disability: If the client cannot adequately act in her own interest because of diminished capacity – e.g., incapacity, minority, unconsciousness, mental impairment, elderly with diminished capacity – the lawyer may take reasonably necessary protective actions such as seeking court appointment of a guardian ad litem.

2. Preserve Confidences: The application for guardian appointment should not disclose any unnecessary client confidences protected under MRPC 1.6.

F. <u>Safeguarding Property</u> – MRPC 1.15

1. Separation Required: All property of clients and third persons must be held separately from the lawyer's own property and may not be used, commingled, converted, borrowed from, or pledged by the lawyer. A small exception is that a lawyer's funds may be used to pay bank service charges on a trust account.

MPRE Tip: Commingling is a serious fiduciary offense even if the client approves of the "loan" and all funds are repaid.

2. Retainers and Trust Advances: The ABA Model Rules do not distinguish between retainers and advances. In many jurisdictions, availability retainers are client payments that are fully earned when received as compensation for the lawyer taking on the case and being available concerning the matter. Retainers are non-refundable and should not be deposited in a trust account. All other funds that clients advance for future fees and costs must be deposited in trust accounts in the state where the lawyer's office is situated, and must be kept separate from the law firm's regular operating account. In most states, split deposits (part retainer and part earned fees in one check) must be deposited into a trust account.

3. Transfers from Trust: As lawyers bill, they should withdraw that portion from the trust account unless the client objects. The usual prudent approach is to wait 10 or 20 days after sending out a fee statement before transferring the funds between accounts; this gives the client a reasonable time to contest the billing. A lawyer's failure to withdraw uncontested billed fees from the trust account results in impermissible commingling.

MPRE Tip: Any client disputed amount must be left in trust until the dispute is resolved.

4. All Client Property Kept Identifiable and Accountable: Client property must be identifiable, segregated, and held in a secure place such as a locked safe deposit box. Complete records of all client property shall be preserved for five years.

a. Notice of Receipt of Property and Funds: A lawyer shall promptly notify a client of the receipt of funds, securities, or other property, including a settlement check.

b. Identify and Label Securities and Properties: A lawyer shall identify and label securities and properties of a client promptly upon receipt. Such assets shall be placed in a locked safe deposit box or other place of safekeeping as soon as practicable.

c. Third Parties' Claims: If a third party has a lawful claim – usually a lien or unsatisfied judgment – against client funds or other property in the lawyer's possession, the lawyer must not surrender the property to the client. The funds at issue should be interpleaded into the registry of the court for a judicial determination of the third party's claims.

d. Promptly Return Property: At the client's request or at the end of the representation, a lawyer must promptly deliver to the client all the client's property. This includes all client-related assets in the lawyer's possession and any interest earned during custody of the client's funds. If the client disputes the fee and/or other split amount items as calculated by the lawyer, the undisputed portion due the client should be paid. If the dispute cannot be liquidated, the balance may be interpleaded into the registry of a court.

5. Escrow Funds: Escrow and other funds held by a lawyer involving multiple party transactions are treated as client funds subject to these rules. Examples include funds for the closing of a real estate property transfer, or the sale and purchase of a business. This applies regardless of whether the lawyer, the law firm, or the parties view the funds as belonging to clients or non-clients. Many jurisdictions require bar authorities to perform random audits to promote proper client funds management.

G. <u>Declining or Terminating Representation</u> – MRPC 1.16

The rule on declining or terminating representation provision has two sections – one where the lawyer must withdraw and another where withdrawal is optional.

1. Must Terminate/Withdraw – VID: Withdrawal is mandatory if any of the following three **VID** reasons apply.

a. <u>V</u>iolate MRPCs: A lawyer shall withdraw from the representation of a client if the representation would result in a violation of the MRPCs, a court order, or other laws. Examples include a client's malicious harassment of an opponent, refusal to comply with discovery orders, or the lawyer's conclusion that the case cannot be supported by a good faith argument for the extension, modification, or reversal of existing law. [MRPC 3.1]

b. <u>I</u>mpaired Ability to Represent: A lawyer must decline or withdraw from the representation of a client if the lawyer's physical or mental condition materially impairs his ability to represent the client. This could include a lawyer's alzheimers or alcohol and drug overuse and/or addictions.

c. <u>D</u>ischarged: A lawyer must withdraw if discharged by the client.

MPRE Tip: The "must" withdraw rules, especially MRPC violations, are frequently tested.

2. May Terminate/Withdraw – CURBSO: The second prong of the Rule gives a lawyer discretion to withdraw from representing a client. The withdrawal usually must be accomplished without a material adverse effect on the client's interests, but certain specifically approved **CURBSO** grounds allow withdrawal notwithstanding adverse effects. These include:

a. <u>C</u>lient Pursuing <u>C</u>riminal Action: A lawyer may withdraw if the client persists in a course of action involving the lawyer's services that the lawyer reasonably believes is criminal or fraudulent (future actions).

b. Used Lawyer to Commit Crime: A lawyer may withdraw if the client has used the lawyer's services to perpetrate a crime or fraud (past actions).

c. Repugnant Objective: A lawyer may withdraw if the client insists on pursuing an objective the lawyer considers repugnant or very imprudent.

d. Burden on Lawyer Unreasonable: A lawyer may withdraw if the representation will result in an unreasonable financial burden on the lawyer or the client has been unreasonably difficult.

e. Serious Client Failure: This includes a client's unsatisfied commitment to pay fees, refusal to obey a court order, or failure to comply with required discovery. The lawyer should warn the client that withdrawal will occur unless the obligation is satisfied timely. Still, a failure to pay fees when due may be insufficient to justify withdrawal.

f. Other Good Cause for Withdrawal Exists: This is a catchall category where the burden is on the attorney asserting the good cause argument. Client difficulties short of actual discharge, such as non-cooperation in preparing for trial, may fall into this category.

3. Court Order to Continue: Where ordered by a tribunal, a lawyer must continue representation notwithstanding a good cause for terminating the representation.

4. Notice, Surrender, and Refund: A lawyer must take reasonable steps to protect a client's interests. This includes giving reasonable notice of intent to withdraw, allowing time to hire other counsel, surrendering appropriate papers and property to the client, and refunding any unearned advance payment of fees.

a. No Client Prejudice: The withdrawal should not prejudice the client's rights or create a material adverse effect on her interests. A withdrawing lawyer must allow sufficient time before trial so the client can get a new attorney.

b. Return Papers and Property: The lawyer must surrender papers and property to which the client is entitled. The files belong to the client unless the retainer agreement specifically states to the contrary. It makes no difference if the client has not paid a past-due fee or the document in question is the lawyer's own work product. Any unearned fee or cost balance in the trust account shall be refunded.

c. File Lien: In many jurisdictions an attorney's possessory lien provision may apply to the client's judgment award. This lien provision may not be used to hold the client's legal files hostage unless the retention would not prejudice the client. Such a circumstance is rare if the litigation is still going forward with new counsel. If withholding the file materially interferes with the ability of a new lawyer to represent the client, the court or professional authority may order the file transferred to the succeeding attorney.

d. Other Lien Restraints: A lawyer seeking or enforcing a lien to tie up the client's judgment or property must be sure the underlying proceeding is not frivolous [MRPC 3.1] or interposed strictly to embarrass or burden a person [MRPC 4.4].

5. Formal Notice: Many jurisdictions require filing a formal Notice of Withdrawal with the tribunal and a minimum time period before withdrawal may be effective. The notice must specify the trial date and identify any succeeding lawyer. If the client does not have a new lawyer substituting in, the address of the client must be stated. If anyone objects to the withdrawal, the court will hold a hearing. If it is too close to trial or other foreseeable prejudice will result, the court may deny the motion, and the lawyer must stay on the case.

6. Malpractice Concern: Prudence suggests that a lawyer with any concern about a possible present or future malpractice claim should copy the file at her own expense.

7. "Noisy" or "Flag-Waving" Withdrawals: To alert third parties, the Sarbanes-Oxley Act (SOX) allows a noisy withdrawal for a corporate attorney learning of an ongoing client fraud. This aspect of SOX is controversial because most jurisdictions require that a lawyer's withdrawal not create a material adverse effect on a client. A lawyer can withdraw any of her own prior opinions given to third parties that now appear to be fraudulent. It is proper to author a letter to a third party stating that "facts have come to my attention such that you should not rely on my prior opinions," without saying anything negative about the client.

H. Sale of Law Practice – MRPC 1.17

This rule focuses on the sale of a law practice by a retiring or deceased lawyer's estate.

1. Sale Procedure: There are restrictions on confidentiality imposed on any purchase investigation by a potential buyer. If a proposed sale results, notice must be given to clients of the transfer of their account. Client consent for file transfer is required and may be inferred if the client does not affirmatively object within 90 days after receiving notice. A single buyer must purchase the entire practice or an entire practice area; piecemeal sale of client accounts is not allowed.

2. Price and Fees: The sales price may be set at a percentage of future fees collected from the book of business the buyer purchased. The purchaser of the law firm cannot increase client fee charges to finance the acquisition.

I. Duties To Prospective Client – MRPC 1.18

A growing number of jurisdictions recognize some duty to a prospective client. An example is a potential client telephones to discuss whether the lawyer will take on a case thus creating a client – lawyer relationship.

1. Conflict Question: The prospective client must always reveal enough information to allow the lawyer to perform a conflict check and determine if the lawyer is competent and willing to undertake representation of the matter. As long as the discussion stops before "significantly harmful" information is shared, the lawyer will not be personally disqualified from later representing the other side in the same controversy.

2. Screening Possible: Even if "significantly harmful" information has passed, the Rule allows a "screening" procedure. Others in the firm may undertake representation of a party on the other side of the controversy, with written notice to the prospective client and isolation of the attorney who conducted the initial consultation. The isolated attorney must have avoided exposure to more disqualifying information than necessary to reach the conclusion that non-representation was appropriate.

3. Fair Warning: A lawyer receiving a prospective representation inquiry usually may avoid disqualification by affirmatively stating that "our law firm has many clients who may be adverse to your interest in this dispute. Therefore, nothing you disclose in this prospective conversation should be considered confidential unless we enter into a formal written representation agreement." Web site inquiry submission forms should contain a specific disclaimer disavowing an attorney-client relationship until a writing is signed.

4. Duty Not to Mislead: If the client expects that a lawyer will represent her in a matter, the lawyer must affirmatively reject the association expectation.

5. Confidential Information Protected: Even if the lawyer disavows the client representation, MRPC 1.6 protects all preliminary discussions of any harmful information.

RIGOS UNIFORM BAR REVIEW SERIES

PROFESSIONAL RESPONSIBILITY EXAM REVIEW (MPRE)

Chapter 3

Client Relations – Disqualification, Client Funds, and Withdrawal

Question Map

Numbers immediately following the topic are the chapter question numbers. The **boldface** numbers preceded by "F" are the final exam question numbers. For example, for the topic "A. Imputation of Conflicts and Disqualification" below, questions 19 and 26 are in the chapter questions on pages 3-109 and 3-111, respectively; question **F28** is in the final exam on page 7-284.

Chapter 3

Client Relations – Disqualification, Client Funds, and Withdrawal

Questions

1. Metes & Bounds was a law firm that limited its practice to closing real property sales. The firm routinely had sellers pre-sign deeds and buyers endorse negotiable instruments. These items were deposited in a safe in the law firm's office. Unknown to any of the lawyers was that the fuel tank for the furnace used to heat the whole building was located in the basement directly beneath the room in which the safe deposit box was located. An electrical fire began in the basement, and the fuel tank exploded, demolishing the area above, including the safe deposit box and its contents.

Is Metes & Bounds subject to discipline?

- **(A)** Yes, because the law firm did not place the documents in a separate account.
- **(B)** Yes, because the law firm should have investigated whether there were any risks that might demolish the safe deposit box.
- **(C)** No, unless there was a more suitable location to safeguard the pre-signed deeds and endorsed negotiable instruments.
- **(D)** No, unless the law firm did not have malpractice insurance to cover the losses.

2. Olive Optimistic hired Albert Attorney to file a lawsuit for defamation and agreed to pay his standard hourly fee for all time spent. Olive believed her case was worth $500,000. After most of the case was dismissed on summary judgment, Albert strongly recommended that Olive accept the defendant's settlement offer of $50,000. Olive reluctantly accepted, and the defendant paid the $50,000 into Albert's trust account. Albert sent his bill for fees of $30,000 to Olive, who disputed half his bill.

It is proper for Albert to

- **(A)** Give Olive the $50,000 and let her decide how much to pay Albert.
- **(B)** Give Olive $20,000 and transfer $30,000 to his operating account.
- **(C)** Give Olive $20,000, transfer $15,000 to Albert's operating account, and retain $15,000 in the trust account.
- **(D)** Keep the $50,000 in the trust account pending a final resolution of the fee dispute.

3. Francis Flighty was a solo practitioner whose practice was primarily wrongful death actions. One of her clients, Iola Innocent, was killed in an automobile accident by a drunk driver who had just left a bar after drinking for six straight hours. Francis took on the case for a contingency fee of one-third of any and all recoveries. She sued both the driver and the serving bar under a local statute that created liability for alcohol sellers whose over-serving of liquor was responsible for personal injuries. Francis settled the case against the driver for $300,000 and took $100,000 for her fee.

When the case was within one month of trial, the bar serving the liquor filed for bankruptcy, alleging zero unsecured assets. Francis realized that one-third of nothing was nothing and petitioned the court to withdraw, arguing that this was an unreasonable financial burden on a solo practitioner. Her petition contained the names of four experienced attorneys whom Francis claimed had agreed to take on the trial. The court denied the motion. Francis withdrew anyway, and the judge was forced to order a trial continuance.

Is Francis subject to discipline?

(A) No, because Francis provided a number of other substitute counsel who were experienced.
(B) No, because there is no defendant left who could provide any money damages.
(C) Yes, because Francis collected $100,000 on the case and that consideration supports the implied promise to see it through to the end.
(D) Yes, because the court denied the motion.

4. Cathy Cautious was driving down Ventura Highway well under the posted speed limit. Hot Rod Henry was following her in his souped-up 1932 Ford Deuce Coupe and became increasingly frustrated because Cathy was going too slow. Hot Rod pulled into the oncoming lane to pass but misjudged and hit a truck coming in the other direction. His car bounced back into Cathy's lane pushing her car into the ditch. Cathy was injured and retained Alice Attorney by signing a representation agreement.

The document specified Alice was to receive a $5,000 retainer and $10,000 advance against a fee of $250 per hour or 40% of any recovery if higher. Alice spent 20 hours making two telephone calls and writing a three page demand letter resulting in a $100,000 settlement check which Alice deposited into her law firm trust account. Alice sent Cathy a statement indicating she was to receive $70,000 of the settlement. Cathy was outraged that 20 hours of a lawyer time should cost as much as Alice was charging and filed a bar grievance against Alice.

To minimize the risk of professional discipline, Alice should be advised to

(A) Remit $115,000 to Cathy.
(B) Remit $65,000 to Cathy and transfer $40,000 to the law firm operating account.
(C) Remit $70,000 to Cathy and transfer $5,000 to the law firm operating account.
(D) Remit $100,000 to Cathy and transfer $15,000 to the law firm operating account.

5. Terrie Taxing completed law school and then entered an LL.M. degree program in tax law. When she received her LL.M., she went to work for the District Counsel's office of the Internal Revenue Service (IRS). In her position, she handled a number of cases involving ongoing tax audits of Bigbuck Corporation. After three years at the agency, Terrie left to take a well-paying position in the tax department of the law firm that represented Bigbuck Corporation. Four months later, she was assigned the responsibility of preparing the tax-free merger plans of Bigbuck and a company it purchased named Smallbucks.

May Terrie undertake the representation in the tax-free merger?

- **(A)** Yes, because the representation before the IRS concerns a corporate merger.
- **(B)** Yes, unless the IRS denies consent.
- **(C)** No, because Terrie acquired confidential knowledge of the way the IRS operates internally.
- **(D)** No, but another lawyer from the law firm may undertake the representation if Terrie is screened from any participation in the matter.

6. Alise Attorney began her legal career after law school by working for the Anystate Purchasing Agency, a public governmental entity. One of the projects she worked on was a confidential investigation of a contractor who was suspected of overbilling government agencies. In the process, she concluded that the governmental bid and billing instructions were ambiguous and that the contractor's method was arguably justified based upon one interpretation of the instructions. She therefore allowed the overbilling, but changed the language of the instructions to preclude them from being used as a justification for overbilling in the future.

One year later, Alise left the agency and joined a law firm that had a large contractor for a client who dealt with the same agency. She learned that this client had not been using the aggressive interpretation in his billings. Alise concluded that the contractor could amend his prior billings to the agency for the past two years and increase the billing by two million dollars. The partner to whom she reported in the firm wants to propose a one-third contingency fee for representation in the matter.

Is Alise and/or the law firm subject to discipline if they go forward in the representation?

- **(A)** Yes, unless the agency is informed before the law firm begins the representation.
- **(B)** Yes, if the information about the ambiguous instruction in the contractor billing language was confidential information of the agency.
- **(C)** No, because the law firm's client did not have any controversy with the agency in which Alise personally and substantially participated.
- **(D)** No, because any duty she owed to agency terminated when she left its employ.

7. Linda Litigator is representing Debra Difficult in a complex matter in civil litigation. Eighteen months of contentious discovery on both sides has frustrated everyone involved. Debra has become increasingly irritated and is complaining that the discovery is a waste of time and money. She insists that Linda just schedule the matter for trial. Linda is very apprehensive that without further discovery, Debra's claim will not prevail and that the opposing party's counterclaim may be successful. There are other lawyers who have expressed a willingness to take on the representation.

Is it proper for Linda Litigator to ask leave of court to withdraw?

(A) Yes, because Debra Difficult's insistence on foregoing discovery makes it unreasonably difficult for Linda Litigator to represent the client effectively and competently.
(B) Yes, because a lawyer may discontinue representation in civil litigation at any time before trial.
(C) No, unless Debra Difficult consents to the withdrawal.
(D) No, because Linda must follow the client's instructions.

8. Pattie Prosecutor presented the criminal case against Diane Defendant to the grand jury. The grand jury issued an indictment, and another prosecutor in the department charged Diane with conspiracy to launder money. Shortly after the charges were filed, Pattie resigned and joined Able and Beard, a criminal defense law firm. Another attorney in the firm, Alice Able, represents Olivia Other, a co-conspirator who was also indicted in the grand jury and indictment phase of the controversy.

Is it proper for Alice Able to continue to represent Olivia?

(A) Yes, because Prosecutor Pattie was required to provide the defense with any exculpatory evidence.
(B) Yes, unless the prosecution can show potential risk of release of confidential government information.
(C) No, because Pattie had substantial responsibility for the grand jury indictment of Diane Defendant.
(D) No, unless Pattie orally agrees not to allow Alice to use the government's confidential information in defending the case at trial.

9. Laura Lawyer and Connie Client entered into a representation agreement. Pursuant to the agreement, Connie paid Laura a $10,000 advance, which was deposited into the law firm's trust account. The trust account also contained other clients' fee and cost advances. The agreement specified that the law firm would bill for its time and costs monthly, and withdraw the billed amount from the trust account ten days later unless an objection was received from Connie. Laura tendered her billing statements to Connie monthly, but did not withdraw any funds from the trust account until 15 months later, when the matter was finally concluded. The total fees billed were $8,500, and Laura refunded $1,500 by check to Connie. Laura then wrote a check on the trust account payable to the law firm's general operating account for $8,500.

Was Laura Lawyer's conduct proper?

- **(A)** Yes, because Laura tendered accurate monthly fee statements to the client as agreed.
- **(B)** Yes, because Laura deposited the $10,000 retainer into the trust account rather than the operating account.
- **(C)** No, because Laura required the client to make a $10,000 advance payment before any fees had been legitimately earned.
- **(D)** No, because Laura commingled funds.

10. Viola Volunteer recently left a large law firm to start her own solo practice. She applied for and was appointed to undertake the representation of a criminal defendant named Mario Murderer. Viola and Mario had numerous differences of opinion and arguments about how to conduct the defense. Viola gradually developed severe depression about the representation and many proceedings were delayed. The relationship continued to deteriorate, and after one major disagreement, Mario discharged Viola.

Must Viola withdraw from the case?

- **(A)** Yes, with court approval, because the client discharged her.
- **(B)** Yes, with court approval, only if the lawyer's mental depression about the representation materially impairs her duty as an advocate.
- **(C)** No, if Viola believes the client's discharge was primarily for the purpose of delay.
- **(D)** No, unless Viola finds Mario's tactics repugnant, or other good cause for withdrawal exists.

11. Harriet Hungry was a personal injury attorney whose practice emphasized automobile accident victims. One afternoon she received a call from Pattie Prospective, who had just been in an automobile accident with a truck. Pattie told Harriet she had been injured in an accident and the degree of injury she suffered. Pattie then said the truck was owned by 30 Minute Pizza, Inc. Harriet immediately recognized the name "30 Minute Pizza, Inc." as one of the law firm's clients and hung up the phone.

Are Harriet and her law firm subject to discipline if they take on the defense of 30 Minute Pizza, Inc., in the accident with Pattie Prospective?

- **(A)** Yes, because Harriet entered into an attorney-client relationship with Pattie Prospective.
- **(B)** Yes, unless Harriet warned Pattie at the beginning of the conversation that her law firm might represent an adverse party.
- **(C)** No, unless information that was significantly harmful to Pattie was received by Harriet in the telephone conversation.
- **(D)** No, only if Harriet Hungry is timely screened out and receives no salary or partnership share from the law firm during the representation period.

12. Olivia Oldtimer owned and operated a law firm named Oldtimer & Associates, PLLC. Nancy Newcomer was an up-and-coming associate with the firm. Olivia has decided to retire and sell her practice. Nancy has expressed an interest in purchasing the law practice, and they are negotiating the terms.

Which of the following would be proper for Olivia and Nancy?

- I. Sell the law firm at a price of 25% of billings for five years and raise the clients' fees by 25% to cover the purchase.
- II. Olivia is required to sign a non-compete agreement for a five-year period of time.
- III. The purchase must be of the entire practice or an entire area of the practice.
- IV. Specific written consent must be received from every client.

- **(A)** One of the above.
- **(B)** Two of the above.
- **(C)** Three of the above.
- **(D)** All of the above.

13. Connie Corporatelawyer is general counsel of Mega Marketing Inc., a start-up financed by a venture capital company. She received a call from an employee, Alice Accountant, who informed her "in confidence" that "management" was fabricating sales to overstate profits. Connie investigated and determined that the amounts involved are very material, and the fabricated revenue is clearly a violation of law. She discussed the matter with Alice's superior, who merely stated that this accounting practice was being done because of orders from higher authority. Connie reported upward to the president and board of directors, all of whom failed to act to stop the illegal acts. Connie then withdrew and contacted the venture capital company who provided the financing.

Is Connie subject to discipline?

- **(A)** Yes, because disclosing the information learned from Alice to the board of directors of the organization is improper if Alice intended it to be confidential.
- **(B)** Yes, because the disclosure to the venture capital company of the client's confidential information was improper.
- **(C)** No, if the management fraud was reasonably certain to result in substantial injury to the financial interests of Mega Marketing's shareholders and creditors.
- **(D)** No, only if the Mega corporate board of directors approved the disclosure to the venture capital company that was also a client of Connie Corporatelawyer.

14. Caustic Chemicals Corporation was a national distributor of sodium hydroxide headquartered in New York. The corporation had received complaints about their methods and procedures used to dispose of waste chemicals that contained significant pollutants. Caustic hired Connie Cleanup, an attorney who is an expert in the current legal interpretations of satisfactory disposal methods. Connie went around the country to Caustic's plants and gave a three-hour presentation to the disposal engineers on the current disposal legal standards. After the presentation at a plant in Polluteville, Anystate, the plant manager, David Dirty, approached Connie and stated he had regularly disposed of waste in what Connie had just stated was an illegal manner.

It would be improper for Connie to tell the manager

- **(A)** I represent the corporation, not David Dirty.
- **(B)** Communications between them (David Dirty and Connie) may not be protected by the attorney-client privilege.
- **(C)** David Dirty should obtain independent legal counsel.
- **(D)** She (Connie) will not report the offense to corporate upper management.

15. Carol Corporatelawyer is the general counsel for ABC Insurance Company. The shareholders have filed a derivative action alleging in part that the president of the corporation intentionally overstated earnings to keep the market value of the stock higher than it would otherwise have been. The board of directors met and determined that there was not a present adversarial position between the corporation and the president.

Is Carol subject to discipline if she takes on the defense in the shareholder's derivative action?

(A) Yes, because her advocacy on behalf of the president would possibly be materially limited.
(B) Yes, unless the president signs an agreement to disgorge any profit he made on trading his stock options.
(C) No, if the chairman of the board consents in writing to the dual representation.
(D) No, if consent to the dual representation is given by the corporate chairman of the board and the president.

16. Sally Sincere is a personal injury attorney who has taken on the representation of a five-year-old boy, who was seriously injured in an automobile accident, and his family. The boy is suing for physical injury, and the family is suing for alienation of affections. Discovery has been completed in the case, and the attorneys have had detailed discussions pursuant to the court order requiring pre-trial mediation. The defendant's attorney has offered a very generous lump-sum settlement amount, and the boy's mother has refused to consider the offer or propose any meaningful counteroffer. Sally believes strongly that the facts and law of the case are such that the settlement should be accepted and that the mother is holding out for her own selfish monetary interests.

It would be improper for Sally to

(A) Continue to maintain a normal client-lawyer relationship.
(B) Take reasonably necessary protective actions, including consulting with individuals who have the ability to take action to protect the client.
(C) Seek court appointment of a guardian ad litem to make decisions about the best interests of the boy.
(D) File a motion for withdrawal with the court if the court refuses to appoint a guardian ad litem.

17. Carol Collector was a wealthy well-known painting collector. Whenever she attended a painting auction and bid on an item, other collectors bid up the prices because of her participation. To reduce her purchase costs, Carol routinely sends agents to purchase on her behalf. Carol hired Lorrie Lawyer to bid on and purchase a particularly valuable Renaissance-era oil painting. Lorrie was the successful bidder and loaded the painting into her car for transport to her law office. During the trip, a large gasoline truck ran a stoplight and collided with Lorrie's car. A fire developed, and while Lorrie escaped, all the contents of her car were destroyed.

Is Lorrie subject to discipline?

(A) Yes, if there was not insurance coverage for law firm related property in the automobiles of the attorneys.
(B) Yes, if using a personal automobile to transport a valuable antique painting from an auction site to the law firm was not a reasonable way of safeguarding client property.
(C) No, because the painting was not in the law firm's possession until it was delivered to the law firm.
(D) No, unless using a commercial carrier to transport the painting would not have avoided the property destruction.

18. Lucy Lawyer was appointed to represent a 16-year-old minor, Daisy Druggey, charged with the sale and distribution of a controlled substance. Daisy was released on bail. During the investigation and interviews with Daisy, she admitted to Lucy that she was hopelessly addicted to methamphetamine. Both Lucy and a consultant agreed that the addiction made it impossible for Daisy to consider adequately the decisions necessary for a proper defense of the case. The decision was therefore made to apply to the court for the appointment of a guardian ad litem.

Lucy may be subject to discipline if she

- **(A)** Files the motion for appointment unless Daisy affirmatively agrees.
- **(B)** Files the motion for appointment unless Daisy does not object.
- **(C)** Discloses to the court Daisy's drug addiction.
- **(D)** Files the motion at all.

19. Mary Moonlighter was a senior associate in a law firm. She received a telephone call at home from one of the defendants in a matter who was a personal friend. Mary knew that another lawyer from the firm represented the plaintiff. Mary agreed to assist the defendant in representing himself *pro se*. Neither the court nor the law firm was aware of Mary Moonlighter's involvement. Mary used the firm library to do research for the defendant and then retained the fee the defendant paid. Mary did confide her moonlighting to one of the firm's partners, who was a personal friend, but the partner promised not to tell anyone.

Professional discipline may be imposed on

- **(A)** Mary Moonlighter, unless the *pro se* client insisted that Mary do his work.
- **(B)** Mary Moonlighter, unless she had malpractice insurance.
- **(C)** The law firm only because it failed to supervise its employee, Mary Moonlighter.
- **(D)** Both Mary Moonlighter and the law firm because of a conflict of interest, among other violations.

20. Judge Darcy Depressed was assigned to handle a very contentious divorce trial. The case went on for three months, and the hatred between the husband and wife bothered Judge Darcy, and her personal family life deteriorated. She had many discussions with a counselor and ultimately decided it was time to leave the bench. Darcy began to seek a position with a local law firm. She was very impressed by the advocacy skills of one attorney in the divorce and heard at a bar meeting that his law firm had an opening.

Is Judge Darcy subject to discipline if she negotiates with the law firm during the trial?

- **(A)** Yes, even if she makes it clear to the law firm that any decision on hiring her must be made only after she renders her decision on the merits of the case.
- **(B)** Yes, unless the person she negotiates employment with is not the attorney appearing in her court.
- **(C)** No, as long as the individual from the law firm she talks to about employment is not appearing in the judge's court.
- **(D)** No, if the judge informs the opposing party and counsel, and they do not object.

21. Judge Horace Bloomfelt had served as a trial court judge for over a decade. He presided over a jury case involving a contract dispute between Connie Consumer and Big Bucks, Inc. The jury decided in favor of Connie, and Big Bucks appealed. About this time, Horace decided not to stand for reelection because his first of four children was about to enter college, and he needed more income. He subsequently interviewed with, and was hired by, the largest law firm in the county, where his earnings were substantially increased.

One year later, the Supreme Court reversed the jury decision in *Connie Consumer v. Big Bucks, Inc.* and remanded it for a new trial. Connie approached the law firm to inquire if they would take on the case. Big Bucks opposed any involvement by Bloomfelt law firm and filed a motion to disqualify both Bloomfelt personally and the law firm.

If the law firm decides to take the case, they will not be subject to discipline if

(A) Connie can find no other lawyer.
(B) The judge assigned to the retrial approves.
(C) Written notice is given to Big Bucks.
(D) Written notice is given to Big Bucks and the new trial court that lawyer Bloomfelt is being screened out.

22. Mary Marketer was a lawyer who met a prospective client named Patty Possibility at a local community council meeting. They discussed a claim that Patty had against Laura Landlord, the owner of her apartment house. At the end of the meeting, Patty said, "I am glad you are helping me on this case." Mary never talked to Patty again, and the statute of limitations ran on Patty's claim against Landloard.

Is Mary subject to potential civil malpractice liability?

(A) Yes, unless Mary affirmatively rejected Patty's expectation that Mary will undertake representation of the matter.
(B) Yes, if Mary says, "I will have to think about taking on your case."
(C) No, unless a representation agreement is reduced to writing.
(D) No, because Mary did not expressly accept Patty's offer of employment.

23. Lorraine Leaving was a partner in the law firm of Big & Fast, PLLC. She had a small corporate client named Great Expectations that she represented in various business matters. Lorraine left the Big & Fast, PLLC, law firm and took the client, Great Expectations, with her to her new law firm. Alice Aggressive has just been made a partner in Big & Fast and has been offered the representation of a substantial claim against Great Expectations.

Is Alice Aggressive subject to discipline if she takes on the representation against Great Expectations?

(A) Yes, because the disqualification of Lorraine is imputed to the law firm Big & Fast, PLLC, and all its attorneys.
(B) Yes, because Big & Fast, PLLC, would be litigating against one of their prior clients.
(C) No, if no other member of Big & Fast, PLLC, has information related to Lorraine's representation of Great Expectations that would be material to the new claim.
(D) No, because when a client leaves the firm the conflict of interest rules terminate.

24. Patricia Potential's new home fell down because of a negligent architect who was both the creator of the design drawings and the designated in charge person on the construction project. Patricia looked through the yellow pages of the phone directory and called some of the law firm numbers under the category of "professional architectural malpractice." One of the larger firms she called transferred the call to a newly hired associate named Nancy New.

Nancy told Patricia that the law firm represented a number of architectural firms in the city, and if the defendant in her proposed claim was one of their clients, she would have to decline taking on her case. Nancy further told her that anything Patricia communicated to her might be made available to the defense. Patricia then proceeded to tell Nancy her side of the story. Later, Nancy discussed Patricia's conversation with the firm's partner who represents the architectural firm defendant.

Is Nancy personally or her law firm subject to disqualification?

(A) Yes, because they would have a conflict between a present and prior client.
(B) Yes, if they disclosed confidential information that Patricia revealed to Nancy during the conversation.
(C) No, because they did not take on the representation of Patricia.
(D) No, because Nancy conditioned the conversation with Patricia upon an understanding that nothing in their conversation would be held confidential.

25. Carol Cashflow had just opened her own law firm. Many of her first clients were insolvent, and in the first six months she had to write off many receivables, so in effect, she worked without compensation. To guard against this occurring in the future, she drafted a withdrawal stipulation. The stipulation states that if the client fails to pay fees timely, Carol may file the stipulation. The clients will be required to sign the stipulation when Carol undertakes the initial representation.

Is it proper for Carol to withdraw pursuant to the stipulation if a client fails to pay timely?

(A) Yes, if the client signed the stipulation after full disclosure and with an appreciation of the risks.
(B) Yes, because it is unfair to allow a client to exploit a lawyer's time without payment.
(C) No, unless the clients are separately represented prior to the time they signed the stipulation.
(D) No, because a failure to pay fees timely by a client may not be sufficient in and of itself to justify a lawyer's withdrawal.

26. Diane Decedent named Emily Executor as the administrator of her estate upon her death. Emily was a lawyer-partner in a large law firm and a close friend of Olivia Opportunity, another lawyer-partner in the firm. Diane passed away, and Emily began the probate process. The probate court admitted the will and granted Emily broad court-authorized non-intervention powers, including the ability to sell any of Diane's property. Emily has decided to sell Diane's home to Emily's law partner Olivia at a price they both agree is fair.

If Emily, on behalf of the estate, consummates the transaction with Olivia, will she be subject to discipline?

- **(A)** Yes, unless the price and terms are at market.
- **(B)** Yes, because Emily and Olivia are lawyer-partners in the same law firm.
- **(C)** No, because the conflict of interest only applies to Emily, not Olivia.
- **(D)** No, because Emily received court non-intervention powers which includes approval to sell the decedent's home.

27. Paula Plaintiff was injured in an automobile accident. She approached Alice Aggressive to represent her against defendant A, whom Paula claimed was the other driver. The representation agreement stated the fee was to be $200 per hour and costs. Paula gave Alice an advance of $2,500, which was deposited into a trust account. The case was dismissed on a Rule 12 motion. This occurred because Alice named the wrong defendant A based on what Paula had told her, rather than the correct defendant B. Paula hired a new attorney and demanded her $2,500 back at a time when Alice had spent five hours on the case and incurred $500 in legitimate case-related expenses that Paula had approved.

Alice should

- **(A)** Return the full $2,500 because this is the client's demand.
- **(B)** Transfer to her firm's operating account the $1,500, which represents the fees she had earned and the costs incurred, and leave the $1,000 balance in the firm's trust account.
- **(C)** Transfer $500 to her firm's operating account and retain the balance of $2,000 in the firm's trust account.
- **(D)** Leave the full $2,500 in the trust account pending a resolution of the dispute with Paula.

28. Alpha was employed as a trial litigator at First Law Firm. She had personally defended Big Bucks, Inc., in a product liability case. Six months before the trial, Alpha left the defense law firm for a higher-paying position with a firm representing the plaintiff. Beta, a partner in the firm, took over the defense of the case. A plaintiff's law firm partner named Chi was representing the plaintiffs in the same action against Big Bucks. Beta filed a motion to disqualify Chi.

If the court follows the ABA Model Rules, the disqualification motion will likely be:

(A) Granted because the taint is imputed firm-wide.
(B) Granted only if screening is not possible.
(C) Granted, unless Alpha does not participate in the prosecution.
(D) Granted, unless Alpha is screened from the plaintiff's team, and Beta receives written notice and a certificate of the screening details.

29. Carol Client lived in Newstate and got into an automobile accident when she drove out of her driveway. She hired Pattie Personalinjury to file suit against the other driver, Debbie Defendant. Debbie lived in Oldstate, and Pattie's law offices were also located in Oldstate. Carol gave Pattie a retainer of $5,000 as an advance on her fees and litigation costs. Pattie deposited the $5,000 in a federally-insured bank in Newstate, but the account did not pay interest.

Was it proper for Pattie to deposit the $5,000 in the non-interest-bearing account in Newstate?

(A) Yes, because the client Carol lives in Newstate.
(B) Yes, because the retainer is the property of the lawyer, not the client.
(C) No, because Pattie's office is in Oldstate.
(D) No, because the $5,000 was not deposited in an interest-bearing account.

30. Pattie Plaintiff was seriously injured in an automobile accident. She needed extensive medical treatment, and the costs for the procedures were quite large. To finance these expenses, Pattie borrowed heavily from Big Buck Bank. Big Buck demanded and Pattie agreed to give the Bank a lien on the funds to be recovered in her personal injury suit.

Lorrie Lawyer filed Pattie's lawsuit against Deep Pocket Defendant. Deep Pocket offered a suitable settlement amount, which Pattie approved. After the settlement documents had been completed, signed, and filed, Deep Pocket gave Lorrie a check for $500,000, which was deposited into her law firm's trust account. Big Buck Bank demanded Lorrie pay them $300,000, but Pattie felt strongly that she owed the Bank no more than $200,000.

Which of the following is the best procedure for Lorrie to follow?

(A) Pay the full $500,000 less her attorney fees to Pattie.
(B) Pay $300,000 to Big Buck Bank and $200,000 less her attorney fees to Pattie.
(C) Assume to arbitrate the dispute between Pattie and Big Buck Bank.
(D) Pay $200,000 less her attorney fees to Pattie and interplead $300,000 into a legal action Lorrie filed to have a court resolve the dispute.

31. Alice and Barbara were lawyers in an office-sharing arrangement. This office facility used a common library and computer network, and both lawyers' names were printed on the front door. They often consulted with each other, cross-referred some cases, and had access to the other's file.

Alice was hired by Paula Plaintiff to sue Debra Defendant for breach of contract. Debra Defendant had previously worked with Barbara on a different matter and had been very pleased with her representation. Accordingly, she asked her if she would take on the defense in the Paula lawsuit.

Is it proper for Barbara to represent Debra?

(A) Yes, because Alice and Barbara are not members of the same law firm.
(B) Yes, if Alice and Barbara believe they can effectively represent their respective clients.
(C) No.
(D) No, unless both Paula and Debra consent to the representation.

32. Sally Student worked as a legal assistant to Judge Steady before she graduated from law school. There was a very complex commercial lawsuit being heard by Judge Steady, and Sally was assigned to do research on a number of technical motions. The jury finally held for the plaintiff in the case.

Shortly thereafter, Sally received news that she passed the bar, and she started work for Alice Appeal's law firm that had previously offered her an associate position conditioned on her passing the bar exam. The defendant in the same complex litigation case that was heard by Judge Steady approached the Alice Appeal law firm. He requested that they handle the appeal of his case and assign Sally to the case.

Is it proper for Sally to handle the appeal?

(A) Yes, because Sally had not been admitted to practice law when she worked for Judge Steady.
(B) Yes, if Sally did not learn any sensitive factual information while working for Judge Steady.
(C) No, if Sally's work on the case in the trial court was personal and substantial.
(D) No, unless Judge Steady approves the representation.

33. Gertrude Government was an attorney working for the Environmental Protection Agency (EPA). She was assigned to handle a case of industrial pollution on land owned by Paula Polluter, who was represented by Mega Law Firm. One night Gertrude was at a bar association dinner meeting and was seated across from Roberta Rainmaker, a senior partner in Mega Law Firm. Gertrude told Roberta she was considering leaving her position with the EPA, and Roberta said, "Come work for us at $10,000 per month." A short negotiation followed. Gertrude subsequently considered her options and accepted a position with a different law firm. During a case she was working on at the new firm, Gertrude used EPA internal information that was available to the public under a formal Freedom of Information Act request.

Is Gertrude subject to discipline?

(A) Yes, because she negotiated for private employment with a lawyer representing a party in a matter in which lawyer Gertrude participated personally and substantially.
(B) Yes, because lawyer Gertrude subsequently used internal EPA information in representing a client.
(C) No, if Gertrude does not use the EPA internal information to the disadvantage of the EPA.
(D) No, because Gertrude did not accept employment with the Mega Law Firm.

34. Othella Other approached a lawyer named Harriet Honesty about representing her in a wrongful discharge case against the local school district. Harriet interviewed Othella and having a bad feeling about her credibility, Harriet told her she needed to do some research before she could decide if she wanted to take the case. Harriet then did some investigation of the school district side of the dispute. After learning the true facts, Harriet decided that Othella's claim was frivolous. As a result she called Othella and informed her she would not take on representation in the case.

Othella found a different lawyer to file the lawsuit. During the trial, a newspaper report attributed testimony to Othella that Harriet knew was perjury, based upon what Othella had told her. Harriet was outraged that Othella would attempt to defraud the local school district and wrote a letter to the court revealing the true facts. A copy of the letter was sent to Othella's lawyer.

Was Harriet's communication proper?

- **(A)** Yes, if Othella's perjury was deemed a criminal violation.
- **(B)** Yes, because disclosure was necessary to avoid perpetration of a fraud on the court.
- **(C)** No, because the information Harriet disclosed was learned during discussions with Othella.
- **(D)** No, because Harriet sent copies of the information in question to both the tribunal and Othella's lawyer.

35. Sally Studious was a 3L at Summer Law School and worked part-time as an intern for a plaintiffs' personal injury firm. She did the input investigation and fact-finding for new clients coming into the law firm. Iola Injured was a new client who had suffered damages in an automobile accident, and Sally interviewed her. The law firm did not offer Sally a full-time position after she graduated, but she was successful in securing a job with a large defense law firm.

Sally passed the bar exam after she graduated and on her first day on the job, she learned the defense firm was defending an insurance company in the Iola Injured case. Her new employer was opposing her old law firm, which was representing Iola Injured. She called her old employer and informed them of the coincidence. They were outraged and filed a motion with the trial court to disqualify anyone from Sally's new defense firm.

The defense law firm's best argument to defeat the disqualification motion is

- **(A)** This is merely a tactical device to deny the insurance company its choice of defense counsel.
- **(B)** Sally was not a lawyer while at the plaintiff's firm, and she can be effectively screened.
- **(C)** Sally was not involved in any trial procedural strategy decisions while at the plaintiff's firm.
- **(D)** The plaintiff's personal injury firm can always take Sally's deposition to determine what she knows about the case.

Chapter 3

Client Relations – Disqualification, Client Funds, and Withdrawal

Answers

MPRE Tip: Put a piece of paper over the answers and "mask down" while working through the questions so you don't accidently peek at the next answer.

1. **/C/** MRPC 1.15(b) specifies that a lawyer must identify and label securities and other property of a client and place them in a safe deposit box. This requirement was complied with, and thus there would only be a violation if there was a more suitable location to safeguard the client's property in question. **(A)** is incorrect; this alternative confuses the attorney's duty to segregate different clients' funds with the duty to safeguard property. **(B)** is incorrect because a lawyer may store client property in her law office, and the danger here does not appear to have been reasonably foreseeable. **(D)** is incorrect because malpractice insurance probably would not cover a premise liability question.

2. **/C/** Funds belonging in part to a client and in part to the lawyer are properly deposited into the trust account. The portion belonging to the lawyer may be transferred to the lawyer's regular account unless the client disputes the billing. The disputed amount shall not be withdrawn until the dispute is resolved. [Comment 3 to MRPC 1.15] **(A)** is incorrect because it is not necessary to transfer all the funds to the client; only the difference between the total recovery and the fees the attorney asserts is due. **(B)** is incorrect since the disputed amount must be withheld. **(D)** is incorrect since the uncontested amounts do not have to be withheld.

3. **/D/** MRPC 1.16(c) specifies that when ordered to do so by a tribunal, a lawyer shall continue in the matter notwithstanding good cause for terminating the representation. **(A)** is incorrect because the issue is whether an attorney can withdraw contrary to the court's decision, not whether other competent counsel who would take on the case exists. **(B)** is incorrect because the issue is whether an attorney can withdraw contrary to the court's decision, not whether a financial burden exists. **(C)** is incorrect because the issue is whether an attorney can withdraw contrary to the court's decision, not whether there was an implied contract between the lawyer and the client.

4. **/C/** The best answer because when a client objects to the proposed fee, the lawyer should transfer the uncontested fee amount from the trust account to the operating account, remit the mutually agreed upon amount to the client and retain the balance in trust pending a reduction of the fee dispute. The $5,000 retainer amount is presumably earned upon receipt and should have been deposited into the law firm operating account upon receipt for the lawyer agreeing to take on the matter, associate their name with the cause, and make themselves available. 60% of the $100,000 and the $10,000 advance are clearly due to the client and the lawyer that was due $250 per hour for the 10 hours spent. **(A)** is incorrect because only the undisputed portion of the fee should be remitted to the client. **(B)** is incorrect because the contested fee in trust should not be transferred to either party but may be impleaded into a court registry if agreement on the amount cannot be reached. **(D)** is incorrect because it is not required that all the contested fee be immediately remitted to the unhappy client [MRPC 1.15].

5. **/A/** A governmental lawyer may be disqualified from representing a client before the agency if the subject of the representation is the same matter that the lawyer handled at the agency; here, Terrie handled ongoing tax audits, not tax-free merger plans. [MRPC 1.11(a)(2)] **(B)** is incorrect because IRS consent is not necessary. **(C)** is incorrect because mere knowledge of the way the agency operates internally is not usually deemed confidential. **(D)** is incorrect because screening would be necessary only if the lawyer were disqualified.

6. **/B/** A lawyer may not use "confidential government information" that was not disseminated to the public in representing a client in subsequent private practice. [MRPC 1.11] This would be an unfair advantage derived solely from the lawyer's prior employment with the agency. **(A)** is incorrect because merely informing the agency is insufficient; informed consent must be confirmed in writing. **(C)** is incorrect because the term "matter" includes any determination, and the government agency itself was a party in the prior dispute. **(D)** is incorrect because it is simplistic, and the government agency is treated as a Rule 1.9 prior client.

7. **/A/** There is a catchall category in MRPC 1.16(b)(7) specifying that a lawyer may withdraw if "other good cause for withdrawal exists" that may apply here. **(B)** is incorrect because a lawyer may not withdraw unless it can be accomplished without a material adverse effect on the client's interest. **(C)** is incorrect because a lawyer may file a motion to withdraw even if the client opposes the withdrawal. **(D)** is incorrect because the area of disagreement here involves litigation strategies to which the lawyer and the client must both agree.

8. **/C/** The best answer because here a lawyer is joining the law firm who previously represented a client with interests adverse to those of the current client. Therefore, Pattie may not represent Olivia, and under the ABA's rules, that disqualification is imputed to all attorneys in the law firm. [MRPC 1.10(a)] **(A)** is not the best answer (even though it is in part an accurate statement) because it does not address the central concern of firm-wide disqualification. **(B)** is incorrect because the government is not required to show prejudice resulting from a violation of the firm-wide impairment and governmental confidential information rules. [MRPC 1.10(a) and 1.11(c)] **(D)** is not the best answer because a disqualified lawyer may be eligible for a screening mechanism, but this requires written notice and much more than a mere oral agreement by the disqualified attorney not to allow another lawyer in the firm to use confidential information.

9. **/D/** A commingling of funds occurs if the funds belonging to the lawyer and the client are in the same account. After a reasonable time, the law firm entitlement to the billed fees left in the client's trust account constitutes commingling of funds. [MRPC 1.15] **(A)** is incorrect because while tendering monthly statements is proper, commingling of funds is not. **(B)** is incorrect because while depositing a client's advance into the trust account is proper, commingling of funds is not. **(C)** is incorrect because there is no prohibition on a lawyer requiring a reasonable retainer fee prior to undertaking representation in a matter.

10. /A/ The best reason for mandatory withdrawal is that the lawyer has been discharged by the client, even if that discharge was wrongful. [MRPC 1.16(a)(3)] Since the lawyer was appointed, it would also seem reasonable to seek court approval. **(B)** is not the best answer because the condition "only if" precludes the other two **VID** reasons for mandatory withdrawal (violate MRPCs and discharge by the client). **(C)** is incorrect because regardless of the possible motive, discharge by the client requires mandatory withdrawal. **(D)** is incorrect because a lawyer may, not must, withdraw if she finds a client's tactics repugnant. [MRPC 1.16(b)(4)]

11. /C/ The best answer because disqualification applies only if the lawyer receives information that is significantly harmful to the prospective client. [MRPC 1.18(c)] **(A)** is incorrect because the facts do not make it clear that Pattie Prospective had a reasonable expectation that a client-lawyer relationship was formed. **(B)** is not the best answer because while such a warning might preclude disqualification, it becomes an issue only if significantly harmful information was conveyed. **(D)** is not the best answer because the screening procedure is necessary only if significantly harmful information was conveyed. Furthermore, even if significantly harmful information was conveyed and a screening mechanism is used, the screened attorney may receive a salary or partnership share from the law firm as long as such compensation is not directly related to the disqualified matter.

12. /B/ The correct answer because only two of the four alternatives are correct. [MRPC 1.17] I is incorrect because the purchaser cannot raise client fees to finance the purchase of the law firm. II is correct because the seller may sign a non-compete agreement as a part of the sale of a law practice even though normally a non-compete agreement by a lawyer is improper. III is correct because the purchase must be of the entire law practice; a buyer may not cherry-pick the clientele and discard those clients who are less lucrative and would find it difficult to secure other counsel. IV is incorrect because written consent to the transfer is not required if clients do not object within 90 days of receiving written notice of the proposed sale; consent will be presumed.

13. /B/ The best answer because a lawyer for a non-public corporate organization who learns of a fraud reasonably certain to result in substantial injury may reveal the fraud externally only if the lawyer's services were being used to further the fraud; here, Connie apparently had no prior involvement in the matter. [MRPC 1.13] **(A)** is not the best answer because the corporate lawyer's duty to the organization overrides the duty to any one constituent, such as a whistleblowing employee. **(C)** is incorrect because mere injury to the corporation is not sufficient to justify external reporting unless the lawyer was being used to further the fraud. **(D)** is not the best answer because if the lawyer represented both clients and their interests have become adverse, the proper procedure would be to withdraw without disclosure.

14. **/D/** It would be improper (and breach of duty to her client) for a corporate lawyer to state that she will not report up the corporate ladder what appears to be a clear violation of law. [MRPC 1.6 and 1.13] **(A)** is incorrect because it would be proper to clarify to the constituent David Dirty that the lawyer represents and must act in the best interest of the corporation, not the constituent, if the illegal act is likely to result in substantial injury to the corporation. **(B)** is incorrect because if the interest of the constituent and the organization becomes adverse, the attorney-client privilege may not be available to shield David Dirty's admissions. **(C)** is incorrect because a lawyer should advise an unrepresented potential or actual adverse party to seek independent legal counsel.

15. **/D/** The best answer because MRPC 1.13(e) specifies that dual representation under Rule 1.7 requires that consent be given by both parties to be represented. Since both the president and corporation are to be jointly represented, both must give consent. **(A)** is incorrect because it states only the general rule conflict problem, not the exception of proper consent. **(B)** is incorrect because the damages and potential cross-claims may exceed the president's profit, and this amount may have to be paid to the shareholders. **(C)** is incorrect because the corporation, through the chairman of the board, is only one of the conflicting parties in the ethical dilemma in which the client's advocacy may be materially limited by the duty owed to another client.

16. **/A/** When it is clear that the client is under a disability with a foreseeable serious consequence, it is not proper for a lawyer to "maintain a normal client-lawyer relationship" because this presupposes the client can make adequately considered decisions. [MRPC 1.14(a)] **(B)** is incorrect because this is proper procedure for a client with diminished capacity. [MRPC 1.14(b)] **(C)** is incorrect because this is proper procedure for a client with diminished capacity. **(D)** is incorrect because seeking to withdraw is not improper if the denial of the motion to appoint a guardian leaves clear MRPC 1.7 and MRPC 1.16(a)(1) violations.

17. **/B/** The best answer because regardless of insurance coverage a lawyer must exercise reasonable safeguards over client property that comes into her possession. [MRPC 1.15(a)] **(A)** is not the best answer because even if there is insurance coverage, a lawyer must exercise reasonable care in safeguarding client property. **(C)** is incorrect because the law firm's duty to safeguard client's property developed as soon as a law firm agent came into possession of the client property. **(D)** is not the best answer because the focus is on the duty of a lawyer to safeguard a client's property in her possession, not on some alternative method of safeguarding, whether or not it would have been successful in avoiding loss of the property.

18. **/C/** The motion involving the client's diminished capacity should not adversely affect the client's interest if such is possible. [MRPC 1.14] Disclosure of a hopeless drug addiction could prejudice the criminal trial and lead to client incarceration. **(A)** is incorrect because client agreement is not always required, and the facts state that the client is unable to make adequately considered decisions. **(B)** is incorrect because client non-objection is not always required, and the facts state that the client is unable to make adequately considered decisions. **(D)** is incorrect because the lawyer may file the motion as long as no client confidences are put at risk.

19. **/D/** The best answer of those given in this convoluted question. Notice that two attorneys from the same law firm are directly representing adverse parties in the same lawsuit. The conflict of interest is imputed to the firm; the lack of knowledge by the other lawyer does not excuse the imputed disqualification rule. One partner's knowledge is sufficient. [MRPC 1.10(a)] **(A)** is not the best answer because both adverse clients would have to agree in writing, and it appears that at least one client is unaware of the conflict. **(B)** is not the best answer because the question of malpractice insurance to cover civil damages is different than whether the attorney or law firm is laboring under an imputed conflict of interest. **(C)** is incorrect because Mary Moonlighter may also be disciplined for violation of MRPCs 1.6, 1.7, 1.9, 1.10, and 8.4.

20. **/A/** A judge is subject to discipline if she negotiates for employment with a lawyer or law firm if they are appearing in her court, and the timing of the case and employment decision do not change the violation. [MRPC 1.12] **(B)** is incorrect because the rule prohibits employment negotiation with anyone from the law firm while any lawyer from the firm is appearing in the judge's court. **(C)** is incorrect because the restraint caused by the judge's seeking employment from a lawyer appearing in her court is applied firm-wide. Notice also that this is the same rationale as alternative B, merely cast in a negative tense. **(D)** is incorrect because this improper conduct may not be excused or waived by the opposing party and/or her counsel.

21. **/D/** The best answer because it is the most complete statement of the screening process that is necessary if the parties will not consent to a former judge's new law firm acting in a subsequent proceeding in a matter in which she formerly served as a judge. [MRPC 1.12] **(A)** is incorrect in that the former judge's potential new client hardship is not determinant. **(B)** is not the best answer because while the new court should be given written notice of the conflict, that alone is insufficient. **(C)** is not the best answer because written notice of the former judge screening given to the opposing party must be accompanied by written notice to the new trial court.

22. **/A/** If the prospective client reasonably believes that a lawyer will represent her in a matter, the lawyer must affirmatively reject the association expectation to avoid creating an attorney-client relationship. [MRPC 1.18] **(B)** is not the best answer because it should be clear that the lawyer is not assuming the responsibility of representation and this statement by the lawyer is ambiguous. **(C)** is incorrect because a prospective client could easily rely upon an oral representation undertaking. **(D)** is incorrect because a formal acceptance is not necessary if the client believes the lawyer-client relationship has commenced.

23. **/C/** If the matter is different and no remaining member of the firm has information that is material to the current matter, the potential prior client conflict terminates [MRPC 1.9(b)]. **(A)** is incorrect because it states the general rule without referring to the exception. **(B)** is incorrect because it states the general rule without referring to the exception. **(D)** is incorrect because the general rule is that the conflict of interest and confidentiality provisions for prior clients continue after termination.

24. /D/ A lawyer may condition conversation with a prospective client on the understanding that no information disclosed during the consultation will prohibit the lawyer from representing a different client in the matter. [Comment 5 to MRPC 1.18] **(A)** is incorrect because this states only the general rule and not the exceptions. **(B)** is incorrect because this states the general rule and not the exceptions. **(C)** is not the best answer because even if the law firm does not take on the representation of a prospective client, there may be a duty of confidentiality.

25. /D/ Withdrawal must be accomplished without prejudice or a material adverse affect on the interests of the client. [Comment 7 to MRPC 1.16] **(A)** is incorrect because the client's right not to be prejudiced by the withdrawal of counsel may not be waived. **(B)** is incorrect because the client's right not to be prejudiced by the withdrawal of counsel exists regardless of the fairness of the situation to the lawyer. **(C)** is incorrect because a withdrawal does not involve a prospective limitation of the lawyer's liability.

26. /B/ There is a prohibition on a lawyer-client **TIC** transaction without informing the estate client of the conflict and recommending the advice of independent counsel [MRPC 1.8], which is imputed to all the lawyers in Emily's firm [MRPC 1.10(a)]. **(A)** is incorrect because even if the price and terms are at market, the requirement that the estate client be advised to seek the advice of independent counsel has not been met. **(C)** is incorrect because the conflict is imputed to all the law firm's partners, including Olivia. **(D)** is incorrect because blanket court approval of non-intervention powers does not usually include specific authorization to sell a home, and even if it did, it does not excuse the imputed ethical violation of not advising the estate client to seek independent counsel.

27. /C/ The best answer because the balance of the undisputed advance in trust should be returned to the client. The costs were agreed to in advance, and a transfer to the operating account of this $500 amount is proper. [MRPC 1.15] **(A)** is incorrect because at least the costs incurred of $500 may properly be paid from trust because they were approved by the client. **(B)** is incorrect because $1,000 of the incurred fees are in dispute, and until resolution of this dispute, that amount should be retained in the trust account. **(D)** is incorrect because at least $500 of the $2,500 in trust is for costs incurred in the claim that should be paid because they were approved by the client.

28. /D/ The ABA Model Rules now allow a screening mechanism as an exception to the firm-wide disqualification rule. **(A)** is incorrect because the ABA has amended MRPC 1.10 to allow screening as an exception to the firm-wide disqualification rule. **(B)** is not as good an answer as (D) as it does not contain the written notice and certification requirements. **(C)** is not the best answer because screening requires written notice and a certificate served on the screened lawyer's prior law firm.

29. /C/ Client funds shall be kept in a separate trust account maintained in the state where the lawyer's office is situated; Pattie's office is in Oldstate, not Newstate. [MRPC 1.15(a)] **(A)** is incorrect because it is not the client's residence that controls the required location of the trust account. **(B)** is incorrect because the ABA's model rules do not distinguish between non-refundable retainers and advances, and the facts do not state that the parties agreed to any particular treatment of the $5,000. **(D)** is incorrect because the ABA's model rules do not require the trust account to earn interest.

30. **/D/** The best alternative because if there is no agreement the lawyer should file an action to have a court resolve the dispute and interplead the contested funds. [Comment 4 to MRPC 1.15] **(A)** is incorrect because the lawyer may have a duty to protect a lawful third-party claim against wrongful interference by the client. **(B)** is incorrect because this would likely breach the duty to protect the client's property from third parties. **(C)** is not the best answer because the lawyer should not unilaterally assume to arbitrate a dispute between the client and a third party.

31. **/C/** The best answer because there are sufficient facts that could lead to the conclusion this office-sharing arrangement constitutes a law firm for conflict of interest disqualification purposes. [MRPC 1.10(a)] It also does not seem that a disinterested lawyer would conclude there would be no adverse effect on the ability to represent, even if written consent is obtained from the obviously opposing clients. [MRPC 1.7] **(A)** is incorrect because whether office sharing constitutes a single law firm for disqualification purposes is a question of fact; here, the facts likely support the conclusion of a single law firm. [MRPC 1.10(a)] **(B)** is incorrect because it is doubtful whether a disinterested lawyer would conclude that there would not be an adverse affect on the two lawyers' representation. [MRPC 1.7(a)] **(D)** is incorrect because it is doubtful that a disinterested lawyer would conclude sufficient disclosure to the adverse clients is possible; if the conclusion is negative, a fully informed client waiver is not possible. [MRPC 1.7(a)]

32. **/C/** A former legal assistant may not act as a lawyer in a matter in which her participation was personal and substantial. [MRPC 1.12(b)] That appears to be the situation here. **(A)** is incorrect because the prohibition applies even if the former legal assistant was not admitted to the bar at the time she worked on the matter. **(B)** is incorrect because there is not an exception if the information is not sensitive and sensitivity, like beauty, is in the eye of the beholder so subject to differing opinions. The more accurate test to evaluate the conflict rule is whether participation was personal and substantial. **(D)** is incorrect because the exception allowing the representation applies if all parties agree. The judge's consent is not necessary.

33. **/A/** A government lawyer shall not negotiate for private employment with an attorney for a party in a matter in which the government lawyer is personally and substantially participating. [MRPC 1.11(c)(2)] **(B)** is incorrect because the information at issue is not confidential since the facts state that it was available to the public under a Freedom of Information Act request. **(C)** is incorrect because the information at issue is not confidential since it is available to the public under a Freedom of Information Act request. **(D)** is incorrect because the negotiation of potential employment with a law firm representing a party is improper for a participating government lawyer, even if employment does not subsequently develop.

34. /C/ The information disclosed was obtained by the lawyer during the time that Othella was a prospective client. Even though the encounter did not result in the formation of an actual attorney-client relationship (because the lawyer affirmatively rejected the association), the potential client's information is considered to be confidential under MRPC 1.6 and may not be disclosed. [MRPC 1.18] **(A)** is incorrect because to override the duty of confidentiality of client's secrets, there must exist one of a number of specifically enumerated exceptions that are not present in these facts. [MRPC 1.6] **(B)** is incorrect because only if the lawyer has formally appeared in the matter is there a duty of disclosure to avoid a fraud on the court under MRPC 3.3. **(D)** is incorrect because merely sending a copy of the lawyer's improper communication of the client's confidences to the client's counsel does not cure the ethical violation.

35. /B/ The best answer because Comment 4 states that law students are included in the category of non-lawyers who do not ordinarily violate MRPC 1.10 imputed disqualification provided they are "screened from any participation in the matter." **(A)** is not the best answer, even if accurate, because it does not contain the screening arrangement that abates the potential risks to loyalty and confidentiality. **(C)** is not the best answer because the confidentiality concerns may be factual and not merely procedural. **(D)** is not the best answer because the prior firm taking the tainted lawyer's deposition does not necessarily eliminate the loyalty and confidentiality concerns.

RIGOS UNIFORM BAR REVIEW SERIES

PROFESSIONAL RESPONSIBILITY EXAM REVIEW (MPRE)

Chapter 4

Counselor, Advocate, and Third Party Dealings

Magic Memory Outline®

RIGOS UNIFORM BAR REVIEW SERIES

PROFESSIONAL RESPONSIBILITY EXAM REVIEW (MPRE)

Chapter 4

Counselor, Advocate, and Third Party Dealings

A. Counselor – TITLE 2

Title 2 focuses on a lawyer functioning not as a partisan, but rather as an advisor, intermediary, preparer of an evaluation for use by a third party, or neutral.

1. Advisor – MRPC 2.1:

a. Independence: A lawyer in an advisory role shall exercise independent professional judgment and present the client with both favorable and unfavorable facts. The lawyer should give the client honest and candid advice, which may refer to relevant moral, economic, social, political, and ethical considerations. If the necessary objective advice is unpleasant, try to put it in as acceptable a form as honesty permits. Sometimes lawyers may have to tell their clients what they don't want to hear.

b. Offering Advice: There is normally no duty to offer advice until asked by the client but any advice given must be candid and objective in stating the lawyer's honest assessment. If the client's action is likely to result in substantial adverse legal consequences, there may be a communication duty under MRPC 1.4. A lawyer should attempt to tell the client that such activity is likely to result in serious legal or ethical problems.

2. Intermediary – MRPC 2.2: The ABA now treats the lawyer intermediary role as a Rule 1.7(b) conflict where there is a "material limitation" on the lawyer concurrently serving as an advocate for two clients. See *supra* at 2-60 for coverage. Many jurisdictions have retained the intermediary role and related restraints in a separate rule.

a. General Rule: A lawyer may act as intermediary between existing clients. The general conflict of interest rules still apply here since parties may have or develop adverse interests; the theoretical difference is that the lawyer is functioning as a counselor, not as an advocate. Examples include putting a transaction together for both a seller and a buyer, or representing two individuals in forming a corporation or partnership without any apparent adverse interest in sight. The lawyer seeks common ground between clients where both benefit rather than seeking to obtain an advantage for one party over the other.

(1) Consultation and Consent: The lawyer consults with each client concerning the implications of the common representation, including the advantages and risks involved and the effect on the attorney-client privilege. Each client must give written consent to the common representation.

(2) Client's Best Interests: The client's best interests controls. The lawyer must reasonably believe the matter can be resolved on terms compatible with each client's best interests. This is an objective standard. The lawyer must also believe that each client will be able to make adequately informed decisions in the matter and there is little risk of material prejudice to any of the clients if the contemplated resolution is unsuccessful.

(3) Impartiality: The lawyer must also reasonably believe that the common representation can be undertaken impartially and without improper effect on other responsibilities the lawyer has to any of the clients.

(4) Attorney-Client Privilege: The prevailing view is that the evidentiary privilege and duty of confidentiality does not attach to communication with commonly represented clients as to one another. Both affected clients should be so advised in advance.

b. Withdrawal: A lawyer shall withdraw as intermediary if one of the clients so requests or any of the above conditions is no longer satisfied. Upon withdrawal, both clients receive Rule 1.9 prior client protections, and the lawyer cannot continue to represent any of the clients in any matter that was a subject of the intermediation.

3. Evaluation for Use by Third Party – MRPC 2.3:

a. Role: This is preparing an evaluation or opinion letter for the primary use of a third party. An example is a lawyer giving an opinion on a client's property title for a buyer or lender. Another is a corporate client planning to sponsor a public stock offering wants its lawyer to author an opinion letter that states the corporation is current on all its state filings. Factual matters limited, excluded, or scope restrictions should be disclosed in the evaluation.

b. Two Requirements: The lawyer must reasonably believe that making the evaluation is compatible with other aspects of the attorney-client relationship. If the evaluation may create adverse effects, the client must give informed consent. The consent to disclose confidential information and secrets in an evaluation may be oral.

c. Uncertainties: The lawyer function here is much like a CPA in an audit role. There may be potential civil negligent misrepresentation liability to third parties who rely on the lawyer's evaluation and thereby suffer losses. Some jurisdictions authorize withdrawing a false evaluation relied upon by a third party. See also MRPC 1.6, 4.1, and 8.4(c).

4. Lawyer Serving as Third-Party Neutral – MRPC 2.4: Lawyers serving non-clients as neutrals in mediation, arbitration, conciliation, escrow, or in a similar capacity must inform unrepresented parties that the lawyer is not representing them. A former neutral may not later become an advocate in the same or related dispute unless all the parties give informed consent that is confirmed in writing. However, a partisan member of an arbitration panel is not prohibited from subsequently representing that party. [MRPC 1.12]

MPRE Tip: The treatment of subsequent representation of a party involved in a prior intermediary and neutral role is related to MRPC 1.9 prior client protections.

B. Advocate – TITLE 3

1. Meritorious Claims and Contentions – MRPC 3.1:

a. Civil Case: The required ethical basis in bringing or defending a civil lawsuit is that lawyers must present a non-frivolous good faith argument in support of their clients' positions. This is similar to Civil Rule 11, under which the court may impose sanctions if an attorney signs a pleading lacking minimal merit and upon notice does not promptly make correction. Civil Rule 11 requires a "reasonable basis," while MRPC 3.1 requires a basis that is "not frivolous." The required ethical standard thus appears lower than the legal threshold.

(1) Not Frivolous: It is not frivolous to advance an action merely because the facts have not been fully substantiated, discovery is necessary to develop vital evidence, or it involves a new legal theory. The fact that the lawyer believes that the client's position ultimately will not prevail also does not necessarily mean a claim or defense is frivolous.

(2) Is Frivolous: The action is frivolous if the lawyer is unable to make a good faith argument for the extension, modification, or reversal of existing law. Also, if the claim was asserted merely to harass or maliciously injure the opposing party, it is frivolous. If the client insists on a frivolous position, the lawyer must withdraw. [MRPC 1.16]

b. Criminal Case: This standard is somewhat relaxed in a criminal case. A frivolous defense may be asserted at least to the extent it forces the state to prove every element required to prosecute the crime.

MPRE Tip: If the client insists on a frivolous position, the attorney must withdraw.

2. Expediting Litigation – MRPC 3.2: A plaintiff is entitled to obtain her day in court. Dilatory practices done with no intent besides delaying proceedings or harassing the opposing side are not allowed. Defendant counsel's dilatory actions must thus have some purpose and rationale other than naked intent to delay.

3. Candor Toward the Tribunal – MRPC 3.3: These restraints focus on the duties the lawyer owes the tribunal as an officer of the court.

a. False Statements of Law / Fact: A lawyer shall not knowingly allow the tribunal to be mislead by making a false statement of law or material fact or fail to correct a previous false statement. Although the lawyer may not have personal knowledge of all factual matters, he should have legal authority. For example, a lawyer cannot cite (or misquote) a case for controlling authority when the case held to the contrary or was overruled. This prohibition includes offering evidence or witness testimony the lawyer reasonably believes to be false other than the testimony of a defendant in a criminal matter.

MPRE Tip: Even under the criminal defendant false evidence introduction exception, the lawyer cannot know for certain that the testimony at issue is false.

b. Adverse Legal Authority Disclosure: A lawyer must also disclose to the tribunal controlling legal authority in the jurisdiction directly adverse to the position of her client. This applies only if the authority is not disclosed by opposing counsel.

c. Later Falsity Discovery: If the client or lawyer offered material evidence that later is discovered to have been false, the lawyer must take reasonable remedial measures.

(1) Persuade Client: The lawyer should first make reasonable efforts to persuade the client to consent to curative disclosure.

(2) Withdrawal: If the client refuses, the lawyer should seek to withdraw.

(3) Required Tribunal Disclosure: Disclosure of the falsity to the tribunal is required if the motion to withdraw is denied or the lawyer's withdrawal will not undo the effect of the false evidence. See also the related FIRST procedures *infra* at 341.

d. Continuing to End of Proceeding: The duty to make disclosure to the court continues to the end of the proceeding, including the trial court appeal period. Thus, withdrawal does not necessarily terminate the duty to disclose to the court. If the lawyer first learns of the fraud after final judgment, the Rule 1.6 confidential duty precludes disclosure.

e. *Ex Parte* Proceeding: In some states a lawyer may appear *ex parte* before a judge without the opposing party or his attorney present. The appearing lawyer shall inform the *ex parte* tribunal of all material facts reasonably necessary to make an informed decision, even if such facts are adverse to the lawyer's client. This enhanced duty of candor is necessary because the usual checks and balances of the adversarial process are missing.

> **MPRE Tip:** Every exam has numerous questions focusing on the above restraints. In the end, the lawyer's duty as an officer of the court prevails over blind obedience to the client's cause.

4. Fairness to Opposing Party and Counsel – MRPC 3.4: These restraints focus on discovery abuses and a lawyer's improper statements at trial.

a. Cannot Interfere with Evidence: A lawyer shall not unlawfully suppress or obstruct another party's pre-trial access to relevant evidence or participate in the alteration, destruction (spoliation), or concealment of a document or physical instrument having potential evidentiary value. The duty to preserve arises when the commencement of a relevant proceeding becomes foreseeable. A lawyer also may not counsel another in doing such an act. There is no duty to disclose voluntarily the existence of evidence, only to preserve it.

b. Falsify Evidence or Witness Inducement: A lawyer shall not falsify evidence or counsel, assist, or induce a witness not to give relevant information, to testify falsely, or to leave the jurisdiction to avoid testifying. Subornation of perjury is the corrupt procurement of false testimony; this is a crime in most jurisdictions. Agents, employees, and relatives of clients may properly be instructed not to voluntarily give information to an opposing party or attorney unless subpoenaed. Only payments of usual expenses, including lost wages, are proper for fact witnesses. In contrast, expert witnesses may be paid at a usual professional hourly rate. Neither type of witness may be paid on a contingent outcome basis.

> **MPRE Tip:** The ethical dilemma between a lawyer's duty not to reveal client secrets (1.6) and the duty not to mislead the tribunal (3.4) is usually resolved in favor of candor to the court.

c. Discovery Standards: In pretrial procedure, a lawyer shall not make a frivolous or unduly burdensome discovery request for facts or documents. A lawyer must also reasonably comply with a legally proper discovery request propounded by an opposing party. Litigation sanctions may be imposed for repeated discovery non-compliance.

d. At Trial:

(1) Improper Arguments: A lawyer shall not allude to any matter that is not relevant or that has not been or will not be supported by admissible evidence. Examples include mentioning the defendant's previous settlement offers to imply culpability or referring to the defendant's enormous wealth in an attempt to inflame the jury.

(2) Closing Arguments: In summing up, a lawyer must not refer to evidence not introduced during the trial, including a criminal defendant's refusal to testify.

e. Personal Opinion During Trial: At trial, a lawyer may usually argue on the analysis of the evidence for or against any position or conclusion, but should not assert personal knowledge or related opinions on the facts, unless the lawyer is also a trial witness.

(1) **Prohibited Statements:** During trial, a lawyer shall not state a personal opinion as to the justness of a cause, credibility of a witness, culpability of a civil litigant, or the guilt or innocence of the accused. The lawyer should not use or imply the word "I," "me," or "we" during trial argument. An example is "Everyone in this courtroom believes the defendant is a liar and not credible." "Everyone" includes the lawyer, so this is improper.

(2) **Witness Questions:** A lawyer may not ask a witness questions that will draw answers that imply another witness was or was not credible. An example is, "Do you think witness B was testifying truthfully?" But in closing arguments, it would not be improper for a lawyer to sum up to the jury with "You saw in cross-examination that C was not truthful."

5. Impartiality and Decorum of the Tribunal – MRPC 3.5:

a. Improper Influence: A lawyer shall not seek to illegally influence a judge, juror, or potential juror. Disruptive, harassing, or abusive conduct in court also is prohibited.

b. *Ex Parte* Communications: *Ex parte* communications with the court or jurors are ordinarily prohibited because the opposing lawyer's position cannot be considered. An exception applies if the lawyer's *ex parte* communication was purely procedural, such as inquiring about a scheduling matter. Even a lawyer not connected with a case must not discuss the case with an impaneled juror. Post-trial communication with jurors in an attempt to prove juror impropriety must not involve coercion, duress, or harassment.

6. Trial Publicity – MRPC 3.6: Extrajudicial trial publicity by lawyers and prosecutors is restricted if it would be disseminated and materially prejudice the proceeding.

a. Prohibited Criminal Case Statements – TOPIC: Prohibited extrajudicial statements and comments by a lawyer that may create a heightened public condemnation of the accused include the **TOPIC** subjects of:

(1) **Test Results:** The performance or results of any investigative test, such as a polygraph examination (lie detector test) or a lab test or failure to submit to such a test.

(2) **Opinion or Future Witness Testimony:** Any opinion as to the guilt or innocence of any suspect or defendant, or the credibility or anticipated testimony of a prospective witness.

(3) **Plea or Confession:** The possibility of a guilty plea or the existence or contents of a confession, admission, or statement given by a suspect or defendant or that person's refusal or failure to make such a statement.

(4) **Inadmissible Evidence:** Information the lawyer knows or reasonably should know is likely to be inadmissible as evidence at trial.

(5) **Character:** Statements about the character, credibility, reputation, or past criminal record of a suspect, or defendant are generally prohibited (except for impeachment purposes in some circumstances).

MPRE Tip: The **TOPIC** prohibited extrajudicial statements are heavily tested on the MPRE.

b. Permitted Disclosures: Out-of-court statements should be limited to the general nature of the claim or defense, the procedural or scheduling status of the case, and public record information, including identities of designated witnesses. A lawyer also has a right to publicly rebut the prejudicial effect of negative publicity generated by another.

c. Safety Information: The public has a right to know about threats to its safety and public security. A public prosecutor involved in a criminal case may **s**tate publically that SIPAW an **i**nvestigation is in progress, identify public record involved **p**arties involved (if allowed by law), request **a**ssistance in obtaining evidence and information, and **w**arn of danger concerning the behavior of a person involved. There must be reason to believe there is a likelihood of substantial harm to an individual or to the public interest.

d. Civil Case Statements: A lawyer's statements that have a substantial likelihood of materially prejudicing an adjudicative proceeding are prohibited in civil matters. This usually involves inadmissible evidence or evidence of a party's character or credibility.

7. Lawyer as Witness – MRPC 3.7: The role of a trial partisan-advocate may conflict with that of an independent witness. Serving as a fact witness subject to cross-examination may also reduce the effectiveness of the lawyer's advocacy role.

a. Improper to Act as Advocate and Witness: A lawyer shall not act as advocate at a trial where the lawyer is likely to be a necessary witness concerning a material contested question of fact or law. Some states limit this prohibition to jury trials.

b. Exceptions: An attorney may be a witness if **HULA**:

(1) Hardship on Client: A lawyer may testify when the evidence is otherwise unobtainable or the lawyer has been called by the opposing party, and/or that disqualification of the lawyer would work a substantial hardship on the client. Some states also require that the likelihood of the lawyer being a necessary witness was not reasonably foreseeable before trial.

(2) Uncontested or Formality: A lawyer may testify if the testimony relates to a minor factual issue that is either uncontested or a mere formality. An example is testifying as a witness to the execution of a will or a corporate document.

(3) Legal Services Rendered Value: A lawyer may testify if the testimony relates to the nature and value of legal services rendered in the case.

(4) Another Firm Lawyer Witness: Unlike the firm-wide disqualification provisions of MRPC 1.10, a lawyer is not disqualified as an advocate merely because another lawyer in the same firm is a witness unless the firm itself has a Rule 1.7 or 1.9 conflict.

8. Special Responsibilities of a Prosecutor – DASH PET - MRPC 3.8: A prosecutor in a criminal case has several elevated duties as the role turns from being an advocate of a private client to being an advocate of the public in the pursuit of justice.

a. Discovery on Lawyer: Prosecutors shall not subpoena a lawyer to secure client evidence in a criminal proceeding. An exception allows such discovery on a lawyer if the evidence is not privileged, it is essential or extremely important, and there is no feasible alternative source.

b. Accused's Right to Counsel: The prosecutor has a duty to advise the accused of the right to counsel and provide the opportunity to obtain a lawyer. The absence of *Miranda* warnings is usually grounds for reversal of a subsequent conviction based upon admissions made during unrepresented interrogation.

c. Supported by Probable Cause: A prosecutor cannot bring a charge or prosecute a criminal case that the prosecutor knows is not supported by probable cause. This includes being able to present believable evidence on every element of the offense.

d. Honor Pretrial Rights of Accused: The prosecutor has a duty to refrain from seeking a waiver of important pretrial rights from an unrepresented accused (rights against self-incrimination, waiver of preliminary hearing, or demand for jury trial).

e. Post-Conviction Duty: The ABA House of Delegates in 2008 voted to require prosecutors to take affirmative steps to remedy a potentially wrongful prior conviction. This applies if new credible legal or factual evidence later comes to light that clearly and convincingly creates substantial doubt about the fundamental fairness of the defendant's guilt. A prosecutor must promptly disclose such information to an appropriate court or other authority. Some argue this puts prosecutor immunity at risk.

f. Extrajudicial Statements: The prosecutor shall not make prohibited extrajudicial statements and must supervise subordinates. Investigators, law enforcement personnel, employees, or other persons assisting or associated with the prosecutor in a criminal case likewise are prohibited from making extrajudicial statements that the prosecutor would be prohibited from making. (See also MRPC 3.6 on page 4-129.)

g. Timely Disclosure of Exculpatory Evidence: The prosecutor must make timely disclosure to the defense of all material exculpatory evidence or information known to the prosecutor that tends to negate the guilt of the accused or tends to mitigate the severity of the offense. During sentencing, the prosecutor has a duty to disclose to the defense and the tribunal all unprivileged mitigating information known to the prosecutor.

9. Advocate in Nonadjudicative Proceeding – MRPC 3.9: A legislative or administrative tribunal or agency will likely give special weight to a lawyer's opinions on a question of law or rulemaking. If the lawyer is giving opinion testimony and simultaneously representing a client with an interest in the subject, disclosure of the attorney-client relationship is required. This permits the agency to make an assessment of any relevant biases of the lawyer. If the jurisdiction allows lawyers to hold public office concurrently, they may not use their public positions to obtain special advantage that is clearly contrary to the public interest.

C. Transactions with Persons Other than Clients – TITLE 4

1. Truthfulness in Statements to Others – MRPC 4.1

a. False Statement: A lawyer shall not knowingly make a false statement of material fact or law to a third person in the course of representing a client. Misrepresentations can also occur by partially true but misleading statements. While a lawyer need not disclose all facts, omissions that are the equivalent of affirmative false statements are improper. A lawyer's "puffery" to any opposing party or counsel in representing estimates of price, value, or dollar settlement maximums are not usually considered statements of fact.

b. Duty to Disclose: There is also a duty to make disclosure of a material fact to a third party when disclosure is necessary to avoid assisting a client's criminal or fraudulent act. Most jurisdictions do not allow disclosures violating MRPC 1.6, but withdrawal may be required. Beyond withdrawal, a lawyer may have to disaffirm affirmatively documents she created that now appear to be fraudulent to avoid being deemed to have personally assisted.

c. Liabilities to Third Parties: Some jurisdictions, including California, have adopted a multi-factor test and held there is potential civil legal liability to unrepresented third parties if it is clear they will rely to their detriment on the lawyer's statements.

2. Communication with Persons Represented by Counsel – MRPC 4.2: A lawyer shall not communicate with a person represented by another lawyer in the same matter unless that person's lawyer consents or direct communication is authorized by law or court order. If the lawyer is contacted by the opposing party, she should say, "I cannot talk to you directly; you need to talk to your own lawyer." Simultaneous communication, such as mailing a letter directed to both the opposing party and his lawyer, is still a violation.

a. Includes: Direct communications by a lawyer about the subject of the representation are prohibited. This might include a lawyer using an investigator to record conversations surreptitiously to obtain damaging admissions from a represented opposing party. If an organization such as a corporation is a party, the Rule protects all employees with managerial responsibility and those personally involved in the wrongdoing.

b. Limited Representation: An opposing party with only limited representation is considered unrepresented unless the opposing lawyer knows of or has received a written notice of appearance. This means the lawyer may usually communicate directly with such a party. This Rule promotes filing a limited Notice of Appearance.

> **MPRE Tip:** Opposing counsel must consent to communication with the opposing party. This absolute "no contact" rule applies even if the opposing party initiates the communication with the lawyer. Opposing parties themselves may usually directly communicate with each other.

3. Dealing with Unrepresented Person – MRPC 4.3: A lawyer shall not state or imply that she is disinterested when dealing with a person who is unrepresented by counsel.

a. Correct Any Misunderstanding: The lawyer shall make reasonable efforts to correct any misunderstanding the unrepresented person has of the lawyer's role in the matter. This rule suggests the lawyer must affirmatively state that (1) she is a lawyer, (2) who represents an identified opposing party, and (3) you should secure your own counsel.

b. Giving Legal Advice: A lawyer should avoid giving legal advice to an unrepresented party if that party is or may be adverse to a current client. Still, a lawyer may negotiate the terms of the transaction or settle a dispute with an unrepresented person.

4. Respect for Rights of Third Person – MRPC 4.4: A lawyer shall not use means that have no substantial purpose other than to embarrass, delay, or burden a third person who is not a party, such as a witness.

a. Depositions: Third parties may be compelled to give deposition testimony, but a lawyer should avoid subjects involving unwarranted intrusions. The lawyer may also not use methods to obtain evidence that are oppressive or violate the legal rights of third parties.

b. Receipt of Inadvertently Sent Documents: A lawyer may receive documents or emails that were mistakenly sent to him by opposing parties or their lawyer. Such disclosure may waive the privileged status of the document unless the "claw back" procedures of CP 26 and 45 are implemented. The lawyer must always promptly notify the sender in order to permit him to consider initiating protective measures. The ABA comments suggest it is best to return such documents unread.

RIGOS UNIFORM BAR REVIEW SERIES

PROFESSIONAL RESPONSIBILITY EXAM REVIEW (MPRE)

Chapter 4

Counselor, Advocate, and Third Party Dealings

Question Map

Numbers immediately following the topic are the chapter question numbers. The **boldface** numbers preceded by "F" are the final exam question numbers. For example, for the topic "A. 2. Intermediary" below, question 17 is in the chapter questions on page 4-140; question **F38** is in the final exam on page 7-287.

a. Cannot Interfere with Evidence – 42, 45 .... **F10**
b. Falsify Evidence or Witness Inducement – 3, 5, 18, 22, 49 .... **F6**
c. Discovery Standards – 35, 53
d. At Trial
(1) Improper Arguments – 36
(2) Closing Arguments – 37, 56
e. Personal Opinion During Trial – 1, 15, 43
(1) Prohibited Statements – 56
(2) Witness Questions – 56

5. Impartiality and Decorum of the Tribunal – 12, 22 .... **F39**
a. Improper Influence – 22, 34, 41, 55 .... **F39**
b. *Ex Parte* Communications – 12, 22, 25, 34

6. Trial Publicity – 1
a. Prohibited Criminal Case Statements
(1) Test Results – 27
(2) Opinion or Future Witness Testimony – 27
(3) Plea or Confession – 13
(4) Inadmissible Evidence – 27
(4) Character – 27, 56
b. Permitted Disclosures – 13, 57
c. Safety Information – 57
d. Civil Case Statements – 27

7. Lawyer as Witness – 9, 58
a. Improper to Act as Advocate and Witness – 9, 58
b. Exceptions
(1) Hardship on Client – 38
(2) Uncontested or Formality – 9, 38
(3) Legal Services Rendered Valuation – 38
(4) Another Firm Lawyer Witness – 38, 47

8. Special Responsibilities of a Prosecutor **F16**
a. Discovery on Lawyer– 48
b. Accused's Right to Counsel
c. Supported by Probable Cause – 23, 39
d. Honor Pretrial Rights of Accused
e. Post-Conviction Duty
f. Extrajudicial Statements Prohibited – 57
g. Timely Disclosure of Exculpatory Evidence – 8, 39 .... **F80**

9. Advocate in Nonadjudicative Proceeding – 7, 28 .... **F99**

C. Transactions with Persons Other Than Clients

1. Truthfulness in Statements to Others – 29, 54
a. False Statement – 59, 61
b. Duty to Disclose – 61
c. Liabilities to Third Parties

2. Communication with Persons Represented by Counsel – 11, 14, 20, 21, 44
a. Includes **F42**
b. Limited Representation

3. Dealing with Unrepresented Person – 29, 46, 59
a. Correct Any Misunderstandings
b. Giving Legal Advice

4. Respect for Rights of Third Person – 22, 25, 29, 60
a. Depositions – 61
b. Receipt of Inadvertently Sent Documents – 62

Chapter 4

Counselor, Advocate, and Third Party Dealings

Questions

1. Attorney represented Joe in a personal injury case against Gary's Bed and Breakfast. Joe had fallen on an icy patch of sidewalk leading to the outdoor hot tub on the premises, breaking his wrist. The case hinged on whether the proprietor Gary knew the sidewalk was icy and was thus negligent in not warning his guests.

During the trial attorney called Gary to the witness stand. Attorney asked Gary, "Isn't it true that you knew the sidewalk was icy?" Gary responded, "No, I didn't know it was icy until I heard Joe fall." "You're lying!" shouted Attorney. "You knew the walk was icy because it had been icy the last three nights. How could you say such a blatant falsehood to me and this court?"

Is Attorney subject to discipline?

- **(A)** Yes, because his shout intimidated the witness.
- **(B)** Yes, because he expressed his personal opinion that Gary was lying.
- **(C)** No, because his shout was a natural reaction to the witness lying.
- **(D)** No, if Attorney could prove that Gary was lying.

2. David Defendant has been charged with criminal trespass and hired Alice Attorney to defend him. Alice does extensive research on the statute in question and related case law interpretations. She discovers a line of case law that may be helpful, but the authority is rather old and the court could conclude that her older case law is contrary to current law.

If Alice Attorney asserts this case authority as a defense, is she subject to discipline?

- **(A)** No, because Alice Attorney is required to be a zealous advocate for the client and should present all arguments favorable to David Defendant.
- **(B)** No, if Alice Attorney has a good faith belief the argument has merit.
- **(C)** Yes, unless the line of case law has sufficient merit to be distinguished from the current law.
- **(D)** Yes, because the court may conclude that Attorney's older case law is contrary to current law.

3. Susan Skier was injured in a skiing race when she suffered a bad fall. Her neck was sprained, and she was under therapy which required taking medicine for a year before her neck returned to normal. A year later, Susan was driving her car in Pleasantville and stopped for a red light. Charlie Careless was in the following car and due to his inattention ran into the back of Susan's car. This aggravated the preexisting weak neck muscles, and Susan was forced to begin therapy and drug treatment again.

Susan went to the yellow pages and picked Bertha Bigrecovery under "personal injury attorneys." Susan explained the prior skiing injury to her neck, and Bertha said that this would hurt the claim recovery if the insurance company learned of it. Bertha said that Susan did not have to volunteer the information, but if it came up in cross-examination, Susan would have to answer truthfully. Susan said, "No, I don't agree with you, and I am not going to let this get in the way of a fat insurance recovery." At trial, Bertha called Susan as a witness. Bertha asked Susan a number of questions about the origin of the neck injury and Susan untruthfully attributed the injury solely to the rear-end accident caused by Charlie.

Is Bertha subject to discipline resulting from Susan's testimonies?

- **(A)** Yes, because Bertha has allowed her client to offer evidence that Bertha knew was false.
- **(B)** Yes, unless Bertha takes reasonable remedial measures.
- **(C)** No, because it was the client Susan who offered the false testimony, not Bertha the lawyer.
- **(D)** No, because Susan insisted upon lying after Bertha the lawyer advised her against it, and lawyers cannot always control a client's actions.

4. Alice and Baker respectively represented the plaintiff and defendant in a complicated and difficult personal injury bench trial. The major area of contention was whether sufficient legal causation existed to link the defendant's breach of duty to the plaintiff's damages. At the end of the trial, the judge declined to render a final decision and stated she would take the matter under advisement.

Four weeks went by without a formal decision. Alice heard that the judge was having difficulty deciding the case because of uncertainty about the controlling law. One week later, no decision had been issued, and Alice and her client were growing increasingly apprehensive. Alice called the trial judge and explained that she had heard rumors about the indecision and suggested that the court reopen the case for additional evidence and allow briefing by both parties. Three days later, both Alice and Baker received an order reopening the case for additional evidence and setting a date for the submission of supplemental briefs.

Was it improper for Alice to communicate with the judge?

- **(A)** No, because Alice did not suggest how the judge should decide the case.
- **(B)** No, because both attorneys were allowed to present additional evidence and submit supplemental briefs.
- **(C)** Yes, because Alice caused the judge to reopen a case that had previously been taken under advisement.
- **(D)** Yes, because Alice communicated with the judge concerning a pending matter without notifying the opposing counsel.

5. Helen Homeowner hired a general contractor named Cheryl Contractor to build a custom-designed personal residence. The specifications and plans were drawn by Alice Architect. When Cheryl submitted her final bill to Helen for the work, Alice refused to approve the construction or issue the Certificate of Completion. Without the certificate, the mortgage company refused to pay advance construction funds to Helen, so she was unable to pay Cheryl.

Cheryl hired Teresa Triallawyer, who filed a lawsuit against Helen for breach of contract and against Alice for professional architectural malpractice. Teresa agreed to accept a fee of 1/3 of any recovery derived from Helen and Alice. Because she was not being paid by Cheryl, Teresa tried to economize on all the expenses required to present the case at trial.

Which of the following will not subject Teresa to potential discipline?

I. Payment of a fact witness' usual salary and travel expenses.
II. Payment to all the fact witnesses 10% of the recovery, distributed among them based upon the ratio of time spent.
III. Payment at $300 per hour to an expert witness architect only if he testifies that Alice Architect was negligent in failing to certify Cheryl's work.
IV. Payment to a testifying expert witness architect in an amount of one-third of any recovery Teresa receives.

(A) I only.
(B) I and II only.
(C) I and III only.
(D) I, III, and IV only.

6. Pattie Proper is a will, gift, trust, and estate lawyer. She prepared a will for Diane Deceased four years ago. Diane's will directs that Diane's husband, Harry, is to be the personal representative and distribute the bequests to himself and Diane's children from a prior marriage.

Diane passed away, and Harry was appointed as personal representative. He duly asked Pattie to act as the estate's counsel in this matter. Pattie prepared and filed with the probate court financial and progress reports based upon information provided by Harry. Six months later, Harry admitted to Pattie that he personally has been embezzling cash receipts that should have gone into the estate. He says that he is no longer doing this and is sorry that the estate report which Pattie presented to the probate court excluded the embezzled cash receipts.

Pattie Proper should

(A) Inform the beneficiaries of Harry's embezzlement.
(B) Inform the probate court.
(C) Do nothing because the embezzlement is a past crime and/or fraud that the client does not want revealed.
(D) File a motion to withdraw and cite "professional ethical concerns" as the reason.

7. Loretta Lobbyist represented a corporation involved in property development as its regulatory lawyer. The corporate president called Loretta and informed her that a state legislative committee was holding hearings on new rule-making procedures that would be adopted in geographic areas where the corporation was planning property developments. The president believed the procedures under consideration would be detrimental to the corporation's interest. Loretta agreed to testify at the hearing and argue against any changes in the rule-making procedures.

Loretta appeared and testified under her own name with no disclosure of the development corporation. While the legislative committee considered Loretta's viewpoint, they adopted the new rule-making procedures that the corporation opposed.

Was Loretta's conduct proper?

- **(A)** Yes, if she was not compensated for the testimony.
- **(B)** Yes, because the duty of confidentiality and attorney-client evidentiary privilege prevented her from revealing the identity of the client without its prior approval.
- **(C)** No, because the attempt to affect the rule-making procedure was unsuccessful.
- **(D)** No, because Loretta did not reveal that she was appearing and testifying on behalf of the property development corporation.

8. There was a robbery by three men at a coffee store late one afternoon. The police were called and within 30 minutes arrested two groups of three men, each in close proximity to the store. Both groups were taken to the local police station. Within 30 minutes, both the Assistant Deputy Prosecutor and the two eyewitness coffee store clerks arrived at the police station. In the lineup, each of the two eyewitnesses identified a different group. The prosecutor and police then encouraged the witnesses to agree, and one witness changed her mind.

The prosecutor charged that group, and at trial, both witnesses testified that they were "reasonably sure these were the three robbers." The public defender assigned to the case was unaware of the other group of men and conducted no relevant discovery.

Is the Assistant Deputy Prosecutor subject to discipline?

- **(A)** Yes, if the jury convicts the defendants.
- **(B)** Yes, because the second group of potential suspects should have been disclosed to the public defender.
- **(C)** No, unless the defense attorney requested the information.
- **(D)** No, if there was a substantial chance that the jury had independent evidence that was the basis for their final decision.

9. Wanda Witness was a lawyer who represented Betty Bigbucks in planning her estate and drafting her will. Betty was elderly and decided to change her testamentary scheme to exclude the children of her husband's prior marriage and give their share to a local charity. Wanda drew the codicil to the will and served as one of the two witnesses attesting to Betty's signature.

Betty passed away, and her will named her son by birth, Ernest, as the executor. Ernest asked Wanda to represent him in the probate and estate administration process. Ernest also told Wanda that the children of his mother's husband's prior marriage had told him that they believed Betty lacked capacity to execute the codicil.

Is it proper for Wanda to undertake representation of the executor in the probate?

- **(A)** Yes, if Wanda's testimony will support the issue of Betty's testamentary capacity.
- **(B)** Yes, because the parties contesting the will can introduce their own witnesses and cross-examine Wanda.
- **(C)** No, because Wanda will be representing an interest adverse to a member of Betty's extended family.
- **(D)** No, because Wanda will likely be called to testify concerning a material contested statement of fact that is in dispute.

10. Francis Famous was a very well-known professional malpractice defense attorney. He defended a case in which a former client of attorney Alice Aggressive sued her for malpractice. Francis took the case to trial, and the jury found against his client Lawyer Alice. Alice then blamed Francis for losing the case.

Alice located another lawyer named Sally Sleazy who filed a malpractice suit against Francis. Francis filed a motion for summary judgment, which the trial court granted. Francis felt his reputation had been damaged and filed a grievance with the state bar association disciplinary authority against Lawyer Sally Sleazy.

Is Sally subject to discipline for filing the lawsuit against Francis?

- **(A)** Yes, if she believed the case would be dismissed on summary judgment.
- **(B)** Yes, if she knew that Francis' reputation would be damaged if the suit was filed.
- **(C)** No, if she believed in good faith the suit had merit.
- **(D)** No, as long as there was a reasonable basis for bringing the lawsuit.

11. Paula Programmer retained lawyer Iola Intellectual Property to bring suit against Acme Computers, Inc., for infringing on software she developed and copyrighted. Iola served Requests for Production of all corporate documents that referred to the software in question. The defendant's corporate attorney refused to produce, and Iola secured an Order to Produce signed by the court. The Defendant still refused to produce, and Iola grew quite frustrated.

Iola went to a bar and grill next to the corporate office and began discussing software development with the defendant's employees who stopped in there after work. One manager admitted to Iola, "Sure, we have studies on that software, but we never give them to the other side in these lawsuits."

Is Iola subject to discipline?

(A) Yes, because she contacted the manager directly.
(B) Yes, only if the manager was separately represented by counsel.
(C) No, because Acme Computer refused to obey a court order.
(D) No, because Iola had the right to take the manager's deposition and inquire into corporate documents related to software development.

12. Carol Client hired a contractor to do a kitchen remodel in her home. Halfway through the job, the contractor walked off the job. Carol hired another contractor to complete the job and retained Alice Attorney to file suit against the original contractor. The case did not settle, so the parties began a jury trial. Alice went to a baseball game on the second night of the trial and was seated next to a person who was a juror in the trial.

To comply with the MRPCs, Alice Attorney

(A) May communicate with the juror concerning the baseball game, but not discuss any matter involving the pending case.
(B) May communicate with the juror concerning the baseball game, but not discuss any matter involving the pending case and must notify the opposing counsel immediately.
(C) May communicate with the juror concerning the baseball game, but not discuss any matter involving the pending case and must notify both the judge and opposing counsel immediately.
(D) May not communicate with the juror at all.

13. Pattie Prosecutor was halfway through a criminal trial in which Kathy Killer was charged with murder. As Pattie was leaving the courtroom for the day, she was stopped by Nancy Newsmaker, a criminal reporter for the Everyday News. Nancy asked Pattie for her "sense of where the trial was at." She replied, "Well, I can't express any opinion as to Kathy's innocence or guilt, but her attorney is suggesting a plea offer reducing murder to a lower homicide offense."

Is Pattie subject to discipline?

(A) Yes, because the statement concerned the ongoing criminal prosecution.
(B) Yes, because her statement mentioned the details of a plea offer (thus implying guilt) to a person who might reasonably be expected to report the statement to the public.
(C) No, as long as the statement did not reveal anything not already in the public court record.
(D) No, as long as the statements she made to the criminal reporter were truthful.

14. Diane Debtor owed $2 million dollars to Carol Creditor on a promissory note. Diane was frequently delinquent in making the required monthly payment, which resulted in many Notices of Defaults being served. Carol retained Alpha as a collection lawyer, and Diane retained Beta to defend the action. While there were a number of communications between the two attorneys, the delinquencies continued. Finally, Alpha filed a Summons and Complaint and served Diane. 30 days expired without an Answer. Alpha then filed a Motion for Default and served Beta. Another ten days went by, and Alpha asked a mutual friend to call Diane and asked her if she was aware her attorney had not responded.

Is lawyer Alpha subject to discipline?

(A) Yes, because Diane was represented by counsel.
(B) Yes, because Alpha did not contact Beta after contacting Diane directly.
(C) No, if such contact was authorized while a Motion for Default was pending.
(D) No, if Alpha also called Beta and left a message stating that she was going to contact her client indirectly through a mutual friend.

15. Alice Aggressive was defending a construction defect case in which a homeowner was complaining that the contractor failed to put fire retardant in the house walls. Apparently, a fire started from an unknown source destroyed all the homeowner's personal possessions. The plaintiff admitted she was a heavy cigarette smoker.

In her closing argument Alice stated, "This fire was caused by defendant's extreme carelessness in smoking over two packs of cigarettes a day. I am sure everyone in this courtroom today will agree she brought this on herself."

Is Alice subject to discipline?

(A) No, because Alice has the right to argue the evidence.
(B) No, if Alice sincerely believed that the homeowner's smoking caused the fire.
(C) Yes, because Alice expressed her opinion as to the conclusion the jury will reach after their deliberations.
(D) Yes, because Alice expressed a personal opinion about the homeowner's culpability.

16. Iola Injured was stopped at a red light in her automobile when Betty Bigbucks rear-ended her car. She suffered back injuries and hired a lawyer, Harriet Honest, to sue Betty's insurance carrier. Iola's doctor, Florence Feelgood, gave extensive trial testimony concluding that Iola had suffered permanent serious back, neck, and soft tissue injuries. The jury agreed and awarded Iola two million dollars.

Two months later, after the appeal period had lapsed, Harriet Honest was skiing in the mountains and observed Iola Injured skiing on an advanced skill level hill. At the bottom of the hill in the chair lift back up line, Harriet asked Iola for an explanation. Iola stated, "Well, I had to pay Dr. Feelgood $100,000 to get her to lie at trial, but we won and you received 30% of the two million." Harriet immediately informed the trial court judge that the testimony of her client and the doctor was fraudulent.

Is lawyer Harriet Honest subject to discipline for the disclosure made to the court?

(A) Yes, because the attorney-client privilege applies to the admission Iola made to her attorney.
(B) Yes, because lawyer Harriet violated her duty to her client not to reveal confidential information.
(C) No, because a lawyer is required to report to the trial court judge evidence entered that is false.
(D) No, unless the fraud was also reported to the medical authorities.

17. Client A decided to start a business with B and C and recommended a lawyer named Sally Startup to create the entity. B and C refused to use Sally, so the three signed a standard partnership form they purchased in a local office supply store. Two years later, two of the owners began to disagree about an unrelated real property use question, and they asked Sally to mediate the land dispute as a neutral. Sally agreed. After several meetings failed to produce a successful compromise, Sally determined there was an impasse and withdrew, since it was clear that the land dispute could not be resolved on terms compatible with each owner's best interest. A later asked Sally to assist A in filing a petition for dissolving the ABC partnership and distributing the assets.

May attorney Sally accept the representation of A?

(A) Yes, if the dissolution of the partnership does not involve the subject of the prior intermediation.
(B) Yes, because Sally had no prior professional relationship with A, B, or C.
(C) No, if Sally was asked to recluse herself by B or C.
(D) No, unless A, B, and C all give written consent to the common representation.

18. Acme Manufacturing Co. is a defendant in a product liability action in which the plaintiff is alleging negligence in failing to inspect the defective product. Critical to the plaintiff is testimony by the company's then quality control inspector, Ike Inspector, concerning the failure to inspect. On the first day of trial, Ike called the corporation's lawyer, Barbara Bulldog and said that a process server for the plaintiff came to his house the previous night after he and his wife were in bed. He apparently saw the process server from his second story window and was very quiet until he left. Barbara told Ike to get packed and check into a hotel for two weeks until the trial was over. Ike decided to go to the Bahamas for two weeks instead.

Is attorney Barbara Bulldog subject to discipline?

- **(A)** Yes, unless Barbara reveals Ike's location if requested to do so by the plaintiff's attorney.
- **(B)** Yes, because Barbara suggested that Ike conceal himself.
- **(C)** No, because a subpoena was never actually served on Ike.
- **(D)** No, because Barbara did not advise Ike to leave the jurisdiction.

19. Sally Subordinate was a plaintiffs' personal injury lawyer who undertook to represent Eunice Unfortunate in an automobile accident lawsuit. Neverpay Insurance Co. hired Diane Dilatory to defend the claim. After many months of broken settlement promises by Diane, Sally finally filed suit. Diane put in a formal Notice of Appearance, but refused to file an Answer until forced to by Sally. Sally began discovery, but Diane refused to cooperate or have her clients submit to depositions, and Sally had to file numerous motions to compel. The delays caused numerous dates on the trial calendar to pass, and the court had to delay the trial four times. Without any monetary recovery, Eunice was unable to afford medical attention and died. Eunice's heirs filed a bar complaint against Diane Dilatory.

Is Diane Dilatory subject to professional discipline?

- **(A)** Yes, because Eunice died without being able to pay for medical attention.
- **(B)** Yes, only if she was sanctioned by the trial court.
- **(C)** No, if a competent lawyer acting in good faith would regard the course of action she followed as having some substantial purpose other than delay.
- **(D)** No, unless it is determined that the dilatory practices of Diane were willful with a view to maximize her own monetary gain.

20. Plaintiff and defendant are involved in a contentious lawsuit. Plaintiff's attorney has made a number of settlement offers in amounts that their side considers quite generous. There has been no response of any substance from the defendant's attorney, which has led to increased frustration and anxiety between plaintiff and plaintiff's attorney.

It is unclear if the defendant's attorney has submitted the offers to the client. In a final attempt to get the case settled, plaintiff's attorney increased the offer amount and sent a new settlement letter to both the defendant's attorney and the defendant personally.

Is the conduct of plaintiff's attorney in sending the letter proper?

(A) Yes, because the defendant's attorney has an obligation to submit all settlement offers to his client.
(B) Yes, if the plaintiff's attorney has clearly indicated in the letter to defendant's counsel that a copy of the letter was going to the client.
(C) No, unless the defendant's attorney gave the plaintiff's attorney permission to send a copy of the letter to her client.
(D) No, because it is unclear if the defendant's attorney has submitted the prior settlement offers to her client as required by ABA Model Rule 1.2(a).

21. Esther Easement lived next door to Nina Neighbor and had used a footpath across Nina's property for 20 years. Nina married Joe Jerk, and he began to complain about Esther crossing over their property. Esther hired Alissa Aggressive to pursue a quiet title action that would record Ester's prescriptive easement over Nina's property. Alissa tried to be as accommodating as possible because the objective was to retain cordial relations between the neighbors. In response, Nina and Joe retained Mary Maddog to represent them.

Negotiations bogged down, and a resolution seemed to be going nowhere quick. Esther told her lawyer Alissa, "This is ridiculous." Alissa responded, "I agree, and I have no answer. Maybe you should try to talk to your neighbor directly and see if the two of you can resolve this directly using the settlement objectives we have decided upon as a framework."

Is Alissa subject to discipline for encouraging a direct contact with the opposing party without going through the opposing attorney?

(A) Yes, because a lawyer shall not directly or indirectly communicate with an opposing party whom she knows is represented by an attorney.
(B) Yes, unless Alissa contacted the attorney for the opposing side and informed her that her client was going to contact the opposing party directly.
(C) No, only if she failed to inform opposing counsel that negotiations between the lawyers had become useless and tendered a formal withdrawal.
(D) No, because Esther and Nina may communicate directly.

22. Alice Attorney represented Denise Defendant in an antitrust lawsuit. The jury found for the plaintiff. Alice has reason to believe that two of the jurors were neither independent nor impartial, but rather had been previously and significantly biased against the defendant. She further believes that they both affirmatively concealed their bias and prejudice during voir dire selection of the jury.

Which of the following methods of investigation will subject Alice to discipline?

I. Hire a private detective to investigate the backgrounds of both jurors.
II. Interview the jurors herself.
III. Interview other jurors to determine if the two questionable jurors said anything in the jury room that might indicate a predisposition or prejudice.

(A) None of the above.
(B) One of the above.
(C) Two of the above.
(D) All three of the above.

23. Petulla Prosecutor is a district attorney in the criminal division with an interest in running for elected office. The police picked up four persons of interest after a robbery, including Mary Meek. After extensive interrogation it became clear that none of them would testify against the others so proof of a conspiracy would be difficult. Petulla believed that Mary is especially susceptible to pressure and might turn on the others if pressed. Therefore, Petulla asked the grand jury to indict Mary for robbery even though no evidence existed to support the indictment.

Is Petulla subject to discipline for this conduct?

(A) Yes, unless the pressure tactic works, and Mary squeals on the other robbers.
(B) Yes, because she does not have sufficient evidence against Mary supported by probable cause.
(C) No, as long as she does not actually prosecute Mary for robbery.
(D) No, because finding a way to indict all persons of interest is consistent with the greater good and public interest against crime.

24. Alice Adversary is a business attorney who represents Dirty Disposal, Inc. She was in a meeting with the corporate president when the sales manager entered the discussion. He explained the availability of a new marketing opportunity in a business venture that would require dumping toxic waste in an area near a river. The new venture would add substantial profits, but involve a small yet significant chance that the disposal would be deadly to the workers involved and/or downriver users. Alice realized the downside risk.

Which of the below acts or conduct by Alice would be improper?

(A) Criticize the sales manager for not considering the downside risks.
(B) Refer to relevant moral and ethical considerations.
(C) Neglect to discuss the legal consequences of the dumping because it would upset both the sales manager and the president.
(D) Keep the plans for the new venture confidential because they are secrets of a client.

25. Iola Involved was a juror in a medical malpractice case. The expert testimony was contradictory and inconclusive, and Iola became confused. Iola had a brother, Larry, who was a lawyer and a cousin, Donald, who was a doctor. At a family picnic on a weekend during the trial, she asked both Larry and Donald a number of technical questions related to uncertainties she had about the procedures and expert testimony. Both Larry and Donald knew Iola was serving as an active juror at the time they gave her advice.

Is Larry subject to discipline?

(A) No, because Larry is a family member of Iola and like his cousin, the doctor, he may advise a member of his family.
(B) No, as long as Larry is not involved as a lawyer in the medical malpractice case.
(C) Yes, regardless of whether Larry was involved as a lawyer in the medical malpractice case.
(D) Yes, unless Larry charged Iola for the advice in which an attorney-client privilege was created.

26. Connie Criminallaw is representing Mega Chemical Corporation which is being investigated by the Environmental Protection Agency (EPA). The allegations are that toxic chemicals were disposed of improperly in violation of the applicable EPA regulations. It is not clear what the government intends to ask for, but some civil and/or criminal sanction seems possible. Mega Chemical's outside auditor has written Connie, seeking to evaluate Mega's litigation exposure so they may decide if a potential liability disclosure should be included in the corporation's annual financial statements. They have asked Connie to author a written evaluation of the potential claim.

Is it proper for Connie to undertake the evaluation?

(A) Yes, even if the client disapproves of the evaluation role because it is not for the client's use.
(B) Yes, with client approval of the evaluation role.
(C) No, unless the client approves of the necessary disclosures.
(D) No, if the lawyer reasonably concludes that truthfully making the evaluation is incompatible with the EPA matter representation.

27. Loretta Loudmouth was representing Paula Plaintiff in a tort action. During a discovery and scheduling conference, the trial judge ruled that the plaintiff's expert Elmer was disqualified and thus ineligible to testify. One week later, Loretta was asked by a TV newsperson to discuss Paula's case. Loretta began to review the case and, in a rambling discussion that went on for two hours, covered a variety of issues. The TV crew taped the whole interview. The final on-the-air summary quoted her on many items, and the defendant's attorney complained to the local state bar association about Loretta's statements.

Which of the following statements made to the newsperson by Loretta were proper?

I. "We believe the complaint is accurate and that the defendant was grossly negligent."
II. "Our expert Elmer believes that res ipsa loquitur applies and that the defendant is thus liable."
III. "The defendant's truck driver refused to take the breathalyzer test, so he must have been driving drunk."
IV. "The defendant and his experts both lied in their depositions, and their lack of credibility is a reflection of their poor character and credibility."

(A) I only.
(B) I and II only.
(C) I and III only.
(D) I, II, III, and IV.

28. Loretta Legislator was a lawyer whose practice was primarily representing property developers. The jurisdiction allows lawyers to serve as part-time legislators and Loretta ran for office and was elected. The state had a law in effect that required property owners to build public parks equal to 20% of the property being developed.

One of Loretta's large clients complained that this made development economically unfeasible. Loretta investigated and after research also concluded that the property owners were being treated unfairly. Loretta therefore co-sponsored legislation that would reduce the public park requirement from 20% to 10% of the land. She did publicly disclose in the legislature that she represented a landowner-developer client that would benefit from the reduction but not their specific identity. The bill was voted down after environmental groups lobbied against its passage.

Is Loretta subject to discipline?

(A) Yes, because the bill was defeated and therefore the bill that Loretta co-sponsored was not in the public interest.
(B) Yes, because Loretta used her public position in an attempt to obtain a special advantage for a private client.
(C) No, because Loretta did not obtain a special advantage for a client that was clearly contrary to the public interest.
(D) No, because an attorney may properly advocate for legislation that benefits a client if another legislator co-sponsors the bill.

29. Ellen Employmentlaw is a lawyer who specializes in human resource law. The senior partner of her law firm asked her to defend Ceilingmart, which had just been sued in a claim alleging numerous human resource violations. One of the lead plaintiffs was Alice Abused. To try to learn more about Alice's personal life, Ellen had a conversation with Alice's neighbor, Nancy. After a few minutes of discussion, Nancy asked Ellen if she represented Ceilingmart. Ellen acknowledged the representation. Ellen did not disclose that Alice had filed suit, and Nancy did not ask.

Was Ellen's conduct in the communications with Nancy proper?

(A) Yes, because she is communicating with an unrepresented party whose loyalty and interest are likely adverse to her client, Ceilingmart.
(B) Yes, because Ellen made no false statements to this third party, and there was no duty to make disclosure of the lawsuit.
(C) No, because she should not have communicated with Nancy at all without Alice's lawyer being present.
(D) No, because this invaded Nancy's right to privacy and solitude.

30. Magna Corporation was sued by Paula Plaintiff, represented by Alice Attorney. The claim was for a low dollar amount, and liability was uncertain. Paula Plaintiff had a prior personal distaste for Magna and its attorney. Still, Magna Corporation had a corporate litigation policy of offering a dollar settlement amount equal to what they expected their legal expenses to be if the case were to be litigated through trial. Magna's attorney thus requested on three different occasions a meeting with Alice Attorney. Alice refused to respond and filed a motion for an expedited trial.

Was Alice's refusal to meet and/or discuss settlement with Magna's attorney proper?

(A) Yes, unless Alice's motive in pursuing the claim was to financially injure Magna.
(B) Yes, unless most attorneys in the jurisdiction would consider a blanket refusal to communicate any settlement possibilities with opposing counsel to be unprofessional.
(C) No, if most attorneys in the jurisdiction would not consider a blanket refusal to communicate any settlement possibilities with opposing counsel to be unprofessional.
(D) No, if Alice's refusal to communicate any settlement possibilities with opposing counsel was primarily to harass Magna Corporation and their counsel.

31. Adam Attorney represented a driver injured in an accident caused by a truck that ran a stop sign. Had the injured driver been alert, the accident with the truck could have easily been avoided. The jurisdiction where the accident occurred still adheres to contributory negligence rather than the more progressive comparative fault standard.

Adam decided to file the lawsuit on the hope the state Supreme Court would use the case to change the law. One week later the comparative fault principle was again rejected by the jurisdiction's Supreme Court. The defendant's attorney filed a motion alleging the complaint was frivolous and sought litigation sanctions under Court Rule 11. Eighteen days later Adam amended the complaint by replacing the reference to contributory negligence with comparative fault.

Is Adam subject to litigation sanctions?

(A) Yes, because Adam knew the theory was not available.
(B) Yes, because there was not a reasonable basis in law for Adam signing and filing the complaint.
(C) No, because Adam amended the complaint timely.
(D) No, because a good faith argument is lacking.

32. Alice Attorney tried a tort case to a jury on behalf of Paula Plaintiff. Paula took the stand, but did not make an effective or credible witness. While the jury held for the plaintiff, the damage award was quite low. Paula was very disappointed and believed the defendant insurance company "got to" one or more of the jurors. She demanded Alice file a motion with the court awarding her the full damage claim notwithstanding the jury verdict. Alice believes that any such motion has virtually no chance and that she cannot make a good faith argument for the motion.

The proper procedure for Alice is to

(A) Withdraw immediately from the case.
(B) Follow Paula Plaintiff's demand, but insist she sign a waiver of any liability claim against Alice's law firm.
(C) Withdraw from the case after ensuring that it will not have a material adverse effect on Paula's interest.
(D) Disregard Paula's demand, file the judgment, and collect the payment from the insurance company.

33. Harriet Hopeful took on the representation of a malpractice case against a doctor and hospital. After discovery was complete, the defendants filed a motion for summary judgment. The motion documents contained affidavits by medical experts that proved the defendants did not cause the plaintiff's injury. Also attached were portions of deposition testimony given by plaintiff in which she admitted to having a pre-existing injury. In granting defendants' summary judgment and dismissing the case, the court remarked, "In my opinion, plaintiff's attorney's claim as filed did not have a reasonable basis in either fact or law, but I cannot state it was frivolous."

Which of the following statements would be true?

I. Harriet Hopeful is "subject to professional discipline."
II. Harriet Hopeful is "subject to litigation sanction."

(A) I only.
(B) II only.
(C) Neither I or II.
(D) Both I and II.

34. Paula Prosecutor was attempting to convict Debra Defendant for the distribution of marijuana. The jury was impaneled for a month to hear multiple criminal cases. The defense in the Debra case was able to convince the criminal jury there was reasonable doubt and 10 days after the trial began acquitted the defendant. The jury was then discharged from that case and assigned back into the jury pool for 10 more days to be picked for other trials. Paula was so upset that they had acquitted Debra that she wrote each juror a letter and stated that what they had done was outrageous and that they should have more consideration for the many broken families destroyed by the drug traffickers.

Is Paula Prosecutor subject to discipline for her letter?

(A) Yes, because this represents an improper attempt to influence the jurors.
(B) Yes, unless opposing counsel is also allowed to send the jurors his own letter.
(C) No, because the jury has been discharged from the case in question.
(D) No, unless there is a court rule or order in effect that prohibits the lawyer from having direct communications with the jurors after the conclusion of the case.

35. Carol Classaction has filed suit against Frontron, an energy company, and an outside auditor alleging a conspiracy to effectuate financial statement fraud. Pre-trial discovery was initiated, which required production of all working papers the outside auditor had prepared to support the opinions it rendered on the company's financial statements. Frontron corporate attorney, Sally Spoliator, ordered the record custodian to shred the accounting files the plaintiff had requested. The answer to the relevant discovery request given by Sally was "none available."

Is Sally Spoliator subject to discipline?

(A) No, if at the time of answering the discovery request, all the records had been spoliated, so the answer is accurate.
(B) No, if Sally herself did not perform the spoliation.
(C) Yes, unless the defendant can prove that the spoliated records were not relevant.
(D) Yes, even though the degree of prejudice to the plaintiff because of the spoliation is uncertain.

36. Pattie Plaintiff was representing a plaintiff injured in an automobile accident. There were extensive pre-trial negotiations between Pattie and the Insurance Company. The negotiations led to a number of settlement offers with the highest one at $75,000. Pattie rejected the $75,000 offer because she thought she could recover a higher sum at trial or that the Insurance Company would later make an enhanced offer. The case did not settle, and in opening arguments at trial, Pattie said, "Why would the defendant's insurance company offer to settle for $75,000 if he was not fully responsible?"

Does Pattie's statement in opening arguments about the settlement offer subject her to discipline?

(A) Yes, if it influenced the jury in their verdict.
(B) Yes, because any settlement negotiations are not admissible.
(C) No, because it is an accurate statement.
(D) No, because the defendant's attorney may argue against it and introduce his own version of the settlement negotiations.

37. Windy Windfall hired Alice Aggressive to sue a CPA. The CPA had issued fraudulent financial statements upon which Windy relied in making a large investment. The complaint alleged the CPA had committed both fraud and negligence in issuing the incorrect financial statements. The defendant's attorney filed a motion for summary judgment on the fraud count. The trial court agreed with the defendant and dismissed the fraud count, stating that "it is a close question." The trial focused on the negligence count. In closing arguments, Alice stated to the jury, "The judge did not let me tell you about the fraud the CPA perpetrated upon the plaintiff, but it was substantial."

Does Alice's statement in closing arguments about the fraud count subject her to discipline?

(A) Yes, because closing arguments may not refer to evidence not introduced during the trial.
(B) Yes, if it influenced the jury in their final verdict.
(C) No, because the defendant's lawyer may argue against the fraud allegation in her closing arguments.
(D) No, because the comment was factual and did not include any of the fraud allegation details.

38. Acme Incorporated is a defendant in a civil action that alleges the corporation committed an *ultra vires* act. Wanda Witness is the corporate general counsel, but she was not involved in the alleged *ultra vires* act. The case did not settle and is to be tried before a jury. Wanda decided to try the case herself and save the money required to retain outside counsel. Towards the end of the presentation of the plaintiff's case, the plaintiff's attorney called Wanda as a hostile witness to testify about the minutes of the corporate Board meetings that she had prepared.

Is Wanda subject to discipline?

(A) Yes, because a lawyer may not be both an advocate and a witness in the same case.
(B) Yes, even if the testimony relates to a mere formality or the value of legal services provided.
(C) No, if the judge determines that disqualification would work a substantial hardship on the client and being called as a witness was not reasonably foreseeable by Wanda.
(D) No, if there is no other lawyer from the corporation who can testify.

39. Shortly after a bank robbery, a police dragnet picked up Carol Criminal and a number of other suspects in the area. They were taken to the local police station. At a lineup, one of the tellers at the bank identified Carol by saying, "I am not sure, but the bank manager said I need to identify someone, and Carol looks close." A criminal indictment later charged Carol with robbery. During the direct testimony at trial, the teller equivocated on the identification on the stand. During the next break in the trial, the prosecutor admitted to the defense attorney that there was some uncertainty in the lineup identification.

Is the Prosecutor's conduct subject to discipline?

(A) Yes, because the prosecutor's disclosure was not made timely.
(B) Yes, because the Prosecutor revealed evidence to the opponent that could have been damaging to the government's prosecution.
(C) No, because the Prosecutor complied with the obligation to make disclosure.
(D) No, as long as the questionable identification was sufficient to support probable cause.

40. Carol Communicator represented a husband in negotiating and satisfying a past due $11,000 judgment for child support. The husband agreed to deposit the $11,000 in the court registry. Carol communicated directly with the wife and eventually persuaded her to settle her claim for $6,000. Carol then drafted a $6,000 settlement agreement, which the husband and wife both signed. The wife did have a lawyer review the agreement. While the agreement stated the ex-wife was to get $6,000, Carol later added a paragraph at the bottom of the last page directing that the $5,000 be paid to the husband.

Carol then went on the *ex parte* calendar and presented an order disbursing $6,000 to the ex-wife and $5,000 to the ex-husband. She told the judge both the wife and her attorney had approved the agreement that was submitted with the proposed order.

Was Carol's action proper?

(A) Yes, because to disclose to the wife that there was actually $11,000 in the registry would be revealing a client's confidence.
(B) Yes, because the statement to the court was true in that the ex-wife and her attorney agreed to the $6,000 settlement.
(C) No, unless the court determines Carol's duty as a client advocate outweighs the responsibility of candor to the court.
(D) No, because there was a duty of disclosure of adverse facts even if they were harmful to Carol's client.

41. Iola Influence is a lawyer and senior partner of a law firm specializes in bankruptcy law. Once a year, the law firm celebrates the summer solstice with a huge party for all the clerks and associates in the local federal bankruptcy office. All bankruptcy court personnel who attend become part of a raffle drawing for cash prizes. Two-thirds of the bankruptcy court personnel who attend receive at least $500 from the raffle.

Is Iola's activity proper?

(A) Yes, as long as none of the cash raffle prizes are given to a judge.
(B) Yes, if Iola and none of the other attorneys in her firm take part in the raffle and related cash distributions.
(C) No, because this party and raffle appear intended to improperly influence the personnel of the federal bankruptcy court.
(D) No, as long as Iola has no intention to influence the personnel of the federal bankruptcy court.

42. Debra Destroyer is a criminal defense attorney who specializes in murder cases. Carol Cutter was arrested and charged with stabbing Victoria Victim with a knife in a tavern after a long night of heavy drinking. Carol called Debra from jail and Debra agreed to undertake the defense.

The next morning Debra posted Carol's bail and together they drove to Debra's law office to discuss the case. In this meeting, Carol gave Debra a large hunting knife and stated "this is what I used to knife Victoria in the tavern, and I was able to hide it in my car before they arrested me." Debra said, "Leave it with me for safe keeping." Debra never did tell the prosecutor she had the fatal weapon.

Debra is most likely subject to discipline because she:

(A) Did not disclose to the prosecutor that Carol removed the knife from the tavern.
(B) Suppressed the knife by not turning it over to the prosecution.
(C) Took custody of the instrument used in the crime.
(D) Did not give the client advice to destroy the knife.

43. Patty Plaintiff was injured in an automobile accident caused by Debra Defendant. Barbara Bulldog undertook the defense for Debra's insurance company. The major issue in the trial was the extent of the soft tissue injury Patty suffered in the accident. Barbara impeached Patty's and her expert witness doctor's testimony by introducing an industrial insurance claim Patty had filed the year before the accident with Debra. The previous claim description covered the same symptoms in the same muscular area that Patty claimed were caused solely by the later accident with Debra. In closing, Barbara stated:

I. "We have proven the doctor for this insurance fraud is not credible."
II. "Everyone in this courtroom knows this is a fraudulent insurance claim."
III. "Patty's testimony is in direct conflict with her action in the previous industrial insurance claim."
IV. "As between Patty and Debra, who has the better reason to fabricate a story?"

For which of the above statements would Barbara be subject to discipline?

(A) I only.
(B) II only.
(C) I and II only.
(D) I, II, III, and IV.

44. Alice and Connie were in business together as a partnership and began to disagree. Alice retained Betty Lawyer to bring suit against Connie, seeking a partnership dissolution. Connie hired Debra to defend her in the action. While Betty and Debra talked about a settlement, the two former partners were far apart in the dollar amount. It appeared that the case was going to trial.

One Sunday afternoon, Betty attended a local baseball game with her two children. She was quite surprised when Connie and her two children seated themselves directly in the row in front of her. The children were about the same ages and immediately began talking and joking together. Betty and Connie said a few words to each other about the game and their children, but Betty was careful not to mention the lawsuit. As the game was ending, Connie said, "My lawyer was wrong about you, and the last settlement offer Alice made was reasonable. I am going to tell Debra to accept it." Betty did not respond.

The next morning Connie called Debra, explained she and Betty had attended the baseball game, and directed Debra to sign the settlement agreement on her behalf. Debra did as her client instructed, but filed a bar association grievance against Betty.

Is Betty subject to discipline?

(A) Yes, because her discussion with Connie at the baseball game was *ex parte*.
(B) Yes, because she communicated with Connie, knowing that she was represented by Debra.
(C) No, if Betty did not know she would be seated one row above Connie.
(D) No, because Betty discussed only the baseball game and their children.

45. For a number of years, Alice Anderdaughter, CPAs, had conducted a certified audit of Beginron, a diversified energy company. Beginron had financial problems, and top management devised elaborate accounting schemes to conceal the true operating losses. The CPA firm had begun to doubt the veracity of the statements and representations they had received from Beginron's top management.

On October 2004, articles began appearing in the financial publications that alleged Beginron was "cooking the books." About this same time, the lawyer for Alice Anderdaughter, CPAs', head office sent a memo to the field office performing the Beginron audit. The memo reminded the staff that the CPA firm's national "record retention policy" was to shred all workpapers and other documents over two years old supporting the financial statement audit.

On January 1, 2005, the US Department of Justice filed a lawsuit against both Beginron and the auditor Alice Anderdaughter, CPAs.

The summons the CPA firm received on January 2, 2005 with the complaint stated that an answer or notice of appearance must be filed within 60 days. One of the allegations in the complaint stated that the details of the CPA firm's malpractice would be proven by analysis of the CPA's working papers. The CPA firm kept shredding all the documents and on February 28 filed a general denial to the complaint.

On March 15, the plaintiff served on the CPA firm a request to produce their audit working papers. On April 15, the CPA firm responded that none were available because they had all been shredded pursuant to the accounting firm's "record retention policy."

The plaintiff filed a motion for partial summary judgment and for litigation sanctions against the lawyer for the accounting firm.

Should the litigation sanctions be imposed?

- **(A)** Yes, because at least on February 28, 2005, the CPA firm had notice the government had a proceeding pending in which the accounting workpapers had foreseeable potential evidentiary importance.
- **(B)** Yes, because on March 15, 2005, the CPA firm had notice the government had an expectation that the workpapers had potential evidentiary value.
- **(C)** No, unless the lawyer for the accounting firm intended to commit a fraud on the court by document spoliation.
- **(D)** No, unless the lawyer for the accounting firm specifically directed the accounting firm to commit a fraud on the court by document spoliation.

46. Florence Familylaw has a law practice in Splendidtown. Harry Heavyhand retained Florence to negotiate a child support issue with his ex-wife, Sally. Sally had apparently written Harry a number of letters requesting that he pay college support for their children. Florence called Sally on the phone and explained that she represented her ex-husband Harry and that he wanted to "do the right thing for their children." Florence asked Sally who was representing her, and she said, "I have no lawyer." Florence stated, "Well, I represent your ex-husband, whose interest is adverse to yours. I can't give you advice, and you should hire your own lawyer." Sally responded that "I can't afford to pay a lawyer, and what is Harry proposing?" Florence then said, "He is willing to pay $25,000 per child per year for all the children's post-secondary education."

The next day, Sally came into Florence's office and signed the revised child support agreement containing the new college support terms.

Is Florence subject to discipline for directly negotiating with Sally, whose interests are contrary to those of Florence's client?

- **(A)** Yes, because Sally's interest is directly adverse to that of Florence's client Harry.
- **(B)** Yes, because representing both a husband and wife is a fundamentally antagonistic conflict that is not waivable.
- **(C)** No, because Florence advised Sally to retain her own lawyer.
- **(D)** No, because Sally waived the right to complain about Florence representing both parties.

47. Acme Corporation had all their legal work done by the Big & Tall law firm. Sharon Short, an associate of the firm, helped corporate top management during negotiations in an infringement and unfair trade practices dispute with their major competitor. The competitor orally agreed with Sharon that the infringed assets' royalty rate would be subject to negotiations anytime after one year. Two years later Acme tried to open negotiations on the royalty rate, and their competitor claimed they never agreed to anything about renegotiations. Acme filed suit for breach of contract. By this time, Sharon had been promoted to partner status at Big & Tall. Sharon's partner, Patty Partner, signed the summons and complaint. The subsequent pre-trial listing of witnesses included Sharon Short as a witness.

One month before trial, the competitor's attorney filed a motion to disqualify any lawyer from the Big & Tall law firm. The theory was that the law firm would be acting as both a witness and an advocate at trial.

Is Patty Partner properly subject to disqualification?

- **(A)** Yes, because disqualification for one lawyer in a law firm is a disqualification for all lawyers in the law firm.
- **(B)** Yes, because Sharon's testimony does not concern a minor uncontested issue in the case.
- **(C)** No, because Sharon is a necessary witness.
- **(D)** No, because a lawyer or law firm is not usually disqualified merely because another lawyer in the firm will testify as a trial witness.

48. Charlie Criminal is a racketeer whom the government believes controls the local mafia and illegal drug trade. For many years, Charlie has used Larry Lowlife as his sole lawyer. Patty Prosecutor is under a great deal of political pressure to press charges against Charlie and his associates. Every witness she has convinced to come forward and testify has disappeared, and Patty believes Larry is involved in the disappearances. Frustrated, Patty issues a subpoena to Larry Lowlife requiring him to present evidence about Charlie Criminal's illegal activities. Patty Prosecutor justifies the subpoena for the following three reasons.

I. The information sought is not protected from disclosure by any applicable privilege.
II. The evidence sought is essential to the prosecution.
III. There is no other feasible alternative to obtain the information.

If Larry files a bar grievance against Patty Prosecutor, Patty may escape discipline if she can show

(A) Item I above only.
(B) Item I and item II.
(C) Item I and item III.
(D) Item I, item II, and item III.

49. Denise Defense attorney is defending Big Bucks Incorporated in a stockholder derivative action alleging fraudulent financial reporting. Big Bucks relied upon some information provided by their outside auditor, Price Airhouse. The plaintiffs' attorney contacted the auditors and requested an informal private meeting to discuss the history of their involvement in the case. The auditor then called Denise and asked her how they should respond to the request. Denise answered, "Do not talk to their side about this case unless you get served with a subpoena." There was no accountant-client privilege statute in the jurisdiction at the time.

Was Denise's advice to Price Airhouse proper?

(A) Yes, because Price Airhouse was operating as Big Bucks' agent in the matter at issue.
(B) Yes, because it was improper for the plaintiffs' attorney to attempt an informal meeting with the auditors.
(C) No, because Denise interfered with the plaintiffs' attorney's right to meet informally with an important witness.
(D) No, because there was no accountant-client privilege statute in the jurisdiction.

50. Betty Bigmouth was attending a political rally where Pattie Political was making a speech in her hotly contested campaign for mayor. After Pattie had made a few statements about her political policies, Betty jumped up and screamed that Pattie was a liar and a crooked politician. Pattie was very embarrassed by Betty's statements and considered her slander very damaging. Pattie hired Loretta Litigator to sue Betty. Loretta researched the applicable law and concluded there may be a privilege that applied to statements about public affairs of a public figure.

Is it proper for Loretta to file the suit?

(A) Yes, as long as Loretta informs Betty's attorney that there is a privilege that can be asserted as a defense.
(B) Yes, as long as Loretta understands that there is a privilege that can be asserted as a defense and is still willing to pay for the representation.
(C) No, because the privilege means the claim has no chance of ultimately prevailing and thus is frivolous.
(D) No, unless Pattie consents to disclose to the court that there is an absolute privilege.

51. Debra Druggey was arrested for drug distribution by the police in this state. She was charged with one felony count and assigned attorney Barbara Bulldog by the public defender's office. While preparing for trial, Debra confessed to Barbara that she had two prior convictions for narcotic violations in the Next state. Apparently, the prosecutor either failed to check for other offenses outside the jurisdiction or checked under incorrect names. There was a "three strikes" statute in this state requiring the judge to impose a life sentence for the third related conviction. During the sentencing the judge stated, "I find you guilty, but because you are a first-time offender, I am going to sentence you to only two years." Public Defender Barbara stood silent during the sentence hearing.

Is Barbara subject to discipline?

- **(A)** Yes, because Barbara was under a duty to reveal the defendant's prior convictions only if they occurred in the court's jurisdiction.
- **(B)** Yes, because Barbara was under a duty to reveal the prior convictions in Next state.
- **(C)** No, because the information at issue was the confidential information of the client.
- **(D)** No, because the failure to include the prior offenses in the sentencing was not based upon any false statement of the defendant or her attorney.

52. Dorothy Deceptive was defending a professional malpractice case filed by a former client *pro se* against a lawyer named Francis Flighty. Dorothy filed a motion for summary judgment asserting that there are no material facts in controversy, and the controlling state law clearly dictates dismissal. In fact, the controlling state law is far from clear, and a recent Supreme Court decision reversed a very similar summary judgment. Dorothy mentioned the case in her brief, but only discussed some dicta that partially favored her client's position. The *pro se* plaintiff was too busy to research the law and controlling case because she believed the factual questions would control and require a trial. The judge did not have time to research the legal authority stated in the brief in any detail and therefore denied the summary judgment motion on the basis that there were facts remaining for the jury's decision.

Is Dorothy subject to discipline?

- **(A)** Yes, because Dorothy should have disclosed the unfavorable legal precedent.
- **(B)** Yes, because a lawyer must always cite opposing authority.
- **(C)** No, because the summary judgment motion was denied, so there was no harm.
- **(D)** No, because a lawyer has a responsibility to her clients to present only the portion of the law in their favor.

53. Pattie Plaintiff, who was represented by Dorothy Delay, filed a lawsuit against Denise Doctor alleging she was injured by an unspecified act of medical malpractice. The defendant hired Sally Dismissitall to represent her in the action. Sally served a set of Interrogations and Requests for Admission upon Dorothy. 30 days later, when the answers were due, Sally received a call from Dorothy explaining she was behind and needed an extra 10 days to comply with the discovery. Sally agreed and wrote Dorothy a confirming letter. 10 days went by, and nothing had been produced. Dorothy had left a telephone message on Sally's voice mail asking for more time. Sally then noted Pattie's deposition for 15 days later. On the deposition date, Dorothy showed up and stated that Pattie was unable to attend and explained the answers to the discovery requests were not yet complete.

In response, Sally filed a motion to compel and for sanctions with the court to be heard 12 days later. At the hearing, Dorothy explained that Pattie was on vacation, and she had been too busy to complete the discovery requests. The judge entered an order specifying that sanctions would be imposed against both Pattie and Dorothy if the plaintiff did not appear for the deposition, and the discovery requests were not returned within 20 days. 20 days expired without Dorothy presenting the completed discovery or Pattie Plaintiff appearing for her deposition. The trial court judge on motion dismissed the complaint and entered an order requiring both Pattie Plaintiff and Dorothy each to pay one-half of the defense costs.

Was the trial court correct in the sanction imposed upon attorney Dorothy?

- **(A)** Yes, because the lawsuit obviously had no merit.
- **(B)** Yes, because the lawyer and client violated the court's discovery order.
- **(C)** No, because dismissing the complaint was too draconian a measure.
- **(D)** No, because an attorney should not be penalized if her client refuses to comply with a discovery order.

54. Terry Timid was in a bar on a Friday evening. The bar bouncer was told by the bartender that Terry had started a fight and should be bounced out. The bouncer grabbed Terry, who complained that she had done nothing wrong. The bouncer threw her down the stairs thereby causing serious injury rendering Terry unconscious for three days. Terry hired Alice Accommodation to file the suit against the bar and bouncer. The defendants hired Harriet Hardball and told her to do whatever it took to settle the case.

Harriet immediately scheduled a settlement conference with Alice. In the meeting, she stated, "We have three eye witnesses who will testify Terry started the fight after screaming at other customers, so the whole claim is fraudulent." None of this was true, but Terry could not remember any of the details of the evening since she was unconscious for three days due to her injuries. Because of this major uncertainty, Alice recommended and Terry reluctantly accepted a nominal $10,000 cash settlement to dismiss the claim.

Is Harriet Hardball subject to discipline?

- **(A)** Yes, because the payment of $10,000 to settle a fraudulent claim is improper.
- **(B)** No, because settlement bluffing is a generally accepted convention in settlement negotiations.
- **(C)** Yes, because Harriet made a material statement of fact that she knew was false.
- **(D)** No, because Harriet's bluff discovered a fraudulent claim by the plaintiff.

55. Carol Creditor hired Frances Facilitator to file a two million dollar collection lawsuit against a debtor who was in default on a promissory note. The case was assigned to Judge Debra Desperate. One evening during the trial, Frances was having dinner alone in a restaurant, and Judge Desperate walked into the room. Since she was alone, Frances invited the judge to join her and she accepted. During the dinner, the trial was not discussed, but the judge confided that she was having difficulty borrowing $100,000 to pay her daughter's tuition for law school.

The next morning a messenger delivered to the judge's chambers a check for $100,000 from Frances that had a note attached stating, "Hope this helps." Subsequently, the parties settled the collection lawsuit, so it was not necessary for Judge Desperate to make any discretionary decisions in the case.

Is Frances subject to criminal liability for providing the $100,000 to Judge Desperate?

(A) Yes, if Frances' $100,000 advance was intended to influence the Judge in deciding Carol's collection action.
(B) Yes, if Judge Desperate intended to decide for Carol's position after Frances advanced the $100,000.
(C) No, because the judge never made a discretionary decision in the case.
(D) No, if the judge either refused to accept or promptly returned the $100,000 to Frances.

56. A criminal robbery and murder trial is being conducted in front of a jury in Everytown. Prosecutor Pattie is presenting the murder case for the prosecution. Dorothy Defendant, after consultation with her attorney, has elected to claim the Fifth Amendment privilege and not testify in the trial. Her husband testified in the trial that Dorothy was elsewhere at the time and therefore could not have been at the robbery scene. Two other defendants have reached a plea agreement with the prosecution, and Pattie feels their testimony is crucial to proving Dorothy was the ringleader.

During the trial and in closing argument, Prosecutor Pattie stated to the jury:

I. "In 20 years of prosecuting capital crimes, you develop a sense of the truthfulness of a witness. I don't think Dorothy's husband was testifying truthfully about this alibi, and neither should you."
II. "The defendant's two fellow criminals have testified for you that Dorothy shot the victim, leading to the death. If she was innocent, she would have taken the stand and denied it."
III. "The two fellow criminals in this murder trial have told you that the defendant's husband's testimony of an alibi was at least mistaken and likely perjury."
IV. "How reliable is the testimony of the defendant's husband? We have introduced proof that he has been convicted of perjury in the past and that clearly indicates dishonesty."
V. "This criminal has been tried twice before for manslaughter and got off both times. Now is the time to put her away for good."

Which of the above statements by Prosecutor Pattie are proper?

(A) None of the above.
(B) One of the above.
(C) Two of the above.
(D) Three of the above.

57. Paula Prosecutor was the leader of a team of investigators and law enforcement personnel investigating a series of armed robberies in Smallville. In the latest robbery, the store clerk resisted, and one of the robbers shot her dead. The Prosecutor's team arrested a number of defendants. Paula formally charged five people with armed robbery and murder. One of the prosecution investigators working on Paula's team attended a news conference and in response to a television reporter's inquiry stated:

I. "We have arrested and have in custody three of the five defendants. Sally Smith and Julie Jones are still at large and should be considered armed and dangerous."
II. "These three defendants have refused to make a statement about their involvement in this terrible crime or the location of the other two robbers involved in this murder."
III. She then showed photos of Sally and Julie and stated, "Anyone seeing these defendants should please call our office."

For which of the above statements made by the investigator is Paula Prosecutor potentially subject to discipline?

(A) None, unless she directed the investigator to make the extrajudicial statements.
(B) I, II, and III.
(C) II only.
(D) III only.

58. Loretta Lawyer was in a busy bar in Manhattan with a college friend named Victoria Victim. A man named Slugger Snake asked Victoria to dance, and she refused. Slugger kept bothering the two women. Finally Victoria told him, "Leave us alone, you flake." In response, Slugger backhanded Victoria across her face, knocking her across the room. She fell onto a concrete fireplace and cracked her skull. Dozens of people in the bar observed the whole incident. After extensive surgery for her head injury, Victoria hired Loretta Lawyer to bring suit against Slugger. Slugger's attorney brought a motion to disqualify Loretta because she was a fact witness of the event itself.

Should the disqualification be granted?

(A) Yes, because there is a possibility that Loretta will be called as a fact witness.
(B) Yes, unless Loretta has a partner in her law firm who could assume the advocacy role if Loretta is called as a fact witness.
(C) No, as long as the client Victoria Victim consents to Loretta testifying after receiving full disclosure of all the risks of combining the role of advocate and witness.
(D) No, because Loretta is not a necessary witness.

59. Laura Lawyer was retained to defend the management of Big Bucks, Inc. in a wrongful termination claim alleged by Elise Employee. Elise had filed a number of complaints with federal agencies, and the management of Big Bucks was very concerned about creating a negative public impression. Elise did not hire a lawyer. Laura met Elise in a grocery store by accident, and they had a long conversation.

In the conversation, Elise asked, "What does it take to prove wrongful termination?" Laura said, "Well, you should hire a lawyer to represent you who could answer that question." Elise responded, "I have no money to hire a lawyer, but I would like to settle this claim." Laura then said, "I have no personal interest to litigate, only to make you whole. I think I can talk Big Bucks into paying you $50,000. As you know, this is a lot of money." Elise said, "If you can get them to pay that amount, I will take it." Unbeknownst to Elise, Big Bucks had given Laura settlement authority up to $100,000.

Is Laura subject to discipline for her handling of the matter?

- **(A)** Yes, because it is improper for a lawyer to communicate with an adverse party prior to the time she hires a lawyer, and the $50,000 settlement offer was insufficient if the client was willing to pay $100,000.
- **(B)** Yes, because Laura pretended to be objectively disinterested and advised Elise to accept an insufficient settlement.
- **(C)** No, because Laura advised Elise to hire her own lawyer.
- **(D)** No, because Laura only stated her opinion in recommending a settlement she knew Big bucks would accept.

60. Alice Aggressive represented a plaintiff suing a medical doctor for malpractice. Alice was trying to build her case and subpoenaed for a deposition all the patients of the doctor defendant. During the deposition, Alice inquired into each deponent's personal life, including their martial and sexual life and alcohol and drug use. If the answers Alice received from the deponent were at all embarrassing or culpable, she asked the witness if he or she would be willing to testify against the doctor defendant.

Was Alice's questioning such that she should be subject to discipline?

- **(A)** Yes, unless there was a substantial purpose other than to embarrass or unreasonably burden the deponent.
- **(B)** Yes, because the questions included personal information.
- **(C)** No, because such questions may lead to discoverable information.
- **(D)** No, because discovery is intended to uncover all material facts to avoid trial by ambush.

61. Terry Takeadvantage was a plaintiff attorney in a wrongful death action against Mega Pharmaceutical Co. Mega manufactures the drug that killed the plaintiff. Terry has undertaken very extensive discovery on the manufacturing practices of Mega, including requesting copies of all relevant internal memorandums. The defendant responded to all discovery requests by stating that they had no internal memos on their manufacturing process.

Terry received an email copy of a Mega internal memo that had been sent to them. The return email address was Mega's law firm, and Terry was not sure if this was sent in error or someone at Mega's Law Firm was discussed at the stonewalling. The document proved that Mega was aware of the life-threatening potential of the drug, but failed to make corrections to save money. This memorandum had not been previously produced by the defendant.

To comply with professional standards, Terry should

(A) Return the document if he can determine whom the sender was.
(B) Not use the document in pursuing the wrongful death case.
(C) Voluntarily withdraw from representing the plaintiff in the case because he has seen the defendant's "smoking gun" memorandum.
(D) File a motion with the court seeking a holding that the disclosure waived the privileged status of the document and seek sanctions against Mega and their attorney for failure to produce the document in question.

62. Alice Argument was retained as a defense attorney by Dorothy Defendant, whom Patty Prosecutor has charged with homicide. Patty Prosecutor's office was overworked and she argued to Dorothy it was a waste of resources to have to try the case since there were direct eyewitnesses and no question that Dorothy committed the offense. She thus told Alice that her defense of Dorothy was frivolous and sanctions could be imposed against the lawyer personally.

Alice refused Patty's settlement offers and after extensive discovery, insisted upon taking the case to trial. Dorothy did not take the stand. The jury found Dorothy guilty and many jurors commented that the defense presented virtually no case at all. Patty Prosecutor was outraged that she had to assign her limited resources to the case in order to get the conviction. She further believed the defense was too weak to ever carry the jury verdict and that Alice's arguments lacked merit and credibility.

Patty is considering filing a complaint against Alice with the Bar Association. If a complaint is filed, the likely outcome would be that it was proper for Alice to

(A) Assert a frivolous defense, at least to the extent of making the State prove every element required to prosecute Dorothy.
(B) Present evidence at trial of another possible suspect even though she knew such evidence to be false.
(C) Have accepted Patty Prosecutor's original offer of a proposed settlement.
(D) To withdraw from representing Dorothy on the eve of the trial because she was afraid of Patty Prosecutor's threats of a bar complaint being filed against her personally.

Chapter 4

Counselor, Advocate, and Third Party Dealings

Answers

MPRE Tip: Put a piece of paper over the answers and "mask down" while working through the questions so you don't accidently peek at the next answer.

1. **/B/** While MRPC 3.6 might prohibit such statements if made extra-judicially, here the statement is being made in court. MRPC 3.5 might apply if the lawyer's conduct was intended to disrupt a tribunal. MRPC 3.4, in comparison, prohibits a lawyer from stating a personal opinion on the culpability of a civil litigant. This is the best answer. Badgering the witness is also present, and Gary's attorney could object; the court likely would sustain the objection and direct the attorney to move on. **(A)** is incorrect because the lawyer's raised voice does not of itself violate the MRPCs. **(C)** is incorrect because a natural reaction may explain why the violation occurred; it does not, however, justify the violation. **(D)** is not the best answer because while the lawyer could put in evidence of Gary's false testimony, he cannot state his personal opinion on the witness' credibility.

2. **/B/** MRPC 3.1 prohibits an attorney from bringing or defending a position unless there is a non-frivolous basis involving a good faith belief that the argument has merit. Even assuming the case law is contrary to current law, the argument would be permissible as a potential reversal of existing law. **(A)** is incorrect because "all arguments" is too broad, and even zealous advocacy is subject to the good faith, non-frivolous standard. **(C)** is not the best answer because the meritorious claim requirement does not require the attorney to distinguish as long as there is a good faith argument for the reversal of existing law. **(D)** is incorrect because even if the court so concluded, the attorney may still have the required good faith belief that the argument is not frivolous and has merit.

3. **/A/** MRPC 3.1(4)(b) specifies that a lawyer shall not knowingly assist a witness in offering evidence that the lawyer knows is false. While here the falsity is coming from the mouth of the client (rather than from the lawyer), the lawyer knew the client was going to lie at trial. **(B)** is not the best answer. While "the lawyer is required to take reasonable remedial measures after they learn of the falsity," this remedial measure mitigates rather than excuses the breach of the disciplinary rule. **(C)** is incorrect because the lawyer knew that the client was going to lie when she put the witness on the stand. **(D)** is incorrect; while the statements in this alternative may be accurate, they do not excuse the lawyer's violation of her ethical duty not to knowingly put up false evidence in that this is assisting in falsifying evidence. [MRPC 3.4(b)]

4. **/D/** *Ex parte* communication by a lawyer to a judge of a contested matter without at least notifying opposing counsel is a violation of MRPC 3.5(a). **(A)** is incorrect because merely suggesting the matter be reopened is a violation of the rule independent of the decision that the judge ultimately reaches. **(B)** is incorrect because the *ex parte* communication is a violation independent of the subsequent proceedings. **(C)** is not the best answer because it focuses upon the result of the ex parte communication, not the basic impropriety of the communication itself.

5. **/A/** Item I is the only witness compensation method – payment of a fact witnesses costs – that is allowed in most jurisdictions. [MRPC 3.4] Item II is improper because fact witnesses may not be compensated on a contingency basis. Item III is improper because the payment of the fee is contingent upon the nature of the expert's testimony. Item IV is improper because it involves the payment of an expert witness on a contingency basis; this is improper even if the attorney is being compensated on a contingency basis. **(B)** is incorrect because fact witnesses may not be compensated on a contingency basis. **(C)** is incorrect because the payment of the fee is contingent upon the nature of the expert's testimony. **(D)** is incorrect because it involves the payment of an expert witness on a contingency basis; this is improper even if the attorney is being compensated on a contingency basis.

6. **/B/** The best answer because a lawyer shall not knowingly fail to correct a false statement previously made to the tribunal. [MRPC 3.3(a)(3)] While the Rule would allow "reasonable remedial measures," the explanation to the tribunal as to why the estate report misstated receipts might lead to the judge asking questions that would reveal Harry's embezzlement. **(A)** is not the best answer even though in many jurisdictions, the estate attorney owes some duty to the estate beneficiaries. The duty of candor to the tribunal is paramount. **(C)** is incorrect because MRPC 1.6 confidentiality restraints are limited to representation of a client, and the facts state that the lawyer is representing the estate, not Harry. **(D)** is incorrect because withdrawal is not sufficient if the lawyer learns false evidence was offered, there must be reasonable remedial measures including, if necessary, disclosure to the tribunal.

7. **/D/** A lawyer who is representing a client before a legislative body or administrative agency must disclose that the appearance is in a representative capacity, so the consequence of any biases may be considered. [MRPC 3.9] **(A)** is incorrect because the representative capacity should have been disclosed even if the lawyer was not compensated. **(B)** is incorrect because disclosure of the client's identity is not the central issue; the lawyer must at least disclose that she is testifying on behalf of an interested client and not in her own capacity. **(C)** is incorrect because the outcome of the rule-making proceedings is not the central issue. Regardless of the outcome, the lawyer should have disclosed she was appearing and testifying in a representative capacity and not in her own capacity.

8. **/B/** The Assistant Prosecuting Attorney must make timely disclosure to the defense of all information that tends to negate the guilt of the accused or mitigate the magnitude of the offense. [MRPC 3.8(d)] **(A)** is incorrect because a prosecutor must make timely disclosure of exculpatory evidence regardless of the trial's outcome. **(C)** is incorrect because the requirement to disclose applies even if the defense attorney did not request the information. **(D)** is incorrect because probable harmless error in the outcome does not excuse the requirement to make disclosure of exculpatory evidence.

9. **/D/** A lawyer shall not act as an advocate in a trial where the lawyer is likely to be a necessary witness concerning a material contested question of fact; here the lawyer is a necessary witness on the competency question which is the key disputed issue. [MRPC 3.7] **(A)** is incorrect because the party who will benefit from the lawyer's testimony is not the central issue of whether a lawyer should operate in the dual role of advocate and necessary material witness in the same case. **(B)** is incorrect because how the opponents will testify is not the central issue of whether the lawyer should be both the advocate and a material witness. **(C)** is not the best answer because who benefits from the lawyer's testimony does not excuse a lawyer operating in the dual conflicting role of advocate and necessary witness in the same case.

10. /C/ The ethical standard to avoid discipline is a non-frivolous good faith argument that the case had merit. [MRPC 3.1] **(A)** is incorrect because the legal standard for a dispositive conclusion on summary judgment is different from that for an ethical violation. **(B)** is incorrect because the issue here is whether there was a good faith argument to bring the lawsuit, not if there might be some reputational damage resulting from the filing. **(D)** is incorrect because a "reasonable basis" is the legal threshold for Civil Rule 11 sanctions, not the "good faith" ethical standard.

11. /A/ The best answer because a lawyer shall not communicate with a corporate manager that is represented by a lawyer in the same case without the consent of opposing counsel. [MRPC 4.2] **(B)** is not the best answer because where an organization such as a corporation is a party, the "no contact" rule applies to all persons with managerial responsibility. **(C)** is incorrect; the proper procedure would be to bring a Motion of Contempt on the basis that the defendant failed to comply with a previous Order to Produce. **(D)** is incorrect because while Iola did have the right to take depositions, that does not justify violating the "no contact with represented persons" rule.

12. /D/ Communications outside of court with a juror are usually improper regardless of whether the case is discussed or not. [MRPC 3.3 and 3.5] **(A)** is incorrect because limiting the topics discussed does not cure the violation. **(B)** is incorrect because notifying opposing counsel of the *ex parte* juror communication does not cure the violation. **(C)** is incorrect because notifying both opposing counsel and the judge does not cure the violation.

13. /B/ This statement would likely materially prejudice the criminal proceeding, and giving it to a criminal reporter means it is likely that it will be reported in the media. [MRPC 3.6] **(A)** is incorrect because statements about ongoing criminal prosecution that do not materially prejudice the criminal proceeding may be made. **(C)** is not the best answer because the facts do not state that the plea agreement offered has yet been formally entered into the public court record. **(D)** is incorrect because the test is whether the statement could materially prejudice the criminal proceeding.

14. /A/ The best answer because a lawyer may not directly contact a person represented by counsel in a matter unless their counsel approves. [MRPC 4.2] Here the lawyer induced another to violate on ethical rule that the lawyer could not do directly. [MRPC 8.4(a)] **(B)** is incorrect because opposing counsel usually has to pre-approve direct contact with their clients prior to the contact. **(C)** is not the best answer because it does not specify who gave the authorization. **(D)** is not the best answer because leaving a message is not the same as receiving pre-approval.

15. /D/ The best answer because "everyone in this courtroom" includes attorney Alice Aggressive, and a lawyer may not express a personal opinion as to the culpability of a civil litigant. [MRPC 3.4(e)] **(A)** is not the best answer because arguing the evidence is different from expressing a personal opinion as to the culpability of a civil litigant. **(B)** is incorrect because the lawyer's belief does not create an exception to the rule that a lawyer may not express a personal opinion as to the culpability of a civil litigant. **(C)** is not the best answer because a lawyer can usually properly predict about the conclusion the jury will reach.

16. /B/ The best answer because the duty to disclose to the tribunal false evidence entered in the proceeding terminates at the end of the proceeding; here, the lawyer learned of the false evidence later, so disclosure violates the duty of confidentiality. [MRPC 3.3 and MPRE 1.6] **(A)** is incorrect because while the attorney-client privilege would apply as it relates to general disclosure, it does not override the duty of candor which requires disclosure to the tribunal. **(C)** is incorrect because the duty to report to the tribunal terminates with the proceeding, and thus any knowledge the lawyer acquires later need not be reported. **(D)** is not the best answer because whether the doctor's fraud was reported to the medical authorities is irrelevant to the dilemma of a lawyer's duty to report false evidence to the tribunal and the client's confidentiality.

17. /A/ The best answer because a lawyer functioning as a intermediary may not subsequently represent any of the parties in any matter that was the subject of a prior neutral assignment; here the land was a different subject and the subsequent dispute involved a partnership. [MRPC 2.2] **(B)** is not the best answer because the disqualification on future representation only applies if the matter was the subject of the prior intermediation. **(C)** is incorrect because mandatory reclusion applies only if the subsequent matter was the subject of the prior intermediation. **(D)** is not the best answer because a written consent to the subsequent representation is necessary only if the subsequent matter was the subject of the prior intermediation.

18. /B/ A lawyer shall not unlawfully obstruct opposing counsel's access to evidence, including witnesses. [MRPC 3.4(a)] **(A)** is incorrect because subsequent cooperation does not cure the previous unlawful obstruction. **(C)** is incorrect because the fact that the subpoena was not served does not excuse the unlawful obstruction. **(D)** is incorrect because the direction to the key witness to conceal himself was sufficient to constitute unlawful obstruction.

19. /C/ The best answer since this is the criteria stated in Comment 1 to MRPC 3.2 Expediting Litigation. **(A)** is not the best answer – but certainly a compelling distractor – because there normally is no duty to the opposing party and perhaps Eunice should have financed herself any desirable medical attention. **(B)** is incorrect because court sanction is not a prerequisite to professional discipline. **(D)** is not as good an answer as **(C)** because defense lawyers usually find that the passage of time improves their settlement possibilities, and this may maximize the lawyer's monetary gain.

20. /C/ A lawyer cannot communicate directly with an opposing party without the permission of opposing counsel unless authorized by law or court rule. [MRPC 4.2] **(A)** is incorrect because while an attorney has an obligation to submit all settlement offers to the client [MRPC 1.2(c)], this is not opposing counsel's responsibility and the client's lawyer should have the right to choose the details of the time and way to best present the settlement offer to their client. **(B)** is incorrect because this is still direct communication with a represented party and the violation is not excused because one copy of the letter was sent to the opposing party's lawyer. **(D)** is not the best answer because this does not excuse the violation of the "no contact" rule; the correct procedure is likely to inform the court and seek an appropriate order.

21. **/D/** The best answer because while a lawyer shall not communicate with another party who is represented by a lawyer, there is usually no restriction on the clients engaging in direct negotiations. [MRPC 4.2] **(A)** is incorrect because the lawyer has not communicated with a represented opposing party, and there is no rule against giving the client advice if the client decides to negotiate directly with the opposing party. **(B)** is incorrect because there is not a requirement of a direct lawyer-to-lawyer communication, even if an attorney has knowledge that her client plans on contacting the opposing party directly. **(C)** is incorrect because it is not necessary that an attorney withdraw before her client is allowed to contact the opposing party in the litigation.

22. **/A/** The correct answer because all three of the methods of investigation given are proper. (Note that in some jurisdictions, prior leave of court may be required.) A juror may be investigated by a lawyer or a private detective after the jury has been discharged unless prohibited by law or court order, or the lawyer engages in improper conduct during the communication. [MRPC 3.5(c)] Since there appears to be a legitimate purpose for the investigation and interview, the lawyer has a purpose other than embarrassing, delaying, or burdening the members of the jury. [MRPC 4.4(a)] **(B)** is incorrect because it involves a wrong combination of alternatives. **(C)** is incorrect because it involves a wrong combination of alternatives. **(D)** is incorrect because it involves a wrong combination of alternatives.

23. **/B/** A criminal prosecutor must refrain from prosecuting a criminal proceeding against a defendant that the prosecutor knows is not supported by probable cause. [MRPC 3.8(a)] **(A)** is not the best answer because the end does not justify improper means used by a prosecutor. **(C)** is incorrect because the indictment by the grand jury itself has been induced without any probable cause and therefore is improper even if there is not a subsequent prosecution. **(D)** is incorrect because the greater good and public interest against crime does not excuse improper conduct by a prosecutor.

24. **/C/** A lawyer should not be deterred from giving candid advice by the prospect that the advice will be unpleasant or even unpalatable to the client. [MRPC 2.1, section 2 of commentary] A true-false approach may be helpful in this negative question. **(A)** is incorrect because criticism of the venture's proponent would be proper. **(B)** is incorrect because referring to relevant moral and ethical considerations would be proper. If objective advice is unpleasant, a lawyer may put it in as acceptable a form as honesty permits. **(D)** is not the best answer because the new business venture would likely be deemed confidential, so this would not be improper. Note: depending on facts and circumstances not stated in the question, a lawyer might be permitted to reveal the confidence because of the future potential for catastrophic effects.

25. **/C/** A lawyer may not communicate *ex parte* with an impaneled juror about issues that the lawyer know relate to the juror's case. [MRPC 3.5(c)] **(A)** is incorrect because the no *ex parte* juror communication rule does not have an exception for family members. **(B)** is incorrect because *ex parte* juror communications are improper regardless of whether the lawyer was involved in the case in question. **(D)** is not the best answer because jurors are not usually allowed to enter into an attorney-client relationship concerning the matter in which they are serving as a juror.

26. /D/ The best answer because the lawyer must reasonably conclude that truthfully making the evaluation is incompatible with the lawyer's other representations for the client. [MRPC 2.3] **(A)** is incorrect because the interests of the client and the CPA could be in conflict. **(B)** is not the best answer because it omits any confidentiality concern [MRPC 1.6] and the requirement that the lawyer does not believe any incompatibility is present. **(C)** is not the best answer – but is in a close second place – because the client may not appreciate the consequences of the necessary disclosures. Therefore, the alternative of the lawyer's reasonable belief is the better answer because it encompasses MRPC 4.1, duty to third parties, and MRPC 8.4(c), possible misrepresentation by a lawyer.

27. /A/ The only correct combination of alternatives. [MRPC 3.6] I is a proper extrajudicial statement because it is limited to the claim and defense. II is an improper statement because a lawyer shall not comment on anticipated testimony that may be excluded or inadmissible. Here, the court has ruled that the plaintiff's expert is ineligible to testify. III is an improper statement because a lawyer shall not comment upon a test result, including a refusal to submit to the test. IV is an improper statement because a lawyer should not comment upon the character or credibility of a party or witness.

28. /C/ A lawyer legislator may represent private clients as long as she does not obtain a special advantage that is clearly contrary to the public interest; that standard does not appear to be violated in this case, and there was disclosure of the client's interest in the outcome. The specific client identity does not have to be disclosed in most jurisdictions. [MRPC 3.9] **(A)** is incorrect because the bill's passage or defeat is not conclusive as to the lawyer's professional conduct. **(B)** is incorrect because disclosure of the client's potential advantage was made, and the legislation was not clearly contrary to the public interest. **(D)** is incorrect because it disregards the necessary disclosure and requirement that the legislation must not be clearly contrary to the public interest.

29. /B/ A lawyer must not knowingly make a false factual or legal statement to a third party in the course of representing a client, but need not voluntarily disclose all the facts, especially if not asked by the third party. [MRPC 4.3] **(A)** is not the best answer because a lawyer may directly contact a person not represented by a lawyer, and whether the third party is loyal to an adverse party is irrelevant. **(C)** is incorrect because a lawyer may communicate with a third party without opposing counsel being present. **(D)** is incorrect because the facts do not indicate that the lawyer's reason for contacting Nancy was to embarrass or burden a third party.

30. /D/ It is improper for a lawyer to bring or continue to pursue a proceeding if the primary motive is to harass the opposing party and its counsel. [Comments to MRPC 3.1] **(A)** is incorrect because it is not improper to have a motivation of financially helping your client, which often means financially injuring an opposing party. **(B)** is incorrect because the average opinion of most attorneys in the jurisdiction does not determine whether another lawyer's action or inaction constitutes an actionable disciplinary offense. **(C)** is incorrect because the average opinion of most attorneys in the jurisdiction does not determine whether another lawyer's action or inaction constitutes an unprofessional disciplinary offense.

31. /C/ Many states and the Federal Rules allow a lawyer to avoid CR11 litigation sanctions if the offending averment is corrected within 21 days of demand. This "safe harbor" will usually eliminate Rule 11 sanctions. Such sanctions may otherwise apply if the pleading is legally or factually baseless and the attorney did not conduct a reasonable and competent investigation. **(A)** is incorrect because there may have been a not-unreasonable belief by the lawyer that the Supreme Court would reverse the precedent. **(B)** is incorrect because the offending claim was timely dropped. **(D)** is incorrect because the standard for litigation sanctions is a reasonable basis which is higher than a good faith belief.

32. /C/ The best answer because withdrawal is required if a client insists the lawyer must violate a MRPC; here, the absence of a good faith argument violates MRPC 3.1. However, withdrawal must be accomplished without a material adverse effect on the client's interest. [MRPC 1.16] **(A)** is incorrect because it does not protect the client against suffering a material adverse effect to her interests. **(B)** is incorrect because a lawyer may not take a frivolous position lacking a good faith argument and, if the client so insists, must withdraw. [MRPC 3.1] **(D)** is not the best answer because a client has the ultimate direction and authority in actions concerning her case [MRPC 1.2]; if the client direction would cause the lawyer to violate a MRPC, withdrawal is mandatory.

33. /B/ Litigation sanctions could be imposed because a lawyer has a duty to make a sufficient investigation to verify that there is a reasonable basis in both fact and law to any pleading he signs; here, the court has determined that standard was not met. [MRPC 3.1] **(A)** is incorrect because professional discipline may only be imposed if the lawyer cannot make a good faith argument for the extension, modification, or reversal of existing law; here, the court has determined that this minimum required standard was met. **(C)** is incorrect because the lawyer is subject to litigation sanction. **(D)** is incorrect because the lawyer is not necessarily subject to professional discipline.

34. /A/ A lawyer is prohibited from improperly attempting to influence a juror, and while this one case is over, the jurors still are required to sit for criminal cases for 10 more days. [MRPC 3.5] **(B)** is not the best answer because the case is over, but a prosecutor's influence over the jurors continues, and opposing counsel's letter would not likely have an influence over the jurors' future behavior. **(C)** is not the best answer because while the jurors have been discharged from this case, they are still in the criminal jury pool for 10 more days. **(D)** is not the best answer because the primary reason that the communication is a violation is that it was an improper attempt to influence the jurors.

35. /D/ A lawyer shall not obstruct another party's access to evidence or destroy documents having potential evidentiary value. [MRPC 3.4] **(A)** is incorrect because the prohibition is on destruction of evidence, not the accuracy of the discovery answer after the spoliation has been completed. **(B)** is incorrect because a lawyer shall not counsel or assist another person to do such act. [MRPC 3.4] **(C)** is not the best answer because the preferred test is whether the requested documents might lead to discoverable evidence.

36. /B/ Settlement negotiations may not be introduced in the trial and therefore Pattie's opening statement will not be supported by evidence. [MRPC 3.4(e)] **(A)** is incorrect because the test is whether the substance of the opening argument is reasonably expected to be introduced at trial. **(C)** is incorrect because the statement's accuracy is irrelevant if it will not be substantiated by evidence to be introduced during the trial. **(D)** is incorrect because the defendant's attorney will likely not be able to introduce settlement negotiations at trial.

37. /A/ Closing arguments may not refer to evidence not introduced during the trial. [MRPC 3.4] **(B)** is incorrect because it is too difficult to determine the effect of the improper statement, and the reference itself was improper. **(C)** is incorrect because it would be improper for the defendant's attorney to refer to the dismissed count in her closing statements. **(D)** is incorrect because the fraud count had been dismissed and should not have been discussed by the plaintiff's lawyer in closing at all.

38. /C/ This is the best answer because the judge may allow a trial lawyer to testify concurrently as a witness if disqualification would work a substantial hardship on the client and being called as a witness was not reasonably foreseeable. [MRPC 3.7] **(A)** is incorrect because MRPC 3.7 does not dictate an absolute bar to the dual role of advocate-witness even though it is not advised. **(B)** is incorrect because discipline is not usually appropriate if the testimony relates to a mere formality or the value of legal services provided. **(D)** is not the best answer because testimony by other lawyers from the corporation may be allowed, but the lack of other lawyers who can testify does not in and of itself create an exception to the rule.

39. /A/ The best answer because in the middle of a trial is hardly timely disclosure of adverse exculpatory evidence. [MRPC 3.8(d)] **(B)** is incorrect because the criminal prosecutor does not have a duty to withhold from the defense lawyer exculpatory evidence. **(C)** is incorrect because while disclosure was made to the defendant's lawyer, it was not made timely. **(D)** is not the best answer although it might be accurate that the questionable identification was sufficient to support probable cause.

40. /D/ All material facts must be disclosed in an *ex parte* proceeding even though they may help the opposing party and/or be adverse to the presenting lawyer's client. [MRPC 3.3(d)] **(A)** is incorrect because the lawyer's duty to maintain client confidences is qualified by the duty of candor to the tribunal. **(B)** is incorrect because even if the statement made to the court was technically accurate, Carol did not disclose "all material facts," including the addition of the paragraph in the order presented after the wife and her attorney agreed. **(C)** is not the best answer because the rationale – the court deciding the non-disclosure of $5,000 is not improper – is only possible if the court understood the significance of the non-disclosed information.

41. /C/ The best answer because the summer solstice party with such large cash payments made to the bankruptcy court personnel appears objectively to be intended to influence court officials. [MRPC 3.5(a)] **(A)** is incorrect because the rule prohibits improper attempts to influence any official who is associated with a judicial tribunal. **(B)** is incorrect because it is irrelevant who in the law firm made the cash payments if they were intended to influence the court. **(D)** is incorrect because the self-serving interpretation of lack of intent is not controlling if the situation appears to be intended to influence the judicial tribunal.

42. /B/ The best answer because a lawyer may usually take temporary possession of physical evidence used in their client's crimes for a limited examination, but the lawyer must eventually turn the evidence over to the police or prosecutor. [Comment to MRPC 3.4] **(A)** is not the best answer because this information would be covered under the attorney-client privilege and such disclosure would violate MRPC 1.6. **(C)** is not the best answer because taking custody of the knife used in the crime is not necessarily improper as long as it is subsequently turned over to the authorities. **(D)** is incorrect because there would be an ethical and legal violation if the lawyer advised the client to destroy the knife.

43. /C/ In trial a lawyer may not state a personal opinion as to the credibility of a witness or the culpability of a party; "everyone in the courtroom" includes the lawyer. [MRPC 3.4(e)] A lawyer may argue the evidence (alternative III) and suggest a reason or motivation for testimony (alternative IV). **(A)** is incorrect because it is an incorrect combination of alternatives. **(B)** is incorrect because it is an incorrect combination of alternatives. **(D)** is incorrect because it is an incorrect combination of alternatives.

44. /D/ It does not appear that the lawyer Betty discussed the subject of the representation, only the subjects of the baseball game and their children. Therefore, this does not violate the "no contact" rule without permission of the other person's lawyer. [MRPC 4.2] **(A)** is incorrect because ex communication usually involves a lawyer communicating with the judge or jury without the other side present. **(B)** is incorrect because mere communication is not a violation unless it involves the subject of the representation. **(C)** is incorrect because it is not the physical location that is a violation but rather discussion of the subject of the representation without the other person's lawyer's consent.

45. /A/ A lawyer may not unlawfully obstruct another party's pre-trial access to relevant evidence. [MRPC 3.4] Here, the defendant's lawyer had 60 days to analyze the complaint and put in an answer; this created the foreseeability and constructive notice of the plaintiff's expectancy of reviewing the workpapers in formal discovery. Beginning on February 28, the lawyer had a duty not to participate in or even condone destroying evidence that they knew was relevant to the government's case. **(C)** is incorrect because proof of fraudulent intent to commit spoliation is not necessary if a reasonable lawyer would have realized the client was in the process of destroying relevant evidence. **(D)** is incorrect because proof of a lawyer's specific direction to a client to spoliate relevant documents is not necessary if a reasonable lawyer would have realized the client was in the process of destroying relevant evidence and made no attempt to stop the spoliation.

46. /C/ The best answer because a lawyer may negotiate the terms of a transaction with a party adverse to the lawyer's client if she does not give the adverse party legal advice besides a recommendation to seek her own independent lawyer. [MRPC 4.3] **(A)** is not the best answer; although Harry and Sally's interests are adverse, Florence was not representing Sally, only communicating the terms under which Harry would agree. **(B)** is incorrect because Florence was not representing Sally. **(D)** is not the best answer as there was no waiver and Sally did not waive any such nonexistent right.

47. /D/ Absent a MRPC 1.7 or 1.9 conflict of interest, an advocate lawyer is not subject to disqualification merely because another lawyer from the same law firm is a witness. [MRPC 3.7(b)] **(A)** is incorrect because only if the advocacy and witness rules create a MRPC 1.7 or 1.9 conflict of interest is there a disqualification. **(B)** is incorrect because it is not the materiality of the testimony that creates a disqualification, only a MRPC 1.7 or 1.9 conflict of interest. **(C)** is incorrect because whether or not one of the lawyers is a necessary witness does not determine if the other should be disqualified.

48. /D/ The best answer because all three of these showings are necessary if a prosecutor is to avoid violating MRPC 3.8(c) by doing discovery on the defendant's lawyer. The information sought is not protected from disclosure by any privilege, the evidence sought is essential to successful prosecution, and there is no feasible alternative for obtaining the information. **(A)** is incorrect because it is not a complete statement of the necessary factors to justify subpoenaing a client's lawyer. **(B)** is incorrect because it is not a complete statement of the necessary factors to justify subpoenaing a client's lawyer. **(C)** is incorrect because it is not a complete statement of the necessary factors to justify subpoenaing a client's lawyer.

49. /A/ The best answer because a lawyer may request that agents, employees, or relatives of clients not voluntarily give information to an opposing party or her lawyer unless subpoenaed, and it does not appear that the agents' interest will be put at risk if they refuse the request. [MRPC 3.4(f)] **(B)** is not the best answer because it is not improper for an attorney to attempt an informal meeting with a critical witness in a case. **(C)** is incorrect because the defense attorney did not interfere with opposing counsel's right to discovery since a formal deposition could be scheduled by the plaintiff's lawyer. **(D)** is incorrect because a witness' lack of privilege does not create a duty to give an informal interview; again, the plaintiff's lawyer should have scheduled a formal deposition.

50. /B/ The best answer because as long as there is sufficient candid communication to the client of the details and prognosis of the action and potential outcomes [MRPC 1.4], a claim is not frivolous even if the lawyer believes the client's position may not prevail, such as there being a defense that may be asserted negating the claim [MRPC 3.1 Comment 2]. **(A)** is not the best answer because there is no duty to inform the opposing attorney that she has a viable defense that could be asserted. **(C)** is incorrect because the fact that there is a powerful defense that could be asserted does not necessarily make the P's claim itself frivolous. **(D)** is incorrect because there usually is no duty to disclose to the court that the opposing party has a privilege.

51. /D/ The lawyer would only have a duty to reveal the prior convictions if she or her client had represented the nonexistence of same so that it would be necessary to correct a previous false statement. [MRPC 3.3] **(A)** is incorrect because it would not make a difference in which state the proceeding was in; if the falsity originated with Debra or Barbara, it either would have to be revealed or Barbara would have to withdraw. [MRPC 1.16] **(B)** is incorrect because the lawyer has a duty not to reveal client confidential information. [MRPC 1.6] **(C)** is not the best answer – even though a true statement – because the lawyer's duty of candor to the tribunal would override the duty of confidentiality to the client [MRPC 1.6] and at least require the lawyer to withdraw [MRPC 1.16].

52. /A/ The lawyer has a duty of candor towards the tribunal that includes disclosing direct controlling adverse legal authority in the jurisdiction if it is not disclosed by opposing counsel which appears to be the situation here. [MRPC 3.3(a)(3)] **(B)** is not the best answer because this limited duty to disclose applies only if the controlling authority is not presented by the opposing counsel and "always" is too broad. **(C)** is incorrect, the "no harm, no foul" rationale does not excuse what is essentially an attempt to mislead the tribunal. **(D)** is incorrect because while generally a true statement, it goes too far in that a lawyer may not make a false statement of law to a tribunal.

53. /B/ The best answer because the judge has a wide degree of discretion to punish the violation of his own discovery order. [MRPC 3.4] **(A)** is incorrect because the merits of the lawsuit are a separate issue from the failure to comply with a court discovery order. **(C)** is incorrect because a court has a wide degree of discretion in formulating the appropriate remedy when its order is not complied with. **(D)** is incorrect because the order was directed towards both the client and the attorney. Furthermore, the attorney has some duty to convince and perhaps pressure the client to comply with discovery orders and may withdraw if the client exhibits repeated recalcitrance.

54. /C/ A lawyer shall not knowingly make a material false statement to a third person in the course of representing a client. [MRPC 4.1(a)] **(A)** is incorrect because the fact of whether the claim was fraudulent was misrepresented. **(B)** is incorrect because the false statements went well beyond the extent of the "puffing" that is generally accepted in settlement negotiations between lawyers. **(D)** is incorrect because it is not clear if there was a fraudulent claim, and the facts say that Harriet made the false statements to induce the settlement.

55. /A/ The best answer because every jurisdiction has a criminal statute that is applicable to an attempt to bribe a judge. [MRPC 3.5] **(B)** is not the best answer because it focuses on the mental intentions of the judge, not the lawyer (obviously the judge's participation is improper). **(C)** is incorrect because the crime and improper conduct by the lawyer occurred with the advancing of the $100,000 even if the judge subsequently did not make a discretionary decision in the case. **(D)** is incorrect because the crime and improper conduct by the lawyer occurred with the advancing of the $100,000 even if the judge refused to accept or promptly returned the $100,000.

56. /B/ The only correct combination of alternatives. I is improper because a lawyer may not state her own personal opinion of the guilt or innocence of the defendant even indirectly. II is improper because a lawyer must not refer to a criminal defendant's refusal to testify based upon Fifth Amendment grounds. III is improper because a lawyer may not ask a witness questions that imply another witness was not credible, nor comment on such results in closing. IV is proper because a prosecutor may ask the jury to consider a witness's background when they are considering the witness's credibility. [MRPC 3.4] V is improper because a prosecutor may not introduce or comment on the prior criminal record of a defendant. [MRPC 3.6]

57. /C/ Neither the prosecutor nor any of her subordinates may make extrajudicial statements concerning the existence of or defendant's refusal to make a statement. [MRPC 3.6] **(A)** is incorrect because a prosecutor must exercise reasonable care in supervising all subordinates. [MRPC 3.8] **(B)** is incorrect because statements I and III are proper; a prosecutor may comment on safety information, warn of dangers, and request assistance of the public. [MRPC 3.6] **(D)** is incorrect because it is an incorrect combination of alternatives.

58. /D/ Because there were a dozen other witnesses to the altercation in the bar, Loretta is not a necessary witness to facts that are otherwise unobtainable. [MRPC 3.7] **(A)** is incorrect because the mere fact that a lawyer "may" be called is not determinant of the disqualification motion and here the lawyer is not a necessary witness about facts that are otherwise unobtainable. **(B)** is incorrect because Loretta will not be disqualified from the representation. **(C)** is not the best answer because there is no need for client consent since the lawyer is not a necessary witness about facts that are otherwise unobtainable.

59. /B/ The best answer because a lawyer may not pretend, state, or imply that the lawyer is disinterested in dealing with an adverse person who is not represented by counsel. Such a lawyer must affirmatively correct any misunderstanding. [MRPC 4.3] **(A)** is not the best answer because it is not necessarily improper for a lawyer to communicate with an adverse party so long as there is a recommendation to hire her own lawyer, and the lawyer does not pretend to be disinterested. Further, dollar settlement authority is not usually considered a statement of fact. **(C)** is incorrect because merely suggesting the adverse party hire her own lawyer is insufficient if the lawyer also pretends to be disinterested in the matter. **(D)** is incorrect because, while perhaps true as far as it goes, it does not excuse the lawyer's pretending to be disinterested.

60. /A/ The best answer because a lawyer may not embarrass or burden a third party witness unless there is an otherwise substantive purpose thereto. [MRPC 4.4] **(B)** is not the best answer because personal information may be discoverable if it is directly relevant to a material factor at issue in the controversy. **(C)** is not the best answer because under these circumstances most courts would impose a requirement that the question of a third party must be directly relevant, not merely that it may lead to discoverable evidence. **(D)** is incorrect because while discovery is intended in part to avoid trial by ambush, it does not justify a failure to respect the rights of third parties.

61. /D/ The best answer under MRPC 4.4(b) because even inadvertent disclosure may be a waiver of the privileged status of the document. In addition, MRPC 1.2(d) states a lawyer shall not consult a client to engage or assist a client in conduct that is criminal or fraudulent. Therefore, a motion for sanctions appears appropriate. **(A)** is incorrect because MRPC 4.4 allows the receiving lawyer to return an inadvertently sent document, but there is apparently some question if this was inadvertent. **(B)** is incorrect because the lawyer may have a duty of loyalty to the client to use the incriminating document in pursuing the case. **(C)** is incorrect because MRPC 4.4(b) does not require the receiving lawyer of an inadvertently sent document to withdraw from the case.

62. /A/ The rule usually requires the lawyer to have a non-frivolous argument in support of their client's positions. [Comment 2 of MRPC 3.1] The lawyer's obligations are subordinate to a criminal defendant's constitutional rights and counsel can present a claim that would be prohibited by the non-frivolous standard, at least to the extent of making the state prove every element required to prosecute the defendant. [Comment 3 of MRPC 3.1] **(B)** is incorrect because a lawyer may not knowingly present false evidence at trial. [MRPC 3.3(a)(3)] **(C)** is incorrect because the decision to accept a settlement is for the client, not the attorney. [MRPC 1.2(a)] **(D)** is incorrect because withdrawal on the eve of trial would likely not be allowed since it would prejudice the client. [MRPC 1.16(b)(1)]

RIGOS UNIFORM BAR REVIEW SERIES

PROFESSIONAL RESPONSIBILITY EXAM REVIEW (MPRE)

Chapter 5

Law Firms, Marketing, and Professional Integrity

Magic Memory Outline®

RIGOS UNIFORM BAR REVIEW SERIES

PROFESSIONAL RESPONSIBILITY EXAM REVIEW (MPRE)

Chapter 5

Law Firms, Marketing, and Professional Integrity

A. Law Firms and Associations – TITLE 5

1. Responsibilities of Partners, Managers, and Supervisory Lawyer – MRPC 5.1: Law firms are not usually subject to professional discipline – only the involved lawyer(s).

a. Partner Responsibility: A partner or one with comparable managerial authority must ensure the organization has in place quality control policies and procedures that give reasonable assurance that all lawyers in the firm conform to the MRPCs.

b. Supervisory Lawyer Responsibility: A lawyer with direct supervisory authority over an associate lawyer must make reasonable efforts to ensure the associate conforms to the MRPCs. Whether a lawyer may be civilly vicariously liable for negligence damages in non-supervision of another lawyer's conduct is not addressed in this ethical rule.

c. Responsibility for Associates' Acts: A supervisory lawyer is responsible if the lawyer directly orders improper conduct or, with knowledge of the specific improper conduct, ratifies the unethical conduct involved. If she knows of the conduct at a time when the consequences can be avoided or mitigated, she must take reasonable remedial action.

2. Responsibilities of a Subordinate Lawyer – MRPC 5.2:

a. General Rule: Even though a subordinate (associate) lawyer acts under the direction of another person, that associate lawyer is personally bound by the MRPCs.

b. Exception: A subordinate lawyer does not violate the MRPCs if she acts in accordance with a supervisory lawyer's ethical decision, and the question involved a reasonably arguable ethical issue. An example is whether the conflict provisions of MRPC 1.7(b) are put at risk by two different clients' interests that might foreseeably become adverse in the future. Another example is where an associate files a frivolous pleading at the direction of a partner, and reasonably relied on the supervisor's analysis of the relevant factual questions.

MPRE Tip: An associate's reliance on a supervising lawyer's decision is frequently tested.

3. Responsibilities Regarding Non-lawyer Assistants – MRPC 5.3: Any lawyer with supervisory authority over non-lawyer employees (office managers, law school interns, paralegals, investigators, and clerical staff) must review their work, and the lawyer must always maintain a direct client relationship. If the non-lawyer was engaged in conduct that would be a violation of the MRPCs, the supervisory lawyer might be vicariously responsible. Liability applies if the lawyer orders or, with knowledge of the specific conduct, ratifies the conduct involved. The lawyer will be liable if he knows of the conduct at a time when its consequences can be avoided or mitigated, but fails to take reasonable remedial action.

MPRE Tip: ABA Opinion 1203 requires external reporting of clear ethical violations by lawyers in the firm. Simply "reporting up" within the law firm is insufficient.

4. Professional Independence of a Lawyer – MRPC 5.4:

a. Improper to Share Fees with Non-Lawyer – MRPC 5.4(a): A lawyer or law firm shall not share legal fees with a non-lawyer. This is the principal deterrent to multi-disciplinary practice. Even splitting fees with a charity is disallowed. There are four **PEND** exceptions where fee sharing with non-lawyers is permitted.

(1) Purchase of Practice: Under a law firm purchase agreement, the acquisition price may be paid to the seller, if alive. Similarly, payment to the estate of the deceased, disabled, or disappeared lawyer of prior legal fees earned is not improper.

(2) Employee Payment Plans: A firm may include non-lawyer employees in a compensation or retirement plan. This exception is allowed even though the firm's compensation and retirement plan funding sources are derived from the profit from legal fees.

(3) Nonprofit Organization: Court-awarded legal fees may be shared with a nonprofit organization that employed, retained, or recommended the lawyer in the matter.

(4) Death or Disability of Lawyer: A firm or partner may pay the pro-rata law firm capital account benefits to a lawyer's estate or beneficiaries. Such death benefit payments may not extend beyond a reasonable period of time after the lawyer's death.

b. Partnerships – MRPC 5.4(b): A lawyer shall not form a partnership with a non-lawyer if any of the activities of the partnership consist of the "practice of law." The "practice of law" is defined by the jurisdiction in question. The broadest definition is "the application of legal principles and judgments to resolve a problem or how to proceed under the law." This broad definition produces uncertainty as to whether the state could move against others, such as CPAs, financial planners, etc., for the unauthorized practice of law.

c. Improper to Direct Lawyer's Professional Judgment – MRPC 5.4(c): A third party who employed, retained, or recommended a lawyer in a matter or pays the lawyer may not direct, regulate, or exercise influence over the lawyer's professional judgment. This issue arises on the exam if a third party "calls the shots." There should not be any interference with the lawyer's independent professional judgment. Review also MRPC 1.8(f) *supra* at 63.

d. Professional Corporation or Association – MRPC 5.4(d): A lawyer shall not practice law with a non-lawyer (or suspended lawyer). This applies if a non-lawyer owns any interest in the law firm or is a law firm director or officer. An ownership exception allows a fiduciary representative of the estate of a deceased partner to own a nominal interest for a reasonable time during administration of the estate.

5. Unauthorized and Multi-jurisdictional Practice of Law – MRPC 5.5:

a. Unauthorized Practice: A lawyer may not assist a non-lawyer in the performance of any activity that constitutes the unauthorized practice of law, as defined by state law. Counseling with individuals *pro se* litigants is usually allowed but partnership and corporations may not appear *pro se*. Delegation of legal work to non-lawyer assistants is allowed if the lawyer adequately supervises the details of the work and maintains a direct relationship with the client. Unauthorized practice usually includes engaging in the practice of law while on inactive or suspended status. It also typically includes participating in the practice of law with a unadmitted, disbarred, or suspended lawyer.

b. Multi-jurisdiction Practice: A lawyer shall not practice law in a jurisdiction in which she is not admitted. This prohibition includes non-isolated transactions such as opening an office, holding out, or other systematic and continuous presence in the jurisdiction. Local admission may not be required for services provided on a temporary basis in a matter reasonably related to a controversy arising in the lawyer's home jurisdiction, or for mediation and arbitration proceedings in some states like California and New York. Most jurisdictions have *pro hac vice* (for a specific matter) admission in association with local counsel and permission of the tribunal. If the local rule is not met, the lawyer's home state licensing authority may also impose discipline for the unauthorized practice in another state.

6. Restrictions on Right to Practice – MRPC 5.6:

a. Non-compete Agreements: Entering into an employment agreement that restricts the rights of a lawyer to represent firm clients after leaving a law firm is improper. The client has the right to decide its own representation, and may switch lawyers or follow a lawyer to a new firm. A small exception is that a lawyer's non-compete agreement may be given in return for retirement benefits or the sale of a law practice.

b. No Further Representation Clause: A lawyer cannot make or sign an agreement not to represent her client or other persons or claims against the opposing party in the future. For example, a settlement agreement prohibiting the lawyer from bringing future suits against the same corporate defendant is contrary to the public interest. This pro-competitive restriction applies even if the client urges the lawyer to so agree.

7. Responsibilities Regarding Law-related Services – MRPC 5.7: A lawyer may engage in law-related ancillary services (such as title insurance, trust services, or financial planning), but all the MRPCs apply whether services are provided through the law firm or a separate entity. If the provider is a separate entity, the customer must understand the services are not legal representation. Disclosure must affirmatively be made that regular law firm protections, such as the attorney-client privilege may not apply. The customer must know restrictions on conflicts of interest do not necessarily apply. If the customer is also a law firm client, the conflict rules of MRPC 1.7 and transaction **TIC** rules of MRPC 1.8 may apply.

B. <u>Public Service</u> – TITLE 6

1. *Pro Bono* Publico Service – MRPC 6.1: A lawyer should aspire to render *pro bono* public interest legal service by serving people of limited means and charitable organizations at no charge or for a reduced fee. This is not usually mandatory; 50 hours per year is the ABA aspirational goal. Public service representation may not violate the civil sanction provisions of CR 11 or any MRPCs, such as conflicts of interests with other clients.

2. Accepting Appointments – MRPC 6.2: A judge may appoint a lawyer to represent indigents and unpopular parties. The appointment should not be declined except for good cause. Good cause includes representation that would lead to likely violation of the MRPCs (including violation of MRPC 1.1 – competency requirements) or create an unreasonable financial burden on the lawyer. If the client or cause is so repugnant to the lawyer as to impair the client-lawyer relationship or the lawyer's ability to represent the client as an effective advocate, the appointment may also be declined. But mere unpopularity of the matter or disapproval by other clients is not considered good cause.

3. Membership in Legal Services Organization – MRPC 6.3: Legal services organizations serve the public. A lawyer may serve as a director, officer, or member even if the organization serves persons whose interests are adverse to a client of the lawyer's firm. The lawyer must not knowingly participate in a decision or action of the organization if the decision or action would be incompatible with the conflict of interest rules.

4. Law Reform Activities Affecting Client Interests – MRPC 6.4: Participation in a law reform organization is acceptable even where reform measures may affect the interests of a client. If the lawyer learns that the interests of a client may be materially benefited by an organizational decision in which the lawyer participates, the lawyer must disclose that fact to the organization but need not identify the client. Note that there is no duty to disclose circumstances where a client may be hurt by the actions of the organization.

5. Nonprofit and Court-annexed Limited Representation – MRPC 6.5: This provision focuses on a lawyer sponsored by a nonprofit organization or appointed by a court to provide short-term legal services to a client without expectation of continuing representation. Examples are the completion of legal forms in a walk-in clinic or advice given on a hotline. The client must agree to the limited scope of representation and be informed if further assistance of counsel is desirable. The imputed firm-wide disqualification conflict of interest rules [MRPC 1.10] do not apply unless the lawyer has personal knowledge of a conflict.

C. <u>Information About Legal Services</u> – TITLE 7

1. Communications Concerning a Lawyer's Services – MRPC 7.1:

a. Includes: The Rule prohibits false and misleading communications or failure to state information that is necessary to make the statement not materially misleading.

b. Unjustified Expectations: Many states have not adopted the ABA 2003 changes and still require that communications may not create unjustified expectations about results the lawyer can achieve. False statistics, claims to experience, or statements of "influence with the tribunal" may create unjustified expectations. Statements of prior law firm case dollar recoveries should include a disclaimer as to future recoveries.

c. Comparisons: Any comparisons of the lawyer's services with other lawyers' must be factually substantiated or otherwise verifiable. An example is, "We are the best tax lawyers in New York City"; such a marketing statement would be very difficult to verify factually. The burden is on the lawyer to show sufficient support for the statement.

> **MPRE Tip:** False, misleading, or unverifiable marketing is improper. While advertising may not create unjustified expectations for potential clients, good taste is not directly required.

2. Advertising – MRPC 7.2: Commercial speech is usually protected by the 1st and 14th Amendments. *(Bates)* Still, narrowly drawn marketing regulations such as a 30-day ban on mass-disaster blanket mailings are permitted. The prohibitions against promising results, testimonials of service quality, event and scene depictions, and celebrity voice or images controlled or sponsored by a lawyer or firm are included.

a. Use of Public Media: A lawyer may advertise services through public media such as radio, television, web sites, telephone directories, electronic search engines, legal directories, newspaper and other periodicals, and other electronic and written communications.

b. Records of Advertisement Kept: Most jurisdictions (but not the ABA's MRPC since 2003) require retention of a copy or recording of an advertisement for two years after its last dissemination. This includes video, online, or television advertisements. The lawyer has the burden to show the basis of any factual claims advertised.

c. No Compensation for Recommendations: A lawyer may not directly or indirectly compensate an individual or organization for recommending or referring a client, except a bar-approved, nonprofit referral service. A lawyer may pay for reasonable costs of ordinary advertising but cannot give value in return for publicity of a lawyer's achievements reported as a news item. The payment of compensation to for-profit referral services, including paid online legal matching services, is not allowed in many states.

d. Name in Advertisement: In many jurisdictions, advertisements must include the name of the law firm. Some states require publishing the name of at least one lawyer responsible for its content.

3. Referrals – MRPC 7.2: A lawyer may agree to refer clients to another lawyer or non-lawyer professional in return for the undertaking of that person to refer back to the lawyer, as long as nothing of value is given. Reciprocal referral agreements that are not exclusive (do not apply to any and all clients) and do not interfere with the lawyer's professional independent judgment are also usually permissible. The client must be informed of the existence and details of any allowable non-exclusive reciprocal agreement.

> **MPRE Tip:** A common fact patterns may include **SAPP** violations; A lawyer may not <u>s</u>hare legal fees [RPC 5.4], **<u>a</u>**id in unauthorized practice of law [MPRC 5.5], **<u>p</u>**ay a referral fee [MRPC 7.2], or **<u>p</u>**artner with a non-lawyer to engage in the practice of law [MRPC 5.4].

4. Direct Contact with Prospective Clients – MRPC 7.3: The concern is that the lawyer using direct communications to solicit will overwhelm a potential client.

a. Solicitation Breadth and ROFF Exceptions: When significant part of the lawyer's motivation is professional employment, the lawyer may not solicit a prospective client by means of live in-person contact, live telephonic contact, or real-time electronic communication. Such solicitation is permissible, however, if directed to **ROFF**, – **<u>r</u>**elatives, **<u>o</u>**ther lawyers, <u>f</u>ormer clients, or **<u>f</u>**riends.

b. Examples: A lawyer may not solicit a stranger at a social event or use an agent, such as a "runner" or "capper," to pass out business cards at an accident scene or hospital emergency room. In comparison, setting up a booth at a street fair with signs stating "legal questions answered" is not usually a violation since the lawyer waits for the potential client to approach and does not directly solicit.

> **MPRE Tip:** A lawyer giving value as a quid pro quo for legal referrals is frequently tested.

c. Written Solicitation – MRPC 7.3(b) and (c): A lawyer's written offers to represent, such as sending letters to individuals who had a foreclosure action filed against them, are now permissible (*Shapero*), but must state "advertising material." An exception applies if the non-client has indicated that no communication from the lawyer is desired.

5. Communication of Fields of Practice and Specialization – MRPC 7.4: A lawyer may communicate that she practices certain types of law and not others.

a. No "Specialists": A lawyer shall not state or imply that he is a specialist such as a "Tax Specialist Attorney." Historical exceptions include "patent attorney" if the attorney is admitted to practice before the United States Patent and Trademark Office. A "Proctor in Admiralty" designation is also usually allowed.

b. Certification: A lawyer may refer to certifications, awards, or recognition she has been issued, as long as they are not misleading and identify the certifying organization. Included are a viable designation or earned award by a bona fide group that is authorized to issue such certifications. An attorney-CPA may designate her dual credentials. (*Ibanez*)

c. Additional Required Disclosure: Some jurisdictions require that the reference to acceptable credentials must state that the supreme court of the state does not recognize specialties in the practice of law. Some even go further and require a statement that the certificate, award, or recognition is not a requirement to practice law in the state.

MPRE Tip: The exam often combines advertising, solicitation, and specialization designation.

6. Firm Names and Letterheads – MRPC 7.5:

a. Trade Names: Trade names and web sites may be used in most jurisdictions by a law firm in private practice unless they are misleading or imply a connection with a government related agency (e.g., "New York City Legal Clinic" or "IRS Tax Law Firm") or charitable legal service organization (e.g., "Community Legal Center").

(1) Misleading Prohibition: The trade name and any web sites used by the law firm may not be misleading or communicate an unauthorized specialty designation. It is usually considered inherently misleading for a sole practitioner to use the term "and associates" in a firm's trade name if there are no associates in the firm.

(2) Former Partners: A law firm may use the names of deceased or retired partners in the firm name where there has been a continuing succession in the firm's identity.

b. Multiple Offices: A law firm with offices in multiple jurisdictions may use the same firm name on the individual offices' letterhead. If individual attorneys are listed on the letterhead, the jurisdictions in which they are admitted must be specified.

c. Holding Public Office: A lawyer holding a public office shall not use her name in the law firm trade name or in communications on its behalf during any substantial period when the lawyer is not actively and regularly practicing law with the firm.

d. Professional Organization v. Solo Practice: Lawyers practicing out of the same office who are not partners or shareholders of a corporation may not join their names together as "associated." Lawyers may state or imply that they practice in a partnership or other organization only when that is the fact. Solo separate letterheads, cards, pleading papers, etc. are required unless the lawyer is a partner, employee or "of counsel" to the firm. To be avoided are representations suggesting a single entity, joint referrals, and mutual access to confidential information because these typically are characteristics of a law firm.

7. Improper Political Contributions – MRPC 7.6: Political contributions or solicitation of another's contributions by a lawyer is usually not improper. But if such contribution or solicitation is made for the purpose of obtaining assigned work or judicial appointment, it is not allowed. This rule prohibits only political contributions or solicitations that would not be made "but for" the consideration of an appointment or legal work.

D. Maintaining the Integrity of the Profession – TITLE 8

1. Bar Admission and Disciplinary Matters – MRPC 8.1: This communication rule addresses an applicant for admission to the bar or a lawyer in a disciplinary matter.

a. Admission Application: A lawyer's recommendation of an applicant for admission must be accurate and based on personal knowledge following a reasonable investigation as to the applicant's character, fitness, and qualifications. Any misstatements in an applicant's admission application must be corrected by a recommender because a lawyer must not assist an unfit or unqualified candidate in gaining admission.

b. Disciplinary Proceeding: All statements made by participants in any bar proceeding must be true and accurate, with full disclosure. Both an applicant and a lawyer must respond to all lawful state bar admission authority demands for information.

2. Judicial and Legal Officials – MRPC 8.2: The objective is to maintain public confidence in the legal system and the integrity of the involved jurists. A lawyer should defend judges and courts from unjust or uninformed criticism.

a. False or Reckless Statements: Lawyers must not make false or reckless statements about the qualifications, integrity, or record of a sitting judge, public legal officer, or candidate for election or appointment to a judicial or legal office. A lawyer's candid opinions concerning a judge that are objective, factually accurate, and honest are allowed.

b. Lawyer Candidate: A candidate for judicial office must comply with Canon 4 of the Code of Judicial Conduct (CJC). See *infra* at 255.

3. Reporting Professional Misconduct – MRPC 8.3: Under the ABA Model Rules, a lawyer is required to ("shall" or "must") report misconduct of another lawyer. Many jurisdictions reduce the required degree of violation reporting (such as non-mandatory "should" or "may") to reduce potential antagonism between opposing counsels.

a. Knowledge of MRPC Violation: A lawyer with actual personal knowledge of a committed violation of the MRPCs by another attorney shall promptly inform the appropriate authority. The perceived violation must raise a substantial and clear question as to that individual's honesty, trustworthiness, or fitness as a lawyer. A failure to report a serious violation by another lawyer has led to discipline being imposed on the non-reporter. In addition, it is improper to threaten reporting as a bargaining chip in negotiating a settlement.

b. Knowledge of MCJC Violation: A lawyer with actual, personal knowledge of a judge's violation of the code of judicial conduct shall promptly inform the appropriate authority. This is mandatory under the ABA Model Rules, not merely suggestive. The perceived violation must raise a substantial and clear question as to the judge's fitness for office.

c. Appropriate Authority: If the matter is in litigation, the appropriate authority for a lawyer would usually be the trial judge. Otherwise it ordinarily would be the state lawyer disciplinary authority. For reporting a judge, it would be the Judicial Conduct Commission in the jurisdiction.

MPRE Tip: Some states require self-reporting to the state bar under some circumstances.

d. CAD Exceptions: There are three **CAD** situations where reporting misconduct is not allowed: if the information to be reported is protected under the MRPC 1.6 duty of <u>c</u>onfidentiality to clients; if the information was received through an approved lawyers' or judges' <u>a</u>ssistance program, or if a lawyer is retained to <u>d</u>efend the attorney in question.

MPRE Tip: The Rules comments specify that judgment is required in applying the reporting obligation. The "substantial" requirement refers to the seriousness of the offense. Actual knowledge of a clear violation by a lawyer goes beyond "mere suspicion."

4. Misconduct – MRPC 8.4: This catch-all category includes lawyers who:

a. Violate MRPCs: Violate or attempt to violate the MRPCs, knowingly assist or induce another to do the same, or do so through the acts of another, such as a legal assistant.

b. Commit a Criminal Act: Commit a criminal act or act of public moral turpitude that reflects adversely on the lawyer's honesty, trustworthiness, or fitness to practice law.

(1) Included: Qualifying acts include willful failure to file an income tax return, violence (such as an unjustified assault), "indifference to legal obligation," threatening witnesses, jurors, other lawyers, and judges, or other offenses relevant to the practice of law.

(2) Excluded: In comparison, matters of personal morality are usually insufficient. Examples include a single personal use of marijuana, act of marital infidelity, or comparable offenses lacking a specific connection to fitness for the practice of law. Repeated occurrences of minor personal morality offenses may cumulate, thus elevating the level of misconduct and increasing the chances of professional discipline.

c. Engage in Dishonesty or Fraud: This includes engaging in conduct that clearly demonstrates intentional dishonesty, fraud, deceit, misrepresentation, breach of trust or fiduciary duty. This is not limited to the practice of law, and a criminal conviction is not necessary. There is ongoing disagreement about government lawyers pretexting by misstating their identity to obtain information about terrorists or criminal activity.

d. Conduct Prejudicial to Administration of Justice: This includes a significant expression of disrespect to or about a tribunal. Rule Comment 3 makes it clear that conduct or statements in employment or while representing a client that manifest prejudice or bias on the basis of sex, race, age, creed, religion, color, national origin, disability, sexual orientation, or marital status are a violation if they are prejudicial to the administration of justice. Discriminatory peremptory juror challenges do not usually violate the rule.

e. Improperly Influence Government: A lawyer should not state or imply to a client or prospective client an ability to influence improperly a government agency, official, or tribunal. A statement promising to achieve such results is also prohibited by the MRPCs.

f. Knowingly Assist Judge in Violation: Knowingly assist a judge or judicial officer in conduct that is a violation of applicable rules of judicial conduct or other law is prohibited.

g. Abuse of Public Position: Lawyers holding public office assume responsibilities beyond ordinary citizens. They may not use the public position to obtain special advantage for themselves or a client if such action is not in the public interest.

MPRE Tip: Many discrete MPRE offenses also qualify as MRPC 8.4 violations.

5. Disciplinary Authority – Choice of Law – MRPC 8.5: This rule addresses disciplinary power over lawyers in multi-jurisdiction practice.

a. Foreign Lawyer in State: This rule subjects a foreign lawyer admitted to appear under the *pro hac vice* rule to discipline by the local bar authority. *Pro hac vice* status usually requires the sponsorship of an attorney admitted in the jurisdiction. This temporary practice privilege usually is not available to persons who have failed the local bar exam.

b. Lawyer Outside State: Similarly, a state lawyer disciplinary authority may discipline a lawyer who is admitted even if the wrongful action occurred outside the licensing jurisdiction. If there are different rules between the licensing jurisdiction and the jurisdiction in which the violating effect of the conduct occur, the latter jurisdiction's rules control.

RIGOS UNIFORM BAR REVIEW SERIES

PROFESSIONAL RESPONSIBILITY EXAM REVIEW (MPRE)

Chapter 5

Law Firms, Marketing, and Professional Integrity

Question Map

Numbers immediately following the topic are the chapter question numbers. The **boldface** numbers preceded by "F" are the final exam question numbers. For example, for the topic "A. 1. Responsibilities of Partners, Managers, and Supervisory Lawyer" below, question 32 is in the chapter questions on page 5-194; question **F1** is in the final exam on page 7-275.

Chapter 5

Law Firms, Marketing, and Professional Integrity

Questions

1. Mega Law Firm hired a new associate attorney named Tom, who graduated from a law school in Boston and had just passed the bar exam. Tom was assigned to work in the tax department for a senior tax partner. The tax partner explained to Tom that every associate was paid in proportion to the hours that he billed to clients and that this was an important factor to promotions. He further explained that "many associates are able to increase their billable hours by applying a 'difficulty equalizer' of 1.2. So if your time sheets show only 35 hours in a week, you multiply by 1.2 and actually bill the clients 42 hours. The clients don't know how much time you actually spend on a matter, so they will not question the fee statements." Tom was eager to advance within the firm, so he immediately began to follow the partner's billing practices advice.

Is Tom, the associate, subject to discipline?

- **(A)** No, because he merely followed the advice of the senior partner to whom he reported in the law firm.
- **(B)** No, unless the clients object to the "difficulty equalizer" billing method.
- **(C)** Yes, for personally engaging in conduct involving dishonesty, fraud, deceit, or misrepresentation.
- **(D)** Yes, unless Tom reports the tax partner to the appropriate professional authority.

2. Attorney David Defense was defending a professional malpractice lawsuit in a bench trial conducted in the courtroom of Judge Florence Fluid. David was unsatisfied both with Judge Fluid's rulings on his objections during the trial and the Judge's ultimate judgment decision containing adverse Findings of Fact and Conclusions of Law. He left the courthouse very upset and held a news conference with his client. The Reporter inquired why the Judge's decision was so harsh against David and his client. David answered that Judge Florence considered evidence that should have been excluded because she was high on marijuana during the whole trial.

Is attorney David Defense subject to discipline for making this statement?

- **(A)** Yes, if the Judge did not use marijuana, whether or not lawyer David believed the statement to be true.
- **(B)** Yes, if lawyer David knew that the Judge was not high on marijuana every day during the trial.
- **(C)** No, because the trier of fact is supposed to render a verdict based on her independent assessment of all the evidence.
- **(D)** No, because David Defense has a First Amendment right to free speech in judicial proceedings.

3. Larry Lawyer agreed to create a corporation for Shawn Shifty. Shawn told Larry he was going to use the new entity to purchase a bowling alley owned by an estate that was being probated by sitting Judge Grant Anderson, who had been "milking" the estate for five years. Shawn told Larry that this is a secret and "don't tell anyone." He further explained that the bowling alley purchase agreement was for $50,000 less than market value, but Shawn had to pay a bank $40,000 to retire the bank debt on a new Cadillac the judge had purchased. Larry was shocked that a sitting judge would operate in such a manner.

Regarding the duty to report the judge's conduct to the Judicial Commission,

- **(A)** Larry must report the offense because it raises a substantial question about the Judge's fitness for office.
- **(B)** Larry may report the offense because it raises a substantial question about the Judge's fitness for office.
- **(C)** Larry must not report the offense.
- **(D)** Larry may not report the offense even though it raises a substantial question about the Judge's fitness for office.

4. Sally Solicitor, attorney, was at a social cocktail party in her condominium. At the party she struck up a conversation with Paula Prospective. As soon as Paula saw Sally, Paula began to talk about an automobile accident she had been in the previous day. Sally gave Paula a number of opinions concerning how the law would likely be applied to the facts of her case. At the end of the party, Sally gave Paula her business card and told her she would like to handle her case.

Under which of the following circumstances is Sally subject to discipline?

I. Sally is Paula's second cousin.
II. Sally had handled a matter for Paula five years ago.
III. Paula called Sally the next morning telling her to begin work on her case.
IV. Sally called Paula the next morning asking her if she should start working on the case.
V. Sally wrote a letter to Paula the next morning that offered to take the case on.

- **(A)** III, IV, and V.
- **(B)** III and IV.
- **(C)** I, III, and IV.
- **(D)** II, III, and IV.

5. Big Bucks law firm has a department that specializes in handling matters concerning commercial paper. Rebecca Rainmaker is a senior partner at Big Bucks and firm "relationship person" with their client Mary Money. Mary was leaving on a Caribbean holiday and decided to leave a $5 million bearer bond with her law firm for safekeeping. Mary went to the firm and learned that Rebecca was in court, so she gave the bond to Alice Associate. Alice worked directly for Rebecca.

Two weeks later, Mary returned and called Rebecca to arrange a meeting to pick up the bearer bond. Rebecca checked the firm's ledger of client property custody, saw no entry, and said, "What bond?" Mary explained she had left the bond with Alice, who had been laid off the previous week. Rebecca went into Alice's office and found the bond in the in basket on the desk.

Is Rebecca Rainmaker subject to discipline?

- **(A)** Yes, if she failed to supervise Alice Associate and ensure that she complied with the MRPCs.
- **(B)** Yes, because Alice Associate is Rebecca's subordinate lawyer.
- **(C)** No, unless Alice Associate had demonstrated a prior history of mistakes and omissions.
- **(D)** No, as long as the bearer bond was promptly returned to Mary Money.

6. Paula Promoter was an attorney specializing in personal injury soft tissue cases. Paula routinely sought out speaking engagements in front of chiropractic groups. One of Paula's speeches was near the university, and two doctors of chiropractory came up to Paula after her speech. They explained that they were alumni of the university and former players. Because of this, they received a great number of referrals from the university coaching staff. The doctors were hoping that they could extend the referral benefit by bringing a lawyer into the group. After negotiations, Paula agreed, "If you doctors refer substantial patients to me, I will retain you as experts in all my soft tissue cases."

Is Paula subject to discipline for making this agreement?

- **(A)** No, unless Paula shares legal fees with the two chiropractors.
- **(B)** No, because Paula is giving more (all expert work) to the chiropractors than she is getting in return (substantial but not all referrals).
- **(C)** Yes, because the lawyer is giving value for the recommendation.
- **(D)** Yes, because their reciprocal agreement is on a mutually exclusive basis.

7. Bigger Business Brokers Inc. has a small transactional department of buying and selling small business enterprises for commission. Management desired to grow this department in their business and related consulting fees. Bigger uses deal-making employees and brokers with some training and varying degrees of education and experience. To increase their apparent business transactional expertise, Bigger hired Connie Competent, a lawyer with deep legal experience in planning corporations, partnerships, LLC, and related financing deal-making opportunities.

One of Connie's duties was to conduct business entity legal classes for all the Bigger company's marketing people. The company also asked her to author a semi-annual business entity newsletter that was mailed to all of the company's actual and potential clients including local business people. The newsletter advised the company's clients to direct all business enterprise legal questions to the newly-trained Bigger employees, who would answer questions and draft documents at no cost if the customers used the company's services. If the employee is unsure of the legal answer, the question will be referred to lawyer Connie Competent, their expert.

Is Connie Competent subject to discipline?

- **(A)** No, as long as Connie is admitted to practice law in the state.
- **(B)** No, because none of the company's clients are charged for the legal advice and documents.
- **(C)** Yes, because Connie is in effect giving legal advice to persons who are not her clients.
- **(D)** Yes, because Connie is aiding Bigger Business Brokers in the unauthorized practice of law.

8. Maria Marketing was a sole practitioner lawyer trying to build her client list. One of her marketing techniques was to attach large signs on both sides of her station wagon stating, "My aggressive legal representation will make your opponent want to settle. Hire us to file your lawsuit today. Call 123-4567 now." In an attempt to build business, Maria parked the station wagon next to the emergency room at the local county hospital.

Is Maria subject to discipline?

- **(A)** Yes, because the signage is in extremely poor taste.
- **(B)** Yes, because lawyers may not engage in in-person solicitation within 500 feet of a hospital.
- **(C)** No, unless the signs created false expectations.
- **(D)** No, because the First Amendment protects commercial speech.

9. Betty Businessbroker was involved in listing, selling, and buying small businesses. She had developed a robust practice of putting business deals together. She had just put together a purchase and sale of a restaurant that included the real estate. The seller wanted to use a title company to handle the escrow. Betty suggested that the parties use Lucy Lawyer to close the sale and told the buyer and seller that Lucy would charge the same as the title company, but would do a better job. Betty knew that Lucy usually charged substantially more than title companies in the locale so she could divide the overcharge with the referring broker. Lucy accepted the closing, overcharged the engagement, and sent one-third of the fee to Betty.

Is Lucy Lawyer subject to discipline?

- **(A)** Yes, because as escrow she would have a duty to both the seller and buyer, thus creating a conflict of interest.
- **(B)** Yes, because she is a lawyer engaging in conduct involving dishonesty.
- **(C)** No, because she did not solicit or propose the escrow.
- **(D)** No, as long as such escrow functions are not determined to be the practice of law in the jurisdiction.

10. Loretta Lawyer and Wendy Writer were childhood friends who grew up in the same block in a small city. They also both went to Kennedy State University and pledged the same sorority in undergraduate school. Following graduation, Wendy decided to take some time off and become a ski bum. Loretta went directly to law school in Boston. After 18 months, Wendy had enjoyed two skiing seasons and decided it was time to get serious about completing her education. She therefore enrolled in a high quality master's in journalism program. The following June, Loretta graduated from law school with a J.D., and Wendy received an M.S. in journalism.

The two friends stayed close and took a flat together in Boston. Loretta went to work at a law firm, and Wendy became the Legal Editor of the *Boston International World News*. Since they were both trying to advance, they agreed Wendy would give heavy and favorable newspaper coverage to all of Loretta's trials. Loretta in return agreed to inform Wendy of any juicy newsworthy cases or controversies Loretta learned about at the law firm.

Is the agreement between Loretta and Wendy proper?

- **(A)** Yes, as long as Loretta does not give any valuable monetary consideration for new clients that result from the favorable news coverage.
- **(B)** Yes, because Wendy has a duty as a newspaper reporter to cover trials, and the newspaper leaves the detailed trial coverage choices up to the reporter.
- **(C)** No, unless Wendy was the person who proposed the reciprocal agreement, and it was not exclusive.
- **(D)** No, even if Loretta runs and pays a reasonable cost for advertisements in the *Boston International World News*.

11. Sally Settlerlawyer was representing a client in a product liability action. The defendant Big Corporation offered a $600,000 cash settlement if Sally and her client would sign the settlement agreement the defendant drafted. The agreement specified that neither Sally nor her client would discuss the underlying claim or settlement terms and that Sally could not further represent her client or any of the other product liability victims of Big Corporation. Sally's client was very much in favor of accepting the settlement since it was $200,000 higher than the $400,000 they had expected.

Is it proper for Sally to sign the agreement?

(A) Yes, because the client has the sole decision to accept or reject settlement offers.
(B) Yes, because not to accept the offer creates a conflict of interest between Sally and her client.
(C) No, because it restricts a lawyer's ability to represent other victims against Big Corporation.
(D) No, unless the lawyer is independently compensated for the non-compete agreement.

12. Alicia Attorney worked for a law firm for five years after law school. She decided she wanted to try something new and began an investment consulting business. Her consulting business grew, and she stopped practicing law completely, but kept her bar membership. Alicia met Iola Investor and advised her to lend $25,000 to Great Expectations Ltd. on an unsecured basis without recommending that Iola receive independent consultation. Iola was not informed that Alicia owned the majority interest of Great Expectations.

Is Alicia subject to discipline?

(A) Yes, because a lawyer cannot borrow from a client.
(B) Yes, because concealment of the ownership interest is a form of dishonesty.
(C) No, because Alicia was not practicing law.
(D) No, because Iola was not a legal client of Alicia.

13. Gloria Genius passed the New York bar exam and opened a law firm in New York City. Gloria also sat for and passed the Certified Public Accountant exam and received a CPA certificate in New Jersey. In renewing her New Jersey CPA certificate, Janet submitted a false financial statement.

Is Janet subject to discipline as a lawyer in New York for so doing?

(A) Yes, but only if the submitted financial statement leads to a criminal conviction.
(B) Yes, if Janet's behavior is found to involve dishonesty.
(C) No, because Janet's behavior in question did not occur in New York.
(D) No, because Janet's behavior in question did not involve her capacity as a lawyer.

14. Able was licensed in jurisdiction A which requires ("shall" or "must") a lawyer to report known incidents of lawyer professional misconduct, while jurisdiction B's reporting requirement is only suggestive ("may"). Able's corporate client is purchasing property in jurisdiction B, which is where most of the negotiations took place. Able developed personal knowledge that the acquiring company's attorney had violated a substantive ethical provision that would have been a violation in both jurisdictions. However, he decided not to report the attorney's misconduct to the bar association in either jurisdiction.

Is Able subject to discipline?

(A) In jurisdiction A only.
(B) In jurisdiction B only.
(C) In both jurisdictions A and B.
(D) In neither jurisdiction A nor B.

15. Sarah Senior was a partner in a major law firm specializing in white collar criminal defense. She was in charge of the defense of a former CEO of a large corporation charged with financial statement reporting fraud. Sarah hired a new associate, Alice, to assist in the defense for an agreed $25 per hour compensation. Four months later, the case settled and Alice left the firm for a much higher-paying position with another defense firm.

Two months later, the corporate CEO complained about the magnitude of the legal bill for the defense. Sarah reviewed the time slips and discovered that her former associate, Alice, had been triple billing her time. Apparently, the payroll clerk made out the hourly associates' paychecks without requiring approval by the supervising lawyer. Sarah instructed the billing department to give the client credit for all the extra time Alice had billed.

Sarah

- **(A)** Must report Alice's fraudulent time slips to the appropriate professional authority because they involve dishonesty.
- **(B)** May report Alice's fraudulent time slips to the appropriate professional authority because they involve dishonesty.
- **(C)** Is not required to report Alice's fraudulent time slips because Alice has left the law firm, and there was no harm done.
- **(D)** Must not report Alice's fraudulent time slips if the CEO and corporate client insist that the billing information detail is to be kept confidential.

16. Everything Law Firm encouraged their lawyers to specialize in various areas of the law. They had this policy so that the firm could better market their member's expertise.

Which of the below statements in an advertisement would subject an attorney to discipline?

- **(A)** Connie Carpenter, Attorney-CPA.
- **(B)** Paula Pepper, Patent Attorney.
- **(C)** Thelma Taxing, Corporate Tax Specialist Attorney.
- **(D)** Alice Always, accepting only matters in Admiralty.

17. Debra Defendant was representing herself *pro se* in a small claims court action. The case involved a loan made by Mega Bank to Francis Friend in which Mega was trying to secure a judgment against Debra under the theory that she guaranteed the loan. She asked her friend, Alice Attorney, if she had any free advice. Alice responded, "Defend on the basis that the statute of frauds requires guarantees be written." Debra followed Alice's advice and won the case.

Is Alice subject to discipline for assisting a non-lawyer in the practice of law?

- **(A)** Yes, because the legal advice was not rendered through a probono organization approved by the State Bar Association.
- **(B)** Yes, because Alice assisted Debra in the unauthorized practice of law.
- **(C)** No, because Alice was not compensated for her legal advice.
- **(D)** No, because Debra was representing herself *pro se* in the case.

18. Barbara Big Bucks was a wealthy client of lawyer Roberta Recommender. Roberta was quite active in local bar committees and was well respected by her peers. Barbara asked Roberta if she would recommend and sponsor her favorite nephew for admission to the state bar. Barbara told Roberta, "He is a good boy, and last summer he worked in our office and performed very well."

Roberta may properly

I. Write a recommendation letter as instructed.

II. Require Barbara to state her opinions of her nephew in writing.

III. Write a letter containing a positive recommendation if she has no adverse information about Barbara's nephew.

IV. Not write the letter unless she makes her own independent investigation.

(A) Any of the above.
(B) III and IV, but not I or II.
(C) IV, but not I, II, and III.
(D) None of the above.

19. Connie Conflict is a lawyer with a robust personal injury practice. She has a staff of experienced non-lawyer assistants who work on the intake of a new case. These paraprofessionals have graduated from recognized legal assistant programs, and the firm has a very detailed policy and procedures manual. One of the assistants took a new client's file home to research the merits of the claim and misplaced it. Unfortunately, before the file was found, the statute of limitations had run on the client's underlying claim.

Which of the below correctly states Connie's professional responsibilities in the matter? Connie is

(A) Subject to both professional discipline and civil liability under a theory of *respondeat superior*.
(B) Subject to civil liability but not professional discipline unless she failed to adequately supervise the non-lawyer assistant.
(C) Subject to professional discipline but not civil liability.
(D) Subject to neither professional discipline nor civil liability.

20. For which of the following is lawyer A subject to discipline if she fails to report to the disciplinary authority lawyer B's criminal activity?

I. Lawyer A received the criminal information while defending lawyer B in a related malpractice case.

II. Lawyer A received the criminal information while serving as a counselor in a bar-sponsored substance abuse program.

III. Lawyer A received the criminal information from a client who was a party to a prior illegal transaction with lawyer B.

(A) All the above.
(B) Two of the above.
(C) Only one of the above.
(D) None of the above.

21. Attorneys Adam, Baker, and Charlie have decided to join practices together in a Professional Limited Liability Company. They will call the firm "A, B & C Law Services, PLLC." Their letterhead will indicate offices in jurisdiction 1 in which Adam is admitted and jurisdiction 2 in which Baker is admitted. Charlie is admitted in both jurisdiction 1 and 2.

Which of the below is most likely to subject the attorneys to professional discipline?

- **(A)** Attorney Adam wins election as the part-time mayor of the city in which one of the offices is located and continues to practice law.
- **(B)** On the firm's letterhead behind Adams name is the wording "admitted only in jurisdiction 1" and behind Baker's name is "admitted only in jurisdiction 2," but there is no such statement behind Charlie's name.
- **(C)** On the firm's letterhead behind Adams name is the wording "admitted only in jurisdiction 1." Behind Baker's name is "admitted only in jurisdiction 2." Behind Charlie's name is "admitted in both jurisdiction 1 and 2."
- **(D)** Attorney Baker wins election to serve as a part-time judge in jurisdiction 2 and he wants to add "part-time judge" behind his name.

22. Emily Excellence was an attorney who was also properly licensed by the jurisdiction as a Certified Public Accountant (CPA). She had just left a large law firm to start a boutique law firm specializing in tax matters. To promote her new firm, she ran an advertisement on the local television station stating, "Emily Excellence, an attorney-CPA, announces the opening of her law practice limited to tax matters. Effective, thoughtful representation at reasonable fees. Call 123-4567 for a free 20-minute consultation." Emily has kept a videotaped copy of the televised advertisement for two years and a record of when each advertisement was shown.

Is this televised advertisement proper?

- **(A)** Yes.
- **(B)** Yes, even if Emily charges for the initial 20-minute consultation.
- **(C)** No, because Emily's CPA certificate is not issued by the State Bar Association.
- **(D)** No, because the words "effective and thoughtful" are a form of implied comparison with other lawyers.

23. Attorney Diane Divorce has just passed the bar exam and opened her new law practice office. While she was in law school, she worked for a family law firm as a legal intern and learned a lot about operating a divorce practice. In an attempt to jump-start her new practice, she sent a written notice to all her law school classmates stating, "Send me a divorce client, and I will send you $1,000 cash."

Is Diane subject to discipline for mailing the advertisement to her law school classmates?

- **(A)** Yes, because a lawyer is never permitted to compensate a referral source.
- **(B)** Yes.
- **(C)** No, as long as no non-lawyer receives the advertisement or the $1,000 forwarding compensation.
- **(D)** No, if the recommended clients are fully informed of the referral fee arrangement and are given a full opportunity to consult with other lawyers.

24. Iola Injured was seriously injured in a automobile accident and taken to the local hospital. She was accosted in the emergency room by Loretta Lawyer. Loretta told Iola, "We are the best personal injury attorneys in the state and guarantee we will get you the highest recovery possible if you sign this representation agreement now." Iola passed out shortly after Loretta made the solicitation and woke up six hours later. She then called her family lawyer, Priscilla Proper, and explained to her what occurred and told her that she could use the information as she saw fit. One week later, disciplinary counsel from the state bar association called Priscilla to ask for information about Loretta.

Priscilla should:

(A) Decline any comment to the inquiries of the disciplinary counsel because they involve another lawyer that Priscilla had never met, and she was not there.
(B) Decline to report the misconduct to the appropriate disciplinary authority.
(C) Respond to the telephone inquiry from the disciplinary counsel, but decline to report the matter to the appropriate disciplinary authority.
(D) Respond to both the telephone inquiry from the disciplinary counsel and report the misconduct to the appropriate disciplinary authority.

25. Quick & Ready, P.S., is a professional corporation organized under state law that allows law firms to incorporate. Mr. Quick is still active in the practice, but Mr. Ready died last year. There are also six other lawyers who own shares of the corporation, and all practice with the firm. There are twenty additional employees in the firm, four of whom are associate lawyers.

Which of the following is (are) proper?

I. The law firm has appointed Laura Layperson, a non-lawyer, to be the president and managing director of the firm.

II. The non-stockholder lawyers are not eligible for share ownership until they have been with the firm for three years.

III. All new hires – lawyers and non-lawyers – are required to sign an agreement that they will not represent any firm clients for one year after leaving the firm.

IV. Two of the new associates feel strongly about *pro bono* work and want the law firm to give 2% of the fees it earns directly to the American Red Cross.

(A) Only one of the above.
(B) Only two of the above.
(C) Only three of the above.
(D) All four of the above.

26. Able and Baker is a law firm trying to expand the services it provides to its clientele base. The firm is considering offering trust services and financial planning for medium-sized family business owners. Such services are not considered the unauthorized practice of law in the jurisdiction.

Which of the following makes the law firm most likely to be subject to discipline?

(A) Providing such services to both clients and non-clients of the law firm.
(B) Not using an entity that is distinct from the law firm.
(C) A failure to communicate to customers that such services are not legal services and that protections such as the attorney-client privilege and conflict of interest provisions do not apply.
(D) Not adhering to all the rules of professional conduct (MRPCs) applicable to the practice of law in the jurisdiction.

27. Alice Alpha and Betty Beta have decided to start a law firm focusing on immigration law. They have employed a public relations firm to assist them in the initial marketing effort. The public relations firm has recommended to Alice and Betty that they use for the trade name "Department of Immigration Law Firm" and post the name on their letterhead and business cards.

If Alice and Betty adopt this name, are they subject to discipline?

(A) No, because no reasonable person would conclude the law firm is connected to a government agency.
(B) No, because a law firm is entitled to practice law using whatever trade name it desires.
(C) Yes, because lawyers may not put their firm's trade name on letterhead and business cards unless approved by the State Bar Association.
(D) Yes, because potential clients may be misled as to the law firm's authoritative status.

28. Cathy Community was an associate in a law firm who volunteered for service with a law reform organization. The committee that Cathy has been appointed to is working on two small loan company statutory revisions to be submitted to the legislature in the jurisdiction. One proposed statute would require registration of all loan companies, many of which are clients of Cathy's law firm. The other proposed statute would eliminate an interest rate ceiling on loans, which would benefit the small loan companies.

Cathy is subject to discipline unless she discloses to the committee

(A) That the proposed registration statute would be detrimental to some of the law firm's clients.
(B) That the proposed elimination of the interest rate ceiling would benefit some of the law firm's clients.
(C) Neither the detriment nor the benefit of the proposed statutes to any of the law firm's clients.
(D) Both the detriment and the benefit of the proposed statutes to any of the law firm's clients.

29. Gladia Goodhearted was appointed by Judge Commending to represent a client named Olivia Obnoxious. After Gladia accepted appointment and made an initial investigation, she determined that the client was both indigent and asserting a very unpopular cause. She wants to avoid the appointment and withdraws on the basis that the appointment:

I. Will result in an unreasonable financial burden.

II. Will result in a violation of the Rules of Professional Conduct.

III. Will outrage Gladia's other clients because the client and cause are so repugnant.

IV. Will impair her ability to represent the client effectively because the client and cause are so repugnant.

Gladia will be subject to discipline if her reason(s) to withdraw is:

(A) I and II.
(B) I and III.
(C) III only.
(D) All four of the above.

30. Alice Associate was a young associate in Mega Law Firm, PLLC. In her spare time, she volunteered for a legal clinic advice telephone hotline sponsored by a nonprofit bar association. On Saturday afternoon, Alice was in the legal clinic and took a call from Connie Consumer. Connie's problem was that she had a viable legal claim against Big Buck Bank, which happened to be a client of Mega Law Firm.

Which of the conduct by Alice would be proper and/or improper?

I. Rendering legal advice to Connie if she did not know Big Buck Bank was a client of Mega Law Firm, PLLC.

II. Rendering legal advice to Connie if she knew Big Buck Bank was a client of Mega Law Firm, PLLC.

III. Informing Connie of the limited representation role that Alice is playing.

IV. Informing Connie that further assistance of counsel may be necessary to resolve or continue monitoring her legal problem.

	Proper	Improper
(A)	I & III	II & IV
(B)	II & III	I & IV
(C)	I, III, & IV	II
(D)	III & IV	I & II

31. Alicia Associate is a newly hired associate at Heavy Hitter, PLLC, a law firm. Alicia was at the firm for about nine months when Pattie Partner approached her. Pattie emphasized that the firm had a public interest policy supporting *pro bono* activities. Pattie asked Alicia if she would be willing to serve as a volunteer on the local Consumer Complaint Committee. The committee would receive complaints and issue formal reports as appropriate. If she accepts, the committee would consist of Pattie, Alicia, and Volia Volunteer, a layperson who volunteered for the committee.

Is it proper for Alicia to accept Pattie's invitation to serve?

(A) Yes, but service is optional.
(B) Yes, because all lawyers have an obligation to do a reasonable amount of *pro bono* work.
(C) No, because lawyers may not share legal service responsibilities with non-lawyers.
(D) No, because if Alicia is unpaid for her service on the *pro bono* committee, it may affect the competency level at which she will perform.

32. Nancy Newcomer graduated from law school and spent the next year clerking for a judge who sat on the court of appeals. During the clerkship, Nancy spent almost all her time in the library conducting research on criminal law issues. Nancy then went with a general litigation law firm upon completion of her clerkship. At the firm, Nancy reported to Paula Partner. The first day on the job, Paula assigned Nancy to try a case in superior court involving a complex civil dispute. She handed her the file and said, "The case starts tomorrow at 9:00 a.m."

Is Paula subject to discipline?

(A) Yes, if the firm's policies and procedures manual indicates that one of Paula's responsibilities is to supervise new associates.
(B) Yes, if Nancy was not competent to conduct the trial assigned to her.
(C) No, unless Nancy loses the case for the firm's client.
(D) No, because Nancy has a duty to ask questions and seek out assistance if she has trouble handling any assigned case.

33. Lean & Hungry was a law firm that specialized in representing individuals in bankruptcy. The economy in the local area was on an upswing, and the law firm partners felt that they had to find some way to stimulate referrals. There was an opening in the local bankruptcy court for an administrator who would assign court-appointed bankruptcy trustee work to local law firms. Lean & Hungry lobbied and campaigned for and made substantial contributions promoting the appointment of Florence Formerpartner, who previously worked for their law firm. Florence got the administrator's position, and Lean & Hungry immediately began to receive appointments.

Is Lean & Hungry subject to discipline?

(A) Yes, unless no cash was given to Florence.
(B) Yes, because a law firm may not contribute to a candidate who subsequently appoints the firm.
(C) No, unless but for the desire to be appointed, Lean & Hungry would not have made the contributions.
(D) No, because lawyers are encouraged to participate in judicial-style appointments.

34. Judge Justice was assigned a case that involved a complicated evidence question. For help in analyzing the two applicable contradictory evidence theories, the Judge enlisted the assistance of a lawyer-professor who taught evidence at the local law school. The professor prepared a detailed memorandum of authority for the Judge that covered the evidence point in controversy. The Judge decided not to inform the attorneys for the parties of the research because they would have insisted upon commenting on the expert's opinion, which would have delayed the trial. The evidence lawyer-professor agreed with the judge that it would be counterproductive to inform the parties' attorneys.

Is the evidence lawyer-professor subject to discipline?

(A) Yes, unless the Judge decides the matter consistent with the evidence lawyer-professor's position.
(B) Yes, because he assisted a judge in conduct that violated the Code of Judicial Conduct.
(C) No, because the Judge makes all evidence decisions.
(D) No, because the Judge directs all lawyers in her court.

35. Mega Law Firm is a large international law firm headquartered in New York City. The Mega firm has 12 offices in the United States and 3 international offices outside the country. The management of the firm is conducted by a five-person managing committee consisting of senior lawyers from five of the firm's largest offices. All administrative functions are conducted by Alice Administrator, a non-lawyer CPA, who is located in the New York office. Alice reports to the managing committee at least once a month at the regular committee meeting. She is paid $5,000 per month and receives an annual bonus of 1% of the net income of the firm.

Is it proper for Alice to conduct all the administrative functions of Mega Law Firm?

(A) Yes, if Alice does not control the professional legal judgment of the lawyers in Mega Law Firm.
(B) Yes, unless Alice has access to client confidential information.
(C) No, because Mega Law Firm is sharing legal fees with a non-lawyer, Alice.
(D) No, because Mega Law Firm is, in effect, practicing law with a non-lawyer.

36. Aggressive Collector, Inc., is a collection company specializing in pursuing debtors. It is owned in part by Aritha Attorney. The lay staff writes standard collection letters and places telephone calls to harass debtors. If these practices are not successful, the staff writes an aggressive letter on Aritha Attorney's law firm letterhead. The letter states that unless full payment is received within ten days, a formal lawsuit will be filed.

For which of the following is Aritha Attorney most likely subject to discipline?

(A) If one of the debtors complains that the collection agency is engaging in extortion.
(B) If Aritha personally reviews and signs every letter before mailing.
(C) If Aritha failed to supervise the collection business.
(D) If Aritha allows the collection agency personnel to sign the letters without making a personal review.

37. Attorney Alice is a good friend of Carol CPA. They went through college together and both briefly worked at the same business before Alice went to law school. They stayed in touch, and both married men who were fraternity brothers in college. The two couples go on at least one long vacation together each year.

Both succeeded in their professional careers. Alice became a very well-thought-of attorney specializing in creating wills and trusts and probating estates. Carol worked for some time for a national accounting firm before starting her own practice. She specializes in taxes and small business accounting. They entered into an agreement where Alice would refer to Carol all clients who needed tax returns prepared or bookkeeping performed. In return, Carol agreed to refer all her clients who needed legal wills and estate work to Alice. The referrals were to be exclusive, but fees were not shared, no money was exchanged in return for the referrals, and all clients were informed of the two friends' relationship.

Was Alice's conduct in entering this agreement proper?

(A) Yes, because she did not share fees with or engage in the practice of law with a non-lawyer.
(B) Yes, because the clients were informed abut the mutual exclusive referral agreement.
(C) No, because consideration was given in return for the exclusive referral.
(D) No, because this is, in effect, a partnership and the sharing of fees with a non-lawyer.

38. Cathy Cautious was a partner in Quick & Sleepy, LLP, and specialized in appeals. She depended upon her legal assistant to docket all critical discovery and scheduling dates. The assistant had worked for Cathy for over five years and always docketed all the dates accurately. One particularly difficult case was completed on the trial court level by another lawyer in the firm who forwarded the file to Cathy's assistant. Unfortunately, the assistant was distracted and failed to bring the matter to Cathy's attention until after the appeal time period had elapsed.

Is Cathy subject to professional discipline because of the assistant's failure?

(A) Yes, because she had *respondeat superior* responsibility for any omissions of her legal assistant.
(B) Yes, if she was negligent in relying upon the assistant to document the critical dates in the appeal.
(C) No, if lawyers routinely rely upon legal assistants to perform such functions.
(D) No, because the client did not specifically retain Quick & Sleepy, LLP, to handle the appeal.

39. Loretta Lean and Harriet Hungry have just received word that they passed the bar exam and plan to start their own firm in Smallville. Their new law firm was named Lean & Hungry. They did not have any clients, so they are considering placing advertisements in the local newspaper containing the following statements:

I. "Both partners hold J.D. degrees, and Loretta Lean is also a licensed CPA."

II. "Our practice is limited to immigration and tax matters."

III. "We are the only law firm in Smallville that interprets both Spanish and French."

IV. "We take credit cards and are available for weekend consultation."

V. "Contact Loretta Lean for advertisement inquiries."

The attorneys would be subject to discipline for

- **(A)** Three of the above advertising statements.
- **(B)** Only two of the above advertising statements.
- **(C)** Only one of the above advertising statements.
- **(D)** None of the above advertising statements.

40. Teresa Traveler was a lawyer admitted to practice in New York. She developed a practice niche of professional engineering malpractice and she consulted with professional engineering firms across the country when they experienced claims. One of her consultees was Quick & Dirty, a professional engineering firm in Los Angeles, California, that was involved in litigation as a defendant. Quick & Dirty asked Teresa to prepare a short memorandum of law covering their situation. Two weeks later, they received a 30-page document and a bill for $15,000, which Quick & Dirty refused to pay.

Teresa may properly

- **(A)** Practice in California as long as she has no physical presence there.
- **(B)** Practice in California as long as the client approves her representation in writing and pays the bill.
- **(C)** Practice in California, but may not sue for a fee if the client decides not to pay.
- **(D)** Practice in California under the pro hac vice rule if sponsored by a lawyer admitted in California and approved by the tribunal.

41. Roberta Ready was a securities lawyer with White & Green, a large New York-based law firm. Prior to joining White & Green, Roberta worked for the Securities and Exchange Commission (SEC) as a litigator for 20 years. A prospective client, Fast & Loose, Inc., had approached White & Green about handling their SEC work. In a meeting, the prospective client demanded that Roberta explain her background, and she replied that she has "superior access to and influence with SEC staff." The client responded by asking a variety of questions of Roberta about her superior access and influence with the SEC. Roberta's answers were all very positive. Based upon the presentation they had heard in the meeting, Fast & Loose believed Roberta had superior access to and influence with the SEC.

Is Roberta subject to discipline?

- **(A)** Yes.
- **(B)** Yes, if she did not have the "superior access and influence" to the SEC as she implied.
- **(C)** No, because after 20 years with the SEC, she obviously would have developed superior access.
- **(D)** No, because most law firms' meetings with prospective clients involve puffing and emphasizing the positive.

42. Mega Law Firm is the largest firm in Smallville and routinely hires the top graduate from Smallville Law School. The firm represents virtually every large business in the area. Because there are not many new businesses entering the Smallville market, the firm is very protective of its client base. Therefore, when they hired Faith First, the number one student at Smallville Law School, she was required to sign an agreement that stated she would not solicit or do work for any client of Mega for a period of one year after voluntarily or involuntarily leaving Mega Law Firm.

Is Faith First subject to discipline if she signed this agreement?

(A) Yes, unless the law firm informed Faith she would not be employed by Mega unless she signed the agreement.
(B) Yes, because it is an agreement that restricts the right of a lawyer to practice after termination of the relationship.
(C) No, because Mega required the provision as a condition of employment, and Faith did not have the power to negotiate the restriction.
(D) No, because a lawyer may voluntarily relinquish the right to practice, and the restraint was reasonable in terms of subject, area of restraint, and time period.

43. Donna Defenselawyer is an experienced criminal defense attorney. She also does *pro bono* work and serves as the chairperson of a local preschool that her daughter attends. The preschool is expanding and wants to secure a variance from the building code given by the Board of Adjustment. The Chair of the Board of Adjustment is a lawyer named Iola Influenced. Iola and Donna have discussed the merits of the variance. Iola's 17-year-old son was arrested for burglary and Donna offered to take on the defense at no charge because she knew Iola's position on the variance would be critical.

Is Iola subject to discipline if she accepts Donna's offer to handle her son's defense at no charge?

(A) Yes, if Iola knew or it was apparent that Donna's offer was intended to influence improperly her action as a public official.
(B) Yes, only if Iola knew that Donna's offer was intended to influence improperly her action as a public official.
(C) No, unless Donna did not state that she expected Iola to vote to grant the variance.
(D) No, unless Donna expressly stated that she expected Iola to grant the variance.

44. Loretta Loyal had a favorite law school professor named Carol Contracts. They stayed close, and 20 years later, Carol ran for a local judgeship position with Loretta's strong support. Ten more years went by, and Carol developed a mild form of dementia. She is now up for reelection and has drawn opposition from a young ex-prosecutor, Nancy Newcomer, who claims Judge Carol is "over the hill" and "hardly knows where she is some days."

Loretta had a case in front of Carol a year ago and noticed a significant decline in the Judge's ability to concentrate on the witnesses and decide routine motions. Nonetheless, Loretta continued to like and respect Carol and allowed her campaign to quote her as, "I had a case before Judge Carol Contracts, and she is very mentally alert and as good as ever."

Is either or both Loretta or Nancy subject to discipline?

	Loretta	Nancy
(A)	No	No
(B)	No	Yes
(C)	Yes	No
(D)	Yes	Yes

45. Mary Moving was a partner in a large law firm and specialized in trust law instrument creation. One of her best assistants was Emily Experienced. Emily had not yet taken the Bar exam but was a very bright 3L who had worked in a bank trust department before beginning law school. Mary agreed to create a trust instrument for Roberta Rich, who wanted to sign the trust documents on June 10th. Unexpectedly, on June 9th, Mary had to travel to Washington D.C. for a Congressional hearing. Mary arranged for Emily to draft the complicated trust instrument. The trust documents were ready on time, and Roberta signed the documents on June 10th as planned.

Is Mary subject to discipline because of this conduct?

- **(A)** Yes, because a lawyer must not aid a non-lawyer in the unauthorized practice of law.
- **(B)** Yes, unless the trust documents were done competently and in accordance with all of Roberta's instructions.
- **(C)** No, if Roberta consents in writing to Emily drafting the trust instrument.
- **(D)** No, as long as Mary is ultimately responsibly for the trust instrument.

46. Ace Inc., was charged with dumping industrial pollution in violating of the state's environmental laws. The case is scheduled for a hearing before an administrative law judge (ALJ) named Helen Hardnose. Ace's management was shopping for an appropriate attorney to defend the case and heard that Judge Hardnose was friends with a lawyer named Penny Promotion. They called Penny and asked if she would interview for the representation.

In the subsequent interview, Ace's Vice president of Engineering commented on Penny's relative lack of experience in trying environmental pollution cases. The President of the corporation said, "Her friendship with Judge Hardnose is more important than experience, and we can buy experience. Penny, will you take our case?"

Is it proper for Penny to accept this representation?

- **(A)** Yes, because the client had full knowledge of Penny's lack of experience in handling environmental pollution cases.
- **(B)** Yes, because Penny did not claim to have improper influence with the tribunal.
- **(C)** No, because she is incompetent to handle such a representation.
- **(D)** No, because Penny has implied by silence that she has the ability to influence improperly the tribunal's decision.

47. Pattie Politician is an attorney and a partner with Nancy Nimble in the law firm of Nimble & Politician. The jurisdiction in question allows a lawyer to practice law and hold a public office concurrently, but she must recuse herself in matters where she has a conflict of interest.

Pattie ran for the state senate, was elected, and was subsequently appointed to chair the Senate Transportation Committee. The legislature meets for one month a year. An anti-development committee has sponsored a bill that would restrict property development, and the Senate Transportation Committee is considering the bill. Pattie, as chair of the committee, has the choice of which witnesses to call and how to schedule the testimony.

Mega Developer, Inc., has many projects under way that would be adversely affected if the legislation receives a "do pass" recommendation from the Transportation Committee. Mega's President called Nancy Nimble and asked if she would undertake representation of the company in expressing opposition to the proposed bill.

Is Nancy subject to discipline if she undertakes representation of the matter on behalf of Mega Developer?

- **(A)** Yes, unless Pattie has no knowledge of the details of Nancy's representation of Mega Developer and does not share in any fees derived from the representation.
- **(B)** Yes, because of her partner Pattie's position of Chair of the Senate Transportation Committee.
- **(C)** No, if Pattie Politician's name is removed from the name of the law firm.
- **(D)** No, if Pattie is screened out of any of the representation of Mega Developer, Inc.

48. Carol Capone was a mobster from Chicago who had been indicted for income tax evasion. She hired Alice Aggressive to defend the case. Sally Straightarrow was the prosecutor assigned to the case. Alice hired Iola Intimidator to sit in the front row at trial and stare at Sally. During one of the breaks in the trial, Iola approached Sally in the restroom and said, "Lady, you had better back off Carol if you want to avoid big trouble."

Sally was so frightened by the intimidation that she had to be replaced by an assistant prosecutor, Susan Second. Nonetheless, the jury returned a guilty verdict against Carol.

Is Alice Aggressive subject to criminal liability for the actions of Iola Intimidator?

- **(A)** Yes, only if there is proof that Alice induced Iola to intimidate Sally Straightarrow.
- **(B)** Yes, only if there is proof that Alice provided Iola with consideration to intimidate Sally Straightarrow.
- **(C)** No, because the guilty verdict means any intimidation efforts were ineffective.
- **(D)** No, because even though Alice may be subject to contempt by the judge or bar association discipline, criminal liability may not be imposed on an attorney.

49. Roberta Ready and Wanda Willing are partners in a law firm. They began as a simple partnership, but their business became more complex as their clientele grew. They also hired associates, and the business overhead increased. Their CPA, Alice Accountant, has advised them that they should form a professional service (P.S.) corporation or limited liability (L.L.) entity to operate their law firm.

Which of the below advantages may Roberta and Wanda properly realize?

I. Limited liability for malpractice inflicting damages upon clients.

II. Tax advantages such as increased retirement plan contributions.

III. Appoint Alice Accountant the treasurer of their new business as long as Alice does not own any shares in the entity.

IV. Convey an ownership interest in the new entity to their children to shift income.

(A) Three of the above.
(B) Two of the above.
(C) One of the above.
(D) None of the above.

50. Betty Broker is a lawyer and business opportunity broker who lists small businesses for sale and finds appropriate buyers. She has a lawyer friend named Carol Closer who specializes in creating the documentation necessary to close the sale and purchase of a small business.

Carol may properly:

I. Appear with Betty in seminars describing the process involved in the sale or purchase of a small business.

II. Give Betty her law firm business cards so that Betty may distribute them in her office to all people selling or buying a small business, with the understanding Betty will be compensated for any new closings generated for Carol.

III. Agree with Betty that she will refer to her all business sales and purchases if Betty refers to her all closings on all business sales, but no compensation will change hands.

IV. Reward Betty for her non-exclusive referrals by giving her a $500.00 gift certificate at her favorite restaurant for each closing she originated.

(A) One of the above.
(B) Two of the above.
(C) Three of the above.
(D) All four of the above.

51. Sarah Secretary worked for Getum & Quick, a law firm. She was a secretary and paralegal and worked primarily for Gertrude Getum. As Sarah was leaving the office at 5:00 p.m. one afternoon, she observed an automobile accident caused by a truck owned by Acme, Inc. She went to the assistance of the passengers and helped pull an elderly woman from the wrecked car. After some comforting talk, it became clear the elderly woman had suffered only minor physical injuries. Sarah gave her a business card and said, "Call Mr. Quick because he is an expert lawyer in automobile accidents and will get you the best recovery."

The next morning, she told Gertrude Getum about the accident and the conversation she had with the elderly woman. Gertrude said, "You should not have given out your card and solicited that case," but did not discuss the matter with any other personnel at the law firm.

Is Gertrude subject to discipline?

(A) Yes, because she is the supervisor of Sarah and therefore vicariously liable for her wrongdoing.
(B) Yes, because she did not inform Mr. Quick of the situation so he could reject the representation of the accident victim.
(C) No, because Sarah was unaware that she did anything wrong at the time she helped comfort the elderly woman.
(D) No, because as a non-lawyer, Sarah may recommend that a third party consult with a particular attorney.

52. In 1890, Simon DeGrande and Louis Foster founded a law firm in Everystate under the name DeGrande & Foster. Simon and Louis passed away early in the 20th century, but the firm continued. Over the years, there have always been various descendants of the two founders as partners and/or associates at the firm. At the present time, Tammie and Tommy DeGrande are partners at the firm, but there are no lawyers there with the surname of "Foster" who are direct descendants of Louis Foster. Tammie DeGrande has just been offered a lifetime appointment to the Federal judiciary.

If Tammie accepts the appointment, may the DeGrande & Foster law firm continue to use the same trade name?

(A) Yes, as long as Tommy DeGrande remains a partner in the firm.
(B) Yes, unless use of the trade name would be misleading.
(C) No, if Tammie DeGrande accepts the lifetime appointment and surrenders her partnership interest.
(D) No, unless there is a partner at the firm with the last name Foster.

53. Alicia Associate was an associate with White & Gray, a large New York City law firm. She began with the corporate tax department. Six months later, she was assigned to work for a partner named Susan Supervisor in the personal injury department. When she was doing research on the claim being asserted by a new firm client, Iola Injured, Alicia realized the defendant corporation was part of a corporate group that the law firm had previously represented in a somewhat related matter. She immediately informed Susan, who took the position that any conflict was too remote to be concerned about.

Alicia felt to the contrary, and after a short argument, they decided to submit the question to a senior partner who agreed with Susan that there was not a substantial conflict. Alicia kept working on the case and filed the complaint with the court as directed. Six months later, the trial court judge learned of the potential conflict and disqualified White & Gray. White & Gray then sent notice to the client Iola that she would have to find a new lawyer. Iola was outraged because White & Gray had already charged her large fees. She felt that it was not fair that she now had to find and pay to educate a new lawyer about her case so she filed a complaint with the jurisdiction's bar association.

Which of the attorneys is likely subject to discipline?

(A) None of the attorneys.
(B) The senior partner.
(C) The senior partner and Susan Supervisor.
(D) The senior partner, Susan Supervisor, and Alicia Associate.

54. Frances Finance is a Certified Financial Planner (CFP) specializing in closely-held, medium-sized companies. She entered into a partnership with Carol Cautious, a lawyer with deep experience in advising closely-held, medium-sized companies. Their business plan was to locate such closely-held, medium-sized companies that were for sale and match the opportunities up with groups of suitable investors. The role of Frances is to find suitable investors, and Carol does all the legal work involved. They both look for suitable businesses to be purchased that may be for sale at a reasonable price. The partnership charges a flat 5% of the purchase price for their joint services, which the partners divide equally after deducting any related expenses.

Is Carol subject to discipline?

(A) Yes, because she and Frances are partners in a business that, at least in part, consists of the practice of law.
(B) Yes, because she is assisting a person who is not a member of the bar in performing the unauthorized practice of law.
(C) No, because Frances' role is to locate suitable investors, and Carol's role is to do all the legal work involved.
(D) No, only if all the investors are informed of the equal division of the profits between Frances and Carol and do not object.

55. Mega Bank has a very large trust administration department. The Bank makes sure its trust officers do not practice law, so it refers all legal questions to a panel of "approved" outside lawyers. This includes drafting of the original trust documents. To be listed in the "approved" panel, a lawyer must sign a standard listing form that states, "I agree to recommend only Mega Bank's trust department and will not withdraw from representing a referred client prior to execution of a Mega Bank trust document by the client." These approved attorneys are listed in the Bank's widely distributed marketing pieces promoting their trust administration expertise. Mega asks Terri Trustlawyer if he would like to join their approval panel.

Is it proper for Terri Trustlawyer to sign the agreement required to become a member of the panel?

- **(A)** Yes, as long as Terri does not give any consideration in return for the listing.
- **(B)** Yes, as long as Terri is competent to draft trust instruments.
- **(C)** No, because the standard listing form may allow a third party to influence the lawyer's independent professional judgment.
- **(D)** No, because in effect, the lawyer is unethically using a non-lawyer to solicit new clients.

56. Quick & Smart was a law firm with both partners and associates. The partners direct and supervise the associates in the performance of their work on the clients' cases. Sally Subordinate was directed to draft an opposition pleading in response to a plaintiff's motion for summary judgment in a tort action. During the research, Sally came across a recent case that held contrary to the position of the firm's client. Sally immediately informed Paula Partner and stated she believed that the recent case should be disclosed. Paula directed to the contrary and stated that she did not believe the adverse position required disclosure. Sally disagreed but followed Paula's directive.

If the court learns of the non-disclosure of the recent case by Quick & Smart, who may receive discipline?

- **(A)** Only Paula Partner if she knew that the position taken was improper.
- **(B)** Only Sally Subordinate since she signed the improper pleading in question.
- **(C)** Both Paula and Sally because they both were involved in creating the improper pleading in question.
- **(D)** Neither Paula nor Sally unless their client loses the case on the merits.

57. Nancy Newlawyer is a new associate at the law firm of Able, Willing, & Ready, PLLC. As a *pro bono* activity, Nancy volunteered to join the board of the local Tenants' Legal Association. She received the appointment, and the managing partner of Able, Willing, & Ready approved of Nancy going on the board. At the first meeting of the board, Nancy learned that the major issue before the association was a pending resolution that would subject a landlord's tenant eviction to judicial scrutiny. Nancy immediately realized that the major landlord in the area was a client of the law firm.

Which of the following is Nancy's most proper position?

(A) Nancy is subject to discipline if the board of the Association takes a position contrary to one of Able, Willing, & Ready clients.
(B) Nancy will be subject to discipline if she fails to disclose to the board of the Association that their actions will harm a client of Able, Willing, & Ready.
(C) Nancy may join the board of the Association and may participate in the deliberations on the pending resolution if disclosure of the conflict is made to the other board members.
(D) Nancy may join the board of the Association, but should recluse herself concerning any input into the eviction decision.

58. Alice and Betty started a new law firm after they passed the bar exam. Each contributed $20,000 to the new professional limited liability entity. Their agreement specified that on the death of either of them, the remaining owner was legally committed to pay the deceased partner's heirs certain amounts for their equity interests in the firm. Alice died in an accident.

Betty and the law firm

(A) May not allow potential law firm purchasers to review confidential client information.
(B) May raise fees on existing clients to accumulate the buyout money of Alice's ownership interest.
(C) May not pay for Alice's ownership interest using firm funds because that would constitute fee splitting.
(D) May assume the client's consent to a transfer of their accounts and files to Betty unless the law firm is notified to the contrary.

59. Airhouse & Co. was a national discount security brokerage house that was experiencing lagging sales. Management came up with a promotion idea that would both increase sales and recruit a new class of customers. The idea was to begin a "Lawyer Referral Service" panel for all Airhouse clients who needed gift, trust, and estate legal documents prepared. The lawyers listed were required to maintain a minimum balance of $25,000 in a brokerage account at Airhouse & Co.

Laura Lawyer signed up and deposited $25,000 in an account with the understanding she would not have to pay for the legal work referrals she would receive.

Is the lawyer subject to discipline for receiving referrals in this manner?

(A) Yes, because this system involves a non-lawyer participating in the practice of law.
(B) Yes, because lawyers are required to maintain a minimum balance of $25,000 in the brokerage account at Airhouse & Co. to receive the referrals.
(C) No, because neither Airhouse & Co. nor the individual clients pay a fee for referrals.
(D) No, because Airhouse & Co. is functioning as a public lawyer referral service.

60. Pay-in-Advance Health Clinics was a chain of medical offices catering to walk-in patients. To avoid having to carry any unpaid account receivables, the clinics require that all patients pay in cash at the time of or before receiving their medical services. The services provided by the walk-in clinics were frequently inadequate, resulting in the aggravation of many individual patients' injuries. Some of the clinics' prior patients' claims were in litigation.

Loretta Lawyer wanted to attract new clients who received inadequate medical care at Pay-in-Advance Health Clinics. To make herself known to this group, Loretta appeared on television and radio shows, ran advertisements, wrote letters to local newspapers, and went to community council meetings to speak about the inadequate treatment given by the Pay-in-Advance Health Clinics. Loretta's negative statements were widely reported in local newspapers and television news shows.

Are the negative statements about the walk-in clinics made by Loretta Lawyer to the public media proper?

- **(A)** Yes, as long as Loretta did not make any false or misleading statements about her legal services.
- **(B)** Yes, as long as Loretta did not give any consideration to the media for publicizing her statements.
- **(C)** No, because it is improper for a lawyer to make a public statement about matters that are then in litigation.
- **(D)** No, because Loretta's intention in making the public media statements was to solicit new clients.

61. A and B are involved in a bitter divorce. In this process, their lawyers have frequent contentious disagreements. A's lawyer, Alice Abrasive, learned that B's lawyer, Tracy Target, did not truthfully respond to a discovery request and that in a subsequent motion to compel, Tracy lied to the court. The jurisdiction in question would likely deem Tracy's misconduct as raising a substantial question about a lawyer's fitness to practice law and require mandatory reporting to the State Bar Association. Instead, Alice told Tracy, "I should report you to the bar, but if your client accepts my client's offer of settlement, I will forget about reporting you to the bar."

Is Alice Abrasive's action proper?

- **(A)** Yes, as long as Alice's client B consents to the proposed lawsuit settlement.
- **(B)** Yes, as long as Alice's client consents to both the proposed lawsuit settlement and not reporting the misconduct of Tracy Target to the Bar Association.
- **(C)** No, because threatening an ethical complaint against opposing counsel as a bargaining chip is improper.
- **(D)** No, because reporting a lawyer's misconduct to the State Bar Association is mandatory.

62. Attorney Monica Maniac represented a wife in a very bitter divorce against an abusive husband. The trial was very contentious, and Judge Tight had to restrain Monica on a number of occasions. Finally, the court imposed significant sanctions on Monica herself for her disruptive behavior. Both Monica and her client felt the judge was terribly one-sided. After the case was over, Monica held a press conference and stated, "This court under Judge Tight does a terrible injustice to women seeking fairness in a divorce."

Is Monica subject to discipline for her public remarks about Judge Tight?

(A) Yes, because a lawyer must always refrain from public attacks on judges.
(B) Yes, unless Judge Tight actually did make decisions that were unfair.
(C) No, if lawyer Monica is a candidate for the judicial office Judge Tight now occupies.
(D) No, if attorney Monica did not make a false or reckless statement, and her opinion about Judge Tight was her honest opinion.

63. Barbara Busy was an attorney with a large caseload of minor tort incidents. She interviewed a workman injured in an industrial accident two and a half years ago. She and a new associate lawyer, Alice, researched the facts and case law and determined that the client had a strong claim against her former employer. This took five months to complete. Barbara and her associate Alice then drafted the Summons and Complaint. Barbara signed and directed the associate to file the pleading in "the local court" as she was leaving on vacation. Alice filed the pleading in the local federal district court rather than the local state superior court where the defendant corporation was located.

Barbara returned from vacation a month later and reviewed the filings. She then realized that the associate had filed the case in the wrong court and immediately prepared a motion to transfer the case to the right jurisdiction. The motion was denied, and by then the statute of limitations on the claim had run in the correct jurisdiction.

Which of the below is a correct statement of Barbara Busy's professional discipline and legal malpractice exposure?

(A) She is subject to neither professional discipline nor civil malpractice.
(B) She is subject to professional discipline, but not civil malpractice.
(C) She is subject to civil malpractice, but not professional discipline.
(D) She is subject to both civil malpractice and professional discipline.

64. Tom, Dick, and Harry were friends in law school. After they passed the bar exam they planned to open their own individual practices. To reduce the overhead, they decided to practice out of the same office and split the costs. To comply with professional responsibilities in most jurisdictions, the three lawyers may:

Which of the below action may the lawyers do without being subject to discipline?

I. Put all three names on a common office door.

II. Have a common telephone number and answer the phone as "law offices."

III. Put all three names on common letterhead and business cards.

IV. Put all their three names on common pleading papers.

(A) One of the above.
(B) Two of the above.
(C) Three of the above.
(D) All of the above.

65. Self-regulation of the legal profession requires that lawyers initiate a disciplinary investigation when they personally know that there has been a serious violation by another lawyer. Ruth Reporter is a lawyer who has been appointed as a guardian *ad litem* in a child custody case. Ruth believes that one of the child's parents may have embezzled substantial funds from the child's trust fund established by a grandparent. Further, Ruth believes that the attorney for the parent in question was personally involved in the embezzlement.

If the seriousness of the possible offense is substantial, and Ruth decides to report, the least appropriate authority to contact would likely be

(A) The county criminal prosecutor.
(B) The trial judge officiating over the case.
(C) The bar disciplinary authority in the jurisdiction.
(D) The attorney for the parent in question.

66. Robert was an insurance defense lawyer whose marriage to Prudence was becoming difficult. One night he attended an office party at the insurance company and met a claim agent named Carol Captivating. Carol had just completed her divorce from her third husband and had long been interested in Robert. After a few drinks the two left the office party together, and Robert engaged in marital infidelity with Carol. Marital infidelity is a criminal misdemeanor in the state.

Carol later bragged to her friends about the sexual encounter with the "Company's Lawyer Robert." This news eventually got to Prudence, who filed for divorce and also initiated a grievance complaint against Robert with the jurisdiction's bar association disciplinary authority.

Is Robert likely to be disciplined by the bar association?

- **(A)** Yes, because this is a criminal offense in the state.
- **(B)** Yes, only if he is convicted of the offense.
- **(C)** No, because Robert was not engaging in the practice of law during the offense.
- **(D)** No, because the crime of marriage infidelity is not usually considered to be an act of public moral turpitude.

67. Pattie Public is a lawyer who concentrates her practice on unfair business practices. She also serves *pro bono* on the state bar association's unfair business practices committee. One of her clients is Short Term Loans Inc. that makes short-term, high interest rate loans to consumers who usually are unable to borrow elsewhere. In representing her client she became very knowledgeable in all aspects of the state law.

The majority of the bar association's committee has decided to recommend to the legislature some public interest changes in the consumer lending law. One of the proposed changes will benefit Short Term Loans, Inc., but another change will eliminate a statutory exception they have used in the past. Pattie disclosed to the committee that some of the proposed statutory changes will benefit one of her client. Pattie also warned her client that one of the proposed changes will close a loophole in the law they are presently using but did not disclose her client notification to the committee.

Is Pattie subject to discipline?

- **(A)** Yes, because she participated in changing the law that could benefit her client.
- **(B)** Yes, because she failed to disclose to the committee she was going to warn her client of the changes that would adversely impact them.
- **(C)** No, because she disclosed to the law reform committee that her client would benefit from the legislative changes.
- **(D)** No, because she was not acting against the public interest and there was a no responsibility to disclose she was going to warn her client that the change in law will close one of the current loopholes.

Chapter 5

Law Firms, Marketing, and Professional Integrity

Answers

MPRE Tip: Put a piece of paper over the answers and "mask down" while working through the questions so you don't accidently peek at the next answer.

1. **/C/** It is professional misconduct to engage in conduct involving dishonesty, deceit, or misrepresentation. The fee statements prepared by associate Tom were fraudulent and constituted intuitional misrepresentations. [MRPC 8.4(c)] **(A)** is incorrect because all lawyers are required to adhere to the MRPCs. While MRPC 5.2(b) allows a subordinate lawyer to defer to a supervisory lawyer's reasonable resolution of an arguable question, the matter of such fraudulent over-billing can reasonably be answered in only one way. **(B)** is incorrect since the facts do not say the client even knew of the over-billing, much less approved of it. **(D)** is not the best answer; while MRPC 8.3(a) states a lawyer learning of an ethical violation should inform the appropriate professional authority, it does not excuse his own violation of the rules.

2. **/B/** A lawyer shall not make a statement that the lawyer knows to be false concerning the qualifications, integrity, or record of a judge. These words appear to be beyond the honest and candid opinion a lawyer is allowed to state about a judge, absent a showing of personal knowledge and truth in fact. [MRPC 8.2(a)] **(A)** is not the best answer because if the lawyer reasonably believed that the judge used marijuana, the lawyer would not have violated the disciplinary rule. **(C)** is incorrect because the Judge's duty to render a verdict based on an impartial assessment of all the evidence is different from the limitations of the lawyer's statements thereupon. **(D)** is incorrect because a lawyer does not have an absolute right to total freedom of speech.

3. **/C/** MRPC 8.3 specifies that a lawyer having knowledge that a judge has committed an act violating an applicable rule of judicial conduct that raises a substantial question as to the Judge's fitness for office shall promptly inform the appropriate authorities unless the information is protected by MRPC 1.6. The client's participation in the kickback to the Judge was potentially criminal fraud, but the client said "don't tell anyone," and thus, to reveal this confidence would violate MRPC 1.6. **(A)** is incorrect because the report involves the confidential information of the client and thus must not be revealed. **(B)** is incorrect because the report involves the confidential information of the client and thus must not be revealed. **(D)** is not the best answer because "may not" indicates improper behavior, but a failure to comply does not necessarily subject an attorney to discipline. An attorney who discloses a client's past crime is subject to discipline.

4. **/B/** Only items III and IV would subject Sally to discipline. (Note that it was the contract formed during the in-person oral solicitation at the party that violated the rule.) Oral solicitation of a prospective client is not allowed unless the client is a relative, friend or has a prior professional relationship with the attorney. There is usually no restriction on an attorney mailing a letter to a potential client, offering to take on the case. [MRPC 7.3] A, C, and D involve combinations of the alternatives that are incorrect.

5. /A/ MRPC 5.1(b) specifies that a supervisory lawyer shall supervise her direct associates and make reasonable efforts to ensure that each associate conforms to all MRPCs. Here, the associate failed to comply with MRPC 1.15, which requires written notice to the client upon receipt of funds or property and that the client custodial property must be safeguarded, such as keeping securities in a safe deposit box. **(B)** is incorrect because it is too simplistic and the MRPC requires only reasonable efforts; this is not strict liability. **(C)** is not the best answer because the duty to supervise direct subordinates does not arise only upon demonstrated mistakes and omissions. **(D)** is not the best answer because professional discipline may be imposed on a lawyer even if the client did not suffer any actual damages.

6. /C/ MRPC 7.2(c) states that a lawyer shall not give anything of value to a person for recommending the lawyer's services; the promise to retain the chiropractors is sufficient value to violate the rule. **(A)** is not the best answer because "anything of value" includes benefits other than sharing legal fees (although that would also qualify). **(B)** is incorrect because the relative benefits to each party of the agreement are irrelevant to the prohibition against giving "anything of value" for a referral. **(D)** is not the best answer because the agreement is exclusive only on the lawyer's side, not the chiropractor's ("retain you as an expert in all my soft tissue cases"). Mutually exclusive agreements violate the rule, but that does not apply here because the agreement is not mutually exclusive.

7. /D/ A lawyer who assists a person or corporation in giving legal advice has violated MRPC 5.5(b) if the assisted person is not admitted to practice law. Connie is helping the non-lawyers in the company to render legal partnership, corporate, and LLC advice to the public. **(A)** is incorrect because any person rendering legal advice must be a lawyer to avoid a violation of MRPC 5.5(b). **(B)** is incorrect because the rendering of legal advice by lay people is still the unauthorized practice of law whether or not compensation is charged. **(C)** is incorrect because a lawyer may give legal advice to non-clients. If the interest of the advised non-client is adverse to the interests of a client, the lawyer must so inform the non-client. [MRPC 4.3]

8. /C/ The best answer because MRPC 7.1 states an advertisement may not create unjustifiable expectations; "make your opponent want to settle" might make consumers believe that Maria has legal superpowers. **(A)** is not the best answer because good taste is not a required attribute of permissible advertising. **(B)** is incorrect because the facts do not state there was any in-person solicitation of individual potential clients, only a written sign. **(D)** is not the best answer; while the statement of speech protection is true, this does not preclude an attorney from being subject to discipline if an advertisement creates false expectations.

9. /B/ The broadest and best reason to impose discipline [MRPC 8.4(c)] (this result assumes the concealed overcharging and fee division is an ongoing arrangement between the attorney and the business broker). **(A)** is not the best answer because the intermediation role may allow dual representation if both parties are informed of the risks in writing and consent. **(C)** is incorrect because it is not necessary that the lawyer participate directly in soliciting or proposing the engagement if this is an ongoing arrangement. **(D)** is incorrect because lawyers may be subject to discipline for dishonest conduct even if it does not involve the practice of law. (Note that fee splitting with a non-lawyer could also be a disciplinary violation in this question, but that rationale was not presented in any of the alternatives.)

10. /D/ The best answer; MRPC 7.2(b) prohibits giving anything of value to another in consideration of a recommendation of the lawyer's services. While the paid advertising distracter may create legitimate new client inquiries, the thrust of the question is the betterment the lawyer is providing to the reporter (to get juicy newsworthy cases and controversies), which is being returned in the form of "heavy and favorable news coverage" to her trials. Further, the prohibition is to be interpreted broadly and would possibly include favorable media coverage that indirectly recommends the services of a particular lawyer. **(A)** is incorrect because the MRPC 7.2(b) prohibition is broader than monetary consideration and includes "giving anything of value" for the recommendation. **(B)** is incorrect because the focus of MRPC 7.2(c) is upon the lawyer giving value to another person, not whether the other person has other reasons for making the recommendations. **(C)** is incorrect because who proposed the relationship is not relevant.

11. /C/ This restriction, known as a "no further representation clause," is improper because it creates a restriction on an attorney's right to represent other victims against Big Corporation. [MRPC 5.6] **(A)** is incorrect because the question focuses on the lawyer's behavior, not the client's. **(B)** is incorrect because while this ethical dilemma does create a conflict of interest between the lawyer and the client, it is still not proper for the lawyer to agree to such a restriction on their future practice. **(D)** is not the best answer because even if compensated, it is still improper for a lawyer to agree to such a "no further representation clause." [ABA Formal Opinion 93-371]

12. /B/ The best answer because a lawyer who conceals material facts may be guilty of dishonesty regardless of whether she is in public practice of law or the disadvantaged party was or was not a client of the lawyer. [MRPC 8.4(c)] **(A)** is incorrect because a lawyer may, under certain circumstances, borrow from a client, but may not conceal material facts in a transaction that involves dishonesty. **(C)** is incorrect because a lawyer is subject to discipline for dishonesty even if not practicing law. **(D)** is incorrect because the victim was at least a customer of a lawyer who engaged in dishonesty.

13. /B/ A lawyer may be disciplined by her state legal authority for dishonesty even if the occurrence was outside the jurisdiction and even if it does not involve the practice of law. [MRPC 8.5] **(A)** is incorrect; while conviction of a crime is one reason for discipline, it may also be imposed even if no crime is involved. [MRPC 8.4(c)] **(C)** is incorrect because discipline may be imposed for actions occurring outside the licensing jurisdiction. **(D)** is incorrect because discipline may be imposed on a lawyer for behavior not involving her capacity as a lawyer.

14. /D/ If there is a different ethical rule between the licensing jurisdiction and the jurisdiction in which the conduct arose, the latter rule will control. Therefore, if jurisdiction A brings disciplinary charges against Able, it must apply the rule of jurisdiction B. [MRPC 8.3(a) and 8.5(b)] **(A)** is incorrect because the rule of the jurisdiction in which the conduct occurs is to be applied. **(B)** is incorrect because the rule of the jurisdiction in which the conduct occurs is to be applied. **(C)** is incorrect because the rule of the jurisdiction in which the conduct occurs – here B – is to be applied.

15. /A/ The ABA rule is that reporting a lawyer's dishonesty to the appropriate professional authority is mandatory ("shall" or "must"). [MRPC 8.3] **(B)** is incorrect because it suggests that reporting a lawyer's dishonesty is optional ("may"); some jurisdictions allow a lawyer's discretion, but that is the minority, non-ABA position. **(C)** is incorrect because reporting is mandatory even if no harm resulted. **(D)** is not the best answer because a lawyer's duties under the MRPCs may override client directions. (Notice the fraud was by an attorney, not the client, so confidentiality does not trump.)

16. /C/ A lawyer may not state she is a specialist (except Patent and Trademark) unless the issuing organization is approved by a state authority or accredited by the ABA. [MRPC 7.4] **(A)** is incorrect because the CPA certificate is issued by the State Board of Accountancy. **(B)** is incorrect because a lawyer admitted to practice before the U.S. Patent and Trademark office may indicate that specialty. **(D)** is incorrect because MRPC 7.4(c) specifies that a lawyer engaged in admiralty practice may use the designation "Admiralty."

17. /D/ The best answer because *pro se* self-representation is an exception to the unauthorized practice of law rules. [MRPC 5.5] **(A)** is incorrect because whether the legal advice was rendered through a *pro bono* organization is irrelevant to the question of the unauthorized practice of law. **(B)** is incorrect because this involves the *pro se* exception to the unauthorized practice of law. **(C)** is incorrect because the unauthorized practice of law does not depend upon whether the attorney was compensated.

18. /C/ A lawyer may not recommend a bar applicant unless all the statements therein are true and the lawyer has personal knowledge of same; the word of another is not usually sufficient, so an independent investigation is normal. [MRPC 8.1] **(A)** is incorrect because it involves an incorrect combination of alternatives. **(B)** is incorrect because it involves an incorrect combination of alternatives. **(D)** is incorrect because it involves an incorrect combination of alternatives.

19. /B/ The best answer. *Respondeat Superior* will create potential civil liability to the lawyer for the client's damages [common law of negligence], but professional discipline requires some showing of negligence in failure to supervise the non-lawyer paraprofessional directly involved in the problem. [MRPC 5.3] **(A)** is incorrect because it involves the wrong combination of outcomes for the related questions of malpractice civil liability and professional discipline for failure to supervise adequately. **(C)** is incorrect because it involves the wrong combination of outcomes for the related questions of malpractice civil liability and professional discipline for failure to supervise adequately. **(D)** is incorrect because it involves the wrong combination of outcomes for the related questions of malpractice civil liability and professional discipline for failure to supervise adequately.

20. /D/ None of the above is the correct answer because the three alternatives given in the question represent the three exceptions the ABA authorizes to the duty of a lawyer to report a violation of the MRPCs. [MRPC 8.3] Attorneys defending lawyers are not required to report MRPC violations of their clients. Information received in a bar sponsored substance abuse program does not have to be reported. If the information bottoming the violation is the confidential information of a client, reporting is not required absent client consent. **(A)** is incorrect because this alternative involves a wrong combination of correct statements. **(B)** is incorrect because this alternative involves a wrong combination of correct statements. **(C)** is incorrect because this alternative involves a wrong combination of correct statements.

21. /D/ The most likely of the four reasons given to impose professional discipline is if a part-time judge is advertising his judicial office on the letterhead because it implies an influence that could easily lead to misleading expectations. [MRPC 7.1] **(A)** is incorrect because it is usually permissible for a lawyer to hold a public office and concurrently practice law if the law practice is active and substantial. **(B)** is incorrect in that a law firm with offices in multiple jurisdictions should indicate in which jurisdiction the lawyers are admitted. Here it seems a reasonable person would assume Charlie is admitted in both states because there is no limitation indicated. **(C)** is incorrect in that a law firm with offices in multiple jurisdictions should indicate in which jurisdiction the lawyers are admitted.

22. /A/ This televised advertisement appears proper in all respects, and Emily retaining a video of the recording for two years is in accordance with the older advertising retention rule. [MRPC 7.2] **(B)** is not the best answer because if Emily charged for the initial consultation after advertising to the contrary (free for 20 minutes), it might be deemed to be false and misleading. [MRPC 7.1] **(C)** is incorrect in that it is not necessary that the State Bar Association issue the CPA certificate as long as it was earned and issued by a bona fide professional association. The CPA is a professional certification, not a specialty designation. [MRPC 7.4] **(D)** is incorrect because the prohibition on comparisons is only on unproven express comparisons. [MRPC 7.1]

23. /B/ A lawyer may not pay others for referring professional legal work. [MRPC 7.2(b)] **(A)** is incorrect because there are three exceptions to the "no-compensation-for-referral rule": purchase of a law practice in accordance with MRPC 1.17, reasonable costs of advertising, and usual charges of a bar-approved qualified legal referral service. **(C)** is incorrect because the rule prohibiting a payment of forwarding fees applies "to a person," which includes both lawyers and non-lawyers. **(D)** is incorrect because client consent and an opportunity to consult with other lawyers is not listed as an exception to the prohibition on payment of forwarded fees.

24. /D/ The correct behavior is both to respond to the disciplinary counsel's inquiry [MRPC 8.1] and affirmatively report the misconduct to the appropriate professional authority [MRPC 8.3(a)]. If Iola's report is accurate, Loretta's oral in-person solicitation of a prospective client violates MRPC 7.3 unless Iola was a former client, friend, other lawyer, or relative. In addition, the statements made appear to violate MRPC 7.1 which prohibits falsity and misleading statements creating unjustifiable expectations and unsubstantiated comparisons. The issue here is whether a hearsay report by an unconscious patient is sufficient "knowledge" to meet the threshold requirement of mandatory reporting. That decision is for the bar disciplinary counsel to make. **(A)** is incorrect because a lawyer must disclose all facts she knows in connection with a disciplinary matter if so required by disciplinary counsel. **(B)** is partially incorrect because there likely is an affirmative duty to report misconduct to the appropriate professional authority. [MRPC 8.3(a)] **(C)** is incorrect because there likely is an affirmative duty to report misconduct to the appropriate professional authority.

25. /A/ There is only one proper statement here – II – that does not violate a disciplinary rule. I is improper because a non-lawyer may not be a corporate director or officer. [MRPC 5.4(d)(2)] II is proper in that there are no restraints on law firm ownership as it applies to lawyers admitted to practice. III is improper because it restricts the rights of a lawyer to practice after termination of employment with the firm. [MRPC 5.6(a)] IV is improper because while commendable, it would seem to be splitting a fee with a non-lawyer, and the nonprofit exception only applies to an organization that employed, retained, or recommended the lawyer for the matter. [MRPC 5.4(a)(4)] **(B)** is incorrect because it involves a wrong combination of alternatives. **(C)** is incorrect because it involves a wrong combination of alternatives. **(D)** is incorrect because it involves a wrong combination of alternatives.

26. /C/ If the activity is not considered to be the unauthorized practice of law, the burden is on the lawyer to show sufficient communication so that the customers understand that such services are not legal services and that protections such as the attorney-client privilege and conflict of interest provisions do not apply. [MRPC 5.7(a)(2)] **(A)** is incorrect because law-related services may be provided to both clients and non-clients of the law firm. **(B)** is not the best answer because law-related services may be provided by the law firm directly (but all the MRPCs apply). **(D)** is not the best answer because if the customers are aware the entity is not a law firm and protections such as the attorney-client privilege do not apply, all the MRPCs applicable to the practice of law may not apply. But MRPC 8.4 Misconduct may be general grounds for discipline even if a lawyer is technically not practicing law.

27. /D/ The best answer because a lawyer shall not use a firm name, letterhead, or other professional designation if it is misleading or implies a connection with a government entity; here, consumers might conclude that the law firm is authorized by or associated with the federal government's Department of Immigration, which would be a false communication. [MRPC 7.1 and MRPC 7.5(a)] **(A)** is incorrect because the test is whether the advertisement is potentially misleading, not what reasonable people may or may not conclude about the trade name advertisement. **(B)** is incorrect because the allowable use of a trade name by a law firm varies from jurisdiction to jurisdiction. **(C)** is incorrect because most jurisdictions do not require approval by the State Bar Association before a lawyer may put the firm trade name on her business cards or letterhead.

28. /B/ A lawyer participating in a law reform organization must disclose that an existing client would materially benefit from an organization decision. [MRPC 6.4] **(A)** is incorrect because the fact that an organization decision would be detrimental to a client does not have to be disclosed. **(C)** is incorrect because only the benefits to a client must be disclosed. **(D)** is incorrect because only the benefits to a client must be disclosed.

29. /C/ Only item III is an invalid reason for avoiding appointment; a lawyer must take on a fair share of unpopular clients and causes. [Comments to MRPC 6.2] I is accurate because the imposition of an unreasonable financial burden may qualify as a valid reason for withdrawal. [MRPC 6.2(b)] II is accurate because the fact that representation will result in a violation of an MRPC may qualify as a valid reason for withdrawal. [MRPC 6.2(a)] IV is accurate because the client and/or cause repugnancy may qualify as a valid reason for withdrawal if it would impair the effectiveness of the client-lawyer relationship. **(A)** is incorrect because this alternative involves the wrong combination of correct alternatives. **(B)** is incorrect because this alternative involves the wrong combination of correct alternatives. **(D)** is incorrect because this alternative involves the wrong combination of correct alternatives.

30. **/C/** This is the only correct combination of alternatives. I is proper conduct because the firm-wide disqualification rules of MRPC 1.10 do not apply to short-term legal services if the lawyer does not know that the representation involves a conflict of interest. [MRPC 6.5] II is improper conduct because if the lawyer knew of the conflict she may not go forward without contacting the firm and ensuring a proper screening process is in place. III is proper conduct because the lawyer must secure the client's informed consent to the limited scope of the representation. IV is proper conduct because if the short-term limited representation is not complete, the lawyer may offer some advice but must advise the client of the need for further assistance of counsel.

31. **/A/** The ABA believes that "every lawyer should aspire to render at least 50 hours of *pro bono* services per year." [MRPC 6.1] "Should" is not the same as "shall" or "must," so the lawyer has discretion whether to do *pro bono* work. **(B)** is incorrect because a lawyer is encouraged to do a minimum of 50 hours of *pro bono* work a year, but it is not an absolute requirement. **(C)** is incorrect because the fact that laypersons also serve on the same committee does not mean they are sharing in the lawyers' fees, which is prohibited by MRPC 5.4(a). **(D)** is not the best answer because the lawyer must perform *pro bono* representation as a reasonably competent attorney would under the circumstances. [MRPC 1.1]

32. **/B/** A law firm partner with direct supervisory authority over an associate must make reasonable efforts to ensure that the associate's conduct conforms to the MRPCs. [MRPC 5.1] Here, there appears to be a bona fide question whether Nancy has the competency and experience necessary to handle the case. [MRPC 1.1] **(A)** is not the best answer because a supervisory partner cannot disregard her duty to supervise firm subordinates even if the firm's policy and procedure manual does not so direct. **(C)** is incorrect because an ethical rule may be violated even if no damages result. **(D)** is incorrect because the rationale – that a lawyer has a duty to ask questions and seek out assistance – while true does not excuse the duty of a partner to supervise associates in the law firm.

33. **/C/** The basic test of whether the political contribution was to obtain governmental legal engagements or appointments by judges, special masters, receivers, etc., is whether the contribution would not have been made "but for" the desire to be appointed. [Comment to MRPC 7.6] **(A)** is incorrect because the prohibition covers "anything of value that is substantial in relation to other contributions by lawyers." **(B)** is incorrect because there is no blanket rule against law firm contributions and receiving appointments. **(D)** is incorrect because while the rationale may be accurate, the reason for participation in appointments that put professional integrity at risk is the thrust of the question.

34. **/B/** A lawyer (even one working as a law school professor) is subject to discipline if he knowingly assists a judge in conduct that is a violation of the Code of Judicial Conduct. Here, both trial lawyers should have been informed. [MRPC 8.4(f)] **(A)** is incorrect because the facts state that the lawyer-professor knew the judge did not tell the parties' lawyers of the research. **(C)** is incorrect because a lawyer may not knowingly assist a judge in conduct that violates the Code of Judicial Conduct. **(D)** is incorrect because a lawyer may not knowingly assist a judge in conduct that violates the Code of Judicial Conduct.

35. /A/ The best answer because the facts indicate the ultimate management of the law firm is conducted by a five person managing committee consisting of five lawyers. **(B)** is not the best answer because a lawyer has a duty to supervise any non-lawyer assistant to be sure all confidentiality restraints are adhered to. [MRPC 5.1(a) and 5.3] **(C)** is incorrect because a law firm may include non-lawyer employees in a compensation plan, and this does not constitute improper fee splitting. [MRPC 5.4(a)(3)] **(D)** is incorrect because mere administrative management of a law firm and receiving a performance bonus does not mean that a lawyer is practicing law with a non-lawyer unless the non-lawyer has the right to direct or control the lawyer's professional judgment. [MRPC 5.4(a)(3)]

36. /D/ The best answer because this would be most likely considered to be assisting a layperson in the unauthorized practice of law. [MRPC 5.5(a)] While the practice of law is defined by state law, drafting an unsupervised and unreviewed letter on a lawyer's stationary threatening a lawsuit appears to qualify; the lawyer must maintain the direct relationship with the case. **(A)** is incorrect because a written statement that a lawsuit will be filed if payment is not made is not extortion. **(B)** is not the best answer because this could indicate proper supervision over non-lawyer assistants even if the collection business was deemed to be the practice of law. [MRPC 5.3] **(C)** is not the best answer because it implies the collection business is separate and distinct from the practice of law and the lawyer supervises the business.

37. /C/ Exclusive reciprocal referral agreements are deemed to be giving consideration and therefore in violation of MRPC 7.2. **(A)** is incorrect because not sharing fees or engaging in the practice of law with a non-lawyer does not eliminate the exclusive referral agreement violation. **(B)** is incorrect because informing the clients of the mutual referral agreement is only sufficient if it is not exclusive. **(D)** is incorrect because there is nothing improper about a partnership with a non-lawyer (although other MRPC restrictions may apply), and fees were not shared.

38. /B/ The best answer because a lawyer must make reasonable efforts to ensure assistants comply with the professional ethical responsibility of a lawyer; thus, a lawyer is ethically liable only for negligence in failing to supervise assistants. [MRPC 5.3] **(A)** is not the best answer because *respondeat superior* vicarious responsibility suggests strict ethical liability beyond the negligence standard. **(C)** is incorrect because routine practices will not excuse unsupervised delegation that was negligence. **(D)** is incorrect because retaining a lawyer to represent a matter includes all aspects including appeals unless the representation was specifically limited. [MRPC 1.2]

39. /D/ None of the advertising statements listed will subject the attorneys to discipline because they all are not misleading, are verifiable factually, and do not tend to lead to unjustified expectations. [MRPC 7.1 and 7.2] Statement I is proper, assuming the lawyers both hold J.D. degrees, Loretta holds a CPA license, and the local jurisdiction does not require additional statements associated with credential advertising. [MRPC 7.4] Statement II is proper because a statement of practice specialization or limitation to a subject is not the same as claiming "expert" status in an area of practice. [MRPC 7.4] Statement III is proper because while in part a comparison, it may be factually verified and substantiated. Statement IV is proper because these statements are factually subject to verification. Statement V is proper in those jurisdictions that require the name of a lawyer responsible for the advertisement's content to be specified. [MRPC 7.2]

40. /D/ Such a detailed written legal memorandum likely constitutes the practice of law, which is unauthorized under state law and thus probably illegal. [MRPC 5.5] An exception to required in-state admission applies if the lawyer is admitted pro hac vice (for a specific matter) under the sponsorship of a lawyer admitted in California and approved by the tribunal and/or administrative agency. **(A)** is incorrect because the lack of physical presence in a jurisdiction is not conclusive as to whether the acts in question rise to the level of the practice of law. **(B)** is incorrect because client approval of a lawyer's illegal activities is not relevant to whether the practice is ethically proper. **(C)** is incorrect because while a lawyer may sue a client for collection, the legal fees for the unlicensed practice of law may not be collectable since the activity is deemed illegal.

41. /A/ A lawyer shall not state or imply an ability to influence improperly a government agency or official. [MRPC 8.4(e)] **(B)** is not the best answer because the focus is on the improper statements made to the prospective client, not the veracity of the statement. **(C)** is incorrect because "superior access" is not the same as "improper influence," and Roberta is subject to discipline. **(D)** is incorrect because a lawyer's puffing and emphasizing the positive cannot include the ability to improperly influencing a government agency or official.

42. /B/ The best answer because a lawyer is prohibited from agreeing not to represent firm clients who are to be free to choose their own professional advisors; this applies even though the associate had no bargaining power. [MRPC 5.6(a)] **(A)** is not the best answer because the lack of bargaining position and the fact that the position required the lawyer to accept the condition do not excuse the fact that Faith should not have agreed to the improper contract provision. **(C)** is incorrect because the lack of bargaining position and the fact that the employment position required the lawyer to accept the condition do not excuse the fact that Faith should not have agreed to the contract. **(D)** is incorrect because while a lawyer may decide not to continue in a professional practice, and the non-compete restraint may be reasonable as between laypersons it remains improper for a lawyer.

43. /A/ The best answer because a lawyer holding public office assumes heightened responsibilities. This includes a prohibition against engaging in conduct involving dishonesty. [Comments to MRPC 8.4] **(B)** is not the best answer because actual knowledge of the dishonest intention is not necessary if it was apparent that dishonesty would result. **(C)** is incorrect because the lack of a express statement of dishonest intentions is not a prerequisite for discipline. **(D)** is incorrect because dishonest conduct does not require an express statement of the dishonest objective in question.

44. /C/ Loretta's loyalty may be commendable, but a lawyer must not make false statements about the qualifications or record of a sitting judge. [MRPC 8.2(a)] Only if Nancy's statements in the campaign were not objective, factually accurate, and honest would she be subject to discipline. **(A)** is incorrect because it involves a wrong combination of yes or no answers to the questions of whether both lawyers' statements about a judicial official were proper. **(B)** is incorrect because it involves a wrong combination of yes or no answers to the questions of whether both lawyers' statements about a judicial official were proper. **(D)** is incorrect because it involves a wrong combination of yes or no answers to the questions of whether both lawyers' statements about a judicial official were proper.

45. /A/ The preparation of a complicated trust instrument constitutes the practice of law in most jurisdictions. [MRPC 8.4(a)] While a lawyer may delegate work to non-lawyers, the work must be supervised and reviewed, and the lawyer must maintain the direct relationship with the client, which did not occur here. [MRPC 5.3] **(B)** is incorrect because the prohibition against assisting in the unauthorized practice of law does not depend upon the competency of the non-lawyer author of the unauthorized work product. **(C)** is incorrect because a client's consent may not be effective to waive the professional ethical prohibitions imposed on a lawyer against assisting the unauthorized practice of law. **(D)** is incorrect because, while true as far as it goes, the ethical prohibition against a lawyer assisting in (in this case ordering) the unauthorized practice of law remains an MRPC violation.

46. /D/ The best answer because a lawyer may not state or imply that she has the ability to improperly influence the tribunal's decision. [MRPC 7.1(b) and 8.4(e)] **(A)** is incorrect because the MRPCs are focused on protecting the integrity of the judicial system, and a client cannot insist a lawyer violate the competency rule of MRPC 1.1. **(B)** is incorrect because MRPC 7.1(b) and 8.4(e) prohibit a lawyer from implying an ability to influence improperly a tribunal, and remaining silent after such a clearly articulated unjustifiable expectation would seem to be a violation. **(C)** is incorrect because it appears that the client intends to associate with another lawyer who has the requisite competence and experience in the area of law.

47. /B/ The best answer because of the general rule that if one lawyer in the firm has a conflict, it is imputed to all other lawyers in the firm. [MRPC 1.10(a)] A lawyer may not use a public position to obtain special advantages for a client if such action is not in the public interest. [MRPC 8.4(e)] **(A)** is not the best answer because screening is applicable only to lawyers joining or leaving a law firm, not a lawyer holding public office in her legislative capacity. [MRPC 1.10(b) and 1.11(b)] **(C)** is incorrect because a lawyer may hold public office and concurrently use her name in the law firm unless she does not actively and regularly practice law with the firm; the required substantial period of absence would seem to be more than one month a year. [MRPC 7.5(c)] **(D)** is not the best answer because screening is applicable only to lawyers joining or leaving a law firm, not a lawyer holding public office in her legislative capacity. [MRPC 1.10(b) and 1.11(b)]

48. /A/ The best answer because intimidating and threatening a prosecutor is a potential criminal violation in all jurisdictions, and Alice is at least an accomplice. **(B)** is not the best answer because it is not necessary that the attorney gave consideration to induce the intimidation. **(C)** is incorrect because the lawyer is subject to criminal liability regardless of the outcome of the case. **(D)** is incorrect because potential criminal law liability exists even though Alice could (and likely would) receive court sanctions and bar association discipline. [MRPC 8.4(b)]

49. /C/ The correct answer because only one of the alternatives is proper treatment for a lawyer and law firm entity. Alternative I is improper because most jurisdictions do not allow an artificial entity to provide a shield for the malpractice of an attorney. II is proper because incorporation may provide tax advantages such as increased retirement plan contributions. III is improper because a non-lawyer may not serve as a director or officer of a professional organization used for the practice of law. IV is improper because only lawyers may own an interest in an entity used for the practice of law. [MRPC 5.4(d)] **(A)** is not the best answer because the alternative involves an incorrect combination of alternatives. **(B)** is not the best answer because the alternative involves an incorrect combination of alternatives. **(D)** is not the best answer because the alternative involves an incorrect combination of alternatives.

50. /A/ The only correct combination of alternatives. I is proper because this is an acceptable form of advertising as long as all information conveyed is not false, misleading, or tending to create unjustified expectations. [MRPC 7.1] II is improper because a lawyer may not solicit business through an in-person contact with a client personally [MRPC 7.3] or through the acts of another such as a "runner" agent [MRPC 8.4(a)]. III is improper because the referral agreement is reciprocal and exclusive; thus, compensation is deemed to be present. [MRPC 7.3(a)] IV is also likely improper because a lawyer may not give anything of value to another for a recommendation or referral. [MRPC 7.3(a)] Note that $500 is more than *de minimis* and the fact that the referral is from another lawyer does not change the application of the "no compensation for referrals" rule. **(B)** contains an incorrect combination of alternatives. **(C)** contains an incorrect combination of alternatives. **(D)** contains an incorrect combination of alternatives.

51. /B/ A lawyer has to mitigate the effect of a violation of a MRPC; informing Mr. Quick of the in-person solicitation would have allowed him to decline any such representation and thus mitigate the apparent violation of MRPC 7.3(a). **(A)** is incorrect because it suggests an absolute liability standard; a supervisory lawyer is liable for an improper act of a non-lawyer assistant only if he ordered or ratified the improper conduct involved or failed to avoid or mitigate the improper conduct. [MRPC 5.3] **(C)** is incorrect because even if the non-lawyer assistant did not know that her conduct was improper, the supervising lawyer still had a duty to avoid the improper result. **(D)** is incorrect because this non-lawyer was also an employee of a law firm, and the lawyer partners of the firm have a duty to exercise a supervisory authority over non-lawyer employees.

52. /B/ The best answer because MRPC 7.5 allows a law firm to use a trade name unless it would violate the false or misleading prohibitions of MRPC 7.1. **(A)** is not the best answer because a law firm may continue to use the names of deceased partners in the firm name if there has been a continuing succession in the firm's DeGrande identity. **(C)** is incorrect because while a law firm must usually remove a lawyer's name from the firm's trade name if that lawyer goes on the bench, the DeGrande name in question belongs to the firm's founder, Simon DeGrande, not Tammie DeGrande. **(D)** is incorrect because it is not necessary that a partner has the same last name as the trade name if the trade name contains only former partners and it has been continually used. [MRPC 7.5]

53. **/C/** The best answer since the law firm supervising attorney and senior partner were put on notice of the conflict and failed to take some action that would have avoided, corrected, or mitigated the violation. [MRPC 5.1] **(A)** is incorrect because the senior partner and supervising attorney are likely responsible. **(B)** is not the best answer because Susan Supervisor is likely responsible, along with the senior partner, since Alice Associate brought the potential violation to her attention. **(D)** is incorrect because an associate does not violate the MRPCs if a reasonably arguable ethical question is decided by a supervisor. [MRPC 5.2]

54. **/A/** Carol is subject to discipline because she has formed a partnership with a non-lawyer in a business in which one of the activities is the practice of law. [MRPC 5.4(b)] **(B)** is not the best answer because the facts indicate all the activities that constitute the practice of law are performed by lawyer Carol. **(C)** is incorrect because the allocation of duties within the partnership does not change the fact that one of the significant activities of the partnership involves the practice of law. **(D)** is incorrect because the thrust of the ethical question is the nature of the partnership work, not the potential conflict disclosure to the clients.

55. **/C/** A lawyer shall not permit a person who recommends the lawyer to direct or regulate the lawyer's independent professional judgment; the restrictions on non-bank referrals and the lawyer's inability to withdraw from the representation clearly interfere with the lawyer's independent judgment. [MRPC 5.4(c)] **(A)** is incorrect because even if the lawyer does not give anything of value, the required restrictions seem to interfere with the lawyer's independent judgment. **(B)** is incorrect because, competent or not, the required restrictions seem to interfere with the lawyer's independent judgment. **(D)** is not the best answer because the lawyer is not giving any consideration, and listing is apparently not exclusive, so it does not appear to be improper solicitation. [MRPC 7.3]

56. **/A/** The supervisory lawyer remains responsible for an MRPC violation by a subordinate if she knew the subordinate acted improperly. **(B)** is incorrect because a subordinate attorney is not liable if her supervisory attorney decides an ethical issue that is reasonably arguable, which seems the situation here. [MRPC 5.2] **(C)** is not the best answer because a subordinate attorney is not liable if her supervisory attorney decides an arguable issue. **(D)** is incorrect; the question of whether the client finally wins or loses the case on the merits does not determine if the position was reasonably arguable.

57. **/D/** The best answer because a lawyer may join a legal service organization as a director even though the organization's interests are adverse to those of a client of the lawyer's firm, but the lawyer may not participate in a decision adverse to their client. [MRPC 6.3] **(A)** is incorrect because a lawyer is not subject to discipline merely because the organization's position or objectives may be adverse to the interests of a firm's clients. **(B)** is incorrect because a lawyer is not subject to discipline merely because she fails to disclose to the law reform organization that its action may harm a client of the law firm. **(C)** is incorrect because a lawyer may join a legal service organization, but should not participate in deliberating any matter that may adversely affect the interest of any of the law firm's clients.

58. /D/ The best alternative of those presented. This question assumes the rules of MRPE 1.17 apply. Notice must be given to clients of the transfer of their account and client consent for file transferred is required. If a client does not affirmatively object within 90 days after receiving notice of the transfer, consent may usually be inferred. **(A)** is not the best alternative because while there are restrictions on allowing potential buyers to review client's confidential information, it is allowed. **(B)** is incorrect because raising fees to finance a law practice purchase is not allowed. **(C)** is incorrect because the payment to the estate of a deceased partner is not deemed to be splitting legal fees, even though client fees may be the source of the buyout payments.

59. /B/ A lawyer may not directly or indirectly compensate an organization for recommending or referring a client; here, the lawyer is required to keep a $25,000 minimum account, and this indirectly constitutes compensation for referrals in violation of MRPC 7.2(c). **(A)** is not the best answer because the non-lawyer Airhouse & Co. is not participating in the practice of law, but rather merely referring a consumer of legal services to a lawyer. **(C)** is incorrect because while the factual rationale – neither the customer nor Airhouse & Co. are paying a fee for the referral – is correct, the conclusion that participation by the lawyer is proper is incorrect. **(D)** is incorrect because Airhouse is not a not-for-profit organization that is approved by the recognized Bar Association to charge lawyers a fee for referrals.

60. /A/ The best answer because unless the lawyer's marketing statements of fact and law are false or misleading, there is not a violation of the professional advertising rules. [MRPC 7.1] **(B)** is not the best answer because advertising and statements made to the public media may be paid for as long as they are not false or misleading. **(C)** is incorrect because, while MRPC 3.6 prohibits a lawyer from making media statements that have a substantial likelihood of materially prejudicing a present adjudicative proceeding, this lawyer is not presently involved in any such matter. **(D)** is incorrect because statements made to the media do not usually qualify as an in-person solicitation covered under MRPC 7.3.

61. /C/ The best answer because ABA Formal Opinion 94-383 dictates that a lawyer must not threaten opposing counsel with reporting an alleged ethical disciplinary violation in order to gain an advantage or "bargaining chip" in litigation. [MRPC 8.3] **(A)** is incorrect because while the client must always consent to a settlement, this question focuses on the ethics of using a disciplinary action as a "bargaining chip" in negotiating a litigation settlement. **(B)** is incorrect because the facts state the rule in the jurisdiction is that reporting of ethical violations is mandatory, and the client cannot usually negate the lawyer's responsibility to comply with the MRPCs. **(D)** is not the best answer (although clearly in second place) because the primary thrust of the question is a lawyer using a potential bar complaint as a "bargaining chip" in litigation.

62. /D/ The best answer because a lawyer's public statement about the integrity or record of a judge is not improper unless the lawyer knows the statement is false or reckless. [MRPC 8.2] **(A)** is not the best answer because, while true, an accurate comment is not usually considered to be an attack. **(B)** is not the best answer because only if the statements were false or in reckless disregard of the truth would discipline be imposed. **(C)** is not the best answer because, candidate or not, a lawyer must not make false or reckless statements about the qualifications, integrity, or record of a sitting judge.

63. /C/ The only correct combination because while it appears Barbara properly supervised the associate, there likely remains potential vicarious liability under the doctrine of *respondeat superior* for the client's damages resulting from the statute of limitations malpractice mistake of the associate. [MRPC 5.1] **(A)** is incorrect because there does appear to be grounds for a civil malpractice claim. **(B)** is incorrect because there does not appear to be grounds for professional discipline. **(D)** is incorrect because there does appear to be adequate grounds for professional discipline.

64. /B/ Lawyers practicing out of the same office who are not partners or shareholders of a professional corporation may not join their names together on a letterhead or pleading paper. They may all put their names on the office door and use a common telephone number, as long as such use does not represent expressly or implicitly that they are actually associated as law firm partners. [MRPC 7.5] **(A)** is not the best answer because the alternative involves an incorrect combination of alternatives. **(C)** is not the best answer because the alternative involves an incorrect combination of alternatives. **(D)** is not the best answer because the alternative involves an incorrect combination of alternatives.

65. /A/ While the substantiality of the potential offense is clear, the facts do not indicate the degrcc of certainty, and it is possible that there may be a valid explanation. Accordingly, it would seem the least appropriate authority to report to would be the county criminal prosecutor, at least until a further investigation is made. [MRPC 8.3(a)] **(B)** is incorrect because, depending upon the circumstances, the judge officiating over the case might be the appropriate authority. **(C)** is incorrect because, depending upon the circumstances, the bar disciplinary authority in the jurisdiction might be the appropriate authority. **(D)** is incorrect because, depending upon the circumstances, the attorney for the parent in question might be the appropriate authority to determine if the suspicion is accurate.

66. /D/ To be grounds for professional discipline, a crime must be related to a lawyer's trustworthiness in their professional capacity. [MRPC 8.4(b)] Here there is only a matter of personal morality. **(A)** is incorrect because a lack of respect for marital fidelity does not necessarily rise to the level of an act of public moral turpitude. **(B)** is incorrect because even if a lawyer is convicted of this offense, it likely would not rise to the level of an act of public moral turpitude or reflect adversely on his honesty, trustworthiness, or fitness as a lawyer in his professional capacity. **(C)** is not the best answer because a lawyer may be disciplined for criminal or dishonest acts even if they are not committed in his professional capacity.

67. /D/ The best and broadest answer because MRPC 6.4 allows a lawyer to participate in a law reform activity even though the reform activity may affect the interests of a client. A client's material benefit resulting from a decision of the reform activity must be disclosed but mandatory disclosure of a client detrimental affect is not required. **(A)** is incorrect because a lawyer is not prohibited from participating in a law reform activity benefitting the client if disclosure is made. **(B)** is incorrect because disclosure of a resulting client detriment is not required as it is for a client benefit. **(C)** is not the best answer because, while correct, it does not include any rational going to the public interest requirement and the lack of a duty to disclose client detriment.

RIGOS UNIFORM BAR REVIEW SERIES

PROFESSIONAL RESPONSIBILITY EXAM REVIEW (MPRE)

Chapter 6

Judiciary Ethics

Magic Memory Outline®

RIGOS UNIFORM BAR REVIEW SERIES

PROFESSIONAL RESPONSIBILITY EXAM REVIEW (MPRE)

Chapter 6

Judiciary Ethics

A. In General

1. 2007 Amendments: In 2003 the ABA appointed a commission to evaluate the ABA Model Code of Judicial Conduct (CJC or MCJC), which had last been amended in 1990. Based upon the commission's recommendations, extensive substantive and numbering format revisions were approved and adopted by the House of Delegates February 12, 2007. This Third Edition of Rigos Uniform Bar Review Series MPRE Review book is updated to reflect these changes and the recusal holding in *Massey Coal.*

2. Scope of Testing:

a. Direct Judicial Testing: The MPRE exam, unlike local bar exams in many jurisdictions, tests restraints on lawyers serving in the judiciary. The authority tested on the MPRE is the ABA Model Code of Judicial Conduct (MCJC) as revised through the exam date. The ABA Model Rules and Model Code are generally consistent with the MCJC.

b. Related Lawyer Testing: There is related potential crossover testing of at least six substantive MRPC sections.

(1) MRPC 1.12: A judge or her law clerk negotiating for employment with a party appearing in their court is a violation. There is an exception for law clerks who notify the judge of the identity of the law firm they are interviewing with. A former judge shall not represent a party in a matter in which she personally and substantially participated while on the bench unless all parties give informed consent in writing. It may also be possible for the law firm to screen out the tainted prior judge. See *supra* at 108.

(2) MRPC 7.5: In a law firm, a named partner going on the bench is responsible for removing his name from the firm name if the jurisdiction prohibits judges from practicing law. See *supra* at 198.

(3) MRPC 8.2: A lawyer may not make a statement about the qualifications or integrity of a judge that the lawyer knows to be false. The restraint extends to a lawyer's reckless disregard as to the truth or falsity of a statement about a judge. See *supra* at 199.

(4) MRPC 8.3(b): A lawyer who knows that a judge has violated a judicial conduct rule shall report to the judicial authorities if the violation creates a substantial question about a judge's fitness to hold judicial office. See *supra* at 200.

(5) MRPC 8.4(e): A lawyer shall not state or imply an ability to influence improperly a tribunal or judge. See *supra* at 200.

(6) MRPC 8.4(f): A lawyer shall not knowingly assist a judge in conduct that is a violation of the MCJC. See *supra* at 200.

3. Testing Frequency: Expect between five and seven of the MPRE questions to focus on MCJC issues. The rule variations for part-time judges are rarely tested.

4. Call of the Question: The usual fact pattern involves a judge's or a judicial candidate's activity or statement. The call of the question is almost always, "Is it proper (or improper) for Judge to . . . ." This is followed by four alternatives, two of which state, "No, . . ." and two that state, "Yes, ..." The conclusion – no or yes – is followed by a rationale usually beginning with "because . . . ." Thus, the MPRE judicial questions test both the conclusion and the best reasoning. In more than 75% of the questions, one of the "no," "not proper," or "improper" alternatives is the best answer.

B. <u>Judiciary Independence, Integrity, and Impartiality</u> – CANON 1

1. Compliance with Law – MCJC 1.1: This is required of all judges. The overriding MCJC theme is that a judge must act only in a manner that promotes independence, integrity, fairness, and impartiality of the judiciary. The MCJC standards for judges are higher than the MRPCs that are applicable to a mere lawyer.

2. Promote Confidence in the Judiciary – MCJC 1.2: The restraints of the MCJC attempt to promote public confidence in the judiciary. Members of the judiciary are prohibited from activities that may create a perception of bias or impaired integrity, impartiality, or competency. In some circumstances, the MCJC applies to personal non-judicial conduct as well as judicial activities.

3. Avoid Abusing the Prestige of Judicial Office – MCJC 1.3, 2.4: A judge may not abuse the prestige of the judicial office to gain personal advantage or preferential treatment. A judge also should not allow others to convey the impression that some other person or organization can influence the judge, such as a book publisher might for an author. Official court or judicial letterheads may not be used for non-judicial purposes if there is any likelihood it would connote judicial pressure.

> **MPRE Tip:** Many questions suggest halfway measures to cure a questionable situation involving a judge's potential prejudice towards a claim or party. If this creates an appearance of impropriety, the judge's involvement likely is improper. Thus, in a close question, the MPRE alternative that would prohibit the judge's activity is probably the best answer.

C. <u>Performance of Judicial Duties</u> – CANON 2

1. General Adjudicative Duties:

a. Decorum, Respect, and Order – MCJC 2.8: A judge must always remain dignified. This includes being patient and courteous to litigants, counsels, jurors, and witnesses. The judge shall require similar conduct of all his court staff.

(1) Officers in Her Court: The judge must require high professionalism and judicial respect from all lawyers and parties appearing in her court. All such lawyers are deemed to be officers of the court and must in return observe order and decorum in all their appearances and representation in the court's proceedings.

(2) Parties – MCJC 2.6: Every person who is legally interested in a proceeding must be allowed the right to be heard, including *pro se* litigants.

(3) Jurors: A judge must guide the jury, but shall not criticize or commend jurors for their verdict other than in a court order or opinion.

(4) Broadcast / Recording of Proceedings: The general rule is that a judge should prohibit the live broadcasting of a trial. Private parties also should not be allowed to record a trial, although an official court reporter version ordinarily is available. Interested parties may buy the full official transcript of the proceedings.

b. Administrative Duties – MCJC 2.1, 2.3, 2.5, 2.7, 2.12, 2.13:

(1) General Responsibilities: The judge must maintain competency in judicial matters. Any judicial appointments should be made solely on merit. A judge must be prompt in judicial administration and expedite matters and controversies. A judge may encourage parties to settle a matter, but should not coerce any party into settlement.

(2) No Bias or Prejudice: Neither the judge nor any lawyers in her court may manifest bias or prejudice in official proceedings. This includes, but may not be limited to, race, religion, sex, disability, age, national origin, or socioeconomic status.

c. *Ex Parte* Communications – MCJC 2.9: A judge shall not initiate, permit, or consider communications unless opposing counsel (or opposing party, if *pro se*) is present. A lawyer participating in *ex parte* communication with a judge also violates MRPC 8.4. *Supra* at 5-199. Prompt notification to the parties is required if the judge inadvertently receives an *ex parte* communication, such as a misdirected fax. Exceptions allowing *ex parte* communications commonly include:

(1) Disinterested Expert: A judge may consult with a non-involved, disinterested expert on a technical aspect of relevant law. All the parties in the matter must receive advance notice of the consultation and be given reasonable opportunity to object and respond to the advice received.

(2) Mere Procedural: Communications for scheduling purposes and administrative matters normally are not improper if no substance of the case is discussed. A judge should advise the other parties of the details of the procedural communication.

(3) Other Judges and Staff: Substantive communication with other judges and staff, such as law clerks, is not considered to be *ex parte*. Thus, consultation with such people is usually proper even without disclosure to the litigants.

MPRE Tip: *Ex parte* communications by a judge with parties, experts, and other judges are frequently tested.

d. Judge's Immunity: The adjudicative decision-making absolute immunity does not necessarily apply to a judge's administrative functions.

2. Impartiality of Tribunal – MCJC 2.2, 2.4, 2.11: If a judge's impartiality or personal bias because of a factual situation "might reasonably be questioned," the judge should disqualify herself *sua sponte*. The judge should enter on the record any factual matters that might be subject to a future concern about impartiality.

a. Appearance Criteria: The appearance test is the objective perception of a reasonable, independent third party not involved in the controversy. The appearance criteria has a lower threshold than actual impaired independence that produces prejudice.

b. Judge's Duty: It is not necessary for one of the parties to file a "motion to disqualify" or similar. The tainted judge must recuse or disqualify herself *sua sponte.*

c. Recusal and Disqualification Examples: The MPRE question writers are very creative as to potentially prejudicial situations.

(1) Bias or Prejudice Towards Party: If the judge had prior dealings with one of the parties, there may be an appearance of positive or negative bias or prejudice, necessitating recusal. Similarly, if the judge has a business relationship with a party or attorney appearing in her court, there could appear to be an exploitation of the judicial position. Recusal by a judge may be suggested if one of the lawyers or a party in a case before the judge was a heavy judicial campaign contributor creating a significant appearance of bias.

(2) Bias or Prejudice Towards Lawyer: If the judge had a bad personal experience with one of the lawyers before becoming a judge, there may be a perceived bias and prejudice that could bring into question the required impartiality, making recusal appropriate. In comparison, recusal usually is not necessary merely because the judge sanctioned one of the lawyers in a previous case.

MPRE Tip: Disqualification because of a judge's prior contact – directly or through a prior law firm partner – with a party or attorney that creates potential prejudice is frequently tested.

(3) Personal Knowledge of Disputed Facts: If the judge has personal knowledge of key disputed facts in the controversy, it may be difficult to make decisions based solely on evidence presented in the trial, thus requiring recusal. Mere general knowledge, such as that gained from reading a newspaper, is not sufficient grounds for disqualification.

(4) Prior Judge or Firm Involvement: Disqualification applies if the judge or one of her former law firm partners represented any of the parties in the matter. There is no *de minimis* or confidential information threshold. The judge must only have been practicing in the firm during the time period when the firm was associated with the matter.

(5) Material Witness: If the judge's prior involvement was such that she may be called as a material witness, disqualification may be favored. This extends to a case in which a lawyer with whom the judge practiced is a material witness.

(6) Involvement of a Close Family Member: Recusal may be necessary when the judge, or the judge's spouse, has a parent, grandparent, great-grandparent, sibling, child, grandchild, great-grandchild, niece, nephew, aunt or uncle who falls in one of the following categories: 1) party to the action; 2) lawyer for a party to the action; 3) material witness; or 4) any other person with an economic interest in the outcome of the litigation (other than a *de minimis* interest). Note that this list of covered relationships is within the "third degree of relationships" and does not include cousins.

(7) Financial Interest in the Dispute: If the judge personally, as a trustee or close family member (spouse, domestic partner, parent, or child) has more than a *de minimis* economic interest in the subject matter in controversy, disqualification is required. Effective investment conflict-checking software is required. Ownership of stock or a debt instrument in entities such as an insurance company, bank, mutual savings association, or mutual fund that invests in or loans to a party before the court does not create a disqualification.

MPRE Tip: A favorite distractor is to suggest that judge's special qualifications or developed expertise in the matter should excuse the duty to recuse herself *sua sponte.*

d. Remittal and Waiver of Disqualification: A judge may violate any of the above impartiality rules except bias towards a party or lawyer or personal knowledge of disputed facts and still participate in the matter if:

(1) Full Disclosure: The court discloses fully the factual basis of the potential impartiality conflict on the record to all parties and their lawyers.

(2) Agreement: All parties and their lawyers must agree that the conflict is not material. If the basis is a financial interest, the amount in question must not be substantial. The proceedings leading to this agreement must be conducted without participation by the judge so there is no personal judicial influence upon the parties' consent.

(3) Record Required: All the parties and lawyers must agree the judge should not be disqualified outside the presence of a judge. The judge should enter into the written record of the proceeding all details of the disqualifying reasons and the fact there has been an approval of the remittal agreement by all the parties and attorneys.

(4) Non-Waivable Reasons: The reason for the disqualification that is waived may not be prejudicial towards a party, lawyer, or involve personal knowledge of material disputed facts. If any of these situations apply, the judge must recuse himself.

> **MPRE Tip:** The disqualification waiver provision only applies to involvement of a family member or a financial interest that is not material in amount. Personal bias, personal knowledge of disputed facts, and personal or law firm prior involvement may not be waived; *sua sponte* disqualification in those circumstances is mandatory.

3. Information Communication or Use

a. Public Comment on Pending Matters - MCJC 2.10: A judge should not comment publicly about any proceedings not yet concluded if doing so might reasonably be expected to affect the outcome or impair the perceived fairness of the proceedings. While it is especially important to avoid any comment to a news media source, even a casual conversation of the matter with friends usually must be avoided. This duty extends to supervising the judge's staff to insure there is no information leak from them. Still, a judge may usually respond to media allegations concerning the judge's conduct.

b. Non-Judicial Use – MCJC 3.5: Judges shall not disclose or use nonpublic information acquired in their judicial capacity for any non-judicial purpose, such as investment opportunities. This includes information obtained in official court appearances, in camera hearings, grand jury proceedings, or in matters under seal.

c. Public Comment on Completed Matters: Judges should not ordinarily comment to the media on any aspect of a completed case except matters of court procedures. This rule would ordinarily prohibit the judge from commenting to the press or writing a book about the case after the trial is completed.

4. Reporting Duty – MCJC 2.14, 2.15: This duty exists on two levels and is absolutely privileged.

a. Another Judge: A judge who has knowledge indicating a substantial likelihood that a lawyer candidate or another judge has violated the MCJCs shall take appropriate action, including informing the appropriate judicial authorities. The standard is that the alleged violation must raise a substantial question about the judge's honesty or fitness for judicial office. If this threshold is met, there is an affirmative duty to report a violation to the appropriate authority.

b. Attorney: Similarly, a judge may have actual knowledge indicating a substantial likelihood of a lawyer's unethical conduct, physical or mental impairment (such as abuse of drugs or alcohol), or violation of an MRPC. Normally, the situation raises a substantial question as to a lawyer's honesty, trustworthiness, or fitness to practice law. "Appropriate action" shall be taken, which may include a discussion with the lawyer, sanction, or other lawyer discipline. If the lawyer's conduct was serious with implications beyond the current case, the judge may initiate a referral to the appropriate state bar association authority.

D. <u>Personal and Extra-Judicial Activities</u> – CANON 3

The judge's extrajudicial activities must not detract from the dignity and stature of the office or create the appearance of impropriety. The judicial position must not appear to be exploited or compromised. Extrajudicial activities must not cast reasonable doubt on the judge's capacity to act impartially. They also cannot interfere with the judge's judicial duties or increase the likelihood that he will be disqualified frequently in future cases and controversies.

1. Financial Interests – MCJC 3.1, 3.11, 3.12, 3.14: Judges usually may participate and invest in private business enterprises unless such activities would result in frequent disqualifications.

a. Investment Constraints: A judge may not invest in activities or enter into business dealings if they are more than insignificant and involve:

(1) Likely Litigants: Significant business transactions with lawyers or persons likely to come before the court on which the judge serves are improper.

(2) Exploit Judge's Position: Investments or associations that may be reasonably perceived to exploit the judge's judicial position are also improper. This could occur if the judge's participation or association in a business venture is publicized.

b. Avocational Activities and Earnings: A judge generally may earn compensation from writing publications, speaking engagements, and related activities including performing weddings. The compensated activity should not involve any subject that violates the overall constraint of exploiting the judge's position, such as speaking publicly or writing a book about a trial the judge presided over. Reasonable expense reimbursement is permissible. Teaching for a bar association and judicial education groups is to be distinguished from fees received from privately-sponsored seminars by organizations that do not disclose funding sources and all speakers' names.

c. Own and Family Investments: A judge may hold and manage investments of the judge and family members. However, such financial interests shall be managed in a way that minimizes the number of cases requiring disqualification. Investment divestiture – as soon as possible – may be required if the investment creates frequent disqualification.

2. Organization Leadership Positions – MCJC 3.7:

a. Business Entities: A judge may not be a director, officer, partner, manager, or employee of any for-profit business. An exception applies if the business ownership is closely-held by the judge or his family.

b. Not-for-Profit Entities: Leadership positions, other than serving as a legal advisor, are allowed in judicial and law school organizations. This is extended to traditional nonprofit organizations intended to improve the administration of legal justice or fraternal, charitable, and religious organizations. Service in educational organizations, other than law schools, is generally prohibited.

(1) Not Party Before Court: The organization in question cannot be a regular party in adversarial proceedings that would ordinarily come before the judge. Also, the members of the organization cannot frequently represent the same side in litigation, such as a plaintiff's trial lawyers' association.

(2) Not Raise Money: The judge may solicit membership and assist in nominal planning and attend fund-raising events of acceptable nonprofit organizations. Participation in fund-raising activities of a qualified legal organization should be avoided. Direct personal solicitations by a judge for contributions to the organization are improper unless made to family members or other judges not subordinate to the solicitor.

MPRE Tip: Participation in the fund management of legal justice or charitable organizations is allowed; personal fund raising is prohibited.

3. Gifts and Related – MCJC 3.13: The general rule is that gifts, favors, bequests, or loans may not be accepted by a judge. This prohibition applies to gifts received by family members and other potential recipients residing in the judge's household.

a. Public Matters: Normal honorariums paid for public testimonials and appearances, free books and periodicals provided by publishers, regular scholarships or fellowships, and invitations to attend bar-related functions at no cost may usually be accepted.

b. Social Hospitality: Ordinary gifts from relatives and social friends for special occasions such as birthdays, weddings, or anniversaries that could not reasonably be perceived as intended to influence the judge may be accepted. In comparison, judges should not attend events and seminars in which sponsors providing the funding are likely to be involved in litigation that may come before the judge's court.

c. Normal Loans: Loans from lending institutions at market interest rates and other terms available to the general public are not considered a gift or favor. Therefore, a judge could likely oversee a trial involving his home mortgage company as a party.

d. *De Minimis* or Reported: This is a catchall *de minimis* category, but a gift or loan valued over a state-specified amount must be reported on an annual basis.

4. Fiduciary Activity – MCJC 3.8: A judge usually should not be a trustee of a trust, guardian of a person, or executor/administrator of an estate. An exception applies if the fiduciary position is on behalf of a judge's family member, such service does not interfere with judicial duties, and no related proceedings will come before the court on which the judge serves. If a judge serves as trustee or executor/administrator, he is deemed to have a personal financial interest in the assets held by the entity.

5. Testifying as Witness – MCJC 3.3: A judge may provide a non-judicial reference for another person if based on personal knowledge. She may also usually be required to testify as a fact witness if she had prior personal involvement in the matter and can offer no

immunity. However, voluntarily testifying as a character witness abuses the prestige of the judicial office unless the judge is officially subpoenaed. Such testimony would also ordinarily require the judge to disqualify herself from officiating over any aspect of the matter.

6. Affiliation with Discriminatory Organizations – MCJC 3.6: A judge may not belong to, become a member of, or use the facilities of an organization that practices non-religious "invidious discrimination." Unlike older rules that provided time to try to reform the discriminatory practices, immediate resignation is now required. This includes an organization that arbitrarily excludes membership based on constitutionally protected categories of race, sex, gender, religion, ethnicity, national origin, or sexual orientation. An exception allows membership in organizations dedicated to the preservation of religious, ethnic, or cultural values of legitimate common interest to its members.

7. Other Restrictions:

a. Concurrent Practice of Law – MCJC 3.9, 3.10:

(1) General Rule: The general rule is that a judge shall not practice law while on the bench. A judge may act *pro se* on his own behalf and may give legal advice to family members without compensation, including drafting and reviewing documents.

(2) Part-Time or Pro Tempore Judges: Some jurisdictions permit judges to serve part-time, usually for minor violations such as traffic cases or to expedite a backlog of cases. Restrictions on the judge concerning matters such as other legal representation engagements and outside income may be reduced by statute in such jurisdictions. Typically, a part-time judge may practice law, but cannot act as a lawyer in any proceeding related to a case she heard as a judge. The appearance of impartiality should not be put at risk.

(3) Arbitration and Mediation: A sitting judge shall not become involved in his private capacity as an arbitrator or mediator.

b. Government Relations – MCJC 3.2, 3.4:

(1) Appointments: A judge shall not normally accept appointment to a government committee, board, or commission. An exception applies (so appointment may be proper) if the committee or commission involves the objective of the improvement of the law, the legal system, or the administration of justice.

(2) Appearances: Similarly, a judge may not usually appear at a public hearing before an executive or legislative body unless it concerns matters about which the judge has expertise, such as the administration of justice. This same prohibition applies to a judge's consultation with an executive or legislative body. A judge usually may meet with a government official in a *pro se* matter that involves the judge personally.

c. Historical, Educational, or Cultural Events: A judge may be appointed as a representative at historical, educational, or cultural activities and may attend such events.

8. Annual Reporting – MCJC 3.15: Every jurisdiction has some type of periodic public reporting procedure and documents that all judges must usually file at least annually. All material gifts and compensation received from non-judicial activities must ordinarily be reported, including significant expense reimbursements. This includes information such as the date, payer, relationship, and amount received.

E. Political Activity by a Judge – CANON 4

Partisan political activity by a sitting judge is discouraged unless the activity is an effort to improve the legal system or administration of justice. Thus, participation in any not-for-profit organization may be subject to question if the organization has a political agenda.

1. Generally Prohibited Judicial Political Activities – SCOPE – MCJC 4.1: Non-candidate judges usually may not promote partisan political activities. This includes:

a. Speeches: Making speeches for a political organization or a partisan political candidate are not allowed. Speeches on topics such as ideas for concerns about improvement of the law, the legal system, or the administration of justice are allowed.

b. Contributions: Contributions to or solicitations for any political party or partisan candidate are not allowed. A small exception applies if the judge herself is involved as the candidate, and the state in question allows it.

c. Office Holder or Political Leader: A judge or candidate may not hold a political office or act as a leader in a political party or organization while on the bench. However, a candidate for elective judicial office may retain a public office, such as county prosecutor, that is not "an office in a political organization." Other family members are usually free to participate in political organizations.

d. Political Gathering: A non-candidate judge may not attend a partisan political gathering or fundraising event unless it is to celebrate a significant historical or patriotic event. Even purchasing tickets for political party dinners is usually improper. Some states restrict judges from all political membership; however, merely registering to vote or voting under a political party designation is not a violation.

e. Endorsement: A judge may not publicly speak for, endorse, or take a position of opposition to any candidate for partisan public office, even if the candidate is a relative. A judge may privately express her views on candidates.

MPRE Tip: A judge is prohibited from engaging in political activities unless she is a current candidate or acting to improve the legal system or administration of justice.

2. Special Rules for Candidates – SEAT – MCJC 4.2: During the election campaign, a judicial candidate or incumbent for judicial reelection may engage in:

a. Speeches: During their election or reelection period the judge may speak in public at political events, but must be dignified and restrict statements to allowable topics.

b. Endorsements: Endorse or oppose other candidates for the same judicial office such as other seats up for election on the state supreme court.

c. Advertisements: Media advertising and television appearances are allowed. Promotional literature may be distributed.

d. Ticket of Political Affiliation: A candidate in a partisan public judicial election may allow his name to be included on a political party ticket along with other candidates for non-judicial offices. Reasonable contributions to a political organization are allowed during the campaign time period.

MPRE Tip: The above prohibited political **SCOPE** activities for sitting judges and permitted **SEAT** activities for judicial candidates are tested on every exam.

3. Seeking Judicial Appointment – MCJC 4.3:

a. No Political Activity: State judges may be appointed by the governor or other appointing authorities such as the legislature in some jurisdictions. A candidate under consideration for a judicial appointment shall not engage in any political activity to facilitate the appointment if not opposed by another candidate.

(1) Support and Endorsement: It is permissible to seek non-partisan support and endorsements from organizations that regularly make judicial recommendations. An example is a state bar association committee that evaluates candidates based on the recommendations of attorneys who have appeared in the judge's court.

(2) Supply Information: The appointing authority may request normal screening information. The candidate may respond by supplying relevant information, including details about the candidate's experience and qualifications for the appointment.

b. Fund Solicitation: Potential appointees may not establish a campaign committee to solicit or accept funds. This is to be contrasted to a candidate for reelection.

MPRE Tip: A candidate for a judicial appointment is highly restricted compared to a candidate conducting a traditional competitive campaign to win an election or reelection.

4. Conducting Election Campaign – MCJC 4.4:

a. "Candidate" Status: A lawyer becomes a "candidate" when he first (1) publicly announces his intentions, (2) formally files with the election authority as a candidate, or (3) authorizes or accepts support or contributions. A candidate shall maintain the dignity appropriate to judicial office and not use court resources in the campaign.

b. Campaign Committee: A candidate facing opposition should establish an independent committee charged with the responsibility of conducting the campaign.

(1) Committee Activities: The committee normally will solicit support including endorsements and funds from the public, individuals, and other lawyers. These activities may not be done personally by the candidate. The candidate is not allowed to know the identity of contributors to the committee or the amount of their contributions during the campaign (but may learn this information later when the required campaign reports are prepared and signed by the candidate).

(2) Time Limits: There are outer time limits on permitted campaign activities. In most jurisdictions the period begins 1 year before the election and must end between 30 and 90 days after the election. Some jurisdictions specify shorter periods.

(3) Contribution Limits: Every jurisdiction specifies cash and in-kind dollar limitations on the amount that may be made to an individual judicial candidate. A loan to the campaign from someone other than the candidate or his family is not usually allowed.

(4) No Personal Benefit: Funds solicited by the committee are to be used only for campaign purposes. They may not be used personally by the candidate. Any positive fund balance at the end of the campaign may be contributed to the campaign efforts of others or retained for the next election. It should not be converted by the candidate to personal use.

c. Prohibited Campaign Activities – CAMP: Certain activities and statements are not allowed by the judicial candidate, his family, or employees, including:

(1) Cases or Controversies: The candidate shall not make statements about or take a position on cases, controversies, or issues in litigation. This prohibition applies at least to all matters that are likely to come before the court. [MCJC 2.10 and 4.1 (13)]

MPRE Tip: On the exam, this prohibition covers almost any statement about any controversy that may come in front of the court, even if the judge's decision merely affirms existing law.

(2) Accept or Solicit Funds: The candidate may not directly accept or solicit campaign contributions. A campaign committee should be formed to accept funds, and the judge should not be informed of the contribution sources.

(3) Misrepresent Opponents: The judicial candidate must be fair and accurate in statements. She also must not knowingly misrepresent the qualifications, position, record, or other facts concerning an opponent for the judicial position. A judicial candidate is permitted to respond directly and publicly with a factually accurate rebuttal statement to false, misleading, or unfair allegations made by an opponent or third party.

(4) Pledges or Promises – MCJC 2.10: Unlike a legislator, a judge shall not make promises, pledges, or other statements that appear to commit to future judicial conduct or position while in office. An example is: "I will decide all cases that come before me in favor of the right-to-life litigant." Such a future commitment obviously is contrary to the judicial impartiality requirement.

MPRE Tip: The candidate may defend against any attacks on her record by opponents as long as those statements do not violate the above four **CAMP** restrictions.

d. *White* Decision: In *Republican Party v. White*, 536 U.S. 765 (2002), the U.S. Supreme Court held that the Minnesota judicial canons' restriction on a judge or judicial candidate – the "announcement clause" – violates the First Amendment.

(1) Announcement v. Commitment: The *White* decision invalidated state judiciary restrictions that prohibited judges from answering questionnaires from judicial selection bodies or special interest groups regarding disputed legal or political issues. The opinion distinguished the "announcement clause" from the disallowed "commitment" provision. The latter concerns a personal pledge, promise, or commitment to take a particular position on a case, controversy, or issue likely to come before the court.

(2) Rationale: The theory is a judge may "announce" her personal views on a controversy or issue without it constituting a "promise, pledge, or commitment" concerning future decisions that would violate judicial impartiality. Any response to inquiries should include assurances that the judge will keep an open mind and be impartial.

(3) Examples: Included are personal view statements such as "tough on crime," "soft on crime," "pro-business," "anti-business," "pro-life," or "pro-choice." A judicial candidate is now prohibited from answering such personal view questions only if her announcement of position is used in a context that contains a pledge or promise to decide cases in a particular manner. See related MCJC 2.10 *supra* at 251.

e. Campaign Reporting: A report must be filed at interim dates and a final summary at the end of the campaign. The candidate must sign the report and state that it is complete and correct based upon her own review and the advice of the campaign committee chairperson. All contributors' identities and amounts must be disclosed in the report.

f. Extraordinary Contribution Scrutiny: Parties making large contributions to the judge's election should not litigate before their candidate. The U.S. Supreme Court in *Caperton v. Massey Coal Company*, 129 S. Ct. 2252, (2009) censored Judge Brent Benjamin of the West Virginia Supreme Court who received a $3 million campaign contribution from the defendant. Benjamin later twice cast the pivotal vote to overturn a large jury verdict below against the judge's contributor Massey Coal. The court held the constitutional right to due process required recusal because the standard is the probability of a serious risk of actual bias or prejudgment on the part of the jurist. Benjamin's actions created a significant appearance of a lack of judicial impartiality and was thus clearly improper.

5. Judge Running for Non-Judicial Political Office – MCJC 4.5: A judge who decides to run for a non-judicial office in either the primary or the general election must resign her judicial office prior to becoming an official political candidate. Remaining on the bench and disqualification in matters that concern the political office they are campaigning for are insufficient; *sua sponte* resignation is required.

F. Restraints on Judges After Leaving Office

A judge may decide not to run for reelection or may run and lose. If she decides to go into private practice, the below MRPC 1.12 restraints must be followed.

1. Employment Negotiations on Bench:

a. Judge Herself: The judge may not negotiate for post-judicial employment with any party, attorney, or law firm appearing in her court.

b. Judge's Subordinates: The judge's clerks may negotiate for post-judicial employment with a party only after the clerk informs the judge.

2. Subsequent Representation:

a. Same Matter: A former judge may not represent either party in a matter in which the judge participated personally and substantially while on the bench. This disqualification does not result from mere prior administrative responsibility in the matter, such as scheduling that did not go to the merits of the case.

b. Exceptions:

(1) Parties' Consent: All parties to the proceeding may give informed consent to the prior judge's representation of a party after full disclosure that is confirmed in writing.

(2) Screening: If the former judge is disqualified under the above rules, another lawyer in her new law firm may take on the matter in most states. The former judge must be screened from any participation in the matter and cannot receive any portion of the fee received for the representation. Written notice must also be given to all the parties.

RIGOS BAR REVIEW SERIES

PROFESSIONAL RESPONSIBILITY EXAM REVIEW (MPRE)

Chapter 6

Judiciary Ethics

Question Map

Numbers immediately following the topic are the chapter question numbers. The **boldface** numbers preceded by "F" are the final exam question numbers. For example, for the topic "B. 2. Promote Confidence in the Judiciary" below, questions 1, 15, and 32 are in the chapter questions on pages 6-243, 6-247, and 6-254, respectively; questions **F11** and **F56** are in the final exam on pages 7-278 and 7-292, respectively.

A. In General
1. 2007 Amendments
2. Scope of Testing
   a. Direct Judicial Testing
   b. Related Lawyer Testing
      (1) MRPC 1.12
      (2) MRPC 7.5
      (3) MRPC 8.2 - 18
      (4) MRPC 8.3(b)
      (5) MRPC 8.4(c)
      (6) MRPC 8.4(f)
3. Testing Frequency
4. Call of the Question

B. Judiciary Independence, Integrity, and Impartiality
1. Compliance with Law – 12
2. Promote Confidence in the Judiciary – 1, 15, 32 .... **F11, F56**
3. Avoid Abusing the Prestige of Judicial Office – 4, 6, 7 .... **F51**

C. Performance of Judicial Duties
1. General Adjudicative Duties
   a. Decorum, Respect, and Order – 48
      (1) Officers in Her Court
      (2) Parties
      (3) Jurors – 48
      (4) Broadcast / Recording of Proceedings
   b. Administrative Duties – 31
      (1) General Responsibilities – 17
      (2) No Bias or Prejudice – 31

Chapter 6

Judiciary Ethics

Questions

1. All Legal Investors Group consisted of a group of wealthy retired attorneys. They decided to start a savings and loan home mortgage bank that would concentrate on attracting members of the legal profession. To make the advertising program work, All Legal offered a residential mortgage at an interest rate of 1% below market to professionals who refer them business. The below market rate offer was extended to a few people. Judge Homer Homeowner had put in an offer on a house that had just been accepted. He needed a mortgage and had heard about the new "lawyer's home mortgage bank." He applied and was approved at the discount mortgage rate because Judge Homer was an official judge.

Was it proper for Judge Homer to accept the discounted mortgage loan?

(A) No, because the savings and loan company was owned by lawyers.
(B) No, because the loan was extended to Judge Homer at a lower interest rate than that charged non-judges.
(C) Yes, as long as none of the retired attorney owners of All Legal brings on a matter in litigation before Judge Homer.
(D) Yes, because the lower rate was available to any other lawyer in the county.

2. Jessica was an attorney who served on the town council of Smallville, USA for two terms. She then ran for a judge's seat in the city's criminal court and was elected. After four years on the bench, Judge Jessica became increasingly tired of hearing petty criminal cases. The mayor suffered a massive stroke, and the city council scheduled a special election. Judge Jessica was urged by many to run for the open office. She decided, however, that she needed to determine the level of campaign support she could expect from the local political leaders and met with many of them over lunch and dinner.

Is Judge Jessica's conduct proper?

(A) No, unless Judge Jessica disqualifies herself from any case involving any of the political leaders she met with.
(B) No, because Judge Jessica should have resigned her seat on the bench before undertaking any overt political campaigning.
(C) Yes, as long as the local leaders paid for their own lunch or dinner.
(D) Yes, as long as the meetings are not secret, and all the conversations are recorded.

3. Judge John and his wife Alice are both attorneys. Alice is a partner in a law firm, and John serves as a civil division judge in the county's superior court. They have decided to sell their residence and listed the house with a local realtor. At the first open house that the broker held on Sunday, an interested buyer made a full-price offer which they immediately accepted. Later it came to light that the buyer was an attorney with the same law firm as Alice. The following Tuesday, a case that the house-buying lawyer was handling was assigned for trial to Judge John.

Is it proper for Judge John to conduct the trial?

- **(A)** No, because the judge may have a deemed financial interest in a party in the proceeding.
- **(B)** No, unless the judge's wife does all the detailed negotiations of the house sale without telling her husband any of the details.
- **(C)** Yes, because the listing and offering price of the residence were fixed before the attorney or judge learned of the case assignment.
- **(D)** Yes, because the buyer is a partner with the judge's wife in the law firm.

4. Judge Janet is a single woman who first ran for her seat on the bench five years ago. She was reelected last year. Seven years ago while practicing law, she was involved in a nasty divorce from her then husband. Her husband's attorney in the divorce proceeding, Stan Shark, was very aggressive in the case, which grew quite contentious. By the time the divorce case was over, Janet was very upset with Stan's conduct and developed a distaste for Stan's professionalism.

On Monday morning, Judge Janet was assigned a criminal assault case. When the parties and their attorneys arrived in her courtroom, Judge Janet immediately recognized Stan Shark, who was representing the criminal defendant. The trial began, and neither Judge Janet nor Stan Shark said anything about the prior divorce trial.

Is Judge Janet subject to discipline for not disqualifying herself in the criminal assault trial?

- **(A)** No, unless Judge Janet's distaste for Stan affects her conduct of the trial, and the Judge believes she cannot conduct the trial in an impartial manner.
- **(B)** No, because any bias occurred prior to the time she went on the bench.
- **(C)** Yes, but only if Stan Shark files a motion to disqualify Judge Janet.
- **(D)** Yes, since Judge Janet likely has a personal bias against Stan Shark.

Questions 5 – 7 are based on the following:

Laurie Lawschool was the president of the Student Bar Association of All-America Law School. Upon graduation, she went to work for the county prosecutor's office. While there, she was involved in a number of high profile cases. This gave her a platform and public support that allowed her to run for an open superior court position.

5. During the judicial campaign for the open seat on the superior court, Laurie

I. Publicly endorsed other candidates who were campaigning for other open seats on the superior court.

II. Appeared in television and newspaper media campaigns.

III. Indicated that she was a Democrat and allowed the party to include her name on a list of "recommended candidates."

IV. Spoke at the Democratic Party political gathering.

V. Agreed to her name being listed on the Democratic "election ticket."

Laurie is subject to discipline for

(A) None of the above actions.
(B) One of the above actions.
(C) Two of the above actions.
(D) Three of the above actions.

6. Laurie was elected to a seat on the superior court. All-American Law School was very proud of the accomplishments of its alumni, especially those few who had been successful in judicial elections. Accordingly, the law school alumni director asked Laurie to serve as a class representative and participate in a campaign to obtain alumni contributions. A letter signed by Laurie was sent to all members of Laurie's law school class, requesting that they make a large contribution to the law school. If no contribution was received from the individual members of her class, a second letter would go out two weeks later. In this letter, Judge Laurie would firmly remind her classmates they had not affirmatively responded to her first request for a contribution. Some members of her law school class objected.

Were Judge Laurie's actions in the contribution campaign proper?

(A) No, because judges may never participate in non-profit organizations.
(B) No, because such activity by a judge involves judicial influences.
(C) Yes, because the market solicited by Judge Laurie was her classmates who knew her before she went on the bench.
(D) Yes, as long as there were no representations that contributors would be afforded special privileges in Judge Laurie's court.

7. Judge Laurie was asked to teach a class at the law school, and she agreed. The student evaluations for her class were quite strong. Based upon these evaluations, the biggest bar review course offered Laurie the "opportunity" to become an instructor in their course at a compensation of $5000 per class. The bar review course is "for profit" and competes with two other local courses. The course administrator intends to widely advertise the fact that their new instructor is a sitting superior court judge.

Is it proper for Laurie to accept the opportunity?

- **(A)** No, because a judge should not accept moonlighting jobs that involve the law.
- **(B)** No, because instructing a bar review course is always considered an extrajudicial activity.
- **(C)** Yes, if the income she receives from the bar review course is not material to her net worth and is reported.
- **(D)** Yes, unless the bar review course advertisement attempts to exploit Laurie's judicial position.

8. Jamie Ernest was the state senate majority leader of Evergreen state. A senior member of the Evergreen State Supreme Court had a stroke and upon his doctor's advice resigned effective immediately. Governor Pattie Political owed Senator Ernest many political favors and appointed her to fill the then vacant seat on the state supreme court. The appointment had to be approved by a bipartisan committee established by the state bar association to evaluate judicial appointments.

Jamie appeared before the election committee. Evergreen had an abortion case currently on appeal. One of the questions asked was if she would follow the law allowing abortions even though it conflicted with her personal views. Jamie answered that "the supreme court has recently upheld a case convicting a doctor of homicide who performed an abortion. I would follow that precedent."

Was the remark made by Judge Jamie proper?

- **(A)** Yes, because Judge Jamie did not refer to a matter pending or that might come before her court.
- **(B)** Yes, because Judge Jamie was compelled to testify before the bipartisan committee.
- **(C)** No, because her remarks included statements about a position she would take in a case or controversy.
- **(D)** No, because a judge should not discuss political philosophy.

9. Nancy Next was a civil prosecutor in the city of Hangemup, USA. After 10 years of high-profile civil cases, Nancy decided she should run for an open seat on the superior court held by Charlie Criminallaw. Nancy was successful in her campaign and was elected to the bench. The first case she was assigned was a criminal first-degree murder trial. Nancy's only experience was in civil cases, and both the prosecution and the defense filed numerous procedural motions. She felt incompetent in some of these criminal matters and contacted Judge Charlie Criminallaw who had retired. Charlie was able to refer Nancy to many helpful criminal law treatises. These references greatly assisted Nancy in deciding the motions, although she did not inform either counsel of the communications she had with Charlie.

Was it improper for Judge Nancy to consult with retired Judge Charlie under these circumstances?

- **(A)** No, because Charlie Criminallaw was another judge.
- **(B)** No, because a judge may consult a disinterested expert on a legal matter only if the judge informs the attorneys for both parties in the matter.
- **(C)** Yes, because Judge Charlie Criminallaw was no longer on the same court as Judge Nancy.
- **(D)** Yes, because Judge Nancy did not inform all counsel that she had conferred with a third party in deciding upon how to rule upon their motions.

10. Jessica was a partner in a four-person law partnership. She ran for and was elected to the local superior court. When the election results were announced, Jessica negotiated a sellout of her law practice with her former partners. All of Jessica's prior clients were transferred to the remaining partners in return for a cash payoff.

Two months later, Judge Jessica received her docket assignment for the next month. Contained in it was a corporate dispute in which the plaintiff was represented by one of Judge Jessica's former partners. Judge Jessica studied the file and realized this matter had been worked on by her ex-partner prior to her leaving the law firm. However, Judge Jessica did not personally work on the matter or know anything about the case details or the plaintiff.

Is it proper for Judge Jessica to hear and decide the matter?

- **(A)** No, unless Judge Jessica receives a written waiver from both parties in the dispute.
- **(B)** No, because Judge Jessica practiced law with her ex-partner while the matter was being handled by the firm.
- **(C)** Yes, as long as Judge Jessica did not personally participate as a lawyer in the matter.
- **(D)** Yes, because Judge Jessica retained no financial interest in the matter.

11. Josepha Jones was a resident of the Highpoint neighborhood in Everycity, USA. She and her husband had three children who all went to Good Children Preschool. After graduating from law school, Josepha worked for three years as a county prosecuting attorney and then successfully ran for a judgeship on the local court. She was asked to and agreed to serve on the board of directors of Good Children Preschool while Mandy Manners was the manager. Two years after her youngest child completed the Preschool, the manager, Mandy, was arrested. Mandy was later charged with possession of marijuana and requested that Judge Josepha testify at trial about her good character and reliable preschool administration.

Is it proper for Judge Josepha to appear and testify at trial?

(A) Yes, if she is served with a subpoena to give testimony at trial.
(B) Yes, but she may only testify about her opinion of Mandy that was formed before she was elected to the bench.
(C) No, because Josepha, as a judge, is not permitted to act as a character witness while serving in the judiciary.
(D) No, unless Josepha has personal knowledge about Mandy's marijuana use.

12. Judge Rudy Romantic had been on the bench of the local superior court for 12 years when his wife died of cancer. After a reasonable period of mourning, Judge Rudy began to be attracted by middle-age eligible single women. One year after his wife's death, Judge Rudy announced his engagement to Alice Attractive.

Friendly Fred had regularly appeared in Judge Rudy's court in business disputes and considered himself a friend of Judge Rudy. Friendly Fred decided to give Judge Rudy a wedding gift of a world cruise for two with a fair market value of $25,000.

Is it proper for Judge Rudy to accept this gift?

(A) Yes, if Friendly Fred was a close personal friend of Judge Rudy.
(B) Yes, if Judge Rudy reports the wedding present as a social hospitality.
(C) No, because to accept a gift worth $25,000 would create the appearance of impropriety.
(D) No, because Friendly Fred appeared regularly in Judge Rudy's court.

13. Judge Ambitious was on the superior court bench in Opportunityville, USA. The state attorney general announced that she would not seek reelection for another term. The general election for the office is in four months, and Judge Ambitious announced her candidacy for the public office. The minimum required restriction this places on Judge Ambitious is to

(A) Make sure that her conduct of the election campaign does not adversely affect performance of her judicial duties.
(B) Disqualify herself as to any matters involving the attorney general's office unless both parties in the matter do not object to her hearing the case after she makes full disclosure.
(C) Disqualify herself as to any matter involving the attorney general's office and resign her judgeship if there are too many requests for disqualification.
(D) Resign her judicial seat immediately.

14. Jeanette Judge sits on the Court of Appeals in a state bordering a foreign country. One of her oldest friends from law school has just won election as governor of the state. The new governor has approached Jeanette and offered to appoint her to a new committee charged with the responsibility of studying the problems associated with immigrants entering the state illegally.

Is it proper for Jeanette Judge to accept the appointment?

(A) Yes, as long as the position only relates to the law, the legal system, or the administration of justice.
(B) Yes, if it does not detract from Jeanette's judicial duties.
(C) No, if any such illegal immigrants are likely to appear in Jeannette's court.
(D) No, unless Jeanette makes no political speeches while serving on the commission.

15. Connie Cautious began her legal career after law school by working as an assistant county prosecutor. One of her first assignments was to investigate a woman named Susan Smith whom the police had accused of embezzlement. After an investigation, Connie concluded that Susan had no involvement in the embezzlement whatsoever. Five years later, Judge Cautious won election to the local superior court. Her current assignment is on the criminal calendar. The County Prosecutor has brought criminal charges against the same Susan Smith, but the matter involved was not connected in any way to the previous embezzlement investigation.

Is it proper for Judge Cautious to decide the case?

(A) Yes, unless Judge Cautious might be prejudiced against Susan Smith because of the prior embezzlement investigation.
(B) Yes, because no part of the prior embezzlement investigation is involved with or affects the present charges.
(C) No, if Judge Cautious was responsible for determining that the previous investigation was unable to show any involvement by Susan Smith in the embezzlement.
(D) No, if Judge Cautious was responsible for initiating the previous investigation of Susan Smith in the embezzlement.

16. Judge Blowhard was a law school professor before he ran for election to the Court of Appeals in New York City. He was elected to the bench, but missed the intellectually stimulating interchange of law school teaching. The American Law School Bench Relations Committee is scheduling their annual summer convention in Boston and would like to present a CLE seminar on penal reform. They have invited Judge Blowhard to make a presentation.

Which of the following are proper?

I. Judge Blowhard may give the speech in Boston and may accept compensation if reasonable in amount.

II. Judge Blowhard should decline to make the speech.

III. Judge Blowhard may make the speech for compensation and be reimbursed for his and his wife's actual traveling, lodging, and meal expenses.

IV. Judge Blowhard may make the speech, keep the reimbursement for his and his wife's travel, lodging, and meal expenses, but should not accept any compensation for the speech.

(A) I only.
(B) I and III.
(C) I, III, and IV.
(D) I and IV.

17. Judge Stewart Slowtime serves on the trial court and hears cases on its docket. This jurisdiction permits a judge to double-set cases for trial, and Judge Stewart has created a special rule for his court that allows litigants the right to demand three trial postponements.

After three of right postponements, a litigant can file a motion for additional discretionary postponements. Judge Stewart believes granting these postponements promotes settlements and forces attorneys for plaintiffs to be more reasonable in their settlement demands and negotiations.

Are Judge Stewart's actions proper?

(A) Yes, because a plaintiff objecting to postponements can appeal the judge's order.
(B) Yes, because the judge is allowed wide discretion in deciding administrative matters.
(C) No, because a judge should expedite matters on their docket.
(D) No, because a judge does not have an obligation to encourage parties to settle a case short of trial.

18. Alice Ambitious was a struggling lawyer who decided to run against a sitting judge named Sally Smith. Judge Smith was widely considered to be quite active in cases in her court. Many lawyers felt she went too far and her lack of impartiality had been questioned in many cases by numerous attorneys. Alice called a senior staff member of the commission on judicial conduct and inquired whether the judge had ever been disciplined. The staff member told her, "Yes, she has received two reprimands for partiality matters." Alice believed the report as it was consistent with what she had observed about the judge's activist manner. In fact, however, it was Judge Sarah Smith who had been reprimanded and the staff member looked at the wrong file.

Is Alice subject to discipline for publicly stating that Judge Sally Smith had been reprimanded twice for judicial misconduct?

(A) Yes, because Judge Sally Smith had not been disciplined.
(B) Yes, because Alice should have insisted upon examining the commission's records herself.
(C) No, because Judge Sally Smith had voluntarily decided to run in a contested election.
(D) No, because Alice relied upon the senior staff member's information.

19. Judge New won election to the bench after serving for eight years as a criminal prosecutor. One of the first cases she was assigned on the bench involved a complicated shareholder derivative action alleging violation of the federal securities laws. Judge New entertained the first motion to dismiss and realized that she was completely incompetent in the area. She contacted Laura Lawschool, a local law school professor who taught securities law. Laura provided the judge with a written memorandum containing a summary of the law and references to some recent law review articles that were on point with issues expected in the upcoming trial. Judge New informed counsel for both parties of her *ex parte* communication, provided them the citations to the law review articles, and told them they could respond in writing if they liked.

Has Judge New acted in a proper manner?

(A) No, because a judge cannot initiate an *ex parte* communication on a substantive matter.
(B) No, unless Judge New obtains a waiver from both counsel of their right to insist the court not engage in *ex parte* communication.
(C) Yes, unless one (or both) counsel argues that Professor Laura Lawschool harbored a bias in her philosophy about shareholder derivative actions involving federal securities matters.
(D) Yes, even if counsel argues that Professor Laura Lawschool harbored a bias in her philosophy about shareholder derivative actions involving federal securities matters.

20. Judge Harriet Hardline is a Superior Court judge in Everycity, USA. In the last five years, most of her cases have been on the criminal docket. The public defenders began to complain that she gave prison sentences to convicted criminals that were always at the upper end of the sentence guidelines. Judge Harriet is beginning to seek opportunities to publicize her reelection campaign. A newspaper reporter asked Judge Harriet, "Is there any truth to the rumor you are a 'lock-em-up' judge?"

Which of the below responses is improper for the judge?

I. "My sentences have always been within the judicial guidelines."

II. "I believe criminals should be put where they can't injure responsible citizens and, if reelected, I will stand by this."

III. "As you know, Robert Rapist's case starts next Monday in my court, and if the jury convicts him, he will receive a heavy sentence."

IV. "I will always do my best to promote the interests of truth and justice."

V. "So that is that – tell your readers to send money for my reelection campaign."

(A) Only one of the above.
(B) Only two of the above.
(C) Only three of the above.
(D) Only four of the above.

21. Attorney Paula Plaintiff practices primarily personal injury cases in the small rural county of Lowverdict. Judge Stingy is the only civil judge in the county. Judge Stingy had dismissed many of the claims Paula filed and, for the few that got to the jury, instructed the jury to be very conservative in the judgments. Paula believes the judge lacks fairness and unreasonably sides with the defendants. The judicial election for the seat held by Judge Stingy is three months hence, and Judge Georgia Generous has announced her intent to run against the incumbent for the seat. Paula believes Judge Generous would make a far better judge and intends to contribute $1,000 to defeat Judge Stingy.

Is it proper for Judge Generous to accept the $1,000?

(A) Yes, if Paula's contribution is made anonymously.
(B) Yes, Generous may accept the $1,000 from Paula personally as long as it is reported in the campaign finance report.
(C) No, unless Paula contributes the $1,000 to a campaign committee formed for the election of Generous.
(D) No, because Paula regularly appears before the court to which Generous seeks to be elected.

22. Judge Moneybags is married to Mary Moneybags. Mary inherited from her parents one-third of a large shopping center, which is her separate property. The major tenant in the center brought a lawsuit seeking a substantial reduction in the rent. If the tenant's suit is successful, it would create a substantial negative economic effect on the value of the property.

The case was assigned to Judge Moneybags, who immediately realized the situation and promptly informed the parties of his personal connection to his wife's ownership interests. He stated to the lawyers in chambers that he would willingly recuse himself unless both parties agreed to waive the conflict. Mary Moneybags said she had no problem and the tenant's attorney stated orally he would not object. Judge Moneybags decided the case in favor of the shopping center and the plaintiff tenant complained to the judicial commission of a clear bias by the judge during the trial.

Did Judge Moneybags act properly in hearing this case?

(A) Yes, because the parties did not object to the judge hearing the case.
(B) Yes, because Judge Moneybags did not have a direct financial interest in the outcome.
(C) No, unless the remittal agreement was entered into the record.
(D) No, because the judge had an apparent conflict of interest that created an appearance of impropriety.

23. Judge Sally Sincere was serving on the court of appeals after receiving an appointment from the governor. She has participated in and written the lead opinion in a number of criminal sentence decisions appealed to her court for review by the prosecutor. Her opinions have also been subject to criticism by many politicians in the state, who claimed her decisions favored the criminals. Judge Sally agreed to appear on a judicial television show interview with a non-controversial host. Two days before the interview, she was informed that she would receive probative questions about her position.

Judge Sally may state which of the following?

I. The issues raised by those opposing my positions may be appropriate matters for legislative consideration.

II. I continue to believe I decided those cases correctly.

III. I continue to believe I decided those cases correctly and will make consistent decisions in similar cases in the future.

(A) I only.
(B) I and II.
(C) II and III.
(D) I, II, and III.

24. Judge Steady serves on the court of appeals in the jurisdiction of Everystate. The judicial election rules provide for voter approval or disapproval of incumbent judges seeking reappointment every six years. If the voters disapprove of the reappointment, the state governor, with the concurrence of the bar association, appoints a new judge to the seat. Judge Steady wrote some controversial opinions that were critical of handguns and automatic weapons. In response the local chapter of the National Rifle Association has organized an effort to urge voters to vote "not reappoint" for Judge Steady.

Is it proper for Judge Steady to organize a campaign committee to raise contributions and support his campaign for a "reappoint" vote?

(A) Yes, because Judge Steady's candidacy has drawn opposition even though there is no present individual opponent.
(B) Yes, because every Judge is entitled to solicit campaign contributions and promote public support.
(C) No, because it is improper for a judge to take a position on a political issue such as gun control.
(D) No, because the judicial position is not to be filled by a opposing lawyer elected by the voters.

25. Judge Charlie Concerned is a criminal court judge in Pleasantville County. His mother has become increasingly detached and forgetful. The doctor feels it represents the onset of Alzheimers. The family met and decided they needed to establish a guardianship and have asked Charlie to accept the responsibility. The duties of conducting the guardianship are minimal and will not interfere with his judicial duties. It would be necessary for Judge Charlie to prepare and execute pleadings and to appear in the civil division on his mother's behalf.

Is it proper for Judge Charlie to take on the guardianship role?

- **(A)** No, because the role will require the judge to prepare and executc pleadings that will be filed in the same county court system in which he sits.
- **(B)** No, because the role will require the judge to appear in the same county court system in which he sits.
- **(C)** Yes, because the position involves both a close family member and will not interfere with the performance of Judge Charlie's judicial duties.
- **(D)** Yes, unless Judge Charlie receives compensation for the legal services rendered as guardian.

Questions 26 and 27 are based on the following:

Judge Barbara Bored has served for over 20 years on the county's superior court. Since she has been on the bench for so long, she often became involved in scheduling for the superior court docket. One of the other judges became sick in the middle of a trial, and Judge Bored reassigned the trial to another judge who completed the case.

Shortly thereafter Judge Bored resigned her seat and joined her daughter in the Bored & Bored partnership to practice law. The trial decision was appealed, and the court of appeals later remanded the case for a new trial. The defendant in the case has approached attorney Barbara Bored and asked her to represent them in the retrial of the case in Superior Court.

26. If former Judge Barbara Bored takes on the representation in the remanded case, will she be subject to discipline?

- **(A)** No, because any information she learned about the case during the reassignment proceeding was in the public record.
- **(B)** No, because Judge Bored did not act as a judge concerning a substantial matter or decide on the merits of the case.
- **(C)** Yes, because attorney Barbara Bored would have to try the case before a judge of the court on which Judge Bored previously sat.
- **(D)** Yes, because attorney Barbara personally acted officially as a judge concerning an aspect of the case.

27. Barbara is not sure she should take on the representation and asked for an advisory opinion from the proper authority. Independently of the opinion, attorney Barbara decided she would not represent the defendant in the retrial. The defendant was quite disappointed and asked if Barbara's daughter could take on the case in Superior Court.

If the daughter takes on the case, who will be subject to discipline?

(A) Only the daughter, because if a former judge is disqualified, no other lawyer in the same firm may undertake representation in the matter.

(B) Only former Judge Bored, because the daughter was not the former judge.

(C) Neither former Judge Bored nor her daughter as long as Barbara does not participate in the case or received any portion of the fee.

(D) Both former Judge Bored and her daughter, since a partner in a law firm has responsibility for another lawyer's violation of the MRPCs.

28. Judge Carol Criminal had served on the criminal trial bench for the last four years. The new presiding judge in the county decided it would be helpful to broaden the judicial experience of the trial court judges. The next matter Judge Carol was assigned was a complicated product liability case. During pre-trial discovery, the judge was unable to get the attorneys to stipulate to any agreement about the manufacturing process that led to the defective product. Judge Carol became frustrated and sent Clark Kent, her court reporter, to the manufacturing plant to observe the process that created the allegedly defective product. Clark interviewed three staff members and reported back to Judge Carol that the plaintiff's version of the manufacturing process defect was correct.

The trial began, and there was evidence introduced that supported what Clark had learned from the three staff members at the plant and reported to the judge. The judge rendered a verdict for the plaintiff.

Was Judge Carol's conduct proper?

(A) Yes, because the facts were contested, and since it was the judge's duty to decide the case, she had the right to gather the necessary facts.

(B) Yes, because the judge did not engage in the discussions herself, and the judge's verdict was supported by evidence at trial.

(C) No, unless all three witnesses Clark interviewed were witnesses at trial and subject to cross examination.

(D) No, because the judge participated in *ex parte* communication even if the party interviewed did not prevail at trial.

Questions 29 and 30 are based on the following:

Judge Florence Forever is running for retention in the judicial election scheduled for six months in the future. The challenger is a prominent deputy district attorney named Aggressive Albert who has won a few high-profile murder cases. Albert has made some very aggressive negative statements about Judge Florence, and she decided to hire a professional consultant, Pattie Political, to organize her campaign committee.

29. Pattie interviewed Judge Florence to learn about her activities. Judge Florence reported that she had been involved as a subscribing member in the local symphony association for many years both before and after she went on the bench. She told Pattie that she had just been asked to become an honorary director and assist them in their public relations. Pattie said, "Great, the more positive publicity the better."

Which of the following activities would be improper for Judge Florence to do for the symphony association?

I. Continue her honorary directorship position provided she does not give legal advice.

II. Contribute her personal funds to the symphony.

III. Solicit contributions for the symphony.

IV. Attend fund raising events for the symphony.

(A) Only one of the above.
(B) Only two of the above.
(C) Only three of the above.
(D) All four of the above.

30. Pattie Political organized a group of local attorneys to form a reelection campaign committee for Judge Florence.

Which of the below activities are acceptable campaign activities for the committee?

I. Seek public endorsements for the judge's campaign.

II. Seek attorney endorsements for the judge's campaign.

III. Solicit monetary contributions for the judge's campaign.

IV. Transmit the balance of any unused campaign contributions to the personal use of Judge Florence after the election.

(A) All of the above.
(B) Only three of the above.
(C) Only two of the above.
(D) Only one of the above.

31. Judge Fred Firem was a senior state superior court justice. He now presides over only a few civil trials because his administrative duties as senior court administrator have increased in recent years. Fred hired and promoted Florence Forester as a probation officer. Later, he demoted and discharged her. Florence filed a lawsuit against Judge Fred alleging sexual discrimination.

Judge Fred Firem's claim of immunity should be

(A) Upheld, because the Judge's immunity is absolute.
(B) Denied, because the Judge's immunity is not absolute.
(C) Denied, because the decision to demote and discharge Florence was primarily administrative rather than adjudicative in nature.
(D) Upheld, because the threat of vexatious lawsuits by disgruntled ex-employees would interfere with the quality of a judge's decisions.

32. Judge Eunice University was a proud alumna of Good Health University and served as a trustee on the university's board. The university entered into a conditional contract to sell some property to Ernie Entrepreneur, who intended to operate a hospital on the property. This required a "certificate of need," which was denied by the controlling state agency. Ernie sued the state agency. Judge Eunice was assigned the case and held for petitioner Ernie Entrepreneur. This decision was appealed on the basis it was improper for Judge Eunice to decide the case and that she should have acted *sua sponte* to disqualify herself.

Was the judge's behavior improper?

- **(A)** No, unless she participated in the negotiations with Ernie Entrepreneur on behalf of the University.
- **(B)** No, as long as the judge did not vote to approve the contract between the University and Ernie.
- **(C)** No, as long as the judge had no knowledge that the University was contracting with Ernie.
- **(D)** Yes.

33. Judge Tracy Truetower sits on the Everycity Superior Court. The presiding judge has just assigned a criminal racketeering case involving the local mob to another superior court judge named Fred Flaky. After a week of trial, the prosecution had almost completed the presentation of the state's case. Friday afternoon, Judge Tracy worked late and left the courthouse around 8:00 pm. As she walked out, she saw Judge Flaky and the attorney for the defendant mob talking in an adjacent doorway. She observed a large stack of what appeared to be cash changing hands, and Judge Flaky said, "I will take care of it." Unbeknownst to Judge Tracy, the cash was a reimbursement for bar association expenses Judge Flaky had properly paid on behalf of a number of attorneys on a bar committee, including the attorney for the defendant.

Is Judge Tracy under a duty to immediately report the conversation to the appropriate judicial authority?

- **(A)** No, unless the perceived violation raises a substantial question about the judge's fitness for judicial office.
- **(B)** Yes, only if she makes further investigation and determines the judge's involvement raises a substantial question about the judge's fitness for judicial office.
- **(C)** Yes, but only upon proper request by the appropriate authority.
- **(D)** No, because reporting a perceived violation by a fellow judge merely is optional, not an absolute requirement.

34. Judge Sarah Snooper was conducting a criminal jury trial in which the defendant was charged with assault and battery. During the morning break of the second week of trial, Judge Sarah was in a stall in the women's restroom. The two defense attorneys were also in the same restroom, and they began a discussion about the defendant's alibi. Judge Sarah believed that what she heard included client confidences and secrets. Disclosure of a client confidential information by a lawyer without consent is a clear ethical violation in the jurisdiction.

Judge Sarah

- **(A)** Must report the attorneys' violation to the appropriate authority.
- **(B)** Must not report the attorneys' violation to the appropriate authority.
- **(C)** Should call the defendant into her chambers without the attorneys being present and inform him that the attorneys have revealed his confidences and secrets.
- **(D)** May discuss the matter privately with the two attorneys.

35. Judge Otto Outspoken is up for reelection. Two weeks before he began his reelection campaign, he officiated over a civil case in which he granted a directed verdict motion at the end of the plaintiff's case. This decision upheld a contract exculpatory provision between an individual consumer and a professional surveyor. The decision was quite controversial, but the 30-day limit for defendants to appeal expired. Two months after his decision in the case and during his reelection campaign, a television reporter accosted him and asked him questions about his decision in the case.

Which of the below statements by Judge Otto are proper?

I. "If I faced the same contractual provision in another contract, I would hold the same."

II. "In my opinion, courts must enforce such provisions to guarantee the certainty of the law of contracts."

III. "Whether such a contract provision is valid is an appropriate issue for the legislature to consider."

- **(A)** I only.
- **(B)** II only.
- **(C)** III only.
- **(D)** II and III.

36. Judge Temperance presided over a highly contentious civil trial in which Iola Insubordinate was one of the lawyers. One month after the end of the trial, the appropriate state disciplinary authority contacted the judge. The investigator said that a formal grievance had been filed against Iola. They asked if Judge Temperance would provide information about Iola's trial conduct.

Does Judge Temperance have an ethical responsibility to provide the requested information to the investigator?

- **(A)** Yes, only if the Judge previously imposed litigation sanctions on Iola.
- **(B)** Yes, because a judge should assist in administering lawyer discipline.
- **(C)** No, unless the Judge previously imposed litigation sanctions on Iola.
- **(D)** No, because a judge may not act as a character witness for a lawyer.

37. Judge Alice Alumni is an honor graduate of Smallville Law School. The non-profit law school has hired a new Director of Development who wants the law school to have a higher judicial presence in Smallville. The Director met with Judge Alice and requested her assistance. During the meeting they discussed that Judge Alice could:

I. Serve on the law school board of trustees.

II. Serve as a judge of the student moot court competition.

III. Teach a 1L course on civil procedure.

IV. Be listed as a major contributor in a public media campaign designed to raise $50 million to build a new law school building.

Which of the above functions may Judge Alice properly agree to do?

(A) Only one of the above.
(B) Two of the above.
(C) Three of the above.
(D) All four of the above.

38. Roberta Reelection is a sitting judge on Everycity's Superior Court. Her first term in office was controversial because she presided over a murder trial. The jury found the defendant guilty, but Roberta granted judgment notwithstanding the verdict (JNOV) to the defendant. Her reasoning was that the police's failure to give the defendant the *Miranda* warnings produced the confession, and the Prosecutor covered it up until a police officer inadvertently disclosed it in his trial testimony. The local press was outraged and labeled Roberta "the criminal's judge." She has just filed for reelection and has drawn opposition from Holly Hangemup, a former prosecutor.

Which of the following is improper reelection conduct?

I. Roberta states she was an honor graduate from Everycity Law School.

II. Roberta asks the American Civil Liberty Union (ACLU) if they would make a public statement supporting her reelection.

III. Roberta asks the American Civil Liberty Union (ACLU) if they would raise funds for her reelection.

IV. Roberta stated that her judicial decisions were consistent with constitutional requirements.

(A) II and III.
(B) II, III, and IV.
(C) III only.
(D) None are improper.

39. Alice Attorney graduated from law school and passed the bar exam. She then joined a medium-sized law firm where she practiced general commercial litigation. She had occasion to do some arbitration work and really enjoyed it. After considering her future she decided to file for election to an open seat in the local trial court. Alice approached a friend of hers from law school named Betty Bigbucks. Betty is from an old-line family in the community and knows many wealthy professionals. Alice asked Betty if she would raise funds for her campaign.

Is Alice's request proper?

- **(A)** Yes, unless Betty practices law in front of the same court where Alice will serve if elected.
- **(B)** Yes, if all the funds that Betty raises are turned into Alice's campaign committee.
- **(C)** No, unless all the funds raised come from non-lawyers.
- **(D)** No, if Betty informs Alice of the identity of the contributors.

40. Carol Chief is the Presiding Judge of the Easyville City Superior Court. The voters of the city have recently voted down a property tax assessment that would have fully funded the local court system. Because of the reduced funding, it is necessary to lay off two of the elected judges, and this reduction may be in violation of certain federal statutory requirements. Carol contacted the mayor of Easyville and Chair of the State Judicial Committee and requested they seek a declaratory judgment that Easyville is legally required to fund the court system at the prior level.

Is Carol's conduct proper?

- **(A)** Yes, only if she can prove that the decrease in revenue will decrease the quality of legal administration in the city.
- **(B)** Yes, because a judge may appear and consult with political officials concerning matters involving the administration of justice.
- **(C)** No, because a judge may not engage in activities that affect the practice or administration of law.
- **(D)** No, because to avoid the appearance of impropriety in political activity, a sitting judge should accept the decision of the legislative body in submitting the matter of judicial funding to the people.

41. Nancy New practiced law for many years before running for and winning a full-time state senate seat in Pleasant State. The governor has just appointed her to a full-time position on the superior court bench, where she has been assigned a full docket of cases. As she began to examine the pleadings in the matters assigned to her, she noticed at least four cases that represented possible disqualification situations.

Assuming the parties in each case do not affirmatively waive their rights to disqualification, in which of the below must Judge Nancy disqualify herself?

I. A suit against a Boy Scout troop in which Judge Nancy's son is the troop leader.

II. A suit against an investment company in which Judge Nancy's husband's sister is the plaintiff's lawyer.

III. A suit against a retail company represented by a lawyer who was Judge Nancy's partner in a law firm before she left the practice of law to become a full-time senator. The retail company was a client of the law firm while Judge New was there, but the matter did not then exist.

IV. A suit against a property developer represented by Judge's first cousin.

(A) All the above.
(B) I, but not II, III, or IV.
(C) I and II, but not III or IV.
(D) I, II, and III, but not IV.

42. Judge Olivia Opportunity was presiding over a copyright infringement case between two software companies. Massive discovery was undertaken, and much of the trade secret portion was conducted in camera and subject to non-disclosure (gag) orders. In this process, it was disclosed that the defendant, Megahard, Inc., was about to release a new operating system that would revolutionize the software industry.

Is it proper for the Judge to advise his son to purchase Megahard, Inc.'s stock before the information becomes public?

(A) Yes, because this is not the judge's investment.
(B) Yes, as long as disclosure is made of the transaction in the annual report the judge is required to file.
(C) No, unless the judge discloses the transaction to Megahard, Inc., in writing and the company does not object thereto.
(D) No, because a judge must not use non-public information acquired in a judiciary proceeding in his personal business dealings.

43. Attorneys Abbott and Costello entered into a partnership to jointly own and manage an apartment building. Both were lawyers who regularly appeared in the local trial court. For five years, they both managed the investment, including interviewing tenants, collecting rents, and making repairs. Abbott then ran for and was elected to the local trial court bench. The partners then decided that because of the judicial role, Abbott would not be involved in the day-to-day partnership business. They thus signed a management agreement under which Costello received 10% of all rental revenue and prepared a monthly accounting for Abbott.

Did Judge Abbott operate properly in entering into the management contract with Costello?

(A) Yes, as long as reviewing the monthly accounting reports prepared by Costello does not interfere with Judge Abbott's judicial duties.
(B) Yes, because the partnership owning the property was formed before Judge Abbott ran for judicial office.
(C) No, if Costello regularly appears in the local trial court that Judge Abbott sits on.
(D) No, because Judge Abbott should have divested himself of all of his active investments when he won the election.

44. Christine Conservative is a trial court judge in Everytown. The state has a statute prohibiting employment discrimination based upon various reasons, including sexual orientation. Christine's parents had for many years operated a family retirement home business that provided both counseling and residential services for the elderly.

The business has had a 30-year history of not hiring homosexuals and has consistently stated their position that a stable heterosexual marriage is a bona fide employee job qualification factor. After her parents death, Christine and her brother each inherited one-half of the business. Her brother is the president and wants Christine to become partially active in the business.

Is it proper for Judge Christine to continue as an owner and become partially active in the business?

(A) Yes, because the discrimination is a bona fide job qualification.
(B) Yes, unless the business activity interferes with the judge's judicial activities.
(C) No, because the business practices employment discrimination based upon sexual orientation.
(D) No, because a judge may not participate in management of a private business organization.

45. Which of the following activities by a sitting judge are proper:

I. Working as a weekend manager at a pizza restaurant.

II. Privately arbitrating a dispute between two neighbors for a fee.

III. Joining a religious organization that prohibits membership by those applicants who will not commit to that particular religion.

IV. Soliciting contributions during the annual telephone campaign for use by the National Forum for Drug Reform.

V. Directing his or her campaign committee chairperson to begin raising contributions 15 months before the reelection date.

(A) One of the above activities.
(B) Two of the above activities.
(C) Three of the above activities.
(D) Four of the above activities.

46. Judge Pattie Political has served two terms on the local superior court bench, and her current term expires in about 20 months. Some of her advisers have told her they have heard that she may face serious opposition in the reelection. To boost her friendship and voter support, Judge Pattie is considering the following activities.

The Judge may properly:

I. Endorse a very popular candidate running for U.S. Senate in the jurisdiction.

II. Endorse an old friend who is running for a seat on the local school board.

III. Attend a political gathering celebrating the 100th year anniversary of her statehood.

IV. Register to vote as a Democrat.

(A) All of the above.
(B) II, III, and IV.
(C) III and IV.
(D) IV only.

47. Judge Ida Involved was a sitting judge who enjoyed joining and participating in public service and local social organizations. She also had to stand for reelection every third year and thought public exposure would help her name familiarity with the local voters.

Which of the following activities may Judge Ida properly do?

I. Serve on a government commission concerned with the level of a veteran's disability payments.

II. Serve as a official representative at a historical event of the American Legion.

III. Serve as an officer of the board of regents of a local law school.

(A) I, II, and III.
(B) I and II only.
(C) II and III only.
(D) Only one of the above 3 activities is proper.

48. Betty Buyer brought a product liability case against Mega Bucks, Inc., a national manufacturer. Judge Connie Conservative heard the matter. The day-to-day proceedings of the case were widely reported in all the area's newspapers, which aroused public sympathy for the plaintiff. The jury was not sequestered and returned a verdict for plaintiff. The judgment included a very large punitive damage award against the defendants.

Judge Conservative was outraged by both the verdict and the size of the damage award because she believed that there was no relevant evidence of liability presented during the trial. In front of the jury, she criticized the verdict, which she thought to be based on passion and prejudice due in part to the extensive media reporting. The defendant's motion for Judgment Notwithstanding the Verdict (JNOV) was granted, and the media reporters responded by criticizing the judge.

As Judge Conservative was leaving the courthouse, she was approached by a group of determined aggressive reporters. In this confrontational session, the judge explained to the reporters the legal procedure a court must follow in deciding a JNOV.

Is Judge Conservatives' public statements proper to?

	The Jury	The Media Reporters
(A)	No	No
(B)	No	Yes
(C)	Yes	No
(D)	Yes	Yes

49. Jackie Judicious had a law practice specializing in intellectual property. Carol Copier was starting a software company and wanted to incorporate within the new operating system they were creating a number of features arguably developed by others. Carol retained Jackie to analyze all the patent and copyright applications of the other developers. Jackie made the investigation and concluded that Gil's new operating system did not infringe in any material way on any of the features previously developed by the other software developers.

The next year, Jackie was appointed to the jurisdiction's court of appeals. One year later, a group of the other developers brought an infringement action against Copier. Copier's attorney in the case believed the best defense Copier could assert was that she relied upon the advice of a lawyer experienced in software matters in their actions.

Is it proper for Jackie Judicious to voluntarily testify in the infringement action in support of Copier?

- **(A)** Yes, as long as the court in which she will testify is not under her court of appeals jurisdiction.
- **(B)** Yes, because her testimony would not go to Copier's character, only to the factual advice she rendered.
- **(C)** No, because a judge may not testify as a witness.
- **(D)** No, if the final decision in the case could be appealed to her court of appeals.

50. Judge Iola Independent had served two terms as a supreme court judge in Honest State and was up for reelection. She was contacted by a state-associated judicial review committee and asked to complete a questionnaire containing the following questions. Is your personal opinion: (1) In favor of personal choice on abortion or a blanket prohibition on abortion? (2) Prohibit gay/lesbian marriages or allow same sex marriages?

Was it proper for Judge Iola to state his personal position on?

- **(A)** The abortion issue only.
- **(B)** The gay marriage issue only.
- **(C)** Both of the personal positions of the judge would be properly stated.
- **(D)** Neither of the personal positions of the judge are properly stated.

51. Judge Pattie and her siblings owned Greenacres, a 2,000 acre ranch that years ago had been upzoned to allow single family developments. The State is considering imposing a downzoning scheme on the local property owners to return the land to solely agriculture use. Judge Pattie's property was included in the downzone area and she requested a meeting with the Governor.

Is it proper for Judge Pattie to meet with the Governor?

- **(A)** Yes, because the matter involved Judge Pattie's own interests.
- **(B)** Yes, as long as the meeting is not reported by the public media.
- **(C)** No, because a judge must not consult with a public official.
- **(D)** No, unless the matter in controversy involves the administration of justice.

52. Judge Wendy Wealthy inherited numerous rental properties in the city from her father. She owned one third of these properties as a tenant-in-common with her brother and sister. Issues often arise in their property business that requires adjudication in the district court in which Wendy is a judge. Her brother, Tom, had been the property manager for many years, but suffered a stroke last week. The family wants Judge Wendy to assume active management of the family property.

Is it proper for Judge Wendy to accept the business management role?

(A) Yes, because it is her family business.
(B) Yes, if she does not spend any time in the day on the investments.
(C) No, because the judge does not own a controlling interest in the business.
(D) No, if it appears likely that significant disqualifications will be required because of the judge's management and ownership interest.

53. Alice Appointee was an attorney who served in the legislature on a part-time basis. In a committee meeting, she learned the Governor was about to appoint five judges to a new county district just established by the legislature. Carol had always wanted to become a judge, but did not want to have to go through a public campaign.

To facilitate her appointment to the new judicial position, which of the following may Carol properly do?

I. Supply relevant information to a screening committee.

II. Solicit funds.

III. Establish a campaign committee.

IV. Seek an endorsement from the local bar association.

(A) Only one of the above.
(B) Two of the above.
(C) Three of the above.
(D) All four of the above.

54. Charlie Conservative was a mediocre lawyer whose practice consisted of defending oil and gas companies that were accused of pollution. At the urging of some of his clients he ran for Supreme Court in a state where heavy off-shore oil drilling was occurring. The seated judge, Laurie Liberal, had a history of zealously enforcing all environmental laws. Oil polluters contributed $3 million dollars to Charlie's campaign that allowed him to heavily outspend Laurie and he won the seat. One of Charlie's first decisions on the Supreme Court was to cast the crucial vote in overturning a large jury verdict below against the oil polluters who contributed to his winning campaign.

Was Judge Conservative's vote proper?

(A) Yes, if the oil polluters' contribution was made through an independent committee.
(B) Yes, unless it can be shown that the vote to overturn the jury verdict was an error.
(C) No, because Judge Charlie's vote created a clear appearance of a lack of judicial impartiality.
(D) No, if other members of the court also voted to overturn the jury verdict before.

Chapter 6

Judiciary Ethics

Answers

> **MPRE Tip:** Put a piece of paper over the answers and "mask down" while working through the questions so you don't accidently peek at the next answer.

1. **/B/** A judge may only accept a loan from a lending institution at market interest rates and other terms available to the general public. All lawyers who are members of the bar in the county are not "the general public." Unless the standard is met, the loan from All Legal Savings and Loan is considered to be in part an improper gift [MCJC 3.13]. **(A)** is not the best answer because in theory, disqualification would only be necessary if one of the lawyer owners became involved in a matter in front of Judge Homer. **(C)** is incorrect because an individual stockholder of All Legal Savings and Loan could appear in front of Judge Homer. **(D)** is incorrect because the test is the market rates and terms offered to the general public, not other lawyers.

2. **/B/** The best answer because before becoming a candidate for a partisan non-judicial office – either in a primary or general election – a sitting judge shall resign their judicial seat [MCJC 3.13]. **(A)** is incorrect because a disqualification in certain cases would not excuse the judge's improper political conduct. **(C)** is incorrect because who paid for the lunch is irrelevant. **(D)** is not the best answer because merely recording the conversations does not cure the prohibition against political campaigning by a sitting judge.

3. **/A/** The best answer because disqualification is required if a judge's impartiality might be questioned; this includes an economic interest in the subject matter of the controversy, a party, or one of the lawyers [MCJC 2.11]. **(B)** is incorrect because the lawyer's conflict "screening" exception does not apply to the judiciary or any financial dealings conducted by a member of the judge's family. The fact that the wife is a partner of the purchaser does not relieve the judge of the responsibility to disqualify himself. **(C)** is incorrect because the judge still has a perceived tainted financial interest regardless of the transaction's timing and price. **(D)** is incorrect because the thrust of the financial interest disqualification focuses on the judge's interest in the transaction independently of the role or situation of the other parties to the transaction.

4. **/D/** The best answer since a judge should disqualify herself in a proceeding in which the judge's impartiality might reasonably be questioned because of personal bias [MCJC 2.11]. **(A)** is not the best answer because disqualification does not turn on the judge's subjective feelings of impartiality, but rather whether a reasonable objective party would raise the question. **(B)** is not the best answer because when the event creating the potential disqualification occurred is irrelevant (even though seven years does seem like a significant cooling-off period). **(C)** is incorrect because if the appearance of partiality is present, the judge should recluse herself without the attorney having to file a motion to recuse or disqualify the judge.

5. **/A/** Laurie became a "candidate" when she publicly announced her intention to run or filed for the office. The question here is the permissible campaign activities for a new candidate for election to an open seat on the local bench. Although some of the five listed activities may be inappropriate in some circumstances for a re-election candidate, each and every activity listed is specifically approved for a new candidate [MCJC 4.2]. **(B)** is incorrect because it involves an incorrect combination of the allowed alternatives. **(C)** is incorrect because it involves an incorrect combination of the allowed alternatives. **(D)** is incorrect because it involves an incorrect combination of the allowed alternatives.

6. **/B/** The use of the prestige and influence of a judge's office to raise funds for an organization described in this question is improper. While mere participation as an alumna of a law school is not improper, the personal solicitation of funds seems to misuse the prestige and influence of the judge's office, which is improper [MCJC 1.3]. **(A)** is incorrect because "never" is an absolute word – "never say never." **(C)** is incorrect because it seems likely that some of Judge Laurie's classmates are practicing law and will bring matters in superior court. **(D)** is incorrect because the prestige and image of a judge in raising funds may imply quid-pro-quo access or special privilege which is improper.

7. **/D/** The best answer because the basic test of acceptable extrajudicial economic activities by a judge is whether the behavior will exploit the judicial position and the large compensation for teaching a single class seems to be awarding the marketing potential of the judicial position [MCJC 1.3, 3.11, and 3.12]. Note the non-profit education exception of MCJC 3.7 does not apply here. **(A)** is not the best answer because involvement of the law is not the most important factor to be considered whether the position exploits the judge's judicial position. **(B)** is incorrect because it is too simplistic, and "always" is an absolute word. **(C)** is not the best answer because the materiality of the income received by the judge is not as important a factor as exploiting the perceived judicial impartiality.

8. **/C/** The best and broadest answer because a judge or candidate for judgeship should not make a pledge, promise, or commitment about a matter likely to come before her court [MCJC 2.10 and 4.1]. **(A)** is incorrect because the public comment prohibition applies to matters before any court, not just that particular judge. **(B)** is incorrect because while attendance in front of the committee might have been compelled, the judge should have declined to answer that question. **(D)** is not the best answer since the topic of political philosophy is different from a public comment about a matter in litigation pending before any court.

9. **/A/** A judge is permitted to consult with other judges about the law without having to notify the attorneys for both sides in the controversy and such consultation is not considered *ex parte* communications [MCJC 2.9]. **(B)** is not the best answer because a judge is not a "disinterested expert," and there is no requirement to inform the attorneys for both parties in the matter. **(C)** is incorrect because the exclusion from the *ex parte* rule includes consultation from all judges, even if not currently serving on the same court. **(D)** is incorrect because a judge is permitted to consult with other judges without being required to notify the attorneys for both sides in the controversy.

10. /B/ A judge should disqualify herself in a matter where a lawyer with whom she practiced law served as the lawyer during the prior association. The fact that she did not work on the matter during her association is not relevant [MCJC 2.11]. **(A)** is incorrect because disqualification may not be avoided by disclosure and written waiver in these circumstances. **(C)** is incorrect because it is not necessary that the judge personally participated in the matter if one of her partners did during the time period when she was associated with the firm. **(D)** is incorrect because the lack of a financial interest in the matter does not obviate the required judicial disqualification.

11. /A/ The best answer because while judges shall not voluntarily testify as a character witness, they may always be subpoenaed and must appear as a fact witness (or at least file an objection or motion to squash) [MCJC 3.3]. **(B)** is not the best answer because when the opinion as to character was formed is not controlling as to whether the prohibition on judges character testimony applies. **(C)** is not the best answer because it disregards the possibility of an involuntary requirement to testify. **(D)** is incorrect because the lack of personal knowledge about the matter of the expected factual testimony is not relevant to the general prohibition on a judge testifying about a person's character.

12. /C/ While normal wedding presents may be accepted by a judge, the magnitude of the gift – $25,000 – might easily create the appearance of impropriety and create doubt about the impartiality of the judge towards a lawyer who regularly appeared in his court [MCJC 3.13]. **(A)** is incorrect because friendship is not enough to make accepting an otherwise impermissibly large wedding gift proper. **(B)** is incorrect because reporting is not enough to make accepting an otherwise impermissibly large wedding gift proper. **(D)** is not the best answer because the fact that Friendly Fred regularly appears in Judge Rudy's court is not as compelling a problem in this situation as the dollar magnitude of the gift in question.

13. /D/ A sitting judge who decides to run for a non-judicial office must resign her judicial office immediately (actually, the resignation should occur before announcing her candidacy, but that is not one of the given alternatives) [MCJC 4.5]. **(A)** is incorrect because it is the appearance of impropriety that is put at risk, regardless of the effect on any judicial duties. **(B)** is not the best because disqualification unless both parties do not object does not cure the appearance of impropriety. **(C)** is not the best answer in that immediate resignation is required regardless of whether there may be requests for disqualification in the future.

14. /A/ The best answer because a judge should not accept appointment to any quasi-governmental body that concerns factual or legal matters other than improvement of the law, the legal system, or the administration of justice [MCJC 3.7]. **(B)** is not the best answer because this quasi-political appointment could be interpreted as forbidden political activity. **(C)** is incorrect because the appointment should be declined even if none of the immigrants appear in Judge's court. **(D)** is incorrect because appointment to a quasi-political organization should be declined even if a judge makes no political speeches associated with the organization.

15. /A/ If a judge's impartiality towards a party might reasonably be questioned, disqualification is proper [MCJC 2.11]. **(B)** is incorrect because whether the prior investigation is related or not to the present case is irrelevant if the judge's impartiality is adversely influenced by the prior investigation. **(C)** is incorrect because the standard is the perception of an objective third party whether the judge is prejudiced for or against Susan. **(D)** is incorrect because while it might indicate a reason for suggesting the judge may be prejudiced against Susan, the better answer focuses on the potential prejudice itself.

16. /C/ This alternative contains the three true statements. A judge may receive reasonable compensation for making a speech as long as the topic is not a case or controversy and the speech does not erode confidence in the integrity and impartiality of the judiciary [MCJC 3.7 and 3.12]. Further, reimbursement of reasonable expenses incurred by the judge speaker and his spouse is not improper. **(A)** This alternative includes an incorrect or incomplete listing of the correct alternatives. **(B)** This alternative includes an incorrect or incomplete listing of the correct alternatives. **(D)** This alternative includes an incorrect or incomplete listing of the correct alternatives.

17. /C/ The best answer of the alternatives given because a judge must be diligent in judicial administration and expedite matters and controversies on his docket [MCJC 2.5]. **(A)** is incorrect because this does not excuse administrative misconduct by a judge. Further, such matters may be interlocutory and thus not appealable until a final decision on the merits is reached below. **(B)** is not the best answer; while the judge is allowed wide discretion in administrative matters, there still is a duty to be prompt in judicial administration and expedite matters and controversies. **(D)** is not the best answer; while encouraging settlement is not improper, this cannot be at the expense of denying litigants a prompt determination on the merits of their case.

18. /D/ Candidates for judicial office shall not knowingly misrepresent the qualifications or other facts concerning an opponent for a judicial position. Alice did not know the staff member's report was in error, and it was consistent with other sources of information and personal observation; as such, reliance was likely reasonable [MRPC 8.2 and 4.1 (11)]. **(A)** is incorrect because the issue is whether Alice had knowledge of the falsity, not the truth of the statement itself. **(B)** is incorrect because under these circumstances it was probably not reasonable to impose a duty of personal examination of the records absent some reason to suspect that an error may have been made. **(C)** is incorrect; the mere fact a sitting judge decides to run in a contested election does not entitle the challenger to knowingly make misrepresentations about the judge's background or record.

19. /D/ *Ex parte* communication by a judge to an impartial expert on a technical aspect of the law is not improper if all the parties in the matter are notified in advance and allowed an opportunity to respond to the expert's input [MCJC 2.9(2)]. **(A)** is incorrect because a judge can initiate an *ex parte* communication with an impartial expert as long as all parties are notified and allowed an opportunity to respond to the expert's input. **(B)** is incorrect because it is not necessary for the judge to obtain a waiver from the parties as long as they are informed of the *ex parte* communication and allowed an opportunity to respond. **(C)** is incorrect because even if one of the parties is unhappy with the judge's *ex parte* communication, their sole remedy is to respond to the expert's advice.

20. /C/ Three of the five statements made by a sitting judge seeking reelection are improper. Statement I is not improper because it is a mere statement of fact. Statement II is improper because it contains a promise or pledge of future judicial conduct by a judge [MCJC 2.10]. Statement III is improper because the judge is taking a position on a case and controversy in litigation [MCJC 2.10]. Statement IV is not improper because it is a general statement of desirable judicial attitude. Statement V is improper since a candidate may not directly solicit campaign contributions (but may through a campaign committee) [MCJC 4.1]. **(A)** is incorrect because it involves the wrong combination of improper and proper statements. **(B)** is incorrect because it involves the wrong combination of improper and proper statements. **(D)** is incorrect because it involves the wrong combination of improper and proper statements.

21. /C/ A judge may accept a contribution for a judicial election only if given to her campaign committee, and the amount does not exceed the state-dictated maximum; $1,000 is normally allowed [MCJC 4.1(8) and 4.4]. **(A)** is incorrect because even if the contribution is anonymous, it must be given to the campaign committee and not directly to the candidate. **(B)** is not the best answer since a $1,000 cash contribution and donor's identity would have to be reported. The candidate will eventually have to sign the report and thus could learn of the identity of the source and amount of the contribution going to their campaign. The only hard and fast requirement is that the contribution be made to a campaign committee. **(D)** is not the best answer because it is irrelevant whether the contributing lawyer appears frequently in the court to which the candidate is seeking election. Still, an interpretation could be that this is an attempt to influence the judge thus suggesting that the judge should recuse herself in matters involving the contributor.

22. /C/ To abate financial impartiality grounds for disqualification, the judge must obtain from both parties a consent to the waiver of the disqualification and the remittal agreement must be promptly entered into the record [MCJC 2.11(3)]. **(A)** is incorrect because the general rule is recusal by the judge is to be *sua sponte*; it is not necessary that the parties file a motion to disqualify. **(B)** is incorrect because the financial/economic interest in the dispute extends to a judge's spouse, household members, or dependents. **(D)** is not the best answer because the judge's conflict of an financial/economic interest may be waived if it meets certain requirements.

23. /B/ The best answer. Statement I does not commit the judge, but is only a non-enforceable recommendation for legislative referral. Statement II does not refer to a pledge, promise, or commitment of a particular position that directly relates to future cases or controversies. **(A)** is incorrect because statement II is also an acceptable statement. **(C)** is incorrect because statement III commits the judge to a position in a future case or controversy [MCJC 2.10]. Judges are required to rule on the basis of the facts and law presented in an individual case in their court and not on any pre-committed position(s).

24. /A/ An incumbent judge seeking reappointment without a present individual opponent may organize a campaign committee and seek support for reappointment if he is opposed [MCJC 4.3]. **(B)** is incorrect because "every" is an absolute word, and judges who are appointed without an election may not usually start campaign committees or raise or accumulate funds. **(C)** is incorrect because the *White* decision allows a judge to announce personal opinions, and the thrust of the question is on starting a campaign committee and raising funds, not taking position on a potential political issue. **(D)** is incorrect because a judge seeking reappointment who is opposed may organize a campaign committee and promote public support.

25. /C/ A judge may act in a fiduciary capacity for a family member as long as it does not interfere with his judicial duties, and related proceedings will not come before the court on which the judge serves. Here, the judge serves only on the criminal division, and any guardianship proceeding would come on before the civil division. It is thus an exception to the prohibition on judges practicing law, and he is treated more like a part-time judge [MCJC 3.8]. **(A)** is incorrect because merely preparing and executing documents for a family member is an exception to the prohibition upon the practice of law by judges [MCJC 3.10]. **(B)** is not the best answer since any appearance on behalf of the guardianship would be in civil division, not the criminal division in which Judge Charlie serves. **(D)** is not the best answer because a judge may serve as a fiduciary for a family member as long as any compensation is not substantial in amount; here the facts do not state that the judge will receive compensation, so by implication, the amount would not be substantial. In addition, C is a better answer than D because it contains a higher level of argument why the role is not improper.

26. /B/ A former judge may not represent either party in a matter in which the judge participated personally and substantially while previously on the bench. Substantial participation excludes mere administrative responsibility in the matter such as case scheduling and assignment [MRPC 1.12 (a)]. **(A)** is not the best answer because the issue turns more on the extent of the personal involvement of the prior judge than the degree of information that might have been learned by the prior judge. **(C)** is incorrect because there is not a prohibition on an attorney appearing before a judge of a court on which she previously sat. **(D)** is incorrect because here the official action of the prior judge in the proceeding was merely administrative.

27. /C/ The best answer because even if a former judge participated personally and substantially while on the bench and is thus disqualified, another lawyer in her firm may take on the case as long as the former judge is properly screened, does not receive any portion of the fee for the representation, and the parties receive written notice [MRPC 1.12]. **(A)** is not the best answer because the screening mechanism could cure the potential disqualification. **(B)** is not the best answer because the screening mechanism could cure the potential disqualification. **(D)** is not the best answer because the screening mechanism could cure the potential disqualification.

28. /D/ A judge may not herself, or through her staff, engage in *ex parte* communication with one of the parties. The fact that the judge may decide against the party who engaged in the *ex parte* communication does not excuse the court's improper conduct [MCJC 2.9]. **(A)** is incorrect because contested facts do not excuse improper *ex parte* communication. **(B)** is incorrect because the fact the communication was made by the judge's employee and not herself is irrelevant. Similarly, the fact that there was some evidence presented at trial that was consistent with the court's verdict does not excuse the court's improper conduct. **(C)** is not the best answer because even if the three witnesses interviewed *ex parte* did appear at trial, the court's improper conduct was not cured.

29. /A/ The only correct combination of alternatives. A judge may not personally solicit contributions for a non-profit organization, but may participate in minor fund management. **(B)** is incorrect because a judge may serve as a honorary director of a non-profit charitable organization as long as legal advice is not rendered, may contribute her personal funds to the charity, and may attend fund raising events for the non-profit charitable organization [MCJC 3.7]. **(C)** is incorrect because it involves the wrong combination of alternatives. **(D)** is incorrect because it involves the wrong combination of alternatives.

30. /B/ A campaign committee may seek public and attorney endorsements for a judicial candidate. The committee may also solicit monetary contributions for the campaign; however, no portion thereof (even if a balance remains unspent) may be used for the private benefit of the candidate [MCJC 4.4]. **(A)** is incorrect because it is an incorrect combination of alternatives. **(C)** is incorrect because it is an incorrect combination of alternatives. **(D)** is incorrect because it is an incorrect combination of alternatives.

31. /C/ The adjudicative decision-making absolute immunity does not necessarily apply to administrative functions. **(A)** is incorrect because the immunity is limited to adjudicative decision-making. **(B)** is not the best answer because the judge's immunity is only absolute as it relates to adjudicative decision-making functions. **(D)** is incorrect; while this may be true in a few circumstances, it does not serve to distinguish judges from other public officials who hire and fire subordinates.

32. /D/ A violation occurred since a reasonable person, knowing the relevant facts, would expect the judge knew enough of the circumstances of the dispute to create an appearance of partiality, notwithstanding the judge's position that she was unaware of the circumstances. The risk of undermining the public's confidence in the judicial process was clear, and the judge should have disqualified herself [MCJC 2.4 and 2.11]. **(A)** is incorrect because the critical fact creating the need for the judge to disqualify herself was that the university was a party in interest. **(B)** is incorrect because the critical fact creating the need for the judge to disqualify herself was that the university was a party in interest. **(C)** is incorrect because the critical fact creating the need for the judge to disqualify herself was that she was a trustee of the university, a party in interest, and as a trustee is likely charged with constructive knowledge of the transaction.

33. /B/ The best answer because reporting is required only if the reporting judge has actual knowledge that another judge has committed a violation. Here, there are mere suspicious circumstances that should likely be investigated [MCJC 2.15]. **(A)** is not the best answer since it omits actual knowledge by the judge as a prerequisite to mandatory reporting. **(C)** is not the best answer because the reporting duty becomes mandatory upon receiving actual knowledge independently of whether a request is made by an appropriate authority. **(D)** is incorrect because a judge's duty to report violations by another judge is mandatory if the above prerequisites are present.

34. /D/ The best answer because a judge gaining actual knowledge of a lawyer's misconduct must take appropriate action. Under these facts where the jury is going to make the ultimate decision, the appropriate beginning action for the judge might simply be to discuss the matter with the attorneys privately [MCJC 2.15]. **(A)** is incorrect because reporting to the appropriate authority is only one form of action available to the judge. **(B)** is incorrect because the judge may decide the appropriate action is to report, but that is not mandatory. **(C)** is incorrect because this would be *ex parte* communication. If the information the judge heard was associated with perjured testimony, the judge might decide to declare a mistrial.

35. /C/ The best answer because judges campaigning for office should not make pledges or promises of future conduct or state their views on matters which may come before them in the future. Even though the time for appeal has run in this case, the same issue may come before him in another case (particularly when defense lawyers learn this judge is enforcing such provisions). Statement III is only a reference identifying an authority that has the power to control the judge's decision on such an issue; such a statement is not improper [MCJC 2.10]. **(A)** is an incorrect alternative because it involves an incorrect combination of alternatives. **(B)** is an incorrect alternative because it involves an incorrect combination of alternatives. **(D)** is an incorrect alternative because it involves an incorrect combination of alternatives.

36. /B/ A judge has an obligation to take appropriate corrective action if the judge gains actual knowledge of a potential MRPC violation by a lawyer; this would include providing requested information to the appropriate state disciplinary authority [MCJC 2.15]. **(A)** is incorrect because the duty to cooperate in the investigation exists whether or not the judge previously imposed litigation sanctions. **(C)** is incorrect because the duty to cooperate in the investigation exists whether or not the judge previously imposed litigation sanctions. **(D)** is incorrect because providing information to the state bar association is not the same as providing character testimony at trial for a lawyer.

37. /C/ Only three of the four listed functions are proper. I is correct because serving on a non-profit law school board is proper [MCJC 3.7]. II is correct because serving as a voluntary judge in a law school moot court competition is proper. III is likely correct because teaching a standard law school course is proper activity for a judge. IV is incorrect because participation by name in such a large fundraising effort likely exploits the judge's prestige and station of the judge's office. This goes beyond mere planning of fundraising activities or minor fund management assistance. **(A)** is incorrect because it involves an incorrect combination of alternatives. **(B)** is incorrect because it involves an incorrect combination of alternatives. **(D)** is incorrect because it involves an incorrect combination of alternatives.

38. /A/ The only correct combination of the four question alternatives that are improper. I is proper because factual educational accomplishments may be stated by a judge up for reelection. II is improper because the judge herself may not personally solicit public statements of support (although her campaign committee probably could) [MCJC 4.1 (7)]. III is improper because the judge herself may not personally solicit campaign contributions (although her campaign committee probably could). IV is a close call, but the statement is probably proper because judges must swear to uphold the constitution. So the "cases and controversies" category would not seem to include this basic non-controversial orientation to which all judges must conform. **(B)** is incorrect because it involves an incorrect combination of alternatives. **(C)** is incorrect because it involves an incorrect combination of alternatives. **(D)** is incorrect because it involves an incorrect combination of alternatives.

39. /B/ The best answer because if all campaign funds raised go into an independent campaign committee, it avoids the prohibition on the judge directly receiving such funds [MCJC 4.4]. **(A)** is incorrect because a lawyer may generally raise money for a judge's campaign and also practice in the same court later. **(C)** is incorrect because there is no prohibition on a campaign committee receiving money from lawyers. **(D)** is a close call, but the candidate is required to report all contributions after the election in the campaign finance report, and this requires them to learn the identity of the contributors.

40. /B/ A judge may appear at a hearing or contact a political body concerning matters that involve the law and administration of the legal system: the reduction in court funding would seem to qualify [MCJC 3.2]. **(A)** is incorrect because there is no requirement that a judge determine the ultimate detrimental effect on the administration of justice before contacting the responsible political body for relief. **(C)** is incorrect because the judge is not practicing law by merely contacting the mayor and chair of the judicial committee and suggesting they pursue a judicial determination of the funding level. **(D)** is incorrect because a judge may properly question the legality of the political action that had an adverse effect on the legal system and administration of justice.

41. /C/ The best combination of alternatives. I requires disqualification because the judge's child is an officer in an organization that is a party. II requires disqualification because the judge's sibling (through marriage) is acting as a lawyer in the proceeding. III does not require disqualification because the matter was not being handled by the law firm when the judge was there. IV does not require disqualification because a cousin is not considered within the third degree of relationships [MCJC 2.11]. **(A)** is incorrect because it includes incorrect alternatives. **(B)** is incorrect because it includes incorrect alternatives. **(D)** is incorrect because it includes incorrect alternatives.

42. /D/ A judge may not use non-public information acquired in a judicial proceeding in her personal business dealings [MCJC 3.5]. **(A)** is incorrect because tipping off another – especially a close relative like a judge's son – would also be deemed improper use of extrajudicial information. **(B)** is incorrect because disclosure in the judge's annual report does not cure the improper use of information acquired in a judicial proceeding. **(C)** is incorrect because disclosure to the corporation does not cure the improper use of information acquired in the judicial proceeding.

43. /C/ A judge should avoid significant business transactions with lawyers or persons likely to come before him [MCJC 3.11]. **(A)** is incorrect because even though an accurate statement the main problem here is the regular appearances of his partner in front of the judge that adversely reflect on the judge's impartiality. **(B)** is incorrect because the ownership interest should likely have been disposed of when the judge won the election and Abbott knew Costello would be appearing in his court. **(D)** is incorrect because a judge may hold investments while on the bench as long as there is not an adverse reflection on his impartiality.

44. /C/ The best answer because a judge may not become a member of an organization that practices invidious discrimination based upon sexual orientation and should divest herself of the ownership. [MCJC 3.6 and 3.11]. **(A)** is not the best answer because the facts do not state whether such an organization has a legitimate interest in enforcing such discrimination for bona fide job qualifications. **(B)** is incorrect because the violation of the invidious discrimination creates a judicial violation regardless of the impact on her judicial activities. **(D)** is not the best answer because the no-management rule has an exception that applies to family-owned businesses.

45. /A/ The correct answer because only one (number III) of the alternatives presented is proper. I is improper because a judge may not be a manager of a business entity unless the business is closely-held by the judge or his family, and this ownership exception is not stated in the facts [MCJC 3.11]. II is improper because a judge shall not become involved in a private capacity as an arbitrator or mediator [MCJC 3.9]. III is proper because while a judge may not become a member of an organization that practices "invidious discrimination," there is an exception if the organization is religious in nature [MCJC 3.6]. IV is improper because a judge may belong to not-for-profit entities intended to improve the administration of justice, but usually may not participate in solicitating contributions [MCJC 3.7]. V is improper because in most jurisdictions, campaign activities may not begin more than one year before the election [MCJC 4.2]. **(B)** is an incorrect combination of alternatives. **(C)** is an incorrect combination of alternatives. **(D)** is an incorrect combination of alternatives.

46. /C/ The only correct combination of alternatives. I is improper because a judge may not endorse a candidate for public political office [MCJC 4.1]. II is improper because even a candidate for an elected school board position is usually considered a candidate for public office. III is proper; while attending a partisan political gathering is not usually allowed, an exception applies in many jurisdictions if the gathering is celebrating a significant historical or patriotic event. IV is proper because a judge may normally register to vote under a political party designation. **(A)** is an incorrect combination of alternatives. **(B)** is an incorrect combination of alternatives. **(D)** is an incorrect combination of alternatives.

47. /C/ The only correct combination of alternatives. I is improper because a judge may not serve on a government commission unless it is intended to improve the administration of the law, the legal system, or the administration of justice, and none of those exceptions apply here [MCJC 3.4]. II is proper because a judge may usually serve as an official representative at a cultural or historical activity or occasion [MCJC 3.4, comment 2]. III is proper because a judge may usually serve as an officer on the board of a local law school [MCJC 3.7].

48. /B/ The only correct combination of alternatives. A judge may explain to media reporters for public information the judicial procedures of the trial and court that were involved in concluding the matter [MCJC 2.10]. In comparison, a judge should not comment or criticize jurors for their verdict because this may impair jurors' independent judgment in subsequent trials [MCJC 2.8]. **(A)** involves an incorrect combination of alternatives. **(C)** involves an incorrect combination of alternatives. **(D)** involves an incorrect combination of alternatives.

49. /B/ The prohibition on a judge's voluntary testimony applies if the testimony involves the character of a party; here, the judge would merely be a fact witness [MCJC 3.3]. **(A)** is not the best answer because even if the court is under her appellate jurisdiction, a judge may testify as a fact witness. **(C)** is incorrect because a judge may usually testify as a fact witness. There is a restriction only if the judge is testifying as a character witness. **(D)** is incorrect because a judge may testify as a fact witness even if the final decision in the case could be appealed to her court of appeals.

50. **/C/** It is proper for the judge to respond to both of the personal position questions if the positions contained within the questionnaire are not used in a context that also contains a pledge, promise, or commitment to decide cases in a particular matter. The U.S. Supreme Court so held in *Republican Party v. White*, 536 U.S. 765 (2002) [MCJC 2.10]. **(A)** is incorrect because it contains an incorrect combination of alternatives. **(B)** is incorrect because it contains an incorrect combination of alternatives. **(D)** is incorrect because it contains an incorrect combination of alternatives.

51. **/A/** The general rule that a judge may not meet with a public official is subject to an exception if the matter involves the judge's personal legal or economic interests [MCJC 3.2]. **(B)** is not the best answer because the reporting of the meeting is not relevant if the judge was acting in a matter that involved only her private interests. **(C)** is incorrect because while the general rule is that a judge should not meet with a public official, the rule is subject to certain exceptions, one of which is if the matter involves only a private concern of the judge. **(D)** is not the best answer; while an exception exists for meeting with an official on a matter of the administration of justice, the thrust of this question is the exception applicable to a meeting involving the private interests of the judge.

52. **/D/** A judge may own and manage family investments unless the management and financial interest will lead to frequent disqualification of the judge [MCJC 3.11]. **(A)** is not the best answer because the general rule allowing a judge to participate in management of a family business applies only if frequent disqualifications do not result and the facts state administrative matters often arise. **(B)** is not the best answer because a better answer goes to the risk of frequent disqualification. **(C)** is not the best answer because, while true, the exception to business management does not require a particular percentage ownership.

53. **/B/** A candidate for a judicial appointment may supply relevant information to a screening committee and seek endorsement from any organization other than a partisan political organization. Unlike a candidate for election, a candidate seeking appointment may not solicit funds or establish a campaign committee [MCJC 4.3]. **(A)** is incorrect because it includes an incorrect alternative. **(C)** is incorrect because it includes incorrect alternatives. **(D)** is incorrect because it includes incorrect alternatives.

54. **/C/** The best answer because the standard is the probability of a serious risk of actual bias or prejudgment on the part of the jurist. This was the essence of the reasoning the U.S. Supreme Court articulated when they disciplined Judge Brent Benjamin. Benjamin received a $3 million dollar campaign contribution from Massey Coal Co. and subsequently twice cast the deciding vote to overturn the jury verdict below against his contributor [*Caperton v. Massey Coal*, 129 S. Ct. 2252 (2009) and MCJC 2.11]. **(A)** is incorrect because the key issue here is whether the Judge knew the identity of the contributor, not the monetary conduit used. **(B)** is incorrect because the appearance of judicial impartiality was put at risk regardless of the merits of any aspect of the controversy. **(D)** is not the best answer because the judge should have recused himself *sua sponte* regardless of the votes of the other jurists participating in the decision.

RIGOS UNIFORM BAR REVIEW SERIES

PROFESSIONAL RESPONSIBILITY EXAM REVIEW (MPRE)

Chapter 7

Final Exam

Instructions

This chapter contains a simulated MPRE exam. There are 60 questions in random order. On the actual MPRE only 50 questions are counted towards your score. You do not know which questions are only there for validation purposes and which ones actually go into your reported score, so answer them all carefully.

1. Solid Block of Time: It is best to create actual exam conditions. Pace yourself and work as quickly as you can without sacrificing accuracy. The 120 minutes equates to 2 minutes per question. Circle your answer choice on the question. At the end of the first 30 questions, check your time to be sure you are on schedule.

2. Transpose Answers: Save the last 5 minutes of the 120 minutes total time to transfer all your 60 answers to the bubble sheet on the next page.

3. Answer Corrections: Unlike the regular questions in this MPRE review course, the answer rationales for the final exam do not follow the individual questions on the CD-ROM software. Correct your answers after you complete the full exam.

a. Learn from Your Mistakes: When you refer to the answer rationales, be sure to understand why you picked the wrong choice. The fine-line distinctions are critical. Again, it is usually worthwhile to review the answer rationales to all the alternatives because they reinforce the details of the relevant issue being tested. More than one answer rationale may be identical if the alternatives are incorrect for the same reason.

b. Mark Mistakes: When you grade your answer put a red star in the margin alongside every question you missed during your preparation, including this final exam. If you are using the software, make note of the questions you missed on a sheet of paper. Write down why your choice was not the best alternative.

4. Review Mistakes: You should work the marked questions you previously missed in the text and final exam. Do this again the day right before sitting for the actual MPRE.

RIGOS UNIFORM BAR REVIEW SERIES

MPRE PRACTICE EXAM ANSWERS BUBBLE SHEET

During the last five minutes of the exam, carefully transpose your circled answer choices - A, B, C, D, - from the question pages to the answer bubble sheet below.

1	a	b	c	d	31	a	b	c	d
2	a	b	c	d	32	a	b	c	d
3	a	b	c	d	33	a	b	c	d
4	a	b	c	d	34	a	b	c	d
5	a	b	c	d	35	a	b	c	d
6	a	b	c	d	36	a	b	c	d
7	a	b	c	d	37	a	b	c	d
8	a	b	c	d	38	a	b	c	d
9	a	b	c	d	39	a	b	c	d
10	a	b	c	d	40	a	b	c	d
11	a	b	c	d	41	a	b	c	d
12	a	b	c	d	42	a	b	c	d
13	a	b	c	d	43	a	b	c	d
14	a	b	c	d	44	a	b	c	d
15	a	b	c	d	45	a	b	c	d
16	a	b	c	d	46	a	b	c	d
17	a	b	c	d	47	a	b	c	d
18	a	b	c	d	48	a	b	c	d
19	a	b	c	d	49	a	b	c	d
20	a	b	c	d	50	a	b	c	d
21	a	b	c	d	51	a	b	c	d
22	a	b	c	d	52	a	b	c	d
23	a	b	c	d	53	a	b	c	d
24	a	b	c	d	54	a	b	c	d
25	a	b	c	d	55	a	b	c	d
26	a	b	c	d	56	a	b	c	d
27	a	b	c	d	57	a	b	c	d
28	a	b	c	d	58	a	b	c	d
29	a	b	c	d	59	a	b	c	d
30	a	b	c	d	60	a	b	c	d

Chapter 7

Final Exam

Questions

1. Associate was hired by a law firm that specialized in criminal practice. The law firm had taken on the defense in a high profile murder case in Superior Court. While Associate had done some research in the case, she was not appointed second chair for the three-week trial. Supervisor, the lead attorney on the case, chose a different lawyer to provide trial assistance to the supervisor litigator. Associate had unused vacation time and attended the first two days of the trial because of her high interest in the case.

A week later, Associate went to dinner with a friend at a restaurant near the courthouse. In the restaurant, Associate saw Supervisor having dinner with one of the jurors on the case. Associate recognized the juror because she had seen the juror during the first two days of trial and read of her role as jury foreperson in the local newspaper. Associate was quite surprised and upset.

Associate should

- **(A)** Report the situation to the senior partner in the law firm.
- **(B)** Report the situation to the State Bar Association's disciplinary counsel.
- **(C)** Report the situation to the prosecutor.
- **(D)** Report the situation to the judge conducting the trial.

2. Estatelawyer had a practice consisting of probating medium-sized estates. One of her law firm's clients, died unexpectedly. Decedent was a stock market speculator during her life and left a substantial estate to her three nephews and nieces. The nephews and nieces had their own attorney whom they preferred do the legal estate work, but decedent's will specified that estatelawyer was to handle her will probate matters.

Estatelawyer began by sorting through decedent's notes covering the stocks in the portfolio. Estatelawyer came on some rough handwritten notes that discussed the confidential marketing plan of Sleeper, Inc. in which decedent had a large position. Sleeper's stock was at an all-time low value, but decedent's notes made it clear that she believed the company's new product was going to take the market by storm leading to a sharp increase in the stock's price. Estatelawyer determined that it was necessary for the estate to sell some stock to pay debts and the accumulating expenses of administration.

Which of the below is proper?

- **(A)** Estatelawyer may buy the Sleeper stock from the estate at the prevailing market price.
- **(B)** Estatelawyer may buy the Sleeper stock from the estate at the prevailing market price less any costs and commissions that the estate would incur had the estate sold the shares without court approval or consent of the beneficiaries.
- **(C)** Estatelawyer should not buy the Sleeper stock from the estate but may buy the stock on the open market.
- **(D)** Estatelawyer should not buy the Sleeper stock from the estate or from the open market because the information was confidential to the client.

3. Attorney Contingency had a client who owned a small lakefront resort which was damaged by a fire started by the neighbor's son. Owner is good friends with her neighbor and seeks only to rebuild the resort. She has a firm $400,000 bid from a contractor to do the necessary work. Her insurance company has paid her the policy limits of $250,000, so she is short $150,000.

Owner called Attorney and discussed the situation. Owner explained she did not want a windfall, only the full $400,000 it would take to have the resort rebuilt. Attorney then told owner that information about insurance proceeds may not be referred to in a legal action, so it is possible the neighbor would pay more than $150,000. Owner said "great" and, "I will hire you to bring this claim against my neighbor, and your fee will be any settlement above $150,000."

If Attorney agrees to owner's offer, is she subject to discipline?

- **(A)** No, unless the contingent fee agreement is written.
- **(B)** No, as long as the amount Attorney receives as a contingency fee is not unreasonable as compared to the benefit owner receives.
- **(C)** Yes, because Attorney would acquire a proprietary interest in the case.
- **(D)** Yes, because "net fee agreements" are improper.

4. Plaintiff was injured in her automobile when she was rear-ended by a reckless driver, who was intoxicated. Plaintiff hired Attorney Contingency to pursue the case. The fee agreement stated that Attorney was to receive the 40% of any recovery, but that all costs were the responsibility of Plaintiff. Attorney brought suit against Driver on Plaintiff's behalf. It took 12 months to get the case to trial, and Attorney advanced some $300,000 in costs for expert witnesses, discovery, and Plaintiff's medical expenses.

At trial the jury awarded Plaintiff $1,000,000 in total compensation, including all costs. Driver's insurance company sent the $1,000,000 check to Attorney's trust account. Attorney then sent Plaintiff a statement indicating the firm had received $1,000,000 of which she was to receive only $300,000 (60% split or $600,000 less $300,000 costs). Plaintiff was outraged and threatened to hire another lawyer to sue the current Attorney's firm if they did not send her "all the money less the agreed costs."

What is the proper action for the current Attorney's firm to take concerning the funds in the trust account?

- **(A)** Remit nothing to Plaintiff, but pay $300,000 to the law firm's operating account.
- **(B)** Remit $300,000 to Plaintiff and $300,000 to the law firm's operating account.
- **(C)** Remit $700,000 to Plaintiff, $300,000 to the law firm's operating account, and initiate a claim against Plaintiff to determine the reasonableness of the fee.
- **(D)** Leave all the funds in the trust account and either attempt to negotiate a settlement or initiate a legal claim to determine the reasonableness of the fee due from Plaintiff.

5. Lawyer A and Lawyer B both have business practices, and are licensed to practice law in Alpha jurisdiction. Lawyer C is licensed to practice law in Omega jurisdiction. Many of both Lawyer A and Lawyer B's corporate clients have legal matters in Omega. As a result, Lawyer A and Lawyer B employ Lawyer C to handle their clients' matters in Omega jurisdiction without any formal relationship. Monthly, Lawyer C bills Lawyer A and Lawyer B for her time. This dollar amount is included within the overall bill tendered to both Lawyer A and Lawyer B's clients.

Is Lawyer A and Lawyer B's billing agreement proper?

- **(A)** No, because this is fee splitting with a lawyer external to Lawyer A and Lawyer B.
- **(B)** No, unless the corporate clients are fully informed in writing and do not object.
- **(C)** Yes, as long as both the division is in proportion to the services performed, and each lawyer assumes joint responsibility for the representation.
- **(D)** Yes, since it would be illegal for Lawyer A and Lawyer B to practice directly in Omega jurisdiction.

6. Minor was 19 years old and a sophomore at Party Forever University. To assist her in getting admitted to the local pubs that all tried to enforce the prevailing minimum age requirement of 21, she purchased a phony driver's license over the Internet under a false name. Minor was also prone to driving recklessly after she had been drinking. In the last year, she had received two reckless driving citations. A local statute provided that the third such ticket in any year had a minimum one-year jail sentence.

On Saturday night, Minor went pub crawling. When the last establishment closed, she began to drive home intoxicated and was stopped by the police. She gave them her phony driver's license and was again charged with reckless driving. She told the public defender that the charges were against her phony driver's license, not the real one, and that if she had to testify, she would give the false name. The public defender called Minor as a witness and asked her for her name, to which Minor gave the false name.

Is the public defender subject to discipline?

- **(A)** Yes, if Minor committed a crime by obtaining a phony driver's license under a false name.
- **(B)** Yes, only if Minor 's correct name is an issue in Minor's driving.
- **(C)** Yes, because the public defender knowingly introduced false testimony.
- **(D)** No, because the public defender learned of Minor's phony driver's license during the course of legal representation.

7. Doctor referred three patients to Attorney Contingency with significant personal injuries suffered in an automobile accidents. Attorney took all three cases on a contingent fee basis of one-third of the recovery. All three cases settled relatively early in the judicial process, and attorney earned over two million dollars in legal fees. In gratitude to Doctor for referring these three cases, Attorney invited Doctor and her family to a two-week fully-paid deluxe vacation in the Caribbean. Both families went on the vacation, business was not discussed, and everyone had a grand time.

Is Attorney Contingency subject to discipline?

- **(A)** No, because the amount of the gratuity was *de minimis* as compared to the fee benefit bestowed, and the gratuity was not given in cash.
- **(B)** No, unless Doctor and Attorney had a binding agreement requiring Doctor to refer cases for compensation.
- **(C)** Yes, unless Doctor had a legitimate expectation of actually receiving compensation from the referrals.
- **(D)** Yes.

8. Attorney and Accountant, were hired by Owner to prepare a detailed business plan. Owner was considering leaving her employer and starting her own printing business. Based on their advice, Owner decided to open her own business. Both Attorney and Accountant referred all their friends to Owner's printing business, and Owner referred all her friends to Attorney and Accountant for accounting and legal matters.

Is Attorney subject to discipline?

- **(A)** No, as long as no money or in-kind compensation changes hands.
- **(B)** No, as long as Owner's referrals to Attorney are made because Owner reasonably believes Attorney is the best personal injury attorney in the local community.
- **(C)** Yes.
- **(D)** Yes, unless disclosure of the exclusive reciprocal agreement is made to all the patients who are referred and consent obtained.

9. Judge Incumbent is campaigning for a second term on the Everycity Superior Court. Judge is being challenged by an active member of the Republican Party. Judge is concerned and uncertain he will be reelected. He inquired about and was asked to attend a Democratic Party gathering.

Which of the following is the most activities that Judge do during his campaign?

- **(A)** Attend the Democratic political gatherings.
- **(B)** Attend the Democratic political gatherings and identify himself as a member of the Democratic Party.
- **(C)** Attend the Democratic political gatherings, identify himself as a member of the Democratic Party, and contribute $10,000 to the Democratic Party partisan campaign.
- **(D)** Identify himself as a member of the Democratic Party and solicit and accept funds at the political gatherings for his own reelection campaign.

10. Plaintiff staged an automobile accident by slamming on her brakes as a taxi was pulling up behind her. Numerous witnesses saw the whole incident. Plaintiff hired an Attorney who filed suit. The taxi company hired a Lawyer to defend the case. Lawyer did no discovery at all and thus did not learn of the defense that could likely have been effectively presented at trial. Attorney knew of the facts which could have provided the key defense and did not inform Lawyer.

Attorney should

- **(A)** Request permission from Defendant to reveal the critical information to Susan.
- **(B)** Inform the court in camera of the critical information and let the court decide whether the evidence should be passed to Lawyer.
- **(C)** Inform Lawyer directly of the evidence as this is required as a form of fairness to the opposing counsel.
- **(D)** Try the case for Defendant without disclosing the information critical to the defense.

11. Contender was trying to upset Judge in a judicial election. She learned that Judge had attended a Democratic political gathering and had been formally endorsed by the Democratic Party. Contender's political advisors told her that she had to create a big issue if she was to have a chance to win the judicial election. A print and media campaign was started to accuse Judge of "being soft on rapists." Judge at first disregarded the advertising, but his political advisors reported the majority of voters were turning against him and he needed to respond.

Which of the following may Judge say with the least likely chance of discipline?

- **(A)** "I have never acquitted a rapist."
- **(B)** "I have never acquitted a rapist and never will."
- **(C)** "Contender is a liar."
- **(D)** "Contender is a low-end shyster lawyer and not fit to serve on the bench."

12. Plaintiff sued Defendant for breach of contract to pay $100,000 for goods. Defendant hired an attorney to defend the case. The defendant told Plaintiff that the goods did not conform to the contract. Over a month went by after Defendant received service of process of the complaint and her attorney Plaintiff did not even put in a formal Notice of Appearance. The plaintiff attorney filed a motion for a default judgment and it was granted. Plaintiff's attorney subsequently learned that Defendant's attorney failure to appear was caused by her addiction to alcohol that had grown progressively more dehabilitating. It became increasingly clear that Defendant's attorney had become incompetent and not fit to practice law.

Plaintiff's attorney should now

- **(A)** Inform the appropriate professional authority if Defendant's attorney alcoholism raises a substantial question of whether she is fit as a lawyer.
- **(B)** Inform the defendant directly that their counsel was incompetent and that they should have won the lawsuit.
- **(C)** Not inform anyone about the Defendant's attorney's alcoholism unless the client Defendant gives prior approval.
- **(D)** Not inform anyone about the Defendant's attorney's alcoholism even if the client Defendant gives prior approval.

13. A student just passed the bar exam in her jurisdiction. Three weeks later, she was admitted to the state bar association and received her license to practice. Student then joined a group of three other lawyers who rented a large office suite and shared the space and common services.

All four lawyers sharing the office facilities put their individual names on the front door under the caption of "Law Offices of." They all believed that the collection of names was more impressive than individual names. They also started on their business cards and letterheads, "The Able, Berry, Cain, and Dee Law Firm." Their hope was that this would further their collective marketability to clients. They were not in fact associated with each other, but rather continued their separate practices.

Are all lawyers subject to discipline?

- **(A)** Yes, but only if a client complains.
- **(B)** Yes, if the name collection appears to be confusing to the public.
- **(C)** No, because office sharing is not *per se* improper.
- **(D)** No, unless they misrepresent the status of their relationship to their individual clients.

14. Lawyer is the youngest of the family. This family has been a very prominent Democratic power in the County of Everyland for decades. Lawyer's older brother has been a Superior Court judge for 12 years, and he is currently up for reelection. Lawyer has thrown her hat in the ring for the open position of Everyland Country Prosecutor. Her campaign manager has conducted polls in Everyland that indicate it would be tremendously helpful to publicize her familial relationship with her brother and her brother would like to help his little sister if he can.

Which of the following activities would most likely subject Brother to potential judicial discipline?

- **(A)** Make a $500 contribution to Lawyer's campaign.
- **(B)** Privately express his endorsement to a few friends.
- **(C)** Make a public endorsement of his sister's candidacy.
- **(D)** None of the above because Lawyer is his sister.

15. A bookkeeper works at Big Buck Corporation. The corporate outside auditors uncovered a massive embezzlement scheme conducted by Bookkeeper. The Corporation was successful in convincing the Prosecutor to charge Bookkeeper with criminal embezzlement. Bookkeeper approached the best criminal defense attorney in the area. Defender had more work than she could handle, so to induce her to take on the case, Bookkeeper offered to pay her $200 per hour fee plus a bonus of $10,000 if she won an acquittal at trial.

Is Defender subject to discipline if she accepts the representation?

- **(A)** Yes, because the lawyer has a financial interest in the litigation.
- **(B)** Yes, because the lawyer will not receive the $10,000 if Bookkeeper is convicted.
- **(C)** No, unless the total fee to be charged is unreasonable.
- **(D)** No, because the fee for the representation is not calculated on a percentage basis.

16. Robber was apprehended during a bank robbery in which one of her criminal team members killed a bank guard. The accomplice who committed the murder also died in the gunfire exchange. Robber was indicted for felony murder and hired an attorney to defend the case. Attorney is a well-known lawyer who was then also a candidate running for public office. Prosecutor made an offer to Attorney to reduce the charges against Robber to second degree murder if the defendant would plead guilty. Attorney refused the plea offer, insisting on a trial that Prosecutor believed was strictly to promote publicity for her election to public office.

Prosecutor decided to go forward and charge Robber with felony murder. Attorney defended the case, and there was substantial publicity generated.

Should Prosecutor report Attorney's conduct to the appropriate disciplinary authority?

- **(A)** Yes, if Attorney did receive substantial publicity and won the election.
- **(B)** Yes, if Robber was convicted of felony murder.
- **(C)** No, if Prosecutor competently and zealously represented Robber during the trial and sentencing.
- **(D)** No, unless Prosecutor had actual knowledge that Attorney did not accept the plea bargain for personal political reasons.

17. Attorney is representing Merchant in a dispute with her customer. Merchant sent the goods with hidden defects that went undiscovered when Customer received and accepted the goods. Three months later Customer discovered the latent defects and tried to return the goods. Merchant refused to accept the return goods that Customer sent back as defective. At Merchant 's request Attorney filed a collection lawsuit against Customer seeking the full billed price. Customer's lawyer counterclaimed a failure of consideration alleging that the goods were defective. Merchant instructed Attorney to file a motion for summary judgment supported by Merchant's affidavit stating that Customer previously agreed that she accepted the goods with full knowledge of the defects. Customer denied ever saying this and filed an ethical grievance against Attorney demanding that she withdraw.

Is Attorney subject to discipline if she does not withdraw from representing Merchant?

- **(A)** Yes, because she will have refused to follow her client Merchant's order to file the affidavit.
- **(B)** Yes, if Attorney reasonably believes that the motion for dismissal on summary judgment will be denied.
- **(C)** No, unless Alice knows that Merchant's affidavit is false.
- **(D)** No, because a lawyer must accept the client's version of the facts.

18. Victim purchased a defective vacuum cleaner from Big Vacuum Inc. When she turned it on, the machine overheated and exploded, and she suffered substantial injuries. Victim hired a lawyer, who estimated the claim was worth $100,000. During discovery, Lawyer discovered a memorandum written by Big Vacuum's head of quality control warning top management that the particular model was defective and could explode.

When Big Vacuum realized the significance of the memorandum discovered by Lawyer, they offered to settle the claim for $500,000. This amount was greatly in excess of what Victim and Lawyer expected, so they accepted immediately. The attorney for Big Vacuum, drew the settlement agreement and presented it to Attorney. The agreement contained a "no further representation clause" restricting Attorney from taking on any other plaintiffs with the same claim against Big Vacuum. Victim was insistent that Attorney sign the agreement, and Attorney finally agreed.

Is the agreement improper?

- **(A)** Yes as it relates to Big Vacuum's attorney, no for Victim's attorney.
- **(B)** No as it relates to Big Vacuum's attorney, yes for Victim's attorney.
- **(C)** Yes for both Big Vacuum's attorney and Victim's attorney.
- **(D)** No for both Big Vacuum's attorney and Victim's attorney.

19. After law school, Attorney went to work for the State Attorney General's Office. For three years, she worked on securing an indictment in a large burglary case involving multiple mob defendants. Attorney's supervisor was appointed to the bench, and Attorney was assigned to a new supervisor. The chemistry between Attorney and the new supervisor was not good, and she quit the State Attorney General's office. Six months later, she interviewed with the law firm of Defense & Defense. She was hired and one month later learned that another partner was defending one of the defendants in the same burglary case.

Is it proper for Defense & Defense to continue to represent the defendant?

- **(A)** Yes, only if Attorney agrees not to reveal to anyone in the law firm anything she learned about the case when she was at the State Attorney General's office.
- **(B)** Yes, only if the potential conflict is revealed to the prosecutor's office.
- **(C)** No, because Attorney had personal and substantial participation in the matter while at the State Attorney General's office.
- **(D)** No, unless Attorney agrees not to participate personally in the defense.

20. Three lawyers decided to join their separate practices together as partners. The three entered into a partnership agreement that stated if a partner died or retired, the other surviving partners would purchase his or her partnership interest. The price was defined as 25% of the fee billings derived from the former partner's clients over the past four years.

Is the sale provision in the partnership agreement proper?

- **(A)** Yes, if the amount to be paid under the agreement is for a reasonable period of time, and the fees are not raised to make the payments.
- **(B)** Yes, if payment under the agreement is to be made only to a former partner's estate.
- **(C)** No, because the payment would be considered a referral fee.
- **(D)** No, because the payments to the estate would be splitting fees with a non-lawyer.

21. Lawyer A began her legal career after law school by working for the State Department of Consumer Protection. Based upon numerous complaints, Lawyer A prosecuted Mega Motors for knowingly selling automobiles with defective brake cylinders. Mega Motors agreed to a settlement in the litigation that involved installing new brake cylinders in all the automobiles sold without cost. Notice of the settlement was sent to all the automobile purchasers at the addresses shown on the sales documents.

Six months later, Lawyer A left the governmental agency and started a practice with a law school friend of hers, Lawyer B. They used the name of A & B, Attorneys at Law. Shortly thereafter, they were contacted by Victim, who was seriously injured in an automobile accident caused by the defective brake cylinder on a car she purchased from Mega Motors. Victim did not receive the notice of the earlier Department of Consumer Protection action because she moved shortly after purchasing the defective automobile. Victim wants the A & B law firm to bring suit against Mega to recover her damages.

If the law firm takes on the representation of Victim, will they be subject to discipline?

- **(A)** Yes, unless both the Consumer Protection agency and Mega consent.
- **(B)** Yes, because Lawyer A had substantial personal involvement in the prosecution of Mega Motors while working as an attorney for the Department of Consumer Protection in the dispute.
- **(C)** No, as long as Lawyer A's law school friend tries the case, and Lawyer A is effectively screened out.
- **(D)** No, because Victim was not a party to the settlement of the litigation between the State Department of Consumer Protection and Mega Motors.

22. A law school professor had a favorite student. Two years ago, Student had confessed to Professor in confidence that she was convicted of marijuana possession before she started law school. Student is now a 3L and has asked Professor to write a letter of recommendation to the bar admission committee in support of her application. As Professor read the application that Student had filed, she saw that under the question of "prior convictions," Student stated none.

Professor may write a letter of recommendation on Student's behalf without being subject to discipline if Professor

- **(A)** Discloses the prior conviction in the letter.
- **(B)** States that Student had no criminal convictions in this state if Professor thinks that the conviction was in another state.
- **(C)** States in the letter that she has advised Student to revise the application to include some omitted information.
- **(D)** Does not mention the previous conviction because it was told to her in confidence.

23. The local court Judge in Evertown, after serving for 30 years on the bench, decided not to seek reelection. Shortly after she announced her decision, two lawyers announced their candidacy. Lawyer One's advertisements promoted all the successful prosecutions she had won in another state. Lawyer Two did not believe the campaign advertisements and called the County Prosecutor's office in the other state. The clerk told Lawyer Two that no Lawyer One had worked in their office. Lawyer Two then began to accuse Lawyer One of dishonesty and insinuate that she was unfit to serve in the judiciary. Lawyer One had actually prosecuted federal cases in the other state, and the clerk Lawyer Two talked to did not check the federal roster and docket, only the state records.

Is Lawyer Two subject to discipline for making false or reckless statements about Lawyer One?

(A) Yes, because lawyers must not make false statements about candidates for election to the bench.
(B) Yes, because a lawyer must adhere to all the requirements of the Code of Judicial Conduct immediately upon announcing that he is a candidate for office.
(C) No, because Lawyer Two was not yet a judicial officer.
(D) No, because Lawyer Two did not knowingly or recklessly make a false statement about Lawyer one.

24. Lawyer passed the bar exam at the third sitting and was admitted to practice law in the jurisdiction of New York. After trying unsuccessfully to land a legal job in New York, he decided to go into the pizza restaurant business in New Jersey. After two years of operating the pizza restaurant at no profit, Lawyer listed it for sale. Buyer purchased the restaurant based upon financial statements Lawyer provided that Buyer claims were significantly false. Buyer brings a civil action against Man for fraud and seeks rescission.

Is Lawyer subject to potential professional discipline in New York?

(A) Yes, only if Buyer was a legal client of Lawyer and not separately represented in the transaction.
(B) Yes, if the allegations appear to be true.
(C) No, because civil fraud is not a criminal matter.
(D) No, unless Lawyer's acts had some nexus to activities in New York.

25. Great Expectations Ltd. was a closely-held corporation contemplating issuing a public stock offering. The company approached the leading securities lawyer in the area. Lawyer had also been approached by a venture capital fund with an interest in securing her assistance in pursuing a hostile tender offer for Great Expectations. Lawyer realized that if she accepted Great Expectations' employment offer, she would not be able to represent other parties involved in the Great Expectations stock offering. She demanded that Great Expectations pay her $25,000 as a nonrefundable retainer plus $350 per hour. Lawyer put the $25,000 into her law firm's regular operating account and drew out $20,000 as a personal advance. After Lawyer had spent some time on the matter, Great Expectations changed its mind about retaining Lawyer and demanded a refund of the $25,000.

If Lawyer refuses to return the $25,000, is she subject to discipline?

(A) Yes, because $25,000 for no work is prima facie unreasonable.
(B) Yes, because the $25,000 was not deposited into a trust account.
(C) No, as long as Great Expectations was informed that the $25,000 was deposited into the law firm's regular operating account and did not object.
(D) No, because the $25,000 retainer was nonrefundable.

26. Lawyer A and Lawyer B have joined their individual family law practices to form A & B Law Firm. They are trying to increase their billings by soliciting and recruiting new clients. Their marketing director has developed four solicitation plans.

Which of the following would be improper for A & B Law Firm?

(A) Contact all their relatives by phone or in person to solicit their business and referrals.
(B) Set up a booth at a street fair with signs stating "Legal Questions Answered."
(C) Send real-time email electronic communication solicitations to all individuals filing *pro se* divorce petitions.
(D) Mail letters soliciting employment to family counselors in the area and all individuals filing *pro se* divorce petitions stating "advertising material."

27. Lawyer A and Lawyer B are partners in Everytown Law Firm. Lawyer A has represented Multi Motors for many years and currently is working on the defense of a major product liability case involving defective air bags. Apparently, the air bags in the automobile's dashboard suddenly exploded, blinding the driver, who lost control, resulting in the car hitting a pedestrian. Five days later, the pedestrian died, and the personal representative has asked Lawyer B to represent the pedestrian's estate against the driver.

Is it proper for Lawyer B to represent the pedestrian's estate in this matter?

(A) Yes, if Multi Motors gives written consent after full disclosure of all material risks.
(B) Yes, if Multi Motors, the driver, and the pedestrian all give written consent after full disclosure of all material risks.
(C) No, unless Lawyer A and Lawyer B are both effectively screened from any information the other may have in representing their respective clients, and all clients are given notice.
(D) No, because the interests of the estate of the pedestrian and Multi Motors are clearly fundamentally antagonistic, so the conflict cannot be waived.

28. Landlord was tired of Tenant, who refused to move out of her rent-controlled unit. Landlord thus instructed Attorney to file a nuisance lawsuit against Tenant. Landlord told Attorney that Tenant was a drug dealer, but this was untrue, and there was no other reasonable basis for the lawsuit. Landlord hired two witnesses who committed perjury at the trial by claiming they saw Tenant selling drugs. The trial court awarded judgment to Landlord and ordered Tenant evicted from the premises.

One month later, Attorney sent Landlord the bill for the representation. Ten days later, she received Landlord's check along with a note in which she admitted that Tenant did not sell drugs and that she had orchestrated the witness perjury during the trial. Attorney then realized she had been used to assist in perpetrating a fraud on the court. She therefore contacted the trial judge and revealed the contents of the note.

Is Attorney subject to discipline?

(A) Yes, unless the fraud on the court and perjured testimony was the reason the court entered judgment against Tenant.
(B) Yes, because Attorney revealed client confidential information.
(C) No, because a lawyer has a duty of candor to the court to reveal fraudulent evidence that was inadvertently entered.
(D) No, because the attorney-client privilege applies to the client communication since it was intended to be confidential.

29. Attorney spent four years after graduating from law school with the real property conveyance department of Mega Law Firm. Her practice focused on clearing title exceptions, procuring title insurance and closing property transactions. The volume of real estate transactions declined in the last year as the economy softened and Mega reduced Attorney's hours. Attorney ultimately decided to go on her own and opened her own practice specializing in property transactions. Her business grew quickly and she hired Title Expert, a non-lawyer title closing officer to assist her. Attorney agreed that in addition to paying Title Expert a monthly salary, Title Expert would receive 10% of the profit earned from the title closing business.

Is Attorney subject to discipline for entering into the agreement with Title Expert?

- **(A)** No, because the law firm's payments to Title Expert are not deemed to be a sharing of legal fees.
- **(B)** No, if all the clients are fully informed of the relationship and their agreement is confirmed in writing.
- **(C)** Yes, because Attorney is assisting Title Expert in the unauthorized practice of law.
- **(D)** Yes, because Title Expert's compensation is to be received from the closing fees charged to clients by the law firm.

30. A product liability case was assigned to Judge. Over the next year, Judge learned considerable factual details about an unusual chemical reaction in one of the defendant's factories. The case is proceeding on schedule towards trial. Over dinner one Sunday evening, Judge's sister informed her that she owned a substantial block of shares in the defendant corporation. Upon further discussion, it became clear that her sister's financial situation would be substantially affected by the outcome of the trial. Although Judge believes she can conduct the trial in an impartial manner, she called both lawyers into her court and on the record disclosed the financial interest owned by her sister.

Is it proper for Judge to hear the case?

- **(A)** Yes, as long as the Judge sincerely believes her judgment would not be affected by her sister's interest.
- **(B)** Yes, because the Judge now has acquired considerable knowledge about the factual details of the case.
- **(C)** No, because disqualification due to a sibling's financial interest in the outcome of the litigation cannot be waived.
- **(D)** No, unless all parties and their lawyers give consent in a proceeding conducted outside the presence of the judge.

31. Lawyer specializes in employment-related cases. She is approached by Employee, who has just been discharged by her former employer and is very upset by the unfairness of what happened to her. Employee has asked Lawyer to sue her former employer for wrongful discharge. Lawyer contacts the former employer for information who says the employment history at question are none of her business. Lawyer has some reservations about the claim, but files the lawsuit anyway.

Lawyer is least likely subject to professional discipline for filing a frivolous claim if

- **(A)** She did not substantiate all the facts in support of the claim before filing.
- **(B)** She hopes that vital evidence necessary to support Employee's position may be later obtained through discovery.
- **(C)** She knows that Employee desires to bring the action primarily to harass her former employer.
- **(D)** She believes that the claim will ultimately not prevail at trial.

32. A litigation law firm is organized as a partnership. The partners are very busy with their cases, and new associates are left largely on their own to practice law. Small cases are usually assigned to a junior associate to draw the complaint and complete the initial filing that begins the case. The partners do not automatically supervise the associates, but the associates are expected to ask if they have any questions.

A new client hired the law firm to pursue a lawsuit for personal injury against a state government agency that was subject to a one-year statute of limitation. The file was assigned to Associate, who had just passed the bar exam. The state law required that before a plaintiff could pursue a formal legal action against an agency, a formal notice of claim had to be filed with the agency. Associate was not aware of the pre-lawsuit claim requirement until the lawsuit was dismissed for failure to exhaust the internal agency remedies. The one year statutory period by then had elapsed. To avoid embarrassment, Associate told the client that the case was dismissed because it lacked sufficient merit.

Which of the following statements is the most correct?

(A) The law firm is subject to discipline for failure to supervise its associates.
(B) Associate is not subject to discipline for her personal incompetency and intentional false misrepresentations made to the client.
(C) Both the law firm and Associate are subject to potential civil liability for the client's loss.
(D) All the individual partners are subject to discipline for failing to make reasonable efforts to assure all lawyers in the firm conform to the Rules of Professional Conduct.

33. Conglomerate, Inc., is a diversified corporation that is publicly owned and traded on a national stock exchange. The corporate bylaws provide that the corporation is required to defend a director in a lawsuit connected with their corporate activities unless the activity involved fraud. A large shareholder sued Director, a corporate director, because the corporation purchased her property at an alleged fraudulently inflated price. The head of the corporate legal department contacted an experienced corporate director defense attorney. The head of the department explained to the defense lawyer that the corporation will pay all the director's legal fees and that a copy of all billings, documents, and pleadings should be forwarded to him.

May the defense attorney take on the representation of Director?

(A) Yes, because there is only a *de minimis* conflict of interest between Director and the corporation.
(B) Yes, if Director is consulted and consents to the defense arrangements.
(C) No, because a third party is paying for the attorney.
(D) No, because here a third party is trying to control the client-lawyer relationship.

34. Lawyer represents a manufacturing company. A former customer has written a demand letter to the board of directors, but not filed a formal complaint in court. Lawyer undertook representation in the claim and began negotiations with the Plaintiff. Ten months elapsed, and the lawyers had come to a dollar settlement understanding when Lawyer realized that the statute of limitations had run on the former customer's claim. Lawyer still wants to recommend to the board of directors of the manufacturing company that they pay the negotiated settlement because she believes it is the right thing to do and the best interest of justice will be served.

Lawyer should

- **(A)** Inform the board of directors and continue the representation even if the board decides to reject the claim and contest it in litigation.
- **(B)** Inform the board of directors of her recommendation and withdraw from the representation if the board decides to reject the settlement.
- **(C)** Withdraw from representation before the board decides to reject the settlement because she can no longer serve the client objectively.
- **(D)** Take immediate action to promote the settlement she participated in.

35. Two law school friends – Lawyer and Prosecutor – were talking one night over drinks in a bar. Prosecutor informed Lawyer that she was dying of cancer and had one big professional regret. Apparently Prosecutor suppressed exculpatory blood type evidence in a case she was prosecuting. This led to a guilty verdict and a sentence of execution being imposed upon the defendant. At the time, Lawyer encouraged Prosecutor to "remedy" the situation, and called her one month later inquiring about the status of correcting the matter. Prosecutor said that she was "working on it." Prosecutor died a few months later without doing anything about the matter. Four years later, defense attorneys discovered the suppressed lab report indicating the blood type difference of the defendant. Lawyer then willingly signed an affidavit of his prior conversation with Prosecutor and testified for the defense at a motion for a new trial.

Is Lawyer subject to professional discipline?

- **(A)** Yes, unless Lawyer is deemed to have represented Prosecutor as a lawyer during the confession.
- **(B)** Yes, only if Prosecutor did not affirmatively state that the suppression of evidence should remain confidential.
- **(C)** No, Lawyer has no duty to the criminal receiving the sentence.
- **(D)** No, because whatever duty Lawyer had to report the Prosecutor's suppression terminated with the death of Prosecutor.

36. Lawyer was quite conservative in her political beliefs and active in conservative causes involving property rights. A conservative politician became Governor of Neverland State and began to appoint conservative lawyers to the judiciary, including Lawyer. After going on the bench, she was assigned a case in which the local government had downzoned a parcel of property owned by a developer and refused to pay compensation. There are several motions pending in the case addressing various legal issues. After careful consideration, Judge has privately concluded that her personal political views are affecting her objective analysis of the legal issues. However, so far neither side has made a motion to disqualify her.

Must Judge recuse herself?

- **(A)** Yes, because the judge believes she cannot be impartial.
- **(B)** Yes, unless all the parties and the lawyers agree that the bias is not substantial and consent to a waiver in writing.
- **(C)** No, because none of the parties have made a motion to disqualify her from the case.
- **(D)** No, because the only issues in the motions are legal, not factual.

37. Developer develops apartment complexes in the suburbs of Evercity. Her corporate legal work is done by Lawyer. Although right now Developer is not a party to any litigation, Developer retained Attorney to assist her in securing a rezone on a farm she wants to develop. The rezone application is pending before the Board of Adjustment, a city administrative agency.

Lawyer serves on a tenant rights commission that is part of her law firm's *pro bono* efforts. One of the tenants has asked her to sue Developer on behalf of the tenants group, seeking a rent reduction. Some of the rental property that would suffer a rent reduction is owned by Developer.

Is it proper for Lawyer to represent the tenant's group in this matter against Developer?

(A) Yes, because Developer has retained Attorney to represent her.
(B) Yes, because all the questions of fact and issues of law are different in the two claims.
(C) No, unless the tenant group representation is undertaken at no cost on a *pro bono* basis.
(D) No, because Lawyer represents Developer in her corporate matters.

38. Lawyer represented the partnership Ace & Bear in purchasing a small shopping center. Ace was the designated day-to-day managing partner, and Bear's role was primarily to provide the necessary financing. Two years later, a dispute developed over strategic management of the partnership. Ace & Bear sought Lawyer's advice, and they both agreed that Lawyer would serve as a neutral in the dispute. The clients met twice to discuss the facts of the problem with Lawyer mediation. The matter was then settled on the basis of an agreement drawn by Lawyer and signed by Ace and Bear. Six months later, Bear asked Lawyer to represent her in litigation against Ace because Ace fraudulently misrepresented the financial condition of the partnership during the mediation leading to the agreement.

Is it proper for Lawyer to represent Bear in this matter?

(A) Yes, if there is reason to believe Ace misled both Lawyer and Bear in the negotiations leading to the prior agreement.
(B) Yes, because Ace has shown his confidence with Lawyer and Bear in the mediation, thereby waiving his right to disqualify the intermediary-neutral from future participation against his interest.
(C) No, because Lawyer previously acted as an intermediary-neutral in reaching the agreement now in dispute.
(D) No, unless Ace is now represented by independent counsel.

39. Lawyer went to law school with Candidate and developed a good friendship. Ten years later Candidate announced her candidacy for an open seat on the local trial court. Lawyer believes that Candidate would be an excellent jurist. Lawyer also had three trials against her opponent. Lawyer believed that Opponent would be a disaster as a judge.

Which of the below would most likely subject Supporter to discipline?

(A) Publicly oppose the candidacy of Candidate's opponent.
(B) Imply that Opponent lacks the integrity to be on the bench based upon another lawyer's report.
(C) Recruit other endorsements supporting Candidate's candidacy by lawyers likely to appear before Candidate.
(D) Personally solicit monetary contributions to Candidate's campaign committee from other lawyers who are likely to appear before Candidate if she is elected.

40. Lawyer's practice is primarily large-scale complex construction litigation. Because the issues in such cases are often quite technical and involve detailed engineering and accounting questions, almost all the cases are conducted by a judge without a jury.

Lawyer was the dinner speaker at a meeting of contractors. In her speech, she stated, "Our law firm makes certain that we give more cash contributions to these construction trial judges than any other law firm. These judges know that we helped them get elected." The speech itself did not directly result in any new business.

Is Lawyer subject to discipline?

- **(A)** Yes, because Lawyer implied that she may receive favorable consideration from judges whom she contributes to.
- **(B)** Yes, because Lawyer implied that judges make decisions based on the size of the contribution they receive from the lawyers, not the merits of the cases before them.
- **(C)** No, unless Lawyer's communication about judicial influence raises false client expectations.
- **(D)** No, unless this is an attempt to influence a tribunal improperly.

41. Creditor had loaned $25,000 to her neighbor, secured by a promissory note. One year later, the neighbor stopped making the payments, and Creditor hired an old family friend Attorney to pursue a collection lawsuit. Creditor paid Attorney a $1,000 retainer.

Two years later, Attorney had done nothing on the case, and Creditor contacted Attorney B to take the matter over. When Attorney B received the file, she discovered that a key witness had died in the last year; thus, Attorney A's dilatory practices had substantially injured Creditor's case. Attorney B discussed it with Creditor, who said, "I know, but please don't say anything about it because Attorney A is an old family friend and she did refund the $1,000."

Is Attorney B subject to discipline if she does not report her knowledge of Attorney A's conduct to the appropriate authority?

- **(A)** Yes, unless Attorney B believes that Attorney A does not usually neglect such legal matters entrusted to her.
- **(B)** Yes, if Attorney B believes that Attorney A was clearly guilty of professional misconduct.
- **(C)** No, unless Creditor agrees that Attorney B may report the matter to the appropriate authority.
- **(D)** No, because Creditor was satisfied with the return of the $1,000 retainer.

42. Defender is representing a large corporation in defending a case filed by Lawyer who is representing Woman. The case has developed into bitter and protracted litigation. All the settlement offers Lawyer had suggested to Defender were summarily rejected. Further, no meaningful counteroffer was even advanced.

One week before trial, Lawyer ran into the President of the corporation at a civic event and both were initially cordial. At his invitation, Lawyer followed the president into the celebrity room, where he said to her, "Why can't we settle this case for $250,000. You know that your client could easily end up with nothing at trial."

Which of the following responses made by Lawyer is not improper?

- **(A)** I can't discuss the matter with you.
- **(B)** I can't discuss a solution to the matter with you unless you terminate Defender.
- **(C)** I agree, and we have made several generous offers to your lawyer to settle the lawsuit.
- **(D)** If that's the way you feel, why don't you make a better offer to settle?

43. Client is a longtime client of Attorney who is in general practice. Client was seriously injured in an accident involving soft tissue injuries. Attorney undertook the case at a fee of one-third of the recovery and filed the lawsuit. During discovery, Attorney became increasingly concerned about her lack of specialized competency in the area. Attorney thus associated with Attorney B, a trial attorney who specialized in such soft tissue damages. The agreement was to split the total fee 50% to Attorney A and 50% to Attorney B.

Will the two lawyers be subject to discipline for agreeing to the fee division?

(A) Yes, unless they assume joint responsibility or the division of the fee between two lawyers is allocated in proportion to the services performed by each lawyer.
(B) Yes, unless the Client agrees.
(C) No, unless the total fee charged Alice is the same amount in total as the original one-third agreement.
(D) No, if the association of the two lawyers is deemed to create a new law firm.

44. Lawyer had just passed the bar exam and volunteered for appointment to represent indigent defendants. The county has a program operated by the presiding judge of the trial court. Lawyer was appointed to defend Murderer on a capital murder case. Lawyer interviewed the client and researched the law, growing more and more uncomfortable with the case. She finally became convinced that she lacked the knowledge to represent Murderer effectively. The trial is scheduled to begin in five days.

Lawyer may properly

(A) Associate with co-counsel with the client's approval, but without requesting court approval.
(B) Petition the court to appoint experienced co-counsel and allow a continuance to enable co-counsel to become knowledgeable about the case.
(C) Petition the court to allow her to withdraw on the basis she lacks sufficient competency.
(D) Disclose the incompetency and inexperience to the defendant and continue representation if the client signs a written approval.

45. Judge served for three years on the superior court bench hearing child custody and family law cases which she enjoyed. She was then assigned to her next jury trial, which was a serial murder case. The case went on for three months, and the gruesome facts seriously depressed Judge. She decided to do something else with her career and began considering working for a private law firm. She was very impressed by the stature, presence and legal skills of one attorney in the murder case and thought it would be good to work for that firm.

Is Judge subject for employment if she negotiates for employment with the law firm?

(A) Yes, unless the party she contacts is not the attorney appearing in court.
(B) Yes, even if she makes it clear to the law firm that any decision on hiring her must only be made after she renders her decision on the merits of the case.
(C) No, if the judge informs the opposing party and counsel, and they do not object.
(D) No, as long as the individual from the law firm she interviews with is not appearing in the judge's court.

46. Litigious had sued five lawyers for malpractice in the last three years. She was rear-ended in her automobile by a driver who was intoxicated. Litigious went to see Lawyer who specialized in automobile personal injury claims. Lawyer felt that Litigious had a good case, but was fearful Litigious would be dissatisfied with her representation and bring yet another malpractice suit against her. Therefore, she created a written representation agreement that she required Litigious to sign. The agreement contained certain provisions designed to protect Lawyer.

Which of the below provisions in the agreement is not improper?

(A) The client agrees to pay the attorney one-third of any amount recovered.
(B) The client agrees that the attorney may be discharged only after giving the attorney a minimum 30 days notice of termination.
(C) The client agrees that the attorney can withdraw at any time with five days prior notice.
(D) Any claim asserted by the client against the attorney is limited to the fees the client has paid in the engagement.

47. Judge served for five years as a superior court judge hearing jury trials. One summer the senior presiding judge was on vacation, and Judge spent one week substituting for the senior judge. One of the other judges who was assigned a civil case named *Jones v. Smith* disqualified herself. Judge then entered an administrative order transferring the case to another judge and rescheduling the trial preparation calendar.

Judge left the bench and found employment with a large law firm named First & Second and began work. Sometime later the court of appeals remanded the *Jones v. Smith* case to the superior court for a new trial. Apparently, the new trial judge assigned to the case did not allow the defense to call any witnesses. Mr. Smith was very unhappy with the attorney he used in the first trial and decided to retain a new lawyer to handle the remand. He approached Lawyer and asked him if he would take on representation of him in the new trial.

Will Lawyer be subject to discipline if he tries this case on behalf of Mr. Smith?

(A) Yes, because Lawyer would try the case before a judge of the court on which he previously sat.
(B) Yes, because Lawyer acted officially as a judge in assigning the case to the judge whose error created the need for a new trial.
(C) No, because any information that Lawyer learned about the case while acting as a judge was a matter of public record.
(D) No, because Lawyer did not act as a judge concerning a substantial matter or act on the merits of the case.

48. Lawyer agreed to take on the defense of a case in which the police have charged Druggy with trafficking in narcotics. The case proved quite difficult because Druggy was uncooperative and frequently "high on the narcotic drugs" he also sold to his customers. Lawyer was a former prosecutor and able to attack the police handling of the case and interrogation process Druggy was subjected to that was not preceded by the required Miranda warnings. Fearful of losing a motion to suppress, the prosecutor agreed to a plea of a deferred sentence. Druggy was unhappy with any conviction at all and felt Lawyer had not advocated his cause with sufficient vigor. Still, he reluctantly agreed to allow Lawyer to enter the plea and execute the settlement agreement.

Lawyer sent Druggy a bill for $25,000 and Druggy refused to pay. Lawyer then filed a collection action against Druggy and in the Complaint filed with the court stated that Druggy was hard to work with because he was always "high on narcotics," and quoted a sentence from the plea agreement that stated Druggy trafficked in narcotics.

Druggy filed a bar complaint against Lawyer based upon disclosure of what he considered to be his confidential information. Lawyer is

(A) Subject to discipline because a lawyer should not sue a client for fees if the client has a bona-fide reason not to pay.

(B) Subject to discipline because Lawyer revealed that Druggy was hard to work with because he was always high on drugs.

(C) Not subject to discipline because the complaint statement that Druggy trafficked in narcotics was true and contained in the plea agreement.

(D) Not subject to discipline because a lawyer has an unequivocal right to file a fee collection lawsuit against a client who does not pay.

49. Lawyer had just passed the bar exam and decided to start her own law firm. She hired one of her law school friends as an associate. The firm moved into a small office suite in a building owned by a CPA firm. The CPA firm helped organize the law firm administration and began to do all the billing and accounting for Lawyer's law practice. A partner in the CPA firm advised the law firm on business and tax matters. The CPA firm accountants also began to refer some business formation and trust and estate document drafting to Lawyer's new law firm.

Is the business relationship between the CPA firm and Lawyer's law firm proper?

(A) Yes, as long as the accounting firm bills its services to the law firm separately and not as an increase in the rent.

(B) Yes, unless confidential information of the law firm clients may be disclosed to the CPA firm's personnel.

(C) No, because the CPA firm's role in management is so important to the law firm that in effect, the CPAs are directing the lawyers' independent professional judgment and sharing in legal fees.

(D) No, because the law firm's payment for rent and services constitutes consideration for the referral of matters involving business formation and document drafting.

50. Attorney is representing Mega Bucks Corporation in litigation involving a sales agreement with Super Sales Corporation. Three senior executives of Mega Bucks testified at trial that Super Sales' President entered into an oral contract with them agreeing to an exclusive requirement contract. The President of Super Sales denies any such statement was made and affirmatively asserted the Mega Bucks executives had committed perjury. After the defense rested and the jury began deliberations, the three executives admitted in confidence to Attorney that their trial testimony was perjurious.

Attorney should

(A) Do nothing because this information was a client confidence.
(B) Describe the perjury to the tribunal later only if the jury finds for the perjuring party, Big Bucks.
(C) Immediately reveal the perjury to the court.
(D) Withdraw if the executives refuse to allow disclosure of the perjury to the tribunal, but do not reveal the truth to the court because the falsity was by the client, not the lawyer.

51. Judge has served as a trial court judge in Everycity for over 25 years. For much of this time, he has also been an unpaid director of a nonprofit organization dedicated to building shelters for the homeless. As part of the 50th anniversary of the nonprofit organization, the other directors have decided to sponsor a public testimonial dinner in Judge's honor. The $2,000 revenue from the dinner was placed in a public testimonial fund. Most of the funds came from lawyer members who practice in the jurisdiction.

Should Judge accept the $2,000 gift?

(A) Yes, because Judge did not receive compensation for his services to the charity.
(B) Yes, because the gift was incidental to a public testimonial for Judge.
(C) No, because most of the proceeds came from lawyers who practice in the jurisdiction.
(D) No, because the amount of the gift exceeds a *de minimis* amount.

52. Attorney undertook the representation of Employee in a labor dispute with Big Bucks, Inc. securing a $2,500 non-refundable retainer. Attorney researched the facts underlying Employee's claim and became convinced that some of the facts Employee had told her were not true. Further, after studying the laws involved while drafting the formal complaint, the claim seemed even less valid than Attorney originally had felt. Attorney's confidence in the claim declined and she finally concluded she would like to withdraw. The statute of limitations will expire on the claim in 10 days, and Employee insists Attorney at least file the complaint.

Is Attorney subject to discipline if she files the complaint?

(A) Yes, if it is finally determined that Employee's version of the facts is not correct.
(B) Yes, if Attorney is convinced the client's claim lacks sufficient merit to prevail at trial.
(C) No, because an implied condition of retaining the non-refundable $2,500 was that Attorney would file the lawsuit.
(D) No, unless the claim was filed merely to harass or maliciously injure the opposing party.

53. Client approached Lawyer asking her to sue Client's business partners because she had been excluded from the business. Lawyer asked for and received an agreed-upon $5,000 nonrefundable retainer and Client agreed to pay $200 per hour for Lawyer's time. Client alleged her partner embezzled from the business and failed to provide regular financial statements. Lawyer began an investigation and began questioning the veracity of Client's story. Lawyer and Client had a heart-to-heart talk about the merits of the claim. Client finally admitted that she had exaggerated some of the facts to make the claim seem more appealing to Lawyer and agreed that Lawyer could withdraw. Lawyer has spent 20 hours on the representation.

Is it proper for Lawyer to keep the $5,000 retainer?

(A) Yes, but only for the time spent of 20 hours at $200 each.
(B) Yes, if Lawyer can show that $5,000 was not a unreasonable fee amount for a non-refundable retainer in the case.
(C) No, because Lawyer withdrew, so the $5,000 should be returned.
(D) No, because Lawyer was hired to file the claim and failed to do so.

54. Lawyer began his legal career after law school by working for the largest law firm in the state called Mega Law. His associate position was almost exclusively researching legal questions assigned him by partners in the firm. He worked for Mega Law for three years when he moved for the County Prosecutor's office. Lawyer took to courtroom work like a duck to water and proved very effective. Lawyer prosecuted two high profile criminal cases that received very positive media coverage.

A vacancy developed on the Court of Appeals bench and Lawyer was appointed to the open seat. One of the first cases assigned to the new Judge for review was an older case entitled Able v. Baker. Five years earlier, while at Mega Law Firm, the new Judge had researched and prepared a legal brief concerning the potential defenses the client could assert in the same case. Lawyer did not meet the client and knew almost nothing about the case or any confidential information. Neither attorney in the current matter mentioned that they had knowledge of Judge's minimal involvement five years earlier.

Must Judge recluse himself *sua sponte*?

(A) Yes, because Judge worked on the case five years ago.
(B) Yes, unless all the parties and the lawyers agree that Judge should not be disqualified in a remittal agreement.
(C) No, unless Judge has acquired confidential information.
(D) No, as long as the statute of limitations has run on the defense that Judge previously researched.

55. Attorney has a law firm that puts together business deals. One client, Entrepreneur, owns a restaurant and is having trouble raising working capital. Another client of Attorney was a trust that had excess liquid assets in its portfolio. Attorney had both clients come into the office, where the trust loaned the restaurant $800,000 in exchange for an unguaranteed, unsecured promissory note. At the closing of the transaction, Attorney presented a consent agreement stating the law firm had a conflict of interest in the transaction. Both clients signed the document. One year later, the restaurant declared bankruptcy, which caused the trust to lose $600,000.

If the trust files suit against Attorney, the best defense would be

(A) The conflict was disclosed to both clients.
(B) The conflict was disclosed to both clients in writing.
(C) Each affected client gave informed consent, confirmed in writing following authorization from the other client to make any required disclosures.
(D) Full disclosure of the conflict was made.

56. Judge and Man were brother-in-laws and had been best friends since childhood. Before he went on the bench, Judge was in private practice and drew a will for Man, who was one of his business clients. The will contained a testamentary trust for the benefit of Man's wife and their three children. The trust instrument designated Judge as the appointed trustee.

At Man's death, the trust corpus contained assets of over five million dollars, of which two million consisted of the common stock of Microhard, a computer software company. Judge was just assigned a large anti-trust case in which Microhard is the named defendant.

Should Judge recuse himself from officiating over the Microhard case?

(A) No, because Judge has no personal financial interest in the litigation.
(B) No, unless any interest the Judge has in the litigation will affect the Judge's impartiality.
(C) Yes, because the Judge has a deemed financial interest in one of the parties in the litigation.
(D) Yes, because the relatives of the Judge's good friend have an interest in one of the parties in the litigation.

57. Lawyer was the senior partner of a law firm specializing in personal injury cases. She was very good at attracting new clients, but occasionally was too aggressive. The firm's marketing manager developed a marketing poster that could be easily attached to telephone poles. The marketing poster stated, "Last year our law firm recovered an average of $400,000 for our injured clients from insurance companies. We are the best P.I. firm in New York City. Note: Your recovery, if any, will be determined by the individual facts and merit of your case."

If these posters are published, is Lawyer subject to discipline?

(A) Yes, because the comparison with other P.I. law firms in New York City is not factually substantiated.
(B) Yes, because past judgment recoveries and comparisons to other law firms are not allowed.
(C) Yes, because the reference to $400,000 per case recovery creates unjustified expectations.
(D) No, because the U.S. Supreme Court has struck down all restraints on advertising by law firms unless they are in bad taste.

58. Patient underwent a surgical procedure at Homey Hospital. The attending physician made a serious procedural mistake resulting in prolonged medical problems for Patient. Patient hired Lawyer to represent her. Lawyer had a number of discussions with Defender, a lawyer the hospital hired to defend the claim. The negotiations seemed to be going nowhere, and Lawyer finally filed and served a summons and complaint on the hospital's registered agent. No responsive pleading or notice of appearance was received by Lawyer during the proper time.

Is Lawyer subject to discipline if she proceeds to have a default judgment entered against the hospital?

(A) Yes, because Lawyer is required to extend professional courtesy to another attorney.
(B) Yes, because Lawyer had actual knowledge that Homey Hospital had retained counsel.
(C) No, because Lawyer is properly representing her client.
(D) No, unless Lawyer gave written assurances to opposing counsel that she would give actual notice of any motion for a default judgment.

59. Attorney is a business lawyer, and most of her practice is on the defense side. One of her clients, Summa Marketing, is being sued by a consumer group. The consumer group is working the case on a contingency basis and has expressed a desire to settle for an amount Attorney believes is quite reasonable. The President of Summa Marketing is adamant that the lawsuit is a form of blackmail and that a bad precedent would be set if the company paid any settlement at all. Attorney is apprehensive about both the applicable legal precedent and some unknown facts and believes the corporation will lose at trial. The president insists she go forward in the defense.

Must Attorney withdraw as trial counsel in the case?

(A) Yes, because Attorney's judgment about the likely outcome at trial is better than the president's.
(B) Yes, if the president is controlling Attorney's judgment in the decision whether to settle the case.
(C) No, because the client has the sole right to decide whether to accept or reject a settlement offer.
(D) No, if Summa Marketing's defense can be supported by a good faith argument.

60. Aggressive and Tough were law school friends. After they passed the bar exam they started a law firm named Aggressive & Tough. One of their first client, Neighbor, developed cancer from radiation exposure when a nearby nuclear reactor exploded. The plaintiff's team of medical and damage experts concluded the claim was worth $300,000. The defendant offered to settle the case for $750,000, which was immediately and joyfully approved by Neighbor.

When the defendant attorney sent over the settlement documents, they contained a provision stating, "Both Neighbor and Aggressive & Tough, and any or all lawyers connected with the law firm, agree not to discuss any aspect or fact underlying this settlement with anyone and/or take on any other claims against defendant for anyone based upon the nuclear exposure and/or pollution."

If Aggressive & Tough sign this settlement agreement, may they be subject to discipline?

(A) Yes, unless they are independently advised in entering into the agreement.
(B) Yes, because it prohibits the lawyers from bringing an action against the opposing party.
(C) No, as long as the lawyers' percentage of the settlement amount is good and sufficient consideration for their promise not to take on other cases.
(D) No, because it is the client's decision whether to accept or reject an offer of settlement.

RIGOS BAR REVIEW SERIES

PROFESSIONAL RESPONSIBILITY EXAM (MPRE) REVIEW

Chapter 7

Final Exam Answers

Instructions

Following are our unofficial answers with complete answer rationales.

1. Learn From Your Mistakes: When you refer to the answer rationales, be sure to understand why you picked the wrong choice. The fine-line distinctions are critical. Again, it is usually worthwhile to review the answer rationales to all the alternatives because they reinforce the details of the relevant rule being tested. More than one answer rationale may be identical if the alternatives are incorrect for the same reason.

2. Mark Mistakes: When you grade yourself put a red star in the margin alongside every question you missed. If you are using the software, make note of the questions you missed on a sheet of paper. Write down why your choice was not the best alternative.

3. Review Mistakes: You should work the marked questions you previously missed again the day right before sitting for the actual MPRE.

Chapter 7

Final Exam

Answers

1. **/D/** The best answer because this appears to violate the trial prohibition against *ex parte* juror communication. [MRPC 3.5(b)] Associate is required to report a violation committed by another lawyer to the appropriate professional authority. [MRPC 8.3] If the matter is in litigation, the appropriate authority would usually be the trial judge. **(A)** is not the best answer unless there is some question whether the apparent *ex parte* communication was proper. A lawyer must externally report clear violations by lawyers in her own firm. [ABA Opinion 1203 (9/1972)] **(B)** is incorrect because the appropriate authority for a matter in litigation would usually be the trial judge. **(C)** is incorrect because reporting to the trial judge would be preferable to reporting the matter to opposing counsel.

2. **/C/** The best answer because a lawyer may not enter a business transaction with a client unless the terms are reasonable, and the client gives informed consent in writing after having the opportunity to seek the advice of independent counsel. Item C avoids the client transaction and thus is the best answer. [MRPC 1.8(a)] (Note that the MRPC 1.8(b) restriction on the use of information relating to the representation is not present because there is no disadvantage to the client.) **(A)** is incorrect because the alternative does not include client consent in writing or the opportunity to seek independent counsel. **(B)** is not the best answer; while financially attractive, it excludes court or beneficiary approval. The price itself does not preclude the possibility of overreaching. Perhaps another estate asset could be sold to provide the desired liquidity. **(D)** is not the best answer because the rationale – abusing a client's confidence – is not as strong as the prohibited business transaction rationale, and it is not clear whether the client ever intended the Sleeper information to be confidential or that using it is an unauthorized disclosure.

3. **/C/** The best answer because a lawyer may not acquire a proprietary interest in the claim, and this "net fee agreement" is not a reasonable contingent fee. [MRPC 1.8(i)] The danger here is that the lawyer's representation of the client may be materially limited by the lawyer's own financial interest. If the neighbor offers $175,000, it is in the client's interest to accept, while the lawyer may hold out for more. The conflict creates the risk the client may not be made whole. **(A)** is incorrect since the contingent fee characterization is a distractor, and even a contingent fee must be reasonable. **(B)** is incorrect since the contingent fee characterization is a distractor, and any contingent fee agreement must be written. **(D)** is not the best answer since "net fee agreements" are not expressly improper under the MRPC.

4. **/B/** This is likely the best answer because the law firm must leave the disputed portion of the funds in trust pending an outcome. It is clear that the client is due at least $300,000 and that the firm paid $300,000 of costs for which they should be reimbursed. [MRPC 1.15 (c)] **(A)** is incorrect because it is undisputed that the client is entitled to receive at least $300,000 of the total funds in the dispute. **(C)** is incorrect because it is not necessary for the client to receive immediately that portion of the total fee over which the law firm has a bona fide dispute. **(D)** is incorrect in that the law firm may disburse the portion of the total funds that is uncontested. (Note that some commentators suggest that at some point a client disagreement may become so heated that the most prudent procedure is to interplead all the funds into the registry of a court for an independent determination.)

5. **/B/** The best answer because the client must be fully informed (and their agreement confirmed in writing) and must not object to a division of fees between lawyers not in the same firm. [MRPC 1.5(e)] **(A)** is incorrect because this general rule is subject to the exception specified in alternative B. **(C)** is incorrect; the MRPCs require only one of the two conditions – the fee division is in proportion to services performed, or joint responsibility is assumed by all the lawyers – not both. **(D)** is incorrect because a state bar prohibition on non-licensed lawyers practicing in the jurisdiction does not prohibit the hiring of a lawyer licensed in that jurisdiction.

6. **/C/** Where the MPRE poses the dilemma of a lawyer complying with MRPC 1.6 confidentiality and the MRPC 3.3 duty not to use or offer false evidence, the latter professional rule of candor to the tribunal usually controls. The public defender asked Mary for her name on the stand knowing she would respond with a false statement; this is putting on false evidence and treated as a fraud on the court. **(A)** is incorrect because whether the obtaining of the phony license was a crime is irrelevant to the issue of the false testimony at trial. **(B)** is not the best answer and a distractor because the increased jail sentence would result if the proper name were used, and "only if" assumes there is no other reason that the public defender's action was improper. **(D)** is incorrect in that the conclusion is wrong, and when the client's secret information is learned does not affect the prohibition on a lawyer introducing false evidence at trial.

7. **/D/** A lawyer may not directly compensate an individual ("a runner") for recommending or referring a client. [MRPC 7.2] A gift of non-cash benefits qualifies as compensation, and the amount here is not *de* minimis. **(A)** is incorrect because even though many jurisdictions allow truly *de minimis* gifts (holiday ham, free lunch, etc.), the value of this Caribbean trip seems to be much more than *de minimis*, and the rule does not compare the relative benefits. **(B)** is incorrect because the reason the referral was made is irrelevant if compensation was given in return. **(C)** is not the best answer because the referring party's expectation or non-expectation of compensation for the referral is not relevant.

8. /C/ Referrals to an attorney are not improper even if made on an exclusive basis unless the attorney compensates the referring source. A mutual exclusive referral agreement, however, is deemed the equivalent of providing compensation for the referral, which violates MRPC 7.2. **(A)** is incorrect because an exclusive mutual referral agreement is deemed to create compensation even if no money or in-kind compensation is involved. **(B)** is not the best answer because while a one-sided exclusive referral does not violate the rule, it does if the referral relationship is mutual. **(D)** is not the best answer because while disclosure and client consent may mitigate the violation of the "no exclusive" cross-referral rule, it does not excuse it.

9. /B/ The best answer because a judicial candidate can attend a partisan political party gathering and identify himself as a member of the political party. [MCJC 4.2] **(A)** is not the best answer because a judicial candidate can also identify himself as a member of a political party. **(C)** is incorrect because a judicial candidate cannot make a significant contribution to a partisan political party. **(D)** is incorrect because a judicial candidate cannot solicit contributors at a partisan political gathering.

10. /D/ A lawyer shall not obstruct another party's access to evidence, but there is usually no duty to help an opponent discover evidence that may assist the other party's case. [MRPC 3.4] **(A)** is incorrect because it is not necessary that the evidence be revealed to the opposing party. **(B)** is incorrect because there is no duty to inform the court (unless evidence was previously offered that was false). **(C)** is incorrect because MRPC 3.4 places a number of restrictions on entering false evidence or obstructing another party's access to evidence. Except for a prosecutor's duty to disclose exculpatory and mitigating evidence, litigants under MRPC 3.8(d) do not have to make the other party's case.

11. /A/ A judge may usually dispute a false factual allegation by an opponent. This statement is not stating a view on a disputed legal or political issue. [MCJC 2.10] **(B)** is incorrect because this would be promising or committing the judge to future judicial conduct. [MCJC 4.1] **(C)** is incorrect because such a statement attacking the messenger does not represent the required high standards of dignified judicial conduct and thus would have the potential to undermine public confidence in the integrity of judges. **(D)** is incorrect because such a statement attacking the messenger does not represent the required high standards of dignified judicial conduct and thus could easily undermine public confidence in the integrity of judges.

12. /A/ A lawyer who knows that another lawyer has committed a violation of the MRPCs that raises a substantial question as to the lawyer's fitness as a lawyer shall inform the appropriate professional authority. [MRPC 8.3(a)] Here, the lawyer's alcoholism appears to be interfering with competency and adequate preparation required under MRPC 1.1. **(B)** is incorrect because a lawyer may not directly contact a person whom the lawyer knows to be represented by another lawyer. [MRPC 4.2] **(C)** is incorrect because it is not usually necessary to get the client's approval before a lawyer's duty to report under MRPC 8.3 matures, and this does not involve client confidences. **(D)** is incorrect because a lawyer shall report another lawyer's acts that raise a substantial question about her fitness as a lawyer.

13. /B/ Discipline seems most likely if the public becomes confused by the way a sole proprietor lawyer advertises and hold himself or herself out as having an association with the other office sharing lawyer. [MRPC 7.5] **(A)** is incorrect because while a client complaint may create an ethics investigation, it is not determinant of disciplinary counsel's opinion regarding the merits of the complaint. **(C)** is incorrect because whether office sharing is *per se* improper is not as probative an alternative as the danger of public confusion. **(D)** is not the best answer because to have a violation it is not absolutely required to expressly misrepresent the status to clients since apparent association by appearance is possible.

14. /C/. A judge should not make a public endorsement of a political candidate for prosecutor – even if related. Note this is not a judicial election. This is especially appropriate here because a prosecutor may appear in superior court where the judge sits. [MCJC 4.1] **(A)** is not the best answer because a judge may contribute to political campaigns if the judge contributor himself is currently involved as a judicial candidate and it is allowed under state law. **(B)** is incorrect because a judge usually may privately express his/her views on candidates. **(D)** is incorrect because judges are not allowed to make public endorsements of political candidates. Note that the judge's sister is campaigning for a non-judicial position.

15. /B/ A contingency fee may not be proposed, agreed to, or charged for representation in a criminal matter and this alternative best focuses on the contingency nature of the fee. [MRPC 1.5(d)] **(A)** is not the best answer because a contingent fee is not the same as acquiring a proprietary interest in the client's claim. [MRPC 1.8(i)] **(C)** is incorrect because even a reasonable contingency fee may not be charged for representation in a criminal matter. [MRPC 1.5(a)] **(D)** is incorrect because it is not necessary that the whole fee be based upon a percentage basis, only that the total fee be in part contingent upon the outcome of the criminal case.

16. /D/ The best answer because actual knowledge of a lawyer's professional misconduct is required to warrant filing a disciplinary complaint; here, there appears to be mere suspicion. [MRPC 8.3] **(A)** is incorrect; while MRPC 1.8 provides that a lawyer's representation of a client may not be materially limited by the lawyer's own interest, the publicity generated by a murder trial without more does not necessarily indicate misconduct. **(B)** is incorrect because the outcome of the trial is not conclusive as to the motives of the lawyer in making tactical decisions regarding defending a case. **(C)** is not the best answer because the reportable question of a "materially limited" conflict usually arises at the beginning of the representation, before the quality of representation is determined.

17. /C/ The best answer because a lawyer shall withdraw from the representation of a client if the representation will result in violation of the rules of professional conduct and assisting a client in making a false statement qualifies. [MRPC 1.16(a)]. **(A)** is incorrect because a lawyer does not have to follow a client's instructions concerning the means and tactics used to achieve the litigation objectives [MRPC 1.2]. **(B)** is incorrect because a lawyer's belief a motion will be denied does not in and of itself justify withdrawal. **(D)** is incorrect because a lawyer who does not accept every aspect of the client's version of the facts does not necessarily have to withdraw.

18. /C/ A lawyer is prohibited from making or agreeing to an agreement not to represent in the future other persons against a party, even though the client may urge acceptance of same. [MRPC 5.5] Thus, it is improper for both lawyers to so agree. **(A)** is incorrect because Victim's lawyer is also subject to discipline. **(B)** is incorrect because Vacuum's attorney is also subject to discipline. **(D)** is incorrect because both lawyers are subject to discipline.

19. /C/ The general rule of firm-wide disqualification applies because Alice's participation in the matter was personal and substantial, and the facts do not indicate all the requirements for screening allowed in some states (notice to agency and informed consent confirmed in writing) were met. [MRPC 1.11(a)] **(A)** is not the best answer because it omits the required notice to and informed written consent confirmed in writing by the agency. **(B)** is not the best answer because a notification without informed consent confirmed in writing is not sufficient. **(D)** is not the best answer because the tainted lawyer's agreement not to participate in the matter is insufficient unless notice is given to the agency in writing.

20. /A/ The best answer because the RPCs authorize the sale of a law practice, including future payment to the estate of the deceased partner, but does not allow the fees to be raised to finance the purchase. [MRPC 1.17] **(B)** is not the best answer because the payment from the business transfer could be paid to the individual retiring partner, not only to a deceased partner's estate. **(C)** is incorrect because the ownership sale payments would not be considered a referral fee under MRPC 5.4(a)(1). **(D)** is incorrect because payments to the former partner or estate were made in return for the client book of business, not splitting a fee.

21. /D/ A lawyer may not represent a private client in a matter in which the lawyer's involvement was substantial and personal while at a government agency. A "matter" does not include circumstances that are merely related by involving the same types of activities or defendant. Here, the victim suffered substantial physical injuries causing damages way beyond the cost of replacing defective brakes. [MRPC 1.11] **(A)** is incorrect because it is not necessary that either the agency or the defendant approve of the representation. **(B)** is not the best answer (even if true) because it is too superficial and reaches the incorrect conclusion. **(C)** is incorrect because Debra is not disqualified, and thus screening is not necessary.

22. /A/ A lawyer recommending a candidate to be admitted to the State Bar Association is required to correct a misstatement or omission in a bar admission application since the bar is likely relying upon the veracity and integrity of the lawyer's recommendation. [MRPC 8.1] **(B)** is incorrect because while such a statement might or might not be accurate, it is still misleading. **(C)** is not the best answer because merely advising the applicant to correct the misstatement is not sufficient, and the facts do not indicate whether the applicant actually made the correction. **(D)** is incorrect because MRPC 1.6 attaches only to an attorney-client communication that does not ordinarily exist between a law school professor and student. If it did, the professor should not write a letter of recommendation or do so only by stating in the letter that there may exist confidential information that is not being disclosed.

23. /D/ A lawyer must not knowingly or recklessly make false statements about a candidate for judicial office; while Lawyer Two may have made a false statement, it was not done knowingly or recklessly. [MRPC 8.4] **(A)** is incorrect because Lawyer Two did not appear to know the statement was false, and it was not made with a reckless disregard for the truth. **(B)** is incorrect because "all" is too broad a category; "some" of the judicial restraints may apply when a lawyer announces his candidacy for judicial office, but not "all." **(C)** is incorrect because the MRPCs still apply to all lawyers, including those campaigning for a judicial position.

24. /B/ The best answer because if Lawyer's action did involve fraud, deceit, or misrepresentation, it is not necessary that it be related to the practice of law, be a crime, result in a civil judgment, or occur within the jurisdiction to subject the attorney to potential discipline. Such actions go to the essence of a lawyer's character. [MRPC 8.4 and 8.5] **(A)** is incorrect because it is not necessary that the fraudulent transaction be with a legal client. **(C)** is incorrect because it is not necessary that the lawyer's fraud be a criminal matter. **(D)** is incorrect because it is not necessary that the conduct arose in the licensing jurisdiction.

25. /D/ The representation agreement specified that the $25,000 fee was characterized as a nonrefundable retainer. [MRPC 1.15] **(A)** is not the best answer because a variety of factors go into determining whether a fee is not unreasonable; here, the lawyer is a leading security expert and being conflicted out of accepting alternative representation from others interested in Great Expectations, and the opportunities foregone suggest the retainer was not unreasonable. [MRPC 1.5(a)] **(B)** is incorrect because only advances should be deposited into the trust account, not nonrefundable retainers which are usually deemed earned upon receipt. **(C)** is incorrect because the client's approval is not necessary for the law firm to deposit a nonrefundable retainer into its regular operating account since this is proper treatment under MRPC 1.15.

26. /C/ Sending email soliciting legal work to all people filing for divorce is in fact improper direct solicitation [MRPC 7.3]. **(A)** is not the best answer because relatives may be directly solicited. **(B)** is not the best answer because here the client - not the lawyer - initiates the lawyer contact by inquiring at the street fair booth for legal advice. **(D)** is not the best answer because letters are not usually considered improper solicitation particularly if the letter includes the statement, "advertising material."

27. /D/ The best answer; even though the two matters may appear separate, it seems quite doubtful a lawyer would reasonably believe the dual representation would not adversely affect one or both clients. [MRPC 1.7(a)] **(A)** is incorrect because abatement of the conflict by consent is not possible if the matter is in litigation and the clients' interests are directly adverse. **(B)** is incorrect because abatement of the conflict by consent is not possible if the matter is in litigation, and the clients' interests are directly adverse. **(C)** is incorrect because the "screening" exception to the imputed conflict rules within a law firm only applies if one of the lawyers involved is joining or leaving the law firm.

28. /B/ The best answer because the duty to report to the tribunal applies only until the end of the proceeding; therefore, the confidential information learned of after the trial decision may not be revealed. [MRPC 3.3] **(A)** is incorrect because even if the judgment was entered because of the tainted evidence, it cannot be revealed after the proceeding is over. **(C)** is incorrect because the duty to report to the tribunal terminates with the proceeding, thus prohibiting revealing any client confidential knowledge the lawyer acquires later. **(D)** is incorrect because, while the attorney-client privilege might apply as it relates to general disclosure, it does not override the duty of candor to the tribunal.

29. **/A/** The best answer because a law firm may include non-lawyer employees in a profit sharing plan and not violate the fee-splitting rule. [MRPC 5.4(a)(3)] **(B)** is not the best answer because the central issue in this question is whether the payments to the non-lawyer constitute improper fee sharing, not client approval. **(C)** is incorrect because a law firm may include non-lawyers in a compensation plan even though the money funding the compensation plan are derived from the profit earned by way of legal fees. **(D)** is incorrect because the facts do not suggest that the lawyer is not supervising the delegated title closing functions or maintaining a direct relationship with the client.

30. **/D/** The best answer because a financial interest by a close family member of a judge (within the third degree of relationships such as a sibling) may be waived by the parties and their lawyers if the decision is made outside the presence of the judge who enters the agreement in the written record. [MCJC 2.11] **(A)** is incorrect because subjective impartiality is not sufficient without an express waiver by the parties and their lawyers. **(B)** is incorrect because the efficiency of the proceeding does not waive the financial interest disqualification rules. **(C)** is incorrect because an express waiver of the disqualification entered into without the judge's participation may be effective if entered on the record.

31. **/A/** The best answer because the opposing party has made a pre-filing investigation difficult, if not impossible. **(B)** is not the best answer because a mere "hope" that sufficient evidence will be attained must also be reasonable. (C) is not the best answer because if the lawyer knows the client wants to assert the claim primarily for harassment, it is likely the lawyer is acting improperly. (D) is not the best answer because if the lawyer believes the case has no chance there is some possibility that the Lawyer could be charged with professional discipline.

32. **/C/** The best answer because both the law firm and individual lawyer have potential civil liability. Alice is liable for her own negligence and the law firm is vicariously liable for failure to supervise under the tort law doctrine of *respondeat superior*. **(A)** is not the best answer because the ABA model RPCs do not usually subject the law firm to professional discipline, only the involved individual lawyers. **(B)** is incorrect because Alice is subject to discipline for incompetent representation [MRPC 1.1] and false statements to the client. [MRPC 5.2] **(D)** is not the best answer because professional discipline would not normally apply to those firm partners who do not supervise Alice Associate's work. [MRPC 5.1]

33. **/D/** A lawyer should not accept compensation from a third party if there is interference with the client-lawyer relationship; here, the corporate payment of the director's legal fees and potential breach of confidentiality in the documents and pleadings could easily represent significant control interference. [MRPC 1.8(f)] **(A)** is incorrect because the conflict between the corporation and individual constituent seems more than *de minimis*. **(B)** is not the best answer because client consent is effective to abate the conflict only if there is no interference, and here that danger seems clear. **(C)** is incorrect because it is too simplistic, and there could easily be considerable interference with the client-lawyer relationship.

34. **/A/** The client has the final authority over the objectives of the representation, while the lawyer has authority to decide strategy and procedure. [MRPC 1.2(a)] In this situation, the decision to reject or accept the claim appears to be more in the nature of an objective in that it is a major outcome-determinant decision. Clients also have the exclusive right to accept settlements. The lawyer thus should continue the representation. **(B)** is incorrect because seeking to withdraw is not usually appropriate unless the client's objectives are very repugnant to the lawyer. [MRPC 1.16(b)(4)] Withdrawal here may also have an adverse effect on the interests of the client. **(C)** is incorrect because a lawyer is not required to withdraw simply because she anticipated the client would disagree with her on a legal issue. **(D)** is incorrect because this would be working against a client's best interests.

35. **/A/** An attorney learning of a substantial question as to the lawyer's honesty or fitness must ("shall") report that misconduct to the appropriate professional authority. [MRPC 8.3] Lawyer's action in suppressing the blood lab report was clear misconduct and should have been reported as soon as Lawyer learned that Prosecutor did not "remedy" the situation unless Lawyer was representing Prosecutor in the matter. [MRPC 3.8] **(B)** is not the best answer because it would only be correct if Lawyer actually represented Prosecutor in the matter, which does not appear to be the situation. **(C)** is incorrect because the duty to report unethical practices exists merely because of the attorney's wrongdoing independent of any duty owed a third party. **(D)** is incorrect because the attorney's ethical reporting duty vested as of the time Lawyer learned of Prosecutor's offense and that Prosecutor did not immediately correct the matter.

36. **/A/** The best answer because if the judge believes she cannot be impartial in deciding the matter, recusal is mandatory. [MCJC 2.11] **(B)** is incorrect because a waiver and recording in the record by the parties and their attorneys is effective only if the lack of impartiality is due to the involvement of a family member or a financial interest, not a personal bias or partiality by the judge. **(C)** is incorrect because it is not necessary that a motion for disqualification be made; the judge should recuse herself *sua sponte* if she believes that she cannot be impartial. **(D)** is incorrect because if partiality exists, the judge may still be subject to discipline for deciding any aspect of the matter.

37. **/D/** A lawyer may not concurrently act for a client in one matter and against her on another matter at the same time since it could materially limit the advocacy posture. [MRPC 1.7(a)(2)] **(A)** is incorrect because undivided loyalty to the client is put at risk even though the client may hire another lawyer to work on other matters. **(B)** is incorrect because even if the questions of fact and issues of law are different, a lawyer cannot serve two clients whose interests are directly adverse. **(C)** is incorrect because *pro bono* representation may not violate any MRPC, including those dealing with conflicts of interest with other clients.

38. **/C/** In an intermediation, both clients are treated as former clients under MRPC 1.9 and absent approval by both, the mediator-neutral may not represent either client in the same or a substantially related matter. [MRPC 2.4] **(A)** is incorrect because the rule prohibiting representation of a current client in a related matter adverse to the other former client protects all former clients regardless of the detail of the former matter. **(B)** is incorrect because a former client does not implicitly waive his right to object to the intermediary-neutral future participation if it is against his interest. **(D)** is incorrect, because even if the former client is now represented by independent counsel, the protections of Rule 1.9 are still available.

39. /B/ Of the four alternatives this seems the most likely to draw professional discipline because she is relying on mere heresay for authority in making a serious accusation. This suggests recklessness because she lacks personal knowledge of the veracity of the statements. [MRPC 8.2]. **(A)** is not the best answer because a lawyer may support one judicial candidate and oppose another as long as she does not seek to influence the judge by means prohibited by law. [MRPC 3.5] **(C)** is not the best answer because lawyers are usually qualified to issue endorsements of judges running for office if they appear in their court or litigated against them. **(D)** is not the best answer because a lawyer may solicit contributions for a judicial candidate as long as the funds are collected by an election committee and not the contribution solicitor or judge personally.

40. /B/ The best answer because the prejudice to the administration of justice seems to be the worst result that will occur from Barbara's reckless statements creating unjustified expectations. [MRPC 7.1, 8.2(a) and 8.4(d)] **(A)** is not the best answer because Barbara's statements do not seem to be as detrimental to maintaining respect for the legal profession and integrity of the judiciary as alternative B (even though the given rationale would likely support discipline under MRPC 8.4(d)). **(C)** is not the best answer because Barbara's statements are not as detrimental to respect for the legal profession and integrity of the judiciary as alternative B (even though the rationale would likely support discipline under MRPC 7.1). **(D)** is not the best answer because Barbara's statements are not as detrimental to respect for the legal profession and integrity of the judiciary as alternative B (even though the rationale would likely support discipline under MRPC 3.5(a)).

41. /C/ A lawyer is usually required to report misconduct by another lawyer if the violation raises a substantial question as to the lawyer's trustworthiness or fitness as a lawyer. [MRPC 8.3] An exception applies if the information to be reported is protected under the client confidentiality rules. [MRPC 1.6] Because the client has expressly indicated she does not want this matter reported, Attorney B would have to secure Creditor's agreement to initiate the professional complaint. **(A)** is not the best answer because a belief that this is not typical behavior or an indication of general incompetence [MRPC 1.1] or diligence [MRPC 1.3] is for the appropriate professional authority to decide, not the reporting lawyer. **(B)** is incorrect because the reporting attorney's belief as to guilt or innocence is irrelevant to the central concern of the confidentiality exception to the reporting duty. **(D)** is incorrect because the reason the reporting duty is not mandatory here is that the client insists on confidentiality.

42. /A/ "I can't discuss the matter" is the only proper response the lawyer can make here; it is improper to communicate about the subject of the representation with an opposing person represented by another lawyer unless that person's lawyer has given prior consent to the direct communication. [MRPC 4.4] **(B)** is improper because a lawyer should not advise an opposing party to terminate its lawyer. **(C)** is improper because it relays and possibly misrepresents discussions between the lawyer and opposing counsel. **(D)** is improper because a lawyer should not enter into settlement discussions with an opposing party directly if they are represented by counsel.

43. /D/ The best answer because if both lawyers are associated in the same law firm, the fee split is not external so the additional rules on external fee splitting is not required. **(A)** is not the best answer because, while an accurate statement, it does not includes client consent confirmed in writing. **(B)** is not the best answer because it does not include the requirement that the client agreement must be confirmed in writing. **(C)** is not the best answer because it does not address the central focus of the fee division, and the reasonableness of the total fee is not raised in this fact pattern.

44. /B/ The best answer because if an attorney lacks experience and competence, two acceptable options are to associate with co-counsel or withdraw from the representation. The representation was obtained through appointment, and good cause to decline an appointment exists if the lawyer cannot handle the matter competently. Thus it would seem appropriate to petition the court for approval to associate rather than merely seeking approval from the client. [MRPC 6.2] **(A)** is not the best answer since the representation was made by appointment so the motion for withdrawal should likely also be approved by the court. **(C)** is not the best answer because if neglects the fact that the trial is only five days away so withdrawal would likely prejudice the client and it does not include the association of the necessary expertise so the client is not adversely effected. **(D)** is not the best answer even though an attractive distracter, but client consent to incompetent representation is not usually effective for disciplinary purposes since the client does not have the experience to form a judgment on the consequences of the lawyer's incompetence. [MRPC 1.1]

45. /B/ A judge is subject to discipline if she negotiates for employment with a lawyer or law firm that is appearing in her court, and the timing of the case and employment decision do not cure the violation. [MRPC 1.12(b)] **(A)** is incorrect because the rule prohibits employment negotiation with anyone from the law firm while any lawyer from the firm is appearing in the court. **(C)** is incorrect because this improper judicial conduct may not be excused or waived by the opposing party and/or his counsel. **(D)** is incorrect because the restraint on the judge's seeking employment from a lawyer appearing in her court is applied firm-wide.

46. /A/ The best answer because this requirement involves a double negative and a contingency fee of one-third of the recovery is not normally considered to be unreasonable and thus it is likely not improper. [MRPC 1.5(c)] **(B)** is likely improper because the client decides this aspect of the representation, which usually includes the potential termination of the lawyer [MRPC 1.2(a)] **(C)** is likely improper because a lawyer must withdraw immediately from representing a client if she is discharged [MRPC 1.16(a)(3)] **(D)** is likely improper because this is an attempt by the lawyer to prospectively limit her liability. This is acceptable only if the client is independently represented, and the facts do not indicate this requirement was met. [MRPC 1.8(h)(1)]

47. /D/ The best answer because the prohibition on a former judge representing a party in a matter in which the judge participated while on the bench applies only if the participation was substantial and went to the merits of the case; mere scheduling or assignment as here is not usually sufficient. [MRPC 1.12(a)] **(A)** is incorrect because the fact a former colleague would hear the case does not necessarily disqualify the prior judge. **(B)** is incorrect because the fact the reassignment was made to a judge who erred does not disqualify the former judge. **(C)** is not the best answer because whether the case information was public or not is irrelevant to the degree of participation the judge had with the case while on the bench.

48. **/B/** The best answer because the disclosure that David was "always high on narcotics" was confidential information not otherwise in the public domain and likely not necessary to prevail in the fee collection lawsuit. [MRPC 1.6(b)(5)] **(A)** is incorrect because a lawyer does have a right to initiate a collection action against a client but should avoid unnecessary disclosure therein or file the case under seal. **(C)** is not the best answer because the facts do not state that the settlement agreement was filed and thus in the public domain and therefore the information could be classified as a client confidence. **(D)** is not the best answer because one of the requirements when a lawyer sues a client is that revealing client confidences is only proper to the extent reasonably necessary to effectual collection and here the lawyer likely exceeded that limitation.

49. **/B/** The best answer because the client's confidential information held by the law firm must not be compromised in any relationship that could lead to disclosure to anyone other than law firm personnel. [MRPC 1.6] **(A)** is not the best answer because how the CPA firm bills the law firm for the use of the office space and services provided does not usually determine if the relationship is proper. **(C)** is incorrect because improper fee sharing must be direct, and the facts do not indicate the CPA firm is directing the lawyer's judgment in rendering legal services. [MRPC 5.4] **(D)** is incorrect because the facts do not indicate that the law firm's rent and service payments have been artificially raised to disguise referral fees. [MRPC 7.2(b)]

50. **/C/** The best answer because a lawyer must correct material false evidence, such as perjury, that was entered. [MRPC 3.3(a)(3)] **(A)** is incorrect because, even though a client confidence [MRPC 1.6], the evidence entered is now known to be false and must be disclosed to the tribunal. **(B)** is incorrect because the duty to disclose false evidence to the tribunal does not depend on whether it was outcome determinant. **(D)** is incorrect because the duty to disclose false evidence to the tribunal applies equally if the falsity was entered by the lawyer, lawyer's client, or a witness called by the lawyer.

51. **/B/** A judge may serve as an officer, director, trustee, or non-legal advisor to a nonprofit organization and may accept a gift incidental to a public testimonial. The facts do not state that the organization itself is a regular party in front of the judge or that the members frequently take one side in litigation. [MCJC 3.7] **(A)** is incorrect because the judge is not prohibited from receiving compensation if it is reported annually and does not produce the appearance of influencing the judge. **(C)** is incorrect because the mere fact that most of the testimonial funding is from local lawyers does not mean that they intend to influence the judge's decisions. **(D)** is not the best answer because there is no restrictive threshold amount as long as the value of the gift is not so large as to appear to be an attempt to influence the judge.

52. **/D/** This is the only rationale presented that would subject a lawyer to professional discipline for filing a frivolous claim. [MRPC 3.1] **(A)** is incorrect because it is not frivolous to advance a claim simply because the facts have not yet been fully substantiated. **(B)** is incorrect because the fact the lawyer does not believe the claim has sufficient merit to prevail does not necessarily mean the claim is frivolous. **(C)** is incorrect because accepting a non-refundable retainer does not excuse a lawyer who files a frivolous complaint.

53. **/B/** The best answer because the lawyer always has the burden to show that the fee is not unreasonable based upon the particular facts and circumstances in the case. **(A)** is incorrect because the retainer was non-refundable so the time spent could be killed in addition. **(C)** is incorrect because the facts do not indicate any restrictions upon retaining the non-refundable retainer. **(D)** is incorrect because the $5,000 non-refundable was earned by becoming available and being in association with the client's cause and the facts do not indicate an express condition of the representation was the claim be filed.

54. **/A/** The general rule is that a judge should disqualify himself *sua sponte* from cases in which he previously participated or was previously associated with a lawyer who participated substantially in the case which appears to be the situation here. [MCJC 2.11] **(B)** is not the best answer because agreement to waive disqualification may not involve the jurist's personal knowledge of material facts and here it seems the defenses to be asserted may be material in the appellant review. **(C)** is incorrect because it is the materiality of the information that is determinant and this alternative does not include the necessity of the remittal agreement if an exception was to apply. **(D)** is incorrect because the required *sua sponte* disqualification exception goes to the materiality of the prior involvement, not the length of time involved and the defenses asserted below may be at issue in the appellant review.

55. **/C/** The best answer because it states the exact wording of the MRPC and includes the required client informed consent confirmed in writing. The required disclosure of the risks and dangers may require authorization by the other client since their confidential information may be involved. It is also the most precise alternative presented [MRPC 1.7]. **(A)** is not the best answer because it is not as complete and accurate a rationale as alternative C. **(B)** is not the best answer because it is not as complete and accurate a rationale as alternative C. **(D)** is not the best answer because it is not as complete and accurate a rationale as alternative C.

56. **/C/** A judge serving as a fiduciary trustee is deemed to have a financial interest in the corpus of the trust. Since Microhard is a substantial investment of the trust and is also a party in the litigation, Judge should recuse himself. [MCJC 3.8] Depending upon the rule of the jurisdiction, there may be additional restraints upon a judge concurrently engaging in the practice of law as a trustee. **(A)** is incorrect because as a trustee fiduciary, Judge is deemed to have a financial interest in the trust. **(B)** is incorrect because it is the appearance of impartiality that is put at risk when a judge has an actual or constructive financial interest in one of the parties in the litigation. **(D)** is incorrect because it is not the financial interest that the Judge's friend's relatives have that creates the disqualification, but rather the Judge's fiduciary capacity.

57. **/A/** The comparison with other law firms following the dollar judgment recoveries figure could lead a reasonable person to conclude that the comparison can be substantiated; this does not seem reasonably possible, and thus the statement is materially misleading. [MRPC 7.1] **(B)** is not the best answer; the disclaimer eliminates (or at least sharply reduces) the misleading character of past judgment recoveries that may lead to unjustified expectations about results that the lawyer can achieve. **(C)** is not the best answer; while the comparison to other law firms may be objectionable, the past judgment amounts seem proper because of the accompanying disclaimer. **(D)** is incorrect because the courts have not struck down restraints prohibiting false and misleading marketing communications, and "all" is too broad. Good taste is not directly required (but may be subject to discipline under MRPC 8.4 as lawyer misconduct in extreme circumstances).

58. /D/ The best answer because if the lawyer gave express written assurances to opposing counsel that she would give actual notice of a motion for default and did not comply with the representation, it would be unfairness to opposing counsel. [MRPC 3.4] In addition, opposing counsel would likely file a motion to overturn the default, and Marianna would be a foreseeable necessary witness [MRPC 3.7] and could also be charged with engaging in fraud or deceit [MRPC 8.4(c)]. **(A)** is incorrect because, absent a representation to the contrary, professional courtesy does not dictate that notice of the default motion be given unless a written Notice of Appearance pleading is filed. **(B)** is not the best answer because actual knowledge of an opposing counsel is not technically sufficient without a written Notice of Appearance. **(C)** is not the best answer here (but would be if the exception in D did not apply) because nothing in the court rules require notice of default be given to opposing counsel unless he files a formal Notice of Appearance pleading.

59. /D/ The most compelling alternative presented is that a lawyer must (not may) withdraw if the representation of the client would result in a MRPC violation. [MRPC 1.16(a)(1)] It is a professional violation of MRPC 3.1 if a civil lawsuit cannot be supported by a good faith argument so withdrawal under that circumstance is mandatory. **(A)** is not the best answer because while the rationale is likely correct, the conclusion – that the lawyer must withdraw – is incorrect if a good faith argument can be made. **(B)** is incorrect because the president of the client is not a third party trying to control a lawyer. **(C)** is not the best answer because while the rationale is correct – the client decides whether to accept or reject the settlement offer – the focus here is upon conditions under which an attorney must withdraw.

60. /B/ A lawyer is prohibited from making an agreement not to represent her client or other persons in the future against the opposing party. [MRPC 5.6] **(A)** is incorrect because there is no such exception allowed to justify a lawyer agreeing to a "no future representation" provision in a settlement agreement. **(C)** is incorrect because consideration received by the lawyers does not excuse the ethical violation. **(D)** is incorrect because while the client has the right to approve all settlement offers, the lawyer may not permit the client to force them to participate in a violation of the MRPCs.

CHAPTER 8

ACRONYMS

AND

MNEMONICS

RIGOS UNIFORM BAR REVIEW SERIES

MODEL PROFESSIONAL RESPONSIBILITY EXAM (MPRE)

RIGOS ACRONYMS AND MNEMONICS

Client's Decisions: **AJET**

Accept or reject a settlement offer; or in a criminal case,
Jury trial waiver,
Entering a plea,
Testifying at trial

Factors in Determining the Reasonableness of a Fee (case-related): **SANTA**

Skill Required in matter,
Amount Involved,
Novelty and Difficulty,
Time Involved / Opportunities Foregone,
Average Customary Fee

Factors in Determining the Reasonableness of a Lawyer's Fee: **REBER**

Relationship with C,
Expertise of L,
Basis of Fee,
Experience / Reputation of L,
Result of Matter

No Lawyer-Client Business Dealings Unless: **TICC**

Terms of Transaction Are Fair,
Independent Counsel Advice,
Client **C**onsent in Writing

Lawyer **must** Terminate / Withdraw from Representation if **VID**

Violate MRPCs,
Impaired Ability to Represent,
Discharged by Client

Former Judge or Governmental Lawyer Representation

Lawyer **may** Terminate / Withdraw from Representation if: **CURBSO**

Client Pursuing **C**riminal Action,
Used Lawyer to Commit Crime,
Repugnant Objective,
Burden on Lawyer Unreasonable,
Serious Client Failure,
Other Good Cause for Withdrawal Exists

Candor to the Tribunal Violation Procedure: **FIRST**

False Statement made to Tribunal,
Information of Non-truthfulness Received by Lawyer,
Request to Client for Curative Disclosure Unsuccessful,
Seek Permission from Tribunal to Withdraw,
Tribunal Disclosure if Withdrawal is denied or it will not undo False Effect,

Prohibited Lawyer Criminal Case Extrajudicial Statements: **TOPIC**

Test Results,
Opinion or Future Witness Testimony,
Plea or Confession,
Inadmissible Evidence,
Character

Prosecutor's Right to Disclose Publically: **SIPAW**

Safety Information
Investigation is in Progress
Public Record Information
Assistance Request to obtain Evidence and Information
Warn Public or Individuals of Danger

A Lawyer may also be a witness if any of the following reasons apply to: **HULA**

Hardship on Client,
Uncontested or Formality,
Legal Services Rendered Value,
Another Firm Lawyer Witness

Special Responsibilities of a Prosecutor apply to: **DASH PET**

Discovery on Lawyer
Accused's Right to Counsel
Supported by Probable Cause
Honor Pretrial Rights of Accused
Post Conviction Duty
Extrajudicial Statements Prohibited
Timely Disclosure of Exculpatory Evidence

Fee sharing with non-lawyers is only permitted if involving: **PEND**

Purchase of Law Practice,
Employee Payment Plans,
Nonprofit Organization that recommended the Lawyer, or
Death or Disability of Lawyer

A lawyer is prohibited from **SAPP**

Sharing Legal Fees with a Non- Lawyer
Aiding in the Unauthorized Practice of Law
Paying a Referral Fee
Partnering with Non-Lawyer in the Practice of Law

Lawyer – Client Oral solicitation seeking future representation is prohibited other than from: **ROFF**

Relatives,
Other lawyers,
Former clients,
Friends

Three situations where Lawyer is not required to report misconduct: **CAD**

Confidential information of Client,
Assistance program source,
Defense attorney retained

RIGOS UNIFORM BAR REVIEW SERIES

PROFESSIONAL RESPONSIBILITY EXAM REVIEW (MPRE)

TABLE OF REFERENCES TO THE ABA

MODEL RULES OF PROFESSIONAL CONDUCT

RIGOS UNIFORM BAR REVIEW SERIES

PROFESSIONAL RESPONSIBILITY EXAM REVIEW (MPRE)

TABLE OF REFERENCES TO THE ABA

MODEL CODE OF JUDICIAL CONDUCT

RIGOS UNIFORM BAR REVIEW SERIES

PROFESSIONAL RESPONSIBILITY EXAM REVIEW (MPRE)

SUBJECT MATTER INDEX

RIGOS UNIFORM BAR REVIEW SERIES

PROFESSIONAL RESPONSIBILITY EXAM REVIEW (MPRE)

PROGRAM EVALUATION FORM

Once again, thank you for choosing this third edition MPRE Volume of the **Rigos Uniform Bar Review Series**! We hope you feel that these materials have given you the tools and confidence to tackle and score high on the Multistate Professional Responsibility Exam!

We are constantly striving to provide the best possible study materials available. We want to hear from you! If you would kindly take a few minutes to fill out the form below and mail it back to us at 230 Skinner Building, 1326 Fifth Avenue, Seattle WA 98101 or fax to 206-624-0731. Let your voice be heard in the effort to improve the **Rigos Uniform Bar Review Series MPRE Review**. THANK YOU!

****

For each of the categories listed below, please rate **Rigos Bar Review Series MPRE Review** on a scale of 1 to 5.

5 = Excellent 4 = Very Good 3 = Good 2 = Fair 1 = Poor

How do you rate the overall presentation of Rigos Bar Review Series?

Arrangement of Materials	5	4	3	2	1
Colors/Typography	5	4	3	2	1
Writing Style	5	4	3	2	1
Ease of Use	5	4	3	2	1
Professionalism	5	4	3	2	1

How do you rate the Rigos Bar Review Series materials in terms of accuracy (typographical, legal, etc.)?

Chapter Texts	5	4	3	2	1
Magic Memory Outlines®	5	4	3	2	1
Question Distribution Maps	5	4	3	2	1
Questions/Answers	5	4	3	2	1
MPRE Tips	5	4	3	2	1

How do you rate the helpfulness of each component of Rigos Bar Review Series?

Chapter Texts and Acronyms	5	4	3	2	1
Audio Learning Lectures	5	4	3	2	1
Magic Memory Outlines®	5	4	3	2	1
Questions/Answers and Maps	5	4	3	2	1
Final Exam	5	4	3	2	1

How well has Rigos Bar Review Series prepared you for each of the following aspects of the MPRE?

Substantive Knowledge	5	4	3	2	1
Multiple Choice Format	5	4	3	2	1
Time Management/Organization	5	4	3	2	1
Helpful Tips/Common Mistakes	5	4	3	2	1
Confidence Level	5	4	3	2	1

Continued on back of page

What is the likelihood that you would do each of the following?

Recommend Rigos Bar Review Series to others	5	4	3	2	1
Keep Rigos Bar Review Series for future reference	5	4	3	2	1
Buy other Rigos Uniform Bar Review products in the future	5	4	3	2	1

If you felt that some chapters of the Rigos Bar Review Series MPRE Review were better than others, rate them individually below:

Competence, Scope of Representation and Fees	5	4	3	2	1
Confidentiality and Conflicts of Interest	5	4	3	2	1
Disqualification, Client Funds, and Withdrawal	5	4	3	2	1
Counselor, Advocate, and Third Party Dealing	5	4	3	2	1
Law Firms, Marketing, and Professional Integrity	5	4	3	2	1
Judiciary Ethics	5	4	3	2	1

Did you study all of the text?
Yes _____ No ______

Did you work all of the learning and practice questions?
Yes _____ No ______

Did you take the Final Exam?
Yes _____ No ______

Did you prepare a Magic Memory Outline® for all 6 subjects?
Yes _____ No ______

Did you use the Make Your Own Exam software feature?
Yes _____ No ______

Did you pass the MPRE?
Yes _____ No ______ Don't know yet ____ MPRE Score _____

If you have any additional comments, critiques, praise, criticisms, or other suggestions about Rigos Uniform Bar Review Series MPRE Review and how we can improve, please tell us about them below.

____

____

If you wish to, please give us the information below. It will allow us to attribute your comments and to follow up on your concerns.

NAME:______________ PHONE ____________EMAIL:______________

LAW SCHOOL ______________ GRAD DATE:______ ADDRESS: ______________

MPRE SCORE: